The Thinking Fan's Guide
to the World Cup

The Thinking Fan's Guide to the World Cup

Edited by
Matt Weiland and Sean Wilsey

HARPER  PERENNIAL

NEW YORK • LONDON • TORONTO • SYDNEY

HARPER ● PERENNIAL

Quotation from "My Thorny Thoughts" by Taras Shevchenko from *Selections*, translated by John Weir (Toronto: Ukrainian Canadian Press, 1961).

FIRST EDITION

Designed by Linda Byrne and Horacio Herrera-Richmond

Library of Congress Cataloging-in-Publication Data is available upon request.

ISBN-10: 0-06-113226-8
ISBN-13: 978-0-06-113226-1

06 07 08 09 10 DIX/RRD 10 9 8 7 6 5 4 3 2 1

Contents

Contents

Preface

Matt Weiland

Martin Amis once described abroad as "the place where the football fan sheds his diffidence and starts to come alive. There he stands . . . with Union Jack underpants on his head . . . stripped to the waist, fat, pale, ankle-deep in sick, menacing the local women and children, peeing into the fountain, singing 'Fuck the Pope' and 'God Save the Queen', and blind drunk."

My sense of abroad, growing up in the Midwest in the 1970s, was not that place. But I wasn't much less ignorant of the world than the average hooligan: I had a poor sense of geography, and foreign countries were just caricatures: Iran was a scraggly beard and a headband, kind of a demonic Bjorn Borg; the Soviet Union was the angry bear of a thousand flickering filmstrips, endlessly scratching blood from other nations. What I did learn came from writers like Amis—and from soccer. I played competitively through the spring and fall each year, and I came to identify other school teams' strengths by the make-up of their immigrant communities—the Poles were strong defenders, the Vietnamese could dribble but not pass. On weekends I watched tape-delayed European matches broadcast at the end of the UHF dial; through the fuzzy reception I could make out grainy Germans and Italians with bad haircuts and short shorts kicking a nearly invisible ball around a pitch ringed with ads for obscure products (*'Pirelli'*? *'Die Zeit'*?), as smoking coaches and fans in flat caps and holey tweeds huddled under the rain. I loved it the way others loved short-wave radio: *Hello, world!* I didn't even have to speak.

At the residential soccer camp I attended each summer, the coaches, wanting to instill in us a sense of the world beyond America, divided us into teams named after the then-leading lights in European club soccer: Ipswich Town, FC Cologne, Grasshoppers of Zurich. At the end of camp we packed into the auditorium for the ceremonial viewing of *Victory*—popcorn would be popped and passed around, the film would begin and a roomful of sweaty boys would recite each line as catechism. These were good years for the World section of daily papers—the international oil crisis, the Soviet invasion of Afghanistan, the Falkland Islands and Grenada . . . but I knew nothing of all that. I was playing for Ipswich Town on a pristine soccer field in southern Minnesota, and cheering as Michael Caine, Sylvester Stallone, Bobby Moore and Pelé beat the Germans.

By the time the 1982 World Cup came around, I was a die-hard international soccer fan. It turned out that all the stereotypes were true: the South Americans were impetuous, the Germans dull, the English dogged. The players themselves were as amazing to me as anything in the science fiction I devoured. Who could possibly invent names as pleasing and perfect as Karl-Heinz Rummenigge or Kevin Keegan or Dino Zoff? Or Socrates—who had a beard and smoked! England was my favorite: they looked sharp in their black shorts and white shirts, they won their first three matches with ease and they had my fellow Ipswich Town man, Terry Butcher, in defense. But I discovered the pang of disappointment that summer: England, needing to beat host Spain to advance past the group stage, could only manage a 0–0 draw after Keegan missed an easy header in front of the goal, and went out.

My grandfather was no fan of soccer, thinking or otherwise; he called it "the game where they all run around a lot." But when I visited him in Brooklyn after the World Cup that summer, he cheerfully drove me into Manhattan, all the way up the long gray avenues of the East Side to what may have been the only soccer store in the city at the time. It was located in Yorkville, the old German part of the city, and was just one small room, with most of the stock in cardboard boxes behind the counter in the back. My grandfather liked the Argentine jersey, with its bold broad stripes of blue and white. But I did not want that. The owners encouraged me to try the West German one. I did not want that either. All I wanted were a pair of black Umbro shorts and a white England jersey; my grandfather bought me both, and matching socks besides. I traced the stitched outline of the England badge for days, admired the three lions, and wore the shirt to the first day of school that fall. It looked so . . . *abroad.*

Since then, each time the World Cup rolls around I have bought an armful of almanacs and guidebooks and travelogues and histories and settled in for the long happy haul. For the month before the World Cup, the month it lasts and the month after, I quiz family and friends about goalscorers and qualification campaigns, about literacy rates and median ages and GDP; I make lists of clean sheets and red cards and golden goals; I discover dictators and death squads, economic miracles and cycles of boom and bust.

A few years ago, I quit playing competitively but moved to London, where my international soccer fixation only grew. Last year, in an old pub on the Thames on a midsummer's afternoon, I discovered that my friend Sean Wilsey—visiting from New York—was as much an enthusiast as I am. We talked of Eduardo Galeano's *Football in Sun and Shadow,* Bill Buford's *Among the Thugs,* Ryszard Kapuscinski's *The Soccer War*—books by writers with a passion for soccer but a thought and a care for everything else. We confessed our mutual love for the World Cup's sunny internationalism, its sense of a good-hearted world struggling to improve itself and make good. We thought: Couldn't we combine hard facts and great writing into one useful and unusual book, which would include everything one needed to watch the World Cup from first match to the final but also tell us something about the countries themselves? Couldn't we play at being manager, and gather a squad of thirty-two writers to write it? They could contribute a piece of personal history, or reportage, or even an essay on a nation's history or the way it plays the game, but whatever the form, each piece would say something lasting about a nation's past and present. Every World Cup there are loads of features in magazines and newspapers about the teams and the players; we wanted some of that, but we wanted something more: to use soccer as a lens and an excuse to learn something about the wider world.

It felt like the beginning of one of those band-of-heroes movies, when the group is gathered: the swordsmen in *Seven Samurai,* or the gunslingers in *The Magnificent Seven.* Or the soccer players in *Victory* itself: at camp we all cheered the happy ending, but I loved the beginning best, when the British officers pulled together the captured Allies to form a team. Sean and I were managers and out there, somewhere, were our thirty-two writers. Some, like Nick Hornby, who had virtually defined the thinking fan's mania, we could not have imagined doing without. Others we weren't sure about: Would they share our passion? Would they have something to say? And would anyone agree to do it? The response came fast. From north London and northern California, Montevideo and Tokyo, Mexico City and Mozambique, Verona and Chicago, Cardiff and Beirut—almost every writer we asked responded with enthusiasm. Eduardo Galeano even gave us the true soccer patriot's answer: "I will write it if Uruguay qualifies. If not, no."

We asked some of the writers, like Galeano, to write about their own country. Others we assigned to countries based on an experience there, and some we sent to a country of their choosing. For a month we made lists and contacted writers, and by the last stage of qualification, we had assigned each nation that looked likely to qualify. Then we sat back to watch and wait.

And then we started shouting at television screens and commiserating over international phone lines.

In East End pubs in London (me) and at home in New York (Sean), we watched as our careful plans fell apart. I have known the cruel disappointment of a favorite team losing: I still remembered England in '82. But to lose a prized writer from your own book! Nothing had prepared us for that.

Granta editor Ian Jack went out early as Scotland, despite a late improvement in form, managed only a draw against Italy in September. Jack was unfazed: "One should never place too much faith in Scotland."

Uwem Akpan, the young Nigerian writer and Jesuit priest, went out next. Seemingly certain to qualify, Nigeria had only managed a draw and a loss against Angola in qualifying, so needed Angola *not to win* their last qualifying match on October 8th to have a chance of surpassing them. But Angola beat Rwanda 1–0, and Nigeria was out. We were sorry to see them go: the Super Eagles had been such a pleasure to watch in recent World Cups. Akpan had theories. "The crucial match against Angola was played in a semi-desert place called Kano: the idea was that the Angolans would be tired, not being used to playing in that terrain, and we would easily fix them. But our players became tired first because they all play in the temperate zones of Europe!"

We lost Roddy Doyle after Ireland managed only a miserable 0–0 draw against Switzerland on October 12th. I was in a boisterous Shoreditch pub, watching with the Kenyan writer Binyavanaga Wainaina. He was matter-of-fact about it: "Listen, playing in those shirts, they cannot win. Only African teams look good in green." Sean and I conferred: perhaps we could send Doyle to Switzerland and he could write about being a losing Ireland fan there? "I'm not up to it," he said. "I don't know if you saw Ireland play. . . . But, if you did, you'd understand. The last thing I want to write about is football. If you're planning a book on the plague . . ."

The Thai-American writer Rattawut Lapcharoensap went out on November 16th. Thailand had no chance to make the World Cup, but Lapcharoensap is a great soccer fan and had told us about the many Thais working in the hotel business in Bahrain, a country on the brink of qualifying. We were preparing to send Lapcharoensap to Manama when Bahrain lost at home to Trinidad and Tobago. In a miserable empty pub in Clerkenwell, I watched the frenetic match alone, and cursed as Bahrain failed to score. The bartender gave me a strange look and a free pint, but Lapcharoensap was out.

Finally, on a blue November morning in London, we lost Eduardo Galeano. Uruguay needed only to beat Australia in a two-legged playoff to qualify, as they had done to reach the World Cup finals in

2002. They won a tense first leg, 1–0 at home, but in the away leg in front of 82,000 fans in Sydney, the Australians won 1–0 to leave the aggregate score tied. Australia then won on penalties, and Galeano, the inspiration for this book as much as anyone, was out.

Management, as the former England manager Ron Greenwood once said of soccer itself, is all about disappointment. But we're over it. We got to replace the writers we lost with others we like just as much, and like the best soccer teams, our thirty-two writers exhibit a pleasing variety of form and pace, sensibility and style.

Thanks to their efforts, I know more about abroad now than I used to. I know where to find a crocodile skin in Paraguay and where to surf in Portugal. I know something about Polish doubts, Swedish fears, Tunisian superstitions and Serbian food. I know that Ecuadorans excel at speed-walking and that the Japanese have particularly effective toilets. I know that more than two million slaves were shipped from Angola to the Americas and West Indies, and that Mexico is either the richest Third World nation in the world or the poorest First World one. I have learned how to say "penis" in Persian (I think). And I have learned that when it comes to winning the World Cup, a democracy beats a military junta beats a dictatorship.

So here we are then, thinking fans in various states of drunkenness and undress, variously fat and thin, pale and burnt, none of us quite peeing into the fountain but all of us soccer-mad, and all of us alive at the thought of abroad.

The Thinking Fan's Guide
to the World Cup

Introduction

Sean Wilsey

There are many beautiful things about being an American fan of World Cup soccer—foremost among them is ignorance. The community in which you were raised did not gather around the television set every four years for a solid, breathless month. The U.S. has never won. You have not been indoctrinated into unwanted yet inescapable tribal allegiances by your soccer-crazed countrymen. You are an amateur, in the purest sense of the word. So when the World Cup comes around, you can pick whatever team you like best and root for them without shame or fear of reprisal—you can spend the month in paradise.

That's what I do. The world of the World Cup is the world I want to live in. I cannot resist the pageantry and high-mindedness, the apolitical display of national characteristics, the revelation of human flaws and unexpected greatnesses, the fact that entire nations walk off the job or wake up at 3 A.M. to watch men kick a ball. There are countries that have truly multiracial squads—France, England, the United States—while other teams are entirely blond or Asian or Latin American. There are irritating fans: "USA! USA! USA!" (Blessedly few.) There are children who hold hands with each player as he walks onto the field. National anthems play. Men paint themselves their national colors and cry openly at opposing victories. An

1

announcer shouts "GOOOOOOOOOOOOOOOOOOOOOOOOOOOOO-OOLLLLLLLLLLLLLLLLLLLLLLLLLLLLLLLL! GOL GOL GOL!" on the Spanish language channel. A Slovakian tire salesman, an Italian cop or a German concert pianist—having passed the official fitness test and psychological examinations—will moonlight as referee. To quote the book every traveling athlete finds in his hotel room: "Rejoice, and be exceedingly glad: for great is your reward in heaven." Or, as my copy of *Soccer and Its Rules* says: "Are you ready? Ready to cheer the players to victory, marvel at their fitness, speed, and skills, urging them to win every tackle for the ball, ready to explode at a powerful shot? Ready for the excitement of flying wingers, overlapping backs, curling corners, slick one-two passing and goals scored with panache? Ready for another moment in a fantasy world?"

I am ready.

I mark the passage of time in World Cups. I started watching when I was old enough to be a young player, and have now reached the point where I imagine myself as the unlikely thirty-six-year-old substitute who comes in and scores.

My first Cup was in 1990, and I rooted for Cameroon. Cameroon had Roger Milla, who was an old man and only ran when it mattered. He did not need to run. He was wily and stylish enough to walk around the field scoring off defenders young enough to be his children. When Cameroon went out I switched allegiance to Italy. I was in Venice, and Italy was the host nation. I got swept up in the local enthusiasm. When the *Azzurri* made it to the final four, young men jumped into the canals, risking death by infection in order to express their triumph. Then Argentina kicked them out in the semis, despite allegations of cheating. (Ever since Argentina's legendary captain, Diego Maradona, punched the ball into the net and claimed the goal had been scored "a little bit by the hand of God, another bit by the head of Maradona," the Argentines have been the cheater's favorite team.) Finally West Germany—with seasoned attackers like Lothar Matthäus (veteran of five World Cups), and clever defenders like Olaf Thon (nickname: "the Professor")—shut down all Argentine forays and won the whole thing. Tragic but inevitable.

The next World Cup was in America. The world looked to the United States and the United States did not notice. The only part of the tournament to get much attention stateside came when a Colombian defender scored a goal against his own team, flew home in disgrace, and was shot dead in the street by a fan who shouted *"Gol! Gol! Gol!"* as he pumped bullets into the body. So far as I know, no one has ever done this to an Olympic discus thrower for misdirecting his Frisbee.

Italy was still my team, despite the Italians' boring soccer. Italian soccer watchers, I discovered, make better watching than Italian soccer, which entails getting a single goal and then locking into defense for the rest of the game. The Italians even have a word for it: *catenaccio,* which means "door bolt," or, if you're a more literal translator, "ugly chain." That year they ugly-chained it all the way to the final, lost on penalties to Brazil, and I decided to abandon them. Seeing your team go out on penalties is always a tragedy, but it's particularly agonizing when you've watched them make it there without any flying wingers, curling corners, slick one-two passing or goals scored with panache. The *Azzurri* had chintzed their way into the final. I'd supported them through a string of draws and one-goal victories, watched them shut down Brazil for two hours, and then watched them lose. Even the misery was tepid.

During the 1998 World Cup I switched to England. I was converted by watching a young David Beckham score a beautiful goal from a direct free kick, then get ejected from a game for needlessly kicking an Argentine player after the whistle was blown. There was something irresistible about an athlete foolish enough to do this in front of the ref, against a team as good as Argentina. I was hooked: Beckham was a brilliant idiot, and England was my squad. Of course it was the Argentines who continued to the next round.

So then I switched to France. France was the host, and their team was a cultural melting pot, which made it fun to root for them. *Les Bleus* came up against *Gli Azzurri* in the quarterfinals, won heroically in a penalty shootout, then went on to win the whole thing, using their home advantage to beat psyched-out world champions, Brazil. Bliss!

But it was the 2002 World Cup, held jointly by South Korea and Japan, where it all came together for me. I watched the games on Telemundo, the Spanish language channel ("GOOOOOOLLL-LLL!"), and split my allegiance between Japan, England, South Korea and Turkey. Japan had great hair, a player who wore goggles and another who taunted the opposing side *in Italian*. England—with grown-up Beckham (now captain), and my new favorite striker, Michael Owen—was dangerous and disciplined and incredibly unlucky. South Korea humiliated Italy with great determination and well-deserved good fortune. The Turks were ruffians: egregious foulers who made for the best watching of the tournament. Inevitably, Brazil won. The final was against Germany, but the best game of the tournament was the one when Brazil knocked out England with a gorgeous goal by Ronaldinho ("little Ronaldo") off a direct free kick—from midfield. Deus ex machina. A beautiful way to lose.

When the World Cup was over I wasn't ready to stop watching. I *needed* more international soccer. I tried Mexican and European league games on the weekends, but it just wasn't the same. What was at stake? Soccer only mattered when you knew an entire country sat rigid with anxiety in front of its television sets, national hopes and paranoias on full display, yearning for release; when players were playing out of love for country, not money. The team with the biggest payroll is always going to win in league games. Not so in international soccer. America has *always* lost.

So I took advantage of my American ignorance. I went on eBay and bought a video of the 1970 World Cup—the first one to be televised in color—from an obsessive Germany fan with the screen name "Olafthon1" (the Professor must have got there before him). Olaf1, a sort of monastic scholar of soccer, wrote emails that read like doctrinal encyclicals, and advised me on which World Cup I should retroactively attend. After settling on 1970 he warned me that there were two missing games, Uruguay–Sweden and West Germany–Morocco. The former was no great loss, but the latter, he said yearningly, was not only magnificent, but no longer existed, and "nobody can get it." *West Germany–Morocco,* I thought, *lost for all time*—and it's a measure of my zealotry that I later found myself daydreaming about a world space agency that could send out a probe to overtake and intercept the original broadcast and bring it home to earth. Traveling at light speed West Germany–Morocco passed beyond the etheric magnetic sphere of our solar system in just over four hours, placing it, in summer 2006, thirty-six years, three-hundred-and-sixty-four and one quarter days and twenty hours later, $3.40586297e+17$ miles from the earth.

The 1970 World Cup was held in Mexico, beginning the same month and year that I was born. I had no idea who would win. When it arrived I slipped the first of twenty-five tapes into the VCR—Mexico–Soviet Union, 5/31/70—and proceeded to watch the entire tournament, drawing it out over a couple of months. The great games (Czechoslovakia–Brazil), the boring games (Uruguay–Israel) and the weird games (Morocco–Bulgaria). I watched the whole thing alone, like West Germany–Morocco, deep in nostalgic space. But this was not sad. It was glorious and true. *We are all ultimately alone, aren't we?*

The quality was surprisingly good. The fans all looked like farmers. The ads at the edges of the fields were for alcohol, tires and cigarettes. The players wore short shorts and short haircuts. Though not Brazil's Rivelino, who sported a shag and a moustache, and, from my amateur's perspective, played better than Pelé. Despite what history remembers as a legendary performance, Pelé looked to me like a man who spent most of the tournament hobbling to his feet after being fouled, while Rivelino and Jairzinho got the goals. Some of the players on the Swedish team worked *day jobs*. And then there was the commentary: innocent, avuncular, genteel:

"My word he's got a kick like a mule!"

"Rubiños was left like a foundering whale."

"No danger to this big, handsome Belgian goalkeeper. This boy last year was only eight stone. Now he's nine stone. Look what football's done for him."

"The little men from the tiny republic—they're not beaten yet!"

Friends who turned down invitations to watch got into the habit of asking me how the 1970 World Cup was going, who was doing well, if I wanted to place a small bet on the outcome. I detected some mockery, *the mockery of infidels,* but I did not care. I turned to Sweden–Italy for solace, as others might turn to the Bible—which, if you look, has some consolingly apropos passages: "Blessed are they which are persecuted for righteousness' sake: for their's is the kingdom of heaven." And: "When thou prayest, enter into thy closet." Watching the 1970 World Cup by myself, in a dark TV room, doors shut at my wife's request, was like living in a closet, in heaven. It was lonely. But knowing the politics and history that surrounded the competing nations in 1970 made for the best cultural/historical/sociological—maybe even sacramental—experience of my life.

I resisted rooting for Brazil. Rooting for Brazil in soccer is like rooting for America in war. I went for the underdogs, the teams from countries that no longer exist: Czechoslovakia, West Germany, the Soviet Union. Brazil won, of course, providing me, four years ago, in my own private 1970, with several of the most rapturous moments I've ever had in front of a television screen. They won me over. But they weren't the only great team. England was almost as good, if mostly in defense. The West Germans were heroic in their determination. Franz Beckenbauer, the original sweeper, or counter-attacking defender, played in the semifinal with a dislocated shoulder, his arm strapped to his side. And Italy, when sufficiently pressed, and pressed they were, proved capable of inspired soccer, beating West Germany 4–3 in an epic two-hour semifinal—a task that left them sapped for the final, which Brazil won easily, and deservedly. They've taken home the trophy in three of the five World Cups I've seen. After 1970 I finally understood why. As Nick Hornby has written about the champions of 1970: "In a way Brazil ruined it for all of us. They had revealed a kind of Platonic ideal that nobody, not even the Brazilians, would ever be able to find again. . . . 1970 was a half-remembered dream they had once had of themselves."

Soccer's worldwide popularity isn't surprising when you look at what has always motivated humanity: money and God. There's lots of money in soccer, of course. League soccer (like capitalism) is basically the childlike desire to make dreams come true, no matter what the cost, realized by men with enough money to combine commodities like the best Brazilian attacker, Dutch midfielder, British defender and German goalkeeper and turn them loose on whatever the other billionaires can put together—an unfair situation that describes much of the world these days. But God's there, too.

What is soccer if not everything that religion should be? Universal yet particular, the source of an infinitely renewable supply of hope, occasionally miraculous and governed by simple, uncontradictory rules ("Laws," officially) that everyone can follow. In fact, if only for this last reason, soccer's got it over on religion. Unlike God's Commandments or Allah's Shari'a, soccer's Laws are all laws of equality and nonviolence and restraint, and all free to be delayed in their application or even reinterpreted at the discretion of a reasonable arbiter. What the ref says goes, no matter how flagrantly in violation of dogma his decisions may be (and despite the fact that he earns his living as a concert pianist, a middle school math teacher, a tire salesman, or commissioner of penitentiary police—to name the professions of four men on the list for Germany 2006). My official rulebook, after presenting a detailed, Olafthon1-style enumeration of soccer's seventeen Laws, concludes that the ref can throw out any of them in order to apply what it rather mystically calls "the spirit of fair play." Spirit is the only real Law within the boundaries of the soccer field (boundaries which themselves are allowed to vary according to the realities of any given playing situation—unlike, say, the earth's location at the time of Galileo).

The religious undercurrent in soccer runs especially deep in World Cup years. Teams from across the globe converge on the host nation in something of an unarmed, athletic crusade. As in the Crusades, the host nation tends to repel them. There's a weird power in home advantage. Hosts always find a level of success disproportionate to their talents on paper, triumphing over stronger sides, as if exerting a gravitational pull on the game, causing it to be played the way they want to play it, as if, to carry this metaphor to its inevitable conclusion, God were on their side. These unexpected heroics can make for great watching—especially for the impartial amateur. One of the best matches I've ever seen was 2002's second-round clash between co-host South Korea and three-time world champion Italy. This was farther than South Korea had ever advanced, and nobody expected them to do any better. But with the stadium in Daejeon filled with forty thousand people, all wearing matching red shirts and banging monstrous drums, the South Koreans played so passionately that they took Italy into overtime. Christian Vieri, the *Azzurri* striker who usually spent quarterfinals just a quarter-step off offside, was actually playing defensively, and sweating. Ahn Jung Hwan, the South Korean midfielder who eventually won the game with a golden goal, was also sweating, more than I'd ever seen an athlete sweat: great silvery explosions kept flying out of his hair every time he headed the ball. The Italian players were running as hard as children—all after him. It was tribal, ancient, unthinkable. The whole game felt possessed. South Korea, routinely eliminated in the group stage, was cleaning Italy's clock. It was David and Goliath— for two hours. The Italians, a team of dour and disciplined profes- sionals, rather than breaking the opposition's flow, as they'd been trained to do, were being forced to play the game like the South Ko- reans: running, running, running, running and—when Ahn rose up and headed the ball with neck-jerking, spray-showering force, in over tired old Paolo Maldini's head—losing.

I turned off my TV and was surprised I couldn't still hear the cele- brating.

South Korea kept on going, through the quarterfinals, all the way to the semifinals, where they barely lost to Germany. For a while they were the world's team. We all wanted to play soccer like South Korea. But it only took one loss for them to collapse completely, as if the spirit had abandoned them. They gave up the first of three goals in the third place game against Turkey in a record eleven seconds— the fastest score in World Cup history. They'd been propelled as far as they could go, by belief alone, and then they were done.

But the fact that the World Cup could even take place in South Korea and Japan was a victory for tolerance and understanding. In less than half a century South Korea had gone from not allowing the Japanese national team to cross its borders for a World Cup qualifier, to co-hosting the tournament with their former occupier. Give the planet another fifty years and we might see the tournament co-hosted by Israel and Palestine.

And why not? Soccer's universality is its simplicity—the fact that the game can be played anywhere with anything. Urban children kick a can on concrete and rural kids kick a rag wrapped around a rag wrapped around a rag, barefoot, on dirt. Soccer is something to believe in now, perhaps empty at its core, but not a stand-in for anything else.

In the last ten years Brazil has returned to form, playing with the offhand brilliance of 1970. This year they're ranked number one by FIFA, which stands for Fédération Internationale de Football Association (founded in Paris on May 21—my birthday!—1904). After Brazil (who won five World Cups) comes the Czech Republic (who excelled as Czechoslovakia, but never won), the Netherlands (who lost in the final, twice), Argentina (who won two), France (1), Spain (0), Mexico (0), the U.S. (0), England (1), Portugal (0). Germany, despite having won three World Cups, had a terrible year, and couldn't make the top ten. Of course these rankings fluctuate constantly, and are probably meaningless. In the run-up to the World Cup, the U.S. beat Mexico and England lost to Northern Ireland, a team ranked near the bottom in the world, just above Hong Kong. (It's a telling fact that one of the terms of the Chinese takeover of Hong Kong was the nonabolition of the Special Administrative Region's own national soccer team.)

With Germany as host and Brazil dominant we may be heading for a repeat of 2002, with these two powers once again in the final. Then again, styles continue to change, loosen, travel—making it anyone's game. The cosmopolitanism and cross-pollination you'll see in 2006 is historically unprecedented, the result of coaches traveling the world, and great players not returning to their home teams, but living abroad under the influence of whole nations of fans, playing styles, racism, and club owners' pointlessly large sums of money.

The beautiful game—let's call it business and religion combined—will be at its most unfair, frustrating, magnificent and unifying this summer in unified Germany's first World Cup. And for the ninety minutes between the referee's whistles, everything you'll learn in this book will come down to young men with hypertrophied quadriceps and tempers and pride—opportunity for another cool and wise Roger Milla to have his day. Look out for Ronaldinho (he draws a huge salary at FC Barcelona, one of the only league teams collectively owned by the fans, but recently told the press: "this type of contentment doesn't have a price"). Also look out for Pavel Nedved (Czech Republic midfielder, and the most impressive player in Euro 2004), Freddy Adu (America's great hope and Ghana's great loss), Carlos Tévez (Argentina's Olympic hero), Alvaro César Elizondo (an obscure striker on the Costa Rican youth team who, if he gets to play, is sure not to be exhausted from a long season in the European leagues).

What makes the World Cup most beautiful is the world; all of us together. Watching the 1970 tournament, leaping up at incredible plays, shouting by myself, I wished more than anything that I'd actually been there, in the stands, knowing what I could only know about those countries with thirty-two years hindsight. This book sets out to be the best approximation of that ideal experience. Knowledge and wonder.

The joy of being one of the couple of billion people watching thirty-two nations abide by seventeen rules fills me with the conviction, perhaps ignorant, but like many ignorant convictions, fiercely held, that soccer can unite the world.

World Cup 2002:
Recap, Results and Statistics

Recap

Sean Wilsey

The 2002 World Cup was unprecedented, but in highly predictable ways.

Held in Asia for the first time, the tournament was co-hosted by traditional enemies South Korea and Japan, who both cooperated with and attempted to outdo each other, first in stadium construction, and then in the competition itself. France, reigning world champions (1998) and European champions (2000), lost the opening game 1–0 to former colony and World Cup debutants Senegal, failed to score in their subsequent matches and went home after the group stage. It was a performance so ignominious that no one complained when FIFA subsequently abolished the longstanding tradition of automatic qualification for world champions.

In another first-round upset, Portugal was beaten 3–2 by the United States. For all the excitement surrounding Luis Figo, the star of Portugal's "Golden Generation," young Americans like Brian McBride and Landon Donovan were a more tangible menace. The U.S. carried on, drawing with South Korea and beating rival Mexico. Germany crushed Saudi Arabia 8–0 in the group stage, and met the U.S. in the quarterfinals. German goalkeeper Oliver Kahn's psy-ops denied Donovan a sure goal, and the U.S., despite dominating the match, was out. Franz Beckenbauer evaluated Germany's performance like this: "Kahn apart, you could take all of them, put them in a bag and hit them with a stick. Whoever got hit would deserve it."

Argentina, in the "Group of Death" with England, Nigeria and Sweden, was eliminated by a penalty kick from David Beckham (making restitution for his fatal mistakes against them in 1998) and went home with the Portuguese and the French.

Africa barely made an appearance after the group stage, with only Senegal continuing on; while of the Asian teams South Korea and Japan both made it into the knockout round. Japan fell first, to an occasionally thuggish, always inspired Turkey (the team that earned more red and yellow cards than any other), while South Korea eliminated Italy in the most exciting game of the tournament. After forcing the complacent *Azzurri* to run hard for nearly two hours, expat striker Ahn Jung Hwan, who played his club soccer for Perugia, won the match with a golden goal in the 117th minute. South Korea had a new national hero, and the hero's Italian boss, Luciano Gaucci, cancelled his contract: "I have no intention of paying a salary to someone who has ruined Italian football." Four days later, facing Spain, South Korea played another two hours, this time winning on penalties. Spain, with the last eight their second best finish since 1950, had to live with *two* disallowed goals. "I thought the referee would be fairer in a quarterfinal match like this," said coach Jose Antonio Camacho. "We fought to the end and went out because South Korea were luckier than us." In the semifinals, South Korea met Oliver Kahn's Germany. Michael Ballack scored the game's lone goal (only the third in six matches to make it past Lee Woon Jae), and ended their run in front of 66,625 of their drum-beating, crimson-clad, mass-choreographed fans. Guus Hiddink, South Korea's Dutch coach (and recipient of honorary citizenship), was sensibly appreciative: "They showed what support can be: a miracle mix of enthusiasm and non-violence."

Both the co-hosts were more than deserving of their success, persevering against storied sides, taking chances, defending with resolve and running harder than all the other nations in the seventeenth World Cup. If FIFA had put a pedometer on the South Korean and Japanese midfields the footfall count would have been twice that recorded by any of the fifteen European teams in the tournament. The one exception being Turkey. With the Netherlands absent (having been semifinalists under Hiddink in 1998), it fell to the Turks to play Dutch-style "total soccer." Despite a third-place finish Turkey was the second best team in the 2002 World Cup. (In consolation they got stadiums, bridges and streets named after them back home: a boulevard in Adana for left winger Hasan Sas, a park in Istanbul for coach Senol Günes and a stadium in the seaside town of Zonguldak for midfielder Ergün Penbe.)

The best match of the tournament was the quarterfinal between

England and Brazil, which contained equal quantities of intensity, beauty and luck. Michael Owen scored with characteristic elegance on a blistering run after a Brazilian gaffe in the 22nd minute, and England led until first half injury time, when Rivaldo equalized on a Ronaldinho assist. A minute into the restart Ronaldinho delivered an incredible, foot-of-God-like goal from a free kick from midfield. Despite three substitutions, and another forty-seven minutes, England couldn't get through Roberto Carlos and the Brazilian defense.

After the game David Beckham visited the winners' locker room, and (according to *Sports Illustrated*) this exchange ensued:

> BECKHAM: Hi, sorry. I just wanted to know if Ronaldo wanted to swap shirts with me.
> ROBERTO CARLOS (listening): I already traded shirts with him.
> RONALDO (returning with a jersey): Beckham just gave me his.

The game was so good, Beckham traded shirts *twice*.

Before the inevitable letdown of the final, some illuminating statistics:

Top foulers: Dietmar Hamann of Germany and Cafu of Brazil, tied at 19. Top tackler: Torsten Frings of Germany, who efficiently broke the flow of fifty-five opponents (though Slovenia's Zeljko Milinovic, eliminated at the group stage, had the most tackles per hour on the pitch: an astounding 7.33). Most goal saves: Rüstü Receber of Turkey: 34. Most goals allowed: Mohammad Al Deayea of Saudi Arabia: 12. Brazil's Ronaldo took the most shots on goal, 21, but couldn't claim a single assist. South Korea's Seol Ki Hyeon was most often tackled (79 times). Nobody took more shots than Paraguay's Nelson Cuevas, who averaged 8 per game. Italy's Francesco Totti was the tournament's least (and most!) disciplined player, with 18 fouls, 3 yellow cards and 1 red card.

The final was not only significant as the first meeting between the two most successful nations in World Cup history, Germany and

Brazil, but as the last to be adjudicated by Italian referee Pierluigi Collina, the greatest, and with his oddly winning absence of any facial hair, most charismatic ref on the FIFA lists.

Germany, crippled without red-carded playmaker and current captain, Michael Ballack, had to rely on Oliver Kahn's perfection in goal, while praying for Brazilian mistakes. Neither were forthcoming. Ronaldo slipped one past Kahn in the 66th minute, off a Rivaldo ricochet—delivered at such close range that the German blocked but couldn't hold it—and then again in the 78th. Ahead 2–0, a cocky Brazil brought some subtitutes into the game—Juninho, only on for five minutes, looked certain to score—and it became obvious that the champions had the world's two best teams. A better final would've been Brazil starters v. Brazil bench.

Kahn took home the Golden Ball trophy, as the player of the tournament, on the basis of his prior performances. (Before Ronaldo, only Ireland's Robbie Keane had been able to get one past him.) Analyzing the Brazilian's first goal Kahn told the press: "My one and only mistake in seven matches. But that one mistake was brutally punished." For his eight goals Ronaldo took the high-scorer's Golden Shoe.

In celebration, the South Americans used the largest stadium in the world's only Shinto-majority country to produce what must have been the highest rated bit of televangelism in broadcast history, as Kaká, Edmilson and Lucio ripped off their jerseys, revealing undershirts that read—in Portuguese and English—"I belong to Jesus" and "Jesus loves you." Other Brazilian players danced in a conga line. Now, God be praised, they could break the forty days of celibacy imposed by coach Luis Felipe Scolari. As Ronaldo told reporters: "Sex I am going to do in a few moments, but nothing can be so rewarding as the World Cup."

They had won all seven of their games, and an unprecedented fifth world championship: a *pent-campeão!*

Despite their victory, they'd still have to go through qualification four years later.

Results

Group Stage

Group A	Matches	Wins	Draws	Losses	Goals For	Goals Against	Points
Denmark	3	2	1	0	5	2	7
Senegal	3	1	2	0	5	4	5
Uruguay	3	0	2	1	4	5	2
France	3	0	1	2	0	3	1

31-May-02	Seoul	France	0	Senegal	1
01-Jun-02	Ulsan	Uruguay	1	Denmark	2
06-Jun-02	Busan	France	0	Uruguay	0
06-Jun-02	Daegu	Denmark	1	Senegal	1
11-Jun-02	Suwon	Senegal	3	Uruguay	3
11-Jun-02	Incheon	Denmark	2	France	0

Group B	Matches	Wins	Draws	Losses	Goals For	Goals Against	Points
Spain	3	3	0	0	9	4	9
Paraguay	3	1	1	1	6	6	4
South Africa	3	1	1	1	5	5	4
Slovenia	3	0	0	3	2	7	0

02-Jun-02	Gwangju	Spain	3	Slovenia	1
02-Jun-02	Busan	Paraguay	2	South Africa	2
07-Jun-02	Jeonju	Spain	3	Paraguay	1
08-Jun-02	Daegu	South Africa	1	Slovenia	0
12-Jun-02	Seogwipo	Slovenia	1	Paraguay	3
12-Jun-02	Daejeon	South Africa	2	Spain	3

Group C	Matches	Wins	Draws	Losses	Goals For	Goals Against	Points
Brazil	3	3	0	0	11	3	9
Turkey	3	1	1	1	5	3	4
Costa Rica	3	1	1	1	5	6	4
China PR	3	0	0	3	0	9	0

03-Jun-02	Ulsan	Brazil	2	Turkey	1
04-Jun-02	Gwangju	China	0	Costa Rica	2
08-Jun-02	Seogwipo	Brazil	4	China	0
09-Jun-02	Incheon	Costa Rica	1	Turkey	1
13-Jun-02	Suwon	Costa Rica	2	Brazil	5
13-Jun-02	Seoul	Turkey	3	China	0

(continued)

Group Stage *(continued)*

Group D	Matches	Wins	Draws	Losses	Goals For	Goals Against	Points
South Korea	3	2	1	0	4	1	7
United States	3	1	1	1	5	6	4
Portugal	3	1	0	2	6	4	3
Poland	3	1	0	2	3	7	3

04-Jun-02	Busan	South Korea	2	Poland	0
05-Jun-02	Suwon	US	3	Portugal	2
10-Jun-02	Jeonju	Portugal	4	Poland	0
10-Jun-02	Daegu	South Korea	1	US	1
14-Jun-02	Incheon	Portugal	0	South Korea	1
14-Jun-02	Daejeon	Poland	3	US	1

Group E	Matches	Wins	Draws	Losses	Goals For	Goals Against	Points
Germany	3	2	1	0	11	1	7
Ireland	3	1	2	0	5	2	5
Cameroon	3	1	1	1	2	3	4
Saudi Arabia	3	0	0	3	0	12	0

01-Jun-02	Sapporo	Germany	8	Saudi Arabia	0
01-Jun-02	Niigata	Ireland	1	Cameroon	1
05-Jun-02	Ibaraki	Germany	1	Ireland	1
06-Jun-02	Saitama	Cameroon	1	Saudi Arabia	0
11-Jun-02	Yokohama	Saudi Arabia	0	Ireland	3
11-Jun-02	Shizuoka	Cameroon	0	Germany	2

Group F	Matches	Wins	Draws	Losses	Goals For	Goals Against	Points
Sweden	3	1	2	0	4	3	5
England	3	1	2	0	2	1	5
Argentina	3	1	1	1	2	2	4
Nigeria	3	0	1	2	1	3	1

02-Jun-02	Saitama	England	1	Sweden	1
02-Jun-02	Ibaraki	Argentina	1	Nigeria	0
07-Jun-02	Sapporo	Argentina	0	England	1
07-Jun-02	Kobe	Sweden	2	Nigeria	1
12-Jun-02	Osaka	Nigeria	0	England	0
12-Jun-02	Miyagi	Sweden	1	Argentina	1

Group G	Matches	Wins	Draws	Losses	Goals For	Goals Against	Points
Mexico	3	2	1	0	4	2	7
Italy	3	1	1	1	4	3	4
Croatia	3	1	0	2	2	3	3
Ecuador	3	1	0	2	2	4	3

03-Jun-02	Sapporo		Italy	2		Ecuador	0
03-Jun-02	Niigata		Croatia	0		Mexico	1
08-Jun-02	Ibaraki		Italy	1		Croatia	2
09-Jun-02	Miyagi		Mexico	2		Ecuador	1
13-Jun-02	Oita		Mexico	1		Italy	1
13-Jun-02	Yokohama		Ecuador	1		Croatia	0

Group H	Matches	Wins	Draws	Losses	Goals For	Goals Against	Points
Japan	3	2	1	0	5	2	7
Belgium	3	1	2	0	6	5	5
Russia	3	1	0	2	4	4	3
Tunisia	3	0	1	2	1	5	1

04-Jun-02	Saitama		Japan	2		Belgium	2
05-Jun-02	Kobe		Russia	2		Tunisia	0
09-Jun-02	Yokohama		Japan	1		Russia	0
10-Jun-02	Oita		Tunisia	1		Belgium	1
14-Jun-02	Osaka		Tunisia	0		Japan	2
14-Jun-02	Shizuoka		Belgium	3		Russia	2

Final Stage

Round of Sixteen

15-Jun-02	Niigata	Denmark	0	England	3
15-Jun-02	Seogwipo	Germany	1	Paraguay	0
16-Jun-02	Suwon	Spain	1	Ireland	1*
16-Jun-02	Oita	Sweden	1	Senegal	2†
17-Jun-02	Kobe	Brazil	2	Belgium	0
17-Jun-02	Jeonju	Mexico	0	US	2
18-Jun-02	Daejeon	South Korea	2	Italy	1‡
18-Jun-02	Miyagi	Japan	0	Turkey	1

Quarterfinals

21-Jun-02	Ulsan	Germany	1	US	0
21-Jun-02	Shizuoka	England	1	Brazil	2
22-Jun-02	Osaka	Senegal	0	Turkey	1§
22-Jun-02	Gwangju	Spain	0	South Korea	0‖

Semifinals

25-Jun-02	Seoul	Germany	1	South Korea	0
26-Jun-02	Saitama	Brazil	1	Turkey	0

Third place

29-Jun-02	Daegu	South Korea	2	Turkey	3

Final

30-Jun-02	Yokohama	Germany	0	Brazil	2

* *After extra time (Spain won penalty shootout 3–2)*
† *After extra time*
‡ *After extra time*
§ *After extra time*
‖ *After extra time (South Korea won penalty shootout 5–3)*

Statistics

Top Goalscorers

Player	Nation	Matches Played	Goals	Assists	Shots	Shots on Goal	Penalty Goals
Ronaldo	Brazil	7	8	0	28	21	0
Rivaldo	Brazil	7	5	1	21	12	1
Miroslav Klose	Germany	7	5	1	18	9	0
Jon Dahl Tomasson	Denmark	4	4	0	6	5	1
Christian Vieri	Italy	4	4	0	19	11	0
Marc Wilmots	Belgium	4	3	0	11	7	0
Pauleta	Portugal	3	3	0	14	5	0
Papa Bouba Diop	Senegal	5	3	0	14	7	0
Ilhan Mansiz	Turkey	7	3	1	10	4	0
Robbie Keane	Ireland	4	3	0	16	8	1
Michael Ballack	Germany	6	3	4	19	8	0
Fernando Morientes	Spain	5	3	0	12	10	0
Raul	Spain	4	3	0	10	7	0
Henrik Larsson	Sweden	4	3	0	7	4	1

Top Goalkeepers

Player	Nation	Matches Played	Goals Allowed	Average
Oliver Kahn	Germany	7	3	0.43
Marcos	Brazil	7	4	0.57
David Seaman	England	5	3	0.60
Pablo Cavallero	Argentina	3	2	0.67
Shay Given	Ireland	4	3	0.75
Narazaki Seigo	Japan	4	3	0.75
Lee Woon Jae	South Korea	7	6	0.86
Rustu Recber	Turkey	7	6	0.86
Boukar Alioum	Cameroon	3	3	1.00
Iker Casillas	Spain	5	5	1.00

**World Cup 2006:
The Tournament**

Overview

	World Cup Appearances	World Cup Champions	FIFA Ranking	Odds to Win
Angola	0	0	63	400–1
Argentina	13	2	4	8–1
Australia	1	0	48	80–1
Brazil	17	5	1	11–4
Costa Rica	2	0	21	500–1
Côte d'Ivoire	0	0	42	66–1
Croatia	2	0	20	50–1
Czech Republic	8	0	2	25–1
Ecuador	1	0	38	125–1
England	11	1	9	6–1
France	11	1	5	10–1
Germany	15	3	17	7–1
Ghana	0	0	50	250–1
Iran	2	0	19	500–1
Italy	15	3	12	8–1
Japan	2	0	15	150–1
Mexico	12	0	7	40–1
Netherlands	7	0	3	14–1
Paraguay	6	0	30	150–1
Poland	6	0	22	80–1
Portugal	3	0	10	18–1
Saudi Arabia	3	0	33	750–1
Serbia and Montenegro	9	0	47	100–1
South Korea	5	0	29	300–1
Spain	11	0	5	12–1
Sweden	10	0	14	28–1
Switzerland	7	0	36	100–1
Togo	0	0	56	400–1
Trinidad and Tobago	0	0	50	1000–1
Tunisia	3	0	28	300–1
Ukraine	0	0	40	50–1
United States	7	0	7	100–1

Source: *CIA World Factbook, FIFA Almanack of World Football 2006,* William Hill

Population and Players

	Population	Clubs	Registered Players	Registered Players Per Thousand
Angola	11,827,000	100	5,000	0.4
Argentina	39,538,000	2,994	140,000	3.5
Australia	20,090,000	1,200	60,000	3.0
Brazil	186,113,000	6,000	275,000	1.5
Costa Rica	4,016,000	128	2,700	0.7
Côte d'Ivoire	17,298,000	200	11,000	0.6
Croatia	4,496,000	1,186	28,000	6.2
Czech Republic	10,241,000	2,000	241,000	23.5
Ecuador	13,364,000	1,000	11,600	0.9
England	49,138,831	42,000	1,502,000	30.6
France	60,656,000	19,835	796,000	13.1
Germany	82,431,000	26,697	1,318,000	16.0
Ghana	21,946,000	250	15,000	0.7
Iran	68,018,000	2,535	252,000	3.7
Italy	58,103,000	16,123	361,000	6.2
Japan	127,417,000	700	190,000	1.5
Mexico	106,203,000	1,493	208,000	2.0
Netherlands	16,407,000	4,050	528,000	32.2
Paraguay	6,348,000	1,100	200,000	31.5
Poland	38,558,000	7,763	383,000	9.9
Portugal	10,566,000	2,530	40,000	3.8
Saudi Arabia	26,418,000	153	6,400	0.2
Serbia and Montenegro	10,829,000	2,821	251,000	23.2
South Korea	48,641,000	54	2,200	0.0
Spain	40,341,000	33,555	117,000	2.9
Sweden	9,002,000	3,228	124,000	13.8
Switzerland	7,489,000	1,453	90,000	12.0
Togo	5,400,000	565	1,500	0.3
Trinidad and Tobago	1,075,000	135	2,400	2.2
Tunisia	10,075,000	552	26,000	2.6
Ukraine	46,997,000	1,088	27,000	0.6
United States	295,734,000	1,690	160,000	0.5

Source: *CIA World Factbook, FIFA Almanack of World Football 2006,* William Hill

Group Stage

Group A
Germany
Costa Rica
Poland
Ecuador

Group B
England
Paraguay
Trinidad and Tobago
Sweden

Group C
Argentina
Côte d'Ivoire
Serbia and Montenegro
Netherlands

Group D
Mexico
Iran
Angola
Portugal

Group E
Italy
Ghana
United States
Czech Republic

Group F
Brazil
Croatia
Australia
Japan

Group G
France
Switzerland
South Korea
Togo

Group H
Spain
Ukraine
Tunisia
Saudi Arabia

Match Schedule

Group Stage

	Day	Date	German Time	Venue	Match	U.S. Time (EST)
1	Friday	9-Jun-06	6:00 P.M.	Munich	Germany–Costa Rica	12:00 noon
2	Friday	9-Jun-06	9:00 P.M.	Gelsenkirchen	Poland–Ecuador	3:00 P.M.
3	Saturday	10-Jun-06	3:00 P.M.	Frankfurt	England–Paraguay	9:00 A.M.
4	Saturday	10-Jun-06	6:00 P.M.	Dortmund	Trinidad & Tobago–Sweden	12:00 noon
5	Saturday	10-Jun-06	9:00 P.M.	Hamburg	Argentina–Côte d'Ivoire	3:00 P.M.
6	Sunday	11-Jun-06	3:00 P.M.	Leipzig	Serbia & Montenegro–Netherlands	9:00 A.M.
7	Sunday	11-Jun-06	6:00 P.M.	Nuremberg	Mexico–Iran	12:00 noon
8	Sunday	11-Jun-06	9:00 P.M.	Cologne	Angola–Portugal	3:00 P.M.
9	Monday	12-Jun-06	9:00 P.M.	Hanover	Italy–Ghana	3:00 P.M.
10	Monday	12-Jun-06	6:00 P.M.	Gelsenkirchen	United States–Czech Republic	12:00 noon
11	Monday	12-Jun-06	3:00 P.M.	Kaiserslautern	Australia–Japan	9:00 A.M.
12	Tuesday	13-Jun-06	9:00 P.M.	Berlin	Brazil–Croatia	3:00 P.M.
13	Tuesday	13-Jun-06	6:00 P.M.	Stuttgart	France–Switzerland	12:00 noon
14	Tuesday	13-Jun-06	3:00 P.M.	Frankfurt	South Korea–Togo	9:00 A.M.
15	Wednesday	14-Jun-06	3:00 P.M.	Leipzig	Spain–Ukraine	9:00 A.M.
16	Wednesday	14-Jun-06	6:00 P.M.	Munich	Tunisia–Saudi Arabia	12:00 noon
17	Wednesday	14-Jun-06	9:00 P.M.	Dortmund	Germany–Poland	3:00 P.M.
18	Thursday	15-Jun-06	3:00 P.M.	Hamburg	Ecuador–Costa Rica	9:00 A.M.
19	Thursday	15-Jun-06	6:00 P.M.	Nuremberg	England–Trinidad & Tobago	12:00 noon
20	Thursday	15-Jun-06	9:00 P.M.	Berlin	Sweden–Paraguay	3:00 P.M.

	Day	Date	German Time	Venue	Match	U.S. Time (EST)
21	Friday	16-Jun-06	3:00 P.M.	Gelsenkirchen	Argentina–Serbia & Montenegro	9:00 A.M.
22	Friday	16-Jun-06	6:00 P.M.	Stuttgart	Netherlands–Côte d'Ivoire	12:00 noon
23	Friday	16-Jun-06	9:00 P.M.	Hanover	Mexico–Angola	3:00 P.M.
24	Saturday	17-Jun-06	3:00 P.M.	Frankfurt	Portugal–Iran	9:00 A.M.
25	Saturday	17-Jun-06	9:00 P.M.	Kaiserslautern	Italy–United States	3:00 P.M.
26	Saturday	17-Jun-06	6:00 P.M.	Cologne	Czech Republic–Ghana	12:00 noon
27	Sunday	18-Jun-06	6:00 P.M.	Munich	Brazil–Australia	12:00 noon
28	Sunday	18-Jun-06	3:00 P.M.	Nuremberg	Japan–Croatia	9:00 A.M.
29	Sunday	18-Jun-06	9:00 P.M.	Leipzig	France–South Korea	3:00 P.M.
30	Monday	19-Jun-06	3:00 P.M.	Dortmund	Togo–Switzerland	29:00 A.M.
31	Monday	19-Jun-06	9:00 P.M.	Stuttgart	Spain–Tunisia	3:00 P.M.
32	Monday	19-Jun-06	6:00 P.M.	Hamburg	Saudi Arabia–Ukraine	12:00 noon
33	Tuesday	20-Jun-06	4:00 P.M.	Berlin	Ecuador–Germany	10:00 A.M.
34	Tuesday	20-Jun-06	4:00 P.M.	Hanover	Costa Rica–Poland	10:00 A.M.
35	Tuesday	20-Jun-06	9:00 P.M.	Cologne	Sweden–England	3:00 P.M.
36	Tuesday	20-Jun-06	9:00 P.M.	Kaiserslautern	Paraguay–Trinidad & Tobago	3:00 P.M.
37	Wednesday	21-Jun-06	9:00 P.M.	Frankfurt	Netherlands–Argentina	3:00 P.M.
38	Wednesday	21-Jun-06	9:00 P.M.	Munich	Côte d'Ivoire–Serbia & Montenegro	3:00 P.M.
39	Wednesday	21-Jun-06	4:00 P.M.	Gelsenkirchen	Portugal–Mexico	10:00 A.M.
40	Wednesday	21-Jun-06	4:00 P.M.	Leipzig	Iran–Angola	10:00 a.m.
41	Thursday	22-Jun-06	4:00 P.M.	Hamburg	Czech Republic–Italy	10:00 A.M.
42	Thursday	22-Jun-06	4:00 P.M.	Nuremberg	Ghana–United States	10:00 A.M.

(continued)

Group Stage *(continued)*

	Day	Date	German Time	Venue	Match	U.S. Time (EST)
43	Thursday	22-Jun-06	9:00 P.M.	Dortmund	Japan–Brazil	3:00 P.M.
44	Thursday	22-Jun-06	9:00 P.M.	Stuttgart	Croatia–Australia	3:00 P.M.
45	Friday	23-Jun-06	9:00 P.M.	Cologne	Togo–France	3:00 P.M.
46	Friday	23-Jun-06	9:00 P.M.	Hanover	Switzerland–South Korea	3:00 P.M.
47	Friday	23-Jun-06	4:00 P.M.	Kaiserslautern	Saudi Arabia–Spain	10:00 A.M.
48	Friday	23-Jun-06	4:00 P.M.	Berlin	Ukraine–Tunisia	10:00 A.M.

Round of Sixteen

	Day	Date	German Time	Venue	Match	U.S. Time (EST)
49	Saturday	24-Jun-06	5:00 P.M.	Munich	Winner of Group A–Runner-up of Group B	11:00 A.M.
50	Saturday	24-Jun-06	9:00 P.M.	Leipzig	Winner of Group C–Runner-up of Group D	3:00 P.M.
51	Sunday	25-Jun-06	5:00 P.M.	Stuttgart	Winner of Group B–Runner-up of Group A	11:00 A.M.
52	Sunday	25-Jun-06	9:00 P.M.	Nuremberg	Winner of Group D–Runner-up of Group C	3:00 P.M.
53	Monday	26-Jun-06	5:00 P.M.	Kaiserslautern	Winner of Group E–Runner-up of Group F	11:00 A.M.
54	Monday	26-Jun-06	9:00 P.M.	Cologne	Winner of Group G–Runner-up of Group H	3:00 P.M.
55	Tuesday	27-Jun-06	5:00 P.M.	Dortmund	Winner of Group F–Runner-up of Group E	11:00 A.M.
56	Tuesday	27-Jun-06	9:00 P.M.	Hanover	Winner of Group H–Runner-up of Group G	3:00 P.M.

Quarterfinals

	Day	Date	German Time	Venue	Match	U.S. Time (EST)
57	Friday	30-Jun-06	5:00 P.M.	Berlin	Winner of Match 49–Winner of Match 50	11:00 A.M.
58	Friday	30-Jun-06	9:00 P.M.	Hamburg	Winner of Match 53–Winner of Match 54	3:00 P.M.
59	Saturday	1-Jul-06	5:00 P.M.	Gelsenkirchen	Winner of Match 51–Winner of Match 52	11:00 A.M.
60	Saturday	1-Jul-06	9:00 P.M.	Frankfurt	Winner of Match 55–Winner of Match 56	3:00 P.M.

Semifinals

	Day	Date	German Time	Venue	Match	U.S. Time (EST)
61	Tuesday	4-Jul-06	9:00 P.M.	Dortmund	Winner of Match 57–Winner of Match 58	3:00 P.M.
62	Wednesday	5-Jul-06	9:00 P.M.	Munich	Winner of Match 59–Winner of Match 60	3:00 P.M.

Third Place

	Day	Date	German Time	Venue	Match	U.S. Time (EST)
63	Saturday	8-Jul-06	9:00 P.M.	Stuttgart	Runner-up of Match 61–Runner-up of Match 62	3:00 P.M.

Final

	Day	Date	German Time	Venue	Match	U.S. Time (EST) Time (EST)
64	Sunday	9-Jul-06	8:00 P.M.	Berlin	Winner of Match 61–Winner of Match 62	2:00 P.M.

Sites and Stadia

Berlin

Olympiastadion
Home To: Hertha BSC
Architect: Werner March; von Gerkan, Marg und Partner (reconstruction)
Opened: 1936; reconstructed 2004
Seating Capacity: 66,021
Notes: American sprinter Jesse Owens won four gold medals at the 1936 Olympic Games here, and the stadium has staged the German Cup final since 1985. Reconstruction includes a new roof, a vast oval interrupted by the historic Marathon Gate.

Dortmund

Westfalenstadion
Home To: Borussia Dortmund
Architect: Schröder Schulte-Ladbeck Strothmann
Opened: 1974; modernized 2005
Seating Capacity: 60,285
Notes: Known as the "opera house." Originally built for the 1974 World Cup. Some 50,000 cubic meters of earth were excavated for the original stadium, and bomb disposal teams uncovered, defused and removed 34 Second World War bombs.

Frankfurt

Commerzbank Arena
Home To: Eintracht Frankfurt
Architect: von Gerkan, Marg und Partner
Opened: 2005
Seating Capacity: 43,324
Notes: A minimalist supporting structure combined with a flood of natural light through the translucent roof give it a cathedral-like atmosphere. Former stadium was the site of the waterlogged 1974 World Cup semifinal between Poland and West Germany.

Gelsenkirchen

Arena AufShalke
Home To: Schalke 04
Architect: HPP Hentrich, Petschnigg und Partner, Becker und Köpcke AIG
Opened: 2001
Seating Capacity: 48,426
Notes: The most modern stadium in Europe, featuring a removable playing surface, giant video cube, a retractable roof and electronic admission controls. Hosted the Champions League final in 2004.

Hamburg

AOL Arena
Home To: HSV Hamburg
Architect: OS Architekten
Opened: 2000
Seating Capacity: 45,442
Notes: Replaced the old Volksparkstadion, where Germany suffered one of their most painful defeats when Jürgen Sparwasser's goal sealed a 1–0 triumph for the former East Germany at the 1974 World Cup.

Hanover

AWD Arena
Home To: HSV Hamburg
Architect: Schulitz & Partner
Opened: 2004
Seating Capacity: 39,297
Notes: Features a free-standing, 2,500-ton roof supporting structure partly made of ultraviolet permeable foil, to ensure the pitch receives enough light.

Kaiserslautern

Fritz-Walter-Stadion
Home To: FC Kaiserslautern
Architect: Fiebeger Architekten
Opened: 1920; reconstructed 2003
Seating Capacity: 39,820
Notes: Situated on the Betzenberg, a sandstone hillock at the heart of the city, and named after the 1954 World Cup–winning captain.

Cologne

RheinEnergie Stadion
Home To: FC Köln
Architect: von Gerkhan, Marg und Partner
Opened: 2004
Seating Capacity: 40,590
Notes: The steeply banked upper tiers feature a 34 -degree rake, with the pitch separated from the stands by less than eight meters. Four 72-meter masts support the roof and act as trademark illuminated beacons.

Leipzig

Zentralstadion
Home To: FC Sachsen Leipsig
Architect: Wirth + Wirth and Zech Planungs
Opened: 2004
Seating Capacity: 38,898
Notes: The previous Zentralstadion, opened in 1956, was once the largest stadium in Germany with a capacity of 100,000.

Munich

Allianz Arena
Home To: TSV 1860 München and FC Bayern München
Architect: Herzog & de Meuron
Opened: 2005
Seating Capacity: 59,416
Notes: The arena chosen to host the German national team in the opening match boasts a smooth facade formed from translucent, lozenge-shaped cushions, which glow in a variety of colors. Features Europe's largest underground parking lot.

Nuremberg

Franken-Stadion
Home To: FC Nürnberg
Architect: HPP Hentrich Petschnigg & Partner
Opened: 1928; renovated 1991
Seating Capacity: 36,898
Notes: One of three 2006 World Cup stadia (with Berlin and Stuttgart) to still feature an athletics track.

Stuttgart

Gottlieb-Daimler-Stadion
Home To: VfB Stuttgart
Architect: Paul Bonatz; Arat, Siegel & Partner (reconstruction)
Opened: 1933; modernized 1951, 1956, 1974, 1990
Seating Capacity: 47,757
Notes: Germany met Switzerland here in 1950 in the first international on German soil following the end of the Second World War. Forty years later, the stadium hosted the first international since reunification, another match-up between the Germans and the Swiss.

Referees

Name	Age	Nation	Occupation
Esam El Deen Abd El Fatah	40	Egypt	air force major
Khalil Ibrahim Al Ghamdi	35	Saudi Arabia	phys-ed teacher
Carlos Amarilla Demarqui	35	Paraguay	computer technician
Benito Armando Archundia Tellez	40	Mexico	economist
Carlos Alberto Batres Gonzalez	38	Guatemala	lab technician
Matthew Breeze	33	Australia	former police prosecutor
Massimo Busacca	37	Switzerland	company manager
Carlos Chandia Alarcon	41	Chile	entrepreneur
Coffi Codjia	38	Benin	tax inspector
Mourad Daami	43	Tunisia	businessman
Jerome Damon	34	South Africa	schoolteacher*
Frank De Bleeckere	39	Belgium	public relations manager
Massimo De Santis	44	Italy	police inspector
Horacio Elizondo	42	Argentina	phys-ed teacher
Herbert Fandel	42	Germany	concert pianist
Mohamed Guezzaz	43	Morocco	geography teacher
Alain Hamer	40	Luxembourg	banker
Terje Hauge	40	Norway	consultant referee
Valentin Ivanov	44	Russia	university professor†
Toru Kamikawa	42	Japan	professional referee
Jong Chul Kwon	42	South Korea	businessman
Jorge Larrionda	38	Uruguay	construction‡
Claus Bo Larsen	40	Denmark	shipping company manager
Shamsul Maidin	40	Singapore	football association manager

Note: Age is as of beginning of World Cup 2006

Source: Individual country's soccer federation unless otherwise noted
   * Phone conversation with referee
   † Moscow Football Club
   ‡ Referees union

Name	Age	Nation	Occupation
Luis Medina Cantalejo	42	Spain	labor relations specialist
Manuel Enrique Mejuto Gonzalez	41	Spain	civil servant
Markus Merk	44	Germany	former dentist
Lubos Michel	38	Slovakia	car tire sales manager
Subkhiddin Mohd Salleh	39	Malaysia	schoolteacher
Masoud Moradi	40	Iran	businessman
Rene Ortube Betancourt	41	Bolivia	accountant
Graham Poll	42	England	former sales consultant
Eric Poulat	42	France	computer programmer*
Peter Prendergast	42	Jamaica	businessman
Marco Antonio Rodriguez Moreno	32	Mexico	phys-ed teacher†
Roberto Rosetti	38	Italy	kinesipath
Oscar Julian Ruiz Acosta	36	Colombia	lawyer
Alain Sars	45	France	physical therapist
Mark Shield	32	Australia	professional referee
Rodolfo Sibrian	42	El Salvador	English professor
Carlos Simon	40	Brazil	journalist
Modou Sowe	42	Gambia	NA
Kevin Stott	38	United States	junior high math teacher
Kyros Vassaras	40	Greece	travel industry consultant

Woman who answered the referee's home phone
† Phone conversation with referee

World Cup 2006:
The 32 Nations

Angola

Capital: Luanda
Independence: November 11, 1975
   (from Portugal)
Area: 1,246,700 sq km
Population: 11,190,786
Median Age: 18.1 years
Life Expectancy at Birth: 38.4 years
Ethnic Groups: Ovimbundu 37%,
   Kimbundu 25%, Bakongo 13%,
   mestico (mixed European and
   African) 2%, European 1%, other 22%
Religions: indigenous beliefs 47%, Roman
   Catholic 38%, Protestant 15%
Languages: Portuguese (official), Bantu and
   other African languages
Suffrage: NA
Military Obligation: 17 years of age; compulsory
GDP Per Capita: $2,100
Budget: $10 billion
Military Expenditures: $183.58 million
   (10.6% of GDP)
Agriculture: bananas, sugarcane, coffee, sisal, corn,
   cotton, manioc (tapioca), tobacco, vegetables,
   plantains; livestock; forest products; fish
Industries: petroleum; diamonds, iron ore,
   phosphates, feldspar, bauxite, uranium, and
   gold; cement; basic metal products; fish
   processing; food processing; brewing; tobacco
   products; sugar; textiles; ship repair
Currency: kwanza

Source: *CIA World Factbook*

Angola

Henning Mankell

The first time I visited Angola, in the mid 1980s, I was not even aware that I was there. I was living just over the Angolan border, way up in the northwestern corner of Zambia. Narrow sand roads twisted through the endless bush. It was easy to get stuck while driving and I often lost my bearings when I was on my way to some distant village. When I'd stop and get out to ask directions it would sometimes happen that the person I'd spoken to would answer in Portuguese. My heart would beat harder than usual: *Angola!* Then it was imperative to get back to the right side of the invisible border as quickly as possible. A brutal civil war was underway, and the rebel leader Jonas Savimbi's warriors, infamous for indiscriminate violence, were everywhere.

But there was something fascinating about that land beyond the invisible border. This giant Angola, more than 1.2 million square kilometers in size, had been deeply wounded by its long colonial period, and then had been throttled after liberation by a violent civil war to which the Great Powers sent their hired armies to gain as much control as possible. The wars had been going on without interruption for thirty years. A generation of Angolans did not know what it was to live in a country where peace reigned.

When calm at last arrived—when the brutal Savimbi was killed by government forces in 2002—people in the cities began cautiously to repaint their houses. A person who does not believe in tomorrow does not repaint his house. Some of the hundreds of thousands who had fled to neighboring Zambia, Namibia, the Republic of Congo and the Democratic Republic of Congo, as well as Botswana and South Africa, began to return.

I remember the people who lived on the Angolan border, and the refugees. I remember their friendliness, their grief that their country was so ravaged. I remember a housekeeper in Kitwe, in north central Zambia, an Angolan named Maria. Her husband had disappeared, probably dead in the war, and she lived with her two children in a garage. She hoped to be able to return to Angola one day. At the same time she dreaded what she would find. She knew nothing about her parents, nothing of what had happened to her village. That was many years ago. I have tried to find out what happened to Maria. The only thing I know now is that she no longer lives in Kitwe with her children. Somehow, I feel sure, she has made her way home to Angola.

If one arrives in Angola, as one almost always does today, by landing at the airport in coastal Luanda, one can hardly imagine the enormous land area the country covers. Lay Angola over Europe: it covers Spain, Portugal and a good piece of France. Principally the land consists of savannah in the north, but there are dense forests near the border with the Congo and the coast by Namibia in the south is desert.

Huge areas of Angola are very sparsely populated, with only seven people per square kilometer in the country. But they are unevenly distributed: while there are few people in the north and south, the population becomes denser in the central highlands. No one knows, though, how many people are still refugees living elsewhere; many have returned, but many remain refugees. The elephants, lions, leopards and buffalo, most of the animals of the African savannah— they, too, suffered a heartless hunt during the years of war. It is said that elephants can feel when a war zone has calmed. Maybe they will return, too?

The very oldest inhabitants of the country were probably Khoisan-speaking nomads, people who lived as gatherers. Then the great immigration of Bantu-speakers from the Congo Basin came around 1000 B.C. and began to change the ethnographic image of all of southern Africa.

The Portuguese arrived in the sixteenth century. As was the case everywhere, first the coastal areas were colonized and then the regions around the largest rivers. Not much was known about the rest of the country. It was only later that the real ruthless exploitation of Angola's raw materials took off: gold, then uranium, now it is oil. But it was first and foremost the slave trade that plagued Angola's history. In the more than two centuries before Portugal abolished slave trafficking in 1836, Angola may have been the source of as many as 2 million slaves bound for the New World. Most were sold to the Portuguese colony of Brazil. But exactly how many people were sold, killed, starved or drowned we will never know. It is a scar on the Angolan soul that will never fully disappear.

The country's borders were drawn up at the beginning of the twentieth century. In 1951 the Portuguese dictator António de Oliveira Salazar decided that from then on Angola would be an "overseas province." The resistance to colonial oppression had begun, though it was mostly quiet; the Portuguese did not notice the movement just under the surface. A little more than ten years later revolts broke out. On November 11, 1975, the independent Republic of Angola was declared.

Almost immediately thereafter the civil war began. The country went from war to war. Peace was scarcely more than a dream, and only returned when Savimbi was dead. Through those years Angola formed a national football team and joined FIFA, but it failed to qualify for the World Cup. Until 2006.

Angola's qualification for the World Cup finals has been a series of extraordinary moments of good fortune. It started in June 2004, with a 1–0 win at home over Nigeria. At the time, no one dared to believe that this heralded a chance to advance. Nigeria was, after all, the great champion of the African continent. They had appeared in the last three World Cup finals. They could afford a loss; they would exact a terrible revenge on their own home turf.

But that is not how it turned out. In the return match in Nigeria, in June 2005, the Egyptian referee Esam Abd El Fatah blew the final whistle on a game in which Angola managed to pull out a draw. That must have come as a surprise to the mighty Nigerians! It had almost been considered a certainty that Nigeria was the team in the group that would go on to the World Cup in Germany.

Angola's players are known fondly as the Palancas Negras, the "black antelopes." Aside from the striker Pedro Mantorras, who plays for Benfica in Portugal, most of the players are not widely known. Figueirido, who equalized against Nigeria, had been eking out an obscure existence as a professional player in the Azores, for example. Angola has seen many of its football players leave the country to seek their livelihood. It was difficult for the Angolan team managers to find them; harder still to determine how they had developed as players during the time they had been gone. But they had not given up their citizenship, and when they were called home to put on black shorts, red socks and orange jerseys, they did not hesitate.

On October 8, 2005, after twelve qualifying matches over two years, Angola arrived at Amahoro Stadium in Kigali having only to beat Rwanda to qualify ahead of Nigeria—no matter what happened in Nigeria's game against Zimbabwe. It was a nightmarish wait for Angolans who gathered by their radios back in Luanda, Huambo, Lubango, Namibe, Lobito, Benguela, Malanje and every other city and every village. Perhaps even the antelopes themselves stood out on the savannah with pricked ears.

When the first half ended the score was 0–0. Meanwhile, Nigeria had their expected victory over Zimbabwe in Abuja: that game ended with the meaningless score of 5–1. Angola still had to win, even by a single goal; a draw would not be enough.

In the second half nervousness spread among the players. Rwanda, playing only for its honor, came close to scoring on several occasions; a Rwandan strike even hit Angola's goalkeeper João Pereira in the ribs. Everyone agreed that Angola was playing miserably. They were a team at the edge of a breakdown, missing passes and misunderstanding one another. It continued to be scoreless, it all seemed to be ending badly. The coaches began to make desperate replacements. Among others they sent in Ze Kalanga. There were ten minutes left. The Angolans were almost unconscious in their desperation. Then Ze Kalanga made a stunning cross to Fabrice "Akwa" Maieco, who headed it past Rwanda's goalkeeper Nkunzingoma— one bounce on the ground and the ball flew up into the net. Angola ahead! The rest of the game was pure agony for the Angolans, as they struggled to hold on to the lead. Only after five minutes of injury time did Mohamed Guezzaz of Morocco finally call the game.

Coach Luis Oliveira Gonçalvez leapt around and hugged his assistants while the players rolled around on the field at Amahoro Stadium. Some of them cried. Angola had qualified for the 2006 World Cup games in Germany. The black antelopes had taken their greatest leap.

Of course no one expects Angola to get far in the tournament. But a great victory has already been won, even if it brought no gleaming trophy. To go to the finals of the World Cup means an enormous amount to the self-confidence of a country that has been so ravaged by war and deprivation. Their national identity as well as the self-confidence of individual Angolans has received a huge injection of strength. One should not underestimate its significance in the long road that lies ahead. I am not speaking of soccer as political propaganda. It is simpler than that: if people play together on a soccer team they can hardly leave the game and wage war against each other. Good soccer depends upon cooperation; in the same way a country is rebuilt after a catastrophe.

For a long time I have lived in Mozambique, another African country burdened by the yoke of Portuguese colonialism for hundreds of years. As in Angola, soccer is everywhere: on gravel pitches and sandy beaches, on sidewalks and city squares. I have seen soccer balls made of old ladies' purses stuffed with rags, of fishnet filled with grass, of a T-shirt wadded up with tightly compressed pieces of paper. The balls roll and bounce and you can do headers and score goals with them. The mood in the stadium bleachers or around the improvised sandlots is often like a carnival. There can be an unholy amount of noise, but there is seldom rage about a call that goes against the home team. It might sound like a dangerous generalization to maintain that the mood at an African soccer game is *friendlier*. But I'm still going to do it. The sense of friendly play never disappears, no matter how important the game.

Perhaps this is why I am optimistic about Angola's future. The war never killed soccer in Angola. The soccer fields were demilitarized zones, and the face-off between teams conducting an intense yet essentially friendly battle served as a defense against the horrors that raged all around.

Once I visited a refugee camp for Angolans who had been forced to flee the civil war. When the trucks arrived with new contingents of refugees, those who were already in the camp gathered in the hope that some vanished relative would be among the new arrivals. Suddenly a young woman began to shriek and dance. She almost tore her clothes off. She danced around two old people, a man and a woman. The young woman cried and screamed, she patted the old woman on the cheek and took the man's hand. I found out later that these were her parents, whom she had believed to be dead.

That is what true happiness looks like, I thought. I will never forget those three Angolan people who found one another again. For me they are the image of an Angola where people will find themselves again and find the past again, the past that was stolen from them.

Of course they will succeed. Angola is a country that deserves all our support, all our respect. Out of inconceivable suffering they are creating a new world.

Translated from the Swedish by Linda Haverty Rugg

World Cup Record

FIFA Ranking: 63
World Cup Appearances: 0
World Cup Champions: 0
Federation Name: Federacão Angolana de
    Futebol
Confederation: CAF
Founded: 1979
FIFA Affiliation: 1980
Nickname: Palancas Negras (Black Impalas)
Manager: Luis Oliveira Gonçalves
Website: www.fafutebol.com
Stadium: Cidadela, Luanda
Home Uniform: red/black/red
Away Uniform: white and yellow/white/white
Provider: Puma

1930: Did not enter
1934: Did not enter
1938: Did not enter
1950: Did not enter
1954: Did not enter
1958: Did not enter
1962: Did not enter
1966: Did not enter
1970: Did not enter
1974: Did not enter
1978: Did not enter
1982: Did not qualify
1986: Did not qualify
1990: Did not qualify
1994: Did not qualify
1998: Did not qualify
2002: Did not qualify

Matches	Wins	Draws	Losses	GF*	GA*	GD*	Points
0	0	0	0	0	0	0	0

Angola is appearing in the World Cup for the first time

*GF = Goals For   GA = Goals Against   GD = Goal Difference

Path to Qualification for World Cup 2006

Date	Home		Away		Result
12-Oct-03	Chad	3	Angola	1	L
16-Nov-03	Angola	2	Chad	0	W
5-Jun-04	Algeria	0	Angola	0	D
20-Jun-04	Angola	1	Nigeria	0	W
3-Jul-04	Gabon	2	Angola	2	D
5-Sep-04	Angola	1	Rwanda	0	W
10-Oct-04	Angola	1	Zimbabwe	0	W
27-Mar-05	Zimbabwe	2	Angola	0	L
5-Jun-05	Angola	2	Algeria	1	W
18-Jun-05	Nigeria	1	Angola	1	D
4-Sep-05	Angola	3	Gabon	0	W
8-Oct-05	Rwanda	0	Angola	1	W

Angola qualified by finishing first in Group 4 of the African Zone

Argentina

Capital: Buenos Aires
Independence: July 9, 1816 (from Spain)
Area: 2,766,890 sq km
Population: 39,537,943
Median Age: 29.4 years
Life Expectancy at Birth: 75.9 years
Ethnic Groups: white (mostly Spanish and Italian) 97%; mestizo (mixed white and Amerindian ancestry), Amerindian or other non-white groups 3%
Religions: nominally Roman Catholic 92%, Protestant 2%, Jewish 2%, other 4%
Languages: Spanish (official), English, Italian, German, French
Suffrage: 18 years of age; universal and compulsory
Military Obligation: 18 years of age; voluntary
GDP Per Capita: $12,400
Budget: $39.98 billion
Military Expenditures: $4.3 billion (1.3% of GDP)
Agriculture: sunflower seeds, lemons, soybeans, grapes, corn, tobacco, peanuts, tea, wheat; livestock
Industries: food processing, motor vehicles, consumer durables, textiles, chemicals and petrochemicals, printing, metallurgy, steel
Currency: Argentine peso

Source: *CIA World Factbook*

Argentina

Thomas Jones

To pay anyone a proper compliment in the playground back in the mid 1980s, you had to use the word "skill"—an adjective, as in "man, your new skateboard is so skill"—and nobody in the world was more skill than Diego Armando Maradona. In the early summer of 1986, in the buildup to the World Cup in Mexico, his name superseded even "skill" as the highest form of praise on the football pitch and elsewhere—"man, your new skateboard is so maradona." It took me a while to realize that the word referred to a human being, let alone a football player. Then I saw him score in a first-round match against Italy, leaping unfeasibly high into the air outside the left edge of the six-yard box to tap the ball deftly over the outstretched right leg of the Italian captain, Gaetano Scirea, past the outstretched arms of the keeper and into the bottom right-hand corner of the goal. It was evident, even to a benighted nine-year-old from the Home Counties town of Basingstoke (famed for its ring road), that Maradona was not merely skillful, but skill embodied.

He was born on October 30, 1960, in Villa Fiorito, a poor barrio on the outskirts of Buenos Aires. When he was nine years old, the manager of Los Cebollitas ("the little onions"), astounded by the boy's performance, thought he couldn't possibly be as young as he claimed, and asked to see some ID. With Maradona playing for them, Los Cebollitas won 136 matches in a row. He wasn't selected for the 1978 World Cup squad—which was in Argentina, and which Argentina won—because he was thought to be too young. A year afterward, in a game between Argentina and a "world eleven" (Cup winners against an international team made up of the best of the rest) Maradona put away an epic goal against Brazil's Emerson Leão, curling the ball in from outside the box: "Fucking motherfucker," he exclaimed later, recalling his frustration at being excluded from the winning World Cup squad, "why wasn't I on the pitch a year earlier, just a year earlier, was I that much younger, for fuck's sake?"

In Mexico, Maradona didn't score again until a couple of weeks later, the night Argentina played England. This was the first time the two countries had met in a major tournament since the quarter-finals of the 1966 World Cup, when England had beaten Argentina 1–0. Since then, the two nations had gone to war.

On April 2, 1982, while Maradona and his teammates were training for the World Cup in Spain, Argentinian troops landed on the Islas Malvinas, a.k.a. the Falkland Islands, three hundred miles off the coast of Argentina and eight thousand miles from London. Argentina assumed that Britain wouldn't do anything about the invasion, but within days a task force set out from ports around Britain and Gibraltar—another of the United Kingdom's disputed overseas possessions—to reclaim the colony. "I cannot foretell," Margaret Thatcher admitted, "what orders the task force will receive as it proceeds," since it would take a week or two for it to get there.

Jorge Luis Borges, another Argentinian genius, later compared the "Falklands thing" to "two bald men fighting over a comb." By the middle of June, Britain had retaken the islands, and more than nine hundred soldiers (655 Argentinian, 253 British) had lost their lives. My mother, a doctor, was working in a hospital in Portsmouth when the fleet sailed. Many of the nurses had husbands or boyfriends or brothers in the navy, and it was an anxious time for them. I remember being excited that the country was going to war, though relieved that any actual fighting would be taking place a very long way away. And I had a sense that there was something not entirely noble about the enterprise, which probably filtered down from my parents' disapproval. Of the Argentinian dead, many of them teenaged conscripts, more than half had been on board the *General Belgrano,* an old Second World War cruiser that was torpedoed by a British submarine as it was steaming away from the conflict. "Gotcha!" was the *Sun*'s gloating headline the next day.

Victory in the Falklands saw Thatcher's popularity soar in Britain. In Argentina the defeat contributed to the downfall of the right-wing military junta that had ruled the country since 1976. It had been in trouble before the war: with the economy in disarray, the reclaiming of the Malvinas had been in part an attempt to boost public support for the regime—and it worked for a while, until the British nuclear-powered submarines, aircraft carriers, Harrier jump jets and helicopter squadrons arrived. Argentina surrendered on June 14—the day after their football team, the defending champions, lost the opening game of the World Cup in Barcelona, beaten by Belgium, a team that had last qualified in 1970, and had never proceeded beyond the first round.

The Falklands Conflict was ancient history by the time Argentina and England met in Mexico in 1986—or so everyone on both sides insisted before the game. Speaking to reporters before the match, José Luis Brown, Maradona's predecessor as captain, said: "We all had cousins, fathers, nephews in the Malvinas, and some of them didn't come back. Lamentable things, but we shan't be thinking of them." Then he promised the press "a very beautiful game."

Ten minutes into the second half, with his team up by a goal, Maradona received the ball from Hector Enrique inside the Argentine half, seemingly blocked in by Peter Reid and Peter Beardsley, then pivoted through 270 degrees and shot away down the right wing, dancing past Kenny Sansom and Terry Butcher as if both he and the ball were on wires. I wouldn't have been surprised if he'd taken off into the air and started flying. And if he didn't, perhaps it's only because he didn't need to, beating Terry Fenwick, the last of the defenders, and the keeper, Peter Shilton, without defying gravity too. He appeared to be moving through a different time frame from the England players, who arrived to tackle him only once he was already past them. The ball was in the back of the net by the time Butcher hacked Maradona down. Sixteen years later, this performance, eleven dazzling seconds of extraordinary skill—or more than skill, eleven seconds of pure Maradona—was voted Goal of the Century in a FIFA ballot. Maradona called it "the goal you dream of as a kid."

England never came back. As Maradona wrote in his 2000 autobiography, *Yo Soy El Diego:*

More than defeating a football team it was defeating a country. Of course, before the match, we said that football had nothing to do with the Malvinas War but we knew a lot of Argentinian kids had died there, shot down like little birds. This was revenge. It was like recovering a little bit of the Malvinas. In the pre-match interviews we had all said that football and politics shouldn't be confused, but that was a lie. We did nothing but think about that. Bollocks was it just another match!

To my surprise, nobody at school the next day wanted to talk about the goal of the century. All anyone wanted to talk about was the one Maradona had scored four minutes earlier, with his fist, the one that had been slotted home, he told the press after the game, "A little bit by the hand of God, another bit by the head of Maradona." El Diego's one-time fans were seething with fury, as if he'd betrayed them personally. Overnight, his name had become an insult, a byword for cheating. I was baffled.

The Hand of God incident never bothered me; I'd even say I admire it. First, it's amazing that Maradona, five-feet-five inches tall, should have outjumped Shilton, who's well over six foot. And weren't the referee and line judges most at fault, for not spotting the foul but allowing the goal? As Maradona told a BBC journalist a year later: "It was 100 percent legitimate because the referee allowed it and I'm not one to question the honesty of the referee." I've always suspected that the high-minded censure of the Hand of God incident is less about sportsmanship than finding a way to dress up the disappointment and frustration of England's loss. England fans will never be able to forgive Maradona, not for his cheating, but for running round five of our best players like so many wooden posts to score the greatest goal that's ever been scored—and knock us out of the World Cup.

What's unforgivable is that he was both the greatest player in the world and at the same time an outrageous cheat: that he didn't only smash the principles of fair play brazenly in the face with his fist, and revel in the transgression, but less than five minutes later proved that he didn't need to cheat in order to win. He cheated for the hell of it. He could score goals legitimately if he wanted to—not only legitimately, but magnificently—and he could get away with breaking the rules if he wanted to, too.

It's not as if his opponents were so noble themselves: Butcher's late tackle would surely have earned Argentina a penalty if the goal hadn't already been scored. And if Maradona's sense of fair play was a little skewed, some of the blame must go to Butcher's many predecessors, who gave up trying to take the ball off El Diego and simply went for his ankles instead. In 1983, when Maradona was playing for Barcelona, a savage lunge from Andoni Goikoetxea (the so-called "Butcher of Bilbao") fractured his ankle: "*crack,* I felt the axe's blow from behind, I felt my leg seize up, and I knew that everything was destroyed." Three months later Maradona was back on the pitch—but unlikely to pay much attention to pious homilies on the subject of fair play.

"Sometimes I think I almost enjoyed that [goal] more, the first one," Maradona wrote in his autobiography. "Now I feel I am able to say what I couldn't then . . . Bollocks was it the hand of God, it was the hand of Diego! And it felt a little bit like pickpocketing the English." On June 23, 1986, and in the weeks following, our pockets still freshly picked, I kept my feelings to myself, holding back from defending Maradona publicly for fear of having my own ankles broken in the playground.

Argentina went on to win the World Cup in Mexico. In Italy in 1990 they were the runner-up, losing 1–0 in the final to Germany. Then in 1994, Maradona was sent home from the United States for failing a drug test, and banned from playing for fifteen months. Argentina was knocked out in the first round, their fortunes seeming to follow those of their greatest player. The next year, in a stunning upset, the U.S. beat a Maradona-less Argentina 3–0 in the Copa America in Uruguay.

When the ban following his ignominious departure from the 1994 World Cup came to an end in the autumn of 1995, Maradona rejoined Boca Juniors, where he stayed until testing positive for cocaine in August 1997. In 2000 he went to live in Cuba, where he started putting on weight, and by March 2005 he weighed 266 pounds. That month he went to a Colombian surgeon to have his stomach stapled and 112 pounds cut off him. His doctor says it's a miracle he's still alive. He's got a tattoo of another legendary Argentinian, Che Guevara, on his right shoulder: "He was a rebel. So am I." He's friendly with Fidel Castro, Hugo Chávez and Evo Morales, the former coca farmer who was last year elected president of Bolivia, and has become something of a populist rallying point for the left in Latin America, leading a protest in the coastal city of Mar del Plata against a visit from George W. Bush last November.

But Maradona won't be involved with coaching Argentina's 2006 World Cup squad (enigmatic as ever, he declined the invitation from the Argentine Football Assocation). The team, which is ranked fourth in the world, includes some outstanding players. Carlos Tevez, one of several to have been tagged as "the new Maradona," has been voted Latin America's Footballer of the Year for the third year running in a poll by the Uruguayan newspaper *El País*. Juan Román Riquelme, the playmaker, isn't properly appreciated in Argentina, at least according to José Pekerman, the national coach; but he won me over, in my unpatriotic way, in a friendly between Argentina and England last November, taking control of almost the entire match. If Riquelme hadn't been brought off after eighty-four minutes, Michael Owen wouldn't have scored his two late goals, and Argentina would have won the game 2–1. Then there's Lionel Messi, the Barcelona midfielder and star of the FIFA World Youth Championship in 2005, another "new Maradona" like Tevez.

None of them, however, will be wearing the number ten shirt. The line between healthy respect and debilitating superstition is a thin one, and perhaps Argentina won't win the World Cup again until they've learned to stop living in awe of El Diego. An Argentinian player truly worthy of being described as "the new Maradona" would come out onto the pitch wearing the sacred number ten shirt— "bollocks to that, fucking motherfuckers." No one would call him by anything other than his own name, and nine-year-olds across the globe from Buenos Aires to Basingstoke would think that there'd never been a footballer like him.

World Cup Record

FIFA Ranking: 4
World Cup Appearances: 13
World Cup Champions: 2
Federation Name: Asociación del Fútbol Argentino
Confederation: CONMEBOL
Founded: 1893
FIFA Affiliation: 1912
Nickname: Albiceleste (White and Sky Blue)
Manager: José Pekerman
Website: www.afa.org.ar
Stadium: Antonio Vespucio Liberti
Home Uniform: light blue white vertical stripes/dark blue/white
Away Uniform: dark blue/white/white
Provider: Adidas

1930: 2nd place
1934: First round exit
1938: Did not participate
1950: Did not participate
1954: Did not participate
1958: First round exit
1962: First round exit
1966: Quarterfinal exit
1970: Did not qualify
1974: Second phase exit
1978: CHAMPIONS
1982: Second phase exit
1986: CHAMPIONS
1990: 2nd place
1994: Second round exit
1998: Quarterfinal exit
2002: First round exit

Matches	Wins	Draws	Losses	GF	GA	GD	Points
60	30	11	19	102	71	+31	101

Argentina is 4th on the all-time World Cup table

Path to Qualification for World Cup 2006

6-Sep-03	Argentina	2	Chile	2	D
9-Sep-03	Venezuela	0	Argentina	3	W
15-Nov-03	Argentina	3	Bolivia	0	W
19-Nov-03	Colombia	1	Argentina	1	D
30-Mar-04	Argentina	1	Ecuador	0	W
2-Jun-04	Brazil	3	Argentina	1	L
6-Jun-04	Argentina	0	Paraguay	0	D
4-Sep-04	Peru	1	Argentina	3	W
9-Oct-04	Argentina	4	Uruguay	2	W
13-Oct-04	Chile	0	Argentina	0	D
17-Nov-04	Argentina	3	Venezuela	2	W
26-Mar-05	Bolivia	1	Argentina	2	W
30-Mar-05	Argentina	1	Colombia	0	W
4-Jun-05	Ecuador	2	Argentina	0	L
8-Jun-05	Argentina	3	Brazil	1	W
3-Sep-05	Paraguay	1	Argentina	0	L
9-Oct-05	Argentina	2	Peru	0	W
12-Oct-05	Uruguay	1	Argentina	0	L

Argentina qualified by finishing among the top four in the South American Zone

Australia

Capital: Canberra
Independence: January 1, 1901
    (federation of UK colonies)
Area: 7,686,850 sq km
Population: 20,090,437
Median Age: 36.6 years
Life Expectancy at Birth: 80.4 years
Ethnic Groups: Caucasian 92%,
    Asian 7%, aboriginal and other 1%
Religions: Catholic 26.4%,
    Anglican 20.5%,
    other Christian 20.5%, Buddhist 1.9%,
    Muslim 1.5%, other 1.2%,
    unspecified 12.7%, none 15.3%
Languages: English 79.1%, Chinese 2.1%,
    Italian 1.9%, other 11.1%,
    unspecified 5.8%
Suffrage: 18 years of age; universal and
    compulsory
Military Obligation: NA
GDP Per Capita: $30,700
Budget: $221.7 billion
Military Expenditures: $16.65 billion
    (2.7% of GDP)
Agriculture: wheat, barley, sugarcane, fruits;
    cattle, sheep, poultry
Industries: mining, industrial and transportation
    equipment, food processing, chemicals, steel
Currency: Australian dollar

Source: *CIA World Factbook*

Australia

Ben Rice

We are emigrating. My wife, after having been in England more than ten years, has endured one interminably dark and dreary English winter too many, and is homesick for her home country. So we have decided to take our two very young children to live on the other side of the world, in Australia.

I am from time to time overcome with nostalgia, a premature homesickness that has taken me by surprise. I have taken to making lists of the things I will miss about England, things that you cannot get in Australia: dark afternoons huddled around an open fire; lying in long grass in the summer, without fear of snakes; putting on shoes carelessly; swimming wherever you like.

Mostly, though, I am excited about the move. My first book, *Pobby and Dingan,* was written on a trip I made to Lightning Ridge, an opal mining town in New South Wales. The book I'm writing now is based on the experience of living near an Australian golf course, a community of wealthy sea changers, where kangaroos grazed on the greens, and aboriginal kids carried out spectacular raids, joyriding golf carts and running about with stolen flags. At night the melaleuca trees between the fairways creaked in the wind and thrashed about in the lightning like ghosts.

What I find inspiring about Australia has to do with extremes. First there is the extremely long journey you have to make to get there, and the extreme jet lag and disorientation you experience upon arrival. There is the steep contrast between the cultured, progressive way of life in the city, and the rugged, artless life of the outback. There are the extremes of landscape, the way conservative and progressive mindsets rub up against each other, the extreme weather and the idiom—the Australian way of talking, the thing I like most of all about Australia.

An Australian might say, "You don't know the real Australia from a bar of soap." And in many ways he'd be right. I don't see Australia as a real country, but almost an imagined place, a state I carry around in my head. The country where I set my stories is a heightened, exaggerated version of Australia, magical and extreme—I should probably call it *Austrangelia,* or *Australextremis.* Though the real Australia is still a heightened, exaggerated version of anyplace I've ever visited, especially when it comes to football.

Football?

Yes, football. Of course it can't command the same audiences or have the same status that it has everywhere else: Australians have other sports that demand their attention, like "Aussie rules," that baffling fast-paced game where the players wear strange vests, and seem permitted to do anything they like, bounce, kick, throw—kill if necessary—in order to get the ball to go between the posts. They've got rugby league (some refer to it as "egg ball"), cricket and even more eccentric, exaggerated, *Australian* sports. For example, I have played golf on an outback course where the greens were not green or made of grass at all, but red dust or rock, and you had to carry a piece of turf around the course with you to tee off. On previous visits to Oz I have fished, surfed, swum with dolphins and jogged along sandy beaches as long as motorways, with the water lapping at my ankles. At times like this football is the furthest thing from my mind.

But Australians these days are mad about football. The sport has slowly gained popularity in Australia over the last decades, struggling hard to establish itself as Australian. A few years ago, in Lightning Ridge, I got into a conversation about the beautiful game with an opal miner who kept referring to it as "wogball" (in Australia "wog" is slang for a person of Mediterranean descent), and seemed convinced that the whole enterprise was up to its neck in drug dealing and mafia connections.

We were playing pool together in the bowling club, and he'd had more than a few schooners of grog. "Poofs, too, the lot of 'em, by the way," he muttered.

He came closer, his breath reeking, and mouth remarkable for its absence of front teeth. "Mean bastards too. Bloody rough bunch."

The miner was of Polish origin, but his father had been "decent enough" to raise him playing Australian sports, a fact for which he was extremely grateful. Otherwise, he said, he could easily have been linked to the mafia scum who were always rioting and causing trouble after wogball matches in that den of filth and corruption—Sydney.

Initially I considered this view to be nothing more than that of an inebriated eccentric who spent too much time underground in an isolated town. But racist or quasi-racist slander of football was not uncommon in Australia, even in the cities, where the football-eggball rivalry could serve as cover for deeper biases. It's still commonplace to hear diehard "Aussie rules" fans badmouthing the foreign game they fear is robbing their sport of its audience. When a famous Socceroo and broadcaster, Johnny Warren (both a long-time campaigner against prejudice in football and vocal critic of the Oceania qualification system), decided to write a memoir, he gave it the title *Sheilas, Wogs and Poofters* (Sheilas are girls).

But in the years since my trip to Lightning Ridge, football has become the number one sport in Australian schools. And now that the Socceroos have qualified for Germany 2006, football has arrived in Oz. When next summer comes (or rather next winter) and the World Cup begins, Australia is going to feel much closer to the rest of the world, to home.

Had I chosen to move to Australia in 2002, it would have been a very different situation. Soccer, and particularly international soccer, was in something of a wilderness. The national team was still obliged to play the bulk of its international matches in the Oceania Confederation, a grouping of southern nations made up predominantly of small Pacific island states—Tonga, Samoa, Tahiti, the Solomon Islands—with teams that (aside from New Zealand) were far less accomplished and professional than the Socceroos, teams that seemed to have been plucked from the pages of a magic realist novel. In some of these strange and utterly imbalanced matches Australia was often in the sorry position of scoring more than ten goals, which doesn't sound like much of a sob story, until you understand that when the Socceroos met teams from more competitive international confederations, vying for a place in the World Cup, they invariably found themselves ill-prepared for real opposition, and came unstuck. For thirty-two years, Australia has been unable to qualify for the tournament. It has been isolated, living in the wrong world.

The most extraordinary of these Oceania cup fixtures, and a beautiful example of the extreme side of Australia, occurred in April 2001, when the Socceroos broke the world record for the most goals scored in one international match, beating their opponents 31–0.

The unfortunate country on the receiving end of that astonishing world-record-breaking pasting was American Samoa, a tiny archipelago located approximately 2,000 kilometers southwest of Hawaii, 4,500 kilometers from the U.S. coast and 4,000 kilometers from Australia. Google "American Samoa" and before you can find anything much about the geography or the politics of the islands you are sure to come across a reference to the merciless spanking the American Samoans received at the hands of the Socceroos, in Coffs Harbour, New South Wales.

It was always going to be an unbalanced contest. A few days earlier the Aussies had trounced Tonga 22–0. A footballing superpower by no stretch of the imagination, Tonga were nevertheless known to be a considerably stronger force than the American Samoans, who, at the time, were ranked 205th, that is to say, *last,* in the entire world. Still, there is always the hope that in this kind of match the underdog, the rank outsider, the poorer nation, might pull off an amazing coup. And indeed, for the first few minutes, it seemed as if the Pacific islanders could, if not make a close fought thing of it, at least go some way to sparing themselves the indignity of a complete spanking.

Then, ten minutes in, the scoring was opened by Con Boutsianis, colorful Australian midfielder famed less for his football than for driving the getaway car in an armed robbery at a Melbourne restaurant. After that his teammates stamped on the accelerator, stealing a goal every few minutes. By halftime the score was 16–0 and several players were on hat tricks. And at the final whistle Archie Thomson, the Australian striker, had bagged a world record of thirteen goals. There followed a heated dispute among the scorekeepers about whether the final Australian tally was thirty-one or thirty-two. But there was no doubt whatsoever about the Samoan total. It was, as an Australian might say, "stuff-all."

The scale of the victory, due in part to the imbalance in skill between the sides, was also due to the handicaps with which the Samoan team had been saddled prior to the game. Several American Samoan first team players had been prohibited from taking part in the contest because they were not carrying the correct passports, and the islanders were therefore forced at the last minute to draw upon a clutch of teenaged replacements in order to field a side. Add to this setback the fact that the American Samoan team occasionally resembled children learning to ice skate (they had only recently become accustomed to playing the game in football boots), multiply it by the obvious economic and political margin that exists between the two countries, and you begin to comprehend how the Socceroos came to attain such a massive score in an international match.

Australia-dominated as the game certainly was, the islanders occasionally succeeded in launching one or two decent attacks on goal. Once Michael Petkovic, the Australian keeper, was even forced to dive. Meanwhile, at the other end of the pitch, the Samoan keeper, Nicky Salapu, managed to keep the Australian tally from sliding into the forties by making a series of spectacular saves. The next day the *Sydney Morning Herald* declared that Salapu "has quite a decent future . . . as long as he recovers mentally from last night's torture."

And tortuous it surely must have been. Put yourself in the cheesy Nikes of a fictional American Samoan teenager. One minute you are at home doing your homework, reading a little pornography under your duvet, and the next you're being called up from Pago Pago airport by a stressed-out national coach (your uncle perhaps) and told to pack your case immediately because you are going to Australia to play for your country. It is the stuff of teenagers' dreams. That night you would have been pissing yourself with excitement, kept awake with fantasies of striking a blow against the Australians, with a spectacular diving header, a bicycle kick, helping your team to the first victory in the nation's footballing history, and becoming in the process not only the most popular kid at school, but a celebrity, a national hero. Already you might be fantasizing about the post-match parties, the jubilant flight home and of being welcomed back to Pago Pago airport by a parade of beautiful girls in traditional dress, each of them bent on claiming your virginity, before you're signed up for a premiership team and whisked away from the island life into a world of international celebrity.

For that dream to be punctured and then torn to pieces and spat back at you, in the form of thirty-one goals, to then have to go back home to face your guffawing classmates knowing that you played a part in ensuring that your country would be forever commemorated on the Internet as a nation of world-record-breaking losers—well, let's just say it can't have been an easy thing to stomach at such an impressionable age.

Remarkable then that the American Samoans did not lose heart. They did not storm off the field in an adolescent huff. They played the full ninety minutes, though they did come across a trifle dazed afterward: "It was as if they [the Australians] were on motorbikes," one of them said to a reporter. At the final whistle, instead of trashing the stadium or bursting into tears or depositing a turd in their opponents' goal and escaping in a getaway car (borrowed, perhaps, from the Australian who began their ordeal), the American Samoans generously performed a traditional dance—which an Australian journalist noted was as "piss weak as you would expect from a team beaten thirty-one zip." Their coach, Tony Langkilde, was praised by more charitable members of the Aussie media for not allowing himself to become "negged-out" by the whole experience.

"It is a learning curve," he said. "We are a member of FIFA and we have a right to play. We are very happy to be here and to build from here. I do not think we are downhearted. The only way is forward."

When I first read this interview I had just returned from visiting a close family friend who was undergoing treatment for cancer. Amazed by her strength of spirit and courage, the words "I do not think we are downhearted" choked me up completely.

If there was something noble about the American Samoans' strength of spirit, there was also something a little off-putting about the apparently greedy and merciless manner in which my future countrymen piled on the goals against their unfortunate opponents. But look deeper into the recent history of the Australian game and you'll see that the Socceroos had long been suffering from a kind of marginalization themselves.

For many years Australia had been attempting to make FIFA recognize that they are a serious force in world football, and deserved to spend their time playing better opposition than the island teams they routinely encountered in the Oceania Confederation. Isolated and frustrated at having to play at a level so far beneath them, and having failed to qualify for the World Cup in thirty-two years, or convince their own countrymen that they deserved to be taken seriously, the thirty-one (or -two) goals constituted not so much a display of thuggishness or greed, as a desperate cry for help.

So take off those cheesy Nikes and place your feet upon the fragrant, lavender-scented innersoles of a Socceroo's handmade, one-thousand-dollar Diadora football boots.

You are killing the American Samoans. By halftime you have bagged six goals, more than you've scored in an entire season for the Serie A side where you play your club football. If you liked you could wheel on a gas barbie, cook up some prawns, have a few beers, make love to a beautiful woman right here on the pitch, and probably score a few more. But you get no pleasure from this game. It *is* nice to be home, *bloody oath it is,* but despite the vast improvement to your international goals stats, you are miserable. It's a bloody farce. The fans are already barracking for the opposition. Some of them are leaving. Your coach has fallen asleep on the sideline. And one of these American Samoans, you can't fail to notice, is young enough to be your kid.

Your mates back in Italy will just assume football in Australia has an entirely different scoring system. You will *never* be taken seriously. You consider suggesting to the referee that you play without a goalkeeper, that you play blindfolded, that you withdraw half your team from the field, or offer your opponents a twenty goal cushion to make more of a game of it, but you know this will not help; if anything it will only reinforce the amateurishness of the contest. And then it hits you—the only decent way to make the organizers appre-

ciate your plight is by creating a massive comedy scoreline, a scoreline that will hopefully transmit the message that soccer deserves a
proper place in the sporting psyche of the nation.

"The American Samoans are not expected to be at the finals next
year," an Australian journalist noted the morning after the 31–0
game. And he was right, the American Samoans were not there. But
then, neither were the Socceroos. Having topped the Oceania Confederation, Australia went on to play two games against Uruguay for
a place at the World Cup, winding up with a 3–1 loss on aggregate—
and another long wait. This was too much for most Aussie soccer
fans. Fearing the jibes of their eggball-playing colleagues, Socceroo
supporters stayed home from work, logged on to the Internet, like a
clandestine society of extremists, and aired their dismay: "The natural state of Australian soccer is frustration and high blood pressure,"
wrote one blogger the day after the match. "Another four years of ob-
scurity and irrelevance awaits," wrote a second. "I want to curl up
and die," wrote a third.

The next time the organizers of the Oceania Confederation met, a
decision was taken to reorganize the playoffs in order to avoid further comedy score lines. The weaker Oceania teams were divided
into two leagues, and the strongest sides, Australia and New
Zealand, were given an automatic ticket to the second round. This
meant that the Aussies would not have another chance to top their
world record.

In the final stages of qualification for Germany 2006, Australia
played a two-leg series against the Solomon Islands, who had recently dispatched New Zealand. Before the first game, Football Federation Australia had replaced longtime coach Frank Farina with
Dutch tactician Guus Hiddink, the man who had taken the Netherlands to the semifinals of the 1998 World Cup, and done the same
thing for the South Koreans in 2002. When Australia beat the
Solomon Islands (9–1 on aggregate) Hiddink decided his team only
knew how to attack, possibly because they had never needed to do
anything else, and immediately set about instilling a defensive mindset. A few months later Australia would cautiously approach their

two intercontinental playoff matches, against Uruguay again. In the first they were perhaps overcautious, controlling the match but losing 1–0 in Montevideo. They would have to score two on the home leg. Four days later, 83,000 fans turned out at Telstra Stadium in Sydney. Millions more watched on TV. There was certainly nothing imbalanced or farcical about this contest. It was "quite the most pulsating football match ever played on Australian soil," as one football commentator described it. Instead of attacking from the start, and burning themselves out in the first half, Australia played an aggressive but collected game, soaking up a wave of Alvaro Recoba attacks, and waiting for their opportunity to reply. It came in the 34th minute when Harry Kewell miskicked his shot, brilliantly as it turned out, toward Marco Bresciano, who swept it up and put it past the keeper. At 1–0, the aggregate score was 1–1 and the crowd grazed on their fingernails. It went to penalties. Mark Schwarzer, the Australian keeper, made two incredible saves. When John Aloisi stepped up and slotted home the winning goal, Telstra Stadium, already drowned in yellow flags, burst into song: "Can you hear can you hear that thunder?" the fans yelled, as if issuing a warning to Australia's future opponents in Germany. "You better run! You better take cover!"

A minority sport? Not anymore. There can be no greater evidence that wogball's days are numbered than the fact that Aloisi's penalty spot was dug up, frozen and placed in a glass case, like a prize winning barramundi. Qualified at last, Aussie soccer fans were going to cram thirty-two years of partying into one night. Thousands danced in the streets of Sydney, and the next morning the papers were mad for it. Journalists spoke of escape from the demons of the past, of breaking a curse. Finally the Socceroos had escaped the world of magic realist football.

Look ahead to the night of June 17, 2006, the five-star Munich hotel room of Australian goalie Mark Schwarzer. You are an experienced keeper, a starter in the English Premiership, responsible for great saves against Uruguay for the national team. You're used to big matches, tense encounters, holding the line. But tonight, the night before your meeting with Brazil, you cannot sleep. You pace around the hotel room doing a few stretches to calm your nerves. Tomorrow is the biggest game of your life. You're playing the world champions in the World Cup. In spite of your team's low FIFA ranking (number forty-eight), you are here, at the planet's biggest sporting event, and every game starts 0–0. Falling asleep now, you dream of thrashing the South Americans, of making a spectacular save, then putting the ball immediately back into play, kicking it straight to Neil, who heads it to Viduka, who heads it into the back of the Brazilian goal. Or scoring one yourself, running the length of the pitch, weaving between the greatest players on earth—Ronaldinho, Robinho, Ronaldo, Roberto Carlos—then threading one between Julio Cesar's legs, straight into the net. The most magnificent goal in history. . . .

Perhaps all goalies have this dream. But maybe it doesn't quite go that way. Ten minutes in Ronaldo passes to Robinho, who double scissor fakes and passes to Ronaldinho, who threads one through *your* legs, leaves you like a child on a potty, and then runs up the pitch, jubilant, turning somersaults while you dig the ball out of the net, crushed; if that happens then perhaps someone in the crowd behind you will shout out: "Do not be downhearted! Keep moving forward!"

It will be a nineteen-year-old boy. He will be wearing cheesy Nikes. His words will lift your spirits. You will grin at him, and then thump the ball back down the pitch.

World Cup Record

FIFA Ranking: 48
World Cup Appearances: 1
World Cup Champions: 0
Federation Name: Football Federation Australia
Confederation: OFC
Founded: 1961
FIFA Affiliation: 1963
Nickname: Socceroos
Manager: Guus Hiddink
Website: www.footballaustralia.com.au
Stadium: Telstra Stadium and Aussie Stadium, Sydney
Home Uniform: yellow and green/green/green
Away Uniform: all dark blue
Provider: Nike

1930:	Did not enter
1934:	Did not enter
1938:	Did not enter
1950:	Did not enter
1954:	Did not enter
1958:	Did not enter
1962:	Did not enter
1966:	Did not qualify
1970:	Did not qualify
1974:	First round exit
1978:	Did not qualify
1982:	Did not qualify
1986:	Did not qualify
1990:	Did not qualify
1994:	Did not qualify
1998:	Did not qualify
2002:	Did not qualify

Matches	Wins	Draws	Losses	GF	GA	GD	Points
3	0	1	2	0	5	-5	1

Australia is 56th on the all-time World Cup table

Path to Qualification for World Cup 2006

Date					
29-May-04	Australia	1	New Zealand	0	**W**
31-May-04	Australia	9	Tahiti	0	**W**
2-Jun-04	Australia	6	Fiji	1	**W**
4-Jun-04	Vanuatu	0	Australia	3	**W**
6-Jun-04	Solomon Islands	2	Australia	2	**D**
3-Sep-05	Australia	7	Solomon Islands	0	**W**
6-Sep-05	Solomon Islands	1	Australia	2	**W**
12-Nov-05	Uruguay	1	Australia	0	**L**
16-Nov-05	Australia	1*	Uruguay	0	**W**

* 4-2 PSO

Australia qualified by winning the Oceania Zone and beating Uruguay in a home-away series

Brazil

Capital: Brasilia
Independence: September 7, 1822
  (from Portugal)
Area: 8,511,965 sq km
Population: 186,112,794
Median Age: 27.8 years
Life Expectancy at Birth: 71.7 years
Ethnic Groups: white 53.7%, mulatto
  (mixed white and black) 38.5%,
  black 6.2%, other (includes Japanese,
  Arab, Amerindian) 0.9%,
  unspecified 0.7%
Religions: Roman Catholic 73.6%,
  Protestant 15.4%, Spriritualist 1.3%,
  Bantu/voodoo 0.3%, other 1.8%,
  unspecified 0.2%, none 7.4%
Languages: Portuguese (official), Spanish,
  English, French
Suffrage: voluntary between 16 and 18 years
  of age and over 70; compulsory over
  18 and under 70 years of age
Military Obligation: 19 years of age; compulsory
GDP Per Capita: $8,100
Budget: $172.4 billion
Military Expenditures: $11 billion
  (1.8% of GDP)
Agriculture: coffee, soybeans, wheat, rice, corn,
  sugarcane, cocoa, citrus; beef
Industries: textiles, shoes, chemicals, cement,
  lumber, iron ore, tin, steel, aircraft, motor
  vehicles and parts, other machinery and
  equipment
Currency: real

Source: *CIA World Factbook*

Brazil

John Lanchester

"And did you once see Pelé play?"

I've been waiting thirty years for someone to ask me that question and nobody shows any signs of doing so, so it looks as if I'll just have to ask it of myself. The answer is yes. Pelé's club Santos, for which he played for eighteen years, came on a tour of the Far East in the early 1970s, shortly before the great man left for his preretirement spell with the Cosmos in New York. I was twelve and living in Hong Kong and did, in fact, see Pelé play, for the first half anyway, at the football stadium in Happy Valley. I don't remember anything about the game other than the impression Pelé gave of being physically very compact, and of showing great economy of movement—it was as if he had made a private arrangement with himself to spend as much time as possible walking. But he had the kind of presence and talent that gave his walking more impact than other players' rushing about.

One of the World Cup's greatest goals, Brazil's last goal in their 4–1 tonking of Italy in the 1970 final, was scored by a lashing drive from the right back and captain Carlos Alberto—but it was created by Pelé, standing on the edge of the area with the ball at his feet, and so clearly a figure of menace and magic that all he had to do to keep defenders cemented in place was just stand there. While he did that Carlos Alberto was running into position; and then Pelé, still keeping the defender in place, just rolled the ball into Alberto's path, so calmly and elegantly and with such clear intent that it was as if Alberto's shot was merely completing something Pelé had already imagined, sketched out, choreographed.

Pelé still seems to me the greatest footballer there has ever been. I suppose the only source of doubt about that is because the game was slower, more reflective then; the frenetic modern game, in which players run roughly twice as far over the ninety minutes, might have given him less time and space. But I don't believe it would have made much difference to Pelé. He always had all the time he needed, regardless of the pace of the game or how closely he was marked. He seemed to occupy his own space in a way more closely resembling that of a dancer than a footballer.

If Pelé was the best footballer, the team in which he most fully revealed and shared his greatness, the Brazil side of 1970, was the best team. This is not an original view, but it is one I hold deeply. I never saw the 1958 and 1962 teams, which paved the way for the great side; everyone says they were amazing too; but the 1970 team was better. I was eight in 1970 and had just fallen in love with football. As a father myself now, asking around other dads, eight seems to be the age at which this happens, if it happens. I think it may be something to do with the fact that at eight you can start properly playing football, in that skill and stamina levels are both high enough to allow an extended game rather than a short-burst runabout, and also you are psychologically equipped in that it begins to be possible to lose. You can't play football, or any other game, unless you can to some extent cope with losing—or missing tackles, missing open goals, letting the ball into your own goal, and all the rest. At eight, you begin to have the stamina to watch football, too, and that also involves being able to come to terms with losing. At least, I say you watch it, but you don't so much watch football as live through it. As the *New Yorker* writer Adam Gopnik once pointed out, a football match is less of a spectacle than it is an experience. The great games I've seen, especially the great World Cup games—Brazil–Italy in 1982, or England–Germany in 1990, or England–Argentina in 1986 or 1998, or Argentina–Netherlands in 1978, feel less in my memory like things I saw, in the way that I might have seen a movie, than things I lived through, things that happened to me. So at about eight you can play it and you can watch it; you're ready. And then, for me, the Brazil team of 1970 came along.

Why do we fall in love with football? What happens? Most of the writing about being a football fan is about group experiences or collective experiences, the process of being one of a crowd willing your team on. It's the thing caught so beautifully in Nick Hornby's *Fever Pitch,* the way the game sweeps up individual life stories in a bigger collective story, makes you feel part of something. Most football writing is about that experience, one way or another; in the overall run of writing about football, most of it is about the epiphenomenon of being a fan rather than the phenomenon of the game itself. It's strange but true. Golf writing is about playing golf; cricket writing is about cricket, and baseball writing about baseball; but most football writing is about being a fan.

That, I think, is because football is difficult to describe. Its texture is elusive and words make a poor fit with the game's graces and beauties; I don't quite know why. But I think at some deep level that the reason football snags us, and the reason it is difficult to write about—to write directly about what happens on the pitch—is connected through the idea of beauty. Good football is beautiful, with a strangely delicate beauty, a beauty you begin to learn about as you begin to play the game. Every time you kick the ball, it's more likely not to go where you aim it than it is to go there; or to go at the wrong speed, or to bounce too much; or it does go where you aimed it but an opponent was standing there, or the teammate you were aiming it at wasn't looking, or moved away, or failed to control it, or was tackled, or fell over, or immediately gave it away to an opponent. (Let's not forget the opponent. As Jean-Paul Sartre wrote, "in football, everything is complicated by the presence of the opposite team.") It's easier, far far easier, to under-, over-, or mis-hit a pass than it is just to pass. It's easier not to control a ball than to control it, and as for headers, well, it's easier to knock yourself out, score an own-goal, or completely miss the ball than it is to manage even a half-decent header, the kind any semi-pro in a graveyard league can execute faultlessly without thinking.

That's what you learn, as soon as you start to play and watch football: that football is difficult and beautiful, and that the two are related. Players kick the ball to one another, pass into empty space which is suddenly filled by a player who wasn't there two seconds ago and who is running at full pelt and who without looking or breaking stride knocks the ball back to a third player who he surely can't have seen who then, also at full pelt and without breaking stride, crosses the ball at sixty miles an hour to land on the head of a fourth player who has run seventy meters to get there and who, again all in stride, jumps and heads the ball with, once you realize how hard this is, unbelievable power and accuracy toward a corner of the goal just exactly where the goalkeeper, executing some complex physics entirely without conscious thought and through muscle-memory, has expected it to be, so that all this grace and speed and muscle and athleticism and attention to detail and power and precision passion comes to nothing, will never appear on a score-sheet or match report and will likely be forgotten a day later by everybody who saw it or took part in it. This is the beauty and also the strange fragility, the evanescence of football.

No country plays beautiful football as naturally and as consistently as Brazil. That, in a nutshell, is why they are so loved. Not in South America, of course, where they have the status of regional sporting superpower, but by pretty much everyone else in the world. In fact, the Brazil football team is as far as I know unique in sport in being an example of a beloved overdog. In general, sport fans, and especially football fans, hate the overdogs (the Yankees in the United States, Real Madrid in Spain, Juventus in Italy, Man United and Chelsea in England). But Brazil, the only team to have won five World Cups, the only team to have won it outside their own hemisphere (twice), are loved. It's an ideological thing. So a great many football fans have, at the national level, two teams: their own, and Brazil. They are the only favorites who are favorites.

This is not to say that Brazilian football has always been beautiful. Part of the interest and drama of following Brazil has been the four-way oscillation between beauty, ugliness, success and failure. Indeed you could almost plot them as a chart, with the 1970 team the apogee of both beauty and success and the 1982 team, who played a heart-stopping masterpiece in losing 3–2 to Italy in the second round, captained by the chainsmoking doctor Socrates, at the height of beauty but a relatively low (for Brazil) standard of success. (That game against Italy was, I think, the best football match I've ever seen.) There was something so cool about his being called Socrates, too—all part of the strange romance of Brazilian names, most of which, thanks to the complexity and length of people's full monickers, and a deep love of familiar forms of address, tend to be nicknames. And then there are the suffixes to consider. The winning coach from 2002, Luiz Felipe Scolari, is always called Philão—the "ão" suffix meaning "big," thus Philão means "Big Phil." The "inho" suffix means "small." As Alex Bellos points out in his brilliant book *Futebol,* the current Ronaldo was once himself known as Ronaldinho, because there was already another Ronaldo in the side, as well as a Ronaldão. When the current Ronaldinho came along, this could have meant that Brazil was fielding Ronaldão, Ronaldo, Ronaldinho and Ronaldinhozinho: big Ronald, normal-sized Ronald, small Ronald and even smaller Ronald. Instead the former Ronaldo dropped out, the new Ronaldo became Ronaldinho Gaúcho (after his place of origin) and the former Ronaldinho was promoted to Ronaldo, a title he still holds. Perhaps this is no odder than the time England had one player called Trever Steven and two players called Gary Stevens (prompting the immortal chant, to the tune of "Guantanamera": "Two Gary Stevens—there's only two Gary Stevens . . .")

But I digress. The 2002 team had the potential to be world-beaters—which is an odd thing to say about a team which did, by winning the World Cup, actually beat the world, but there was nonetheless something held back and within their shell about them, a sense that players as great as Ronaldo and Roberto Carlos were not fully expressing their talents. Perhaps that was something to do with the coaching style of Philão Scolari; or perhaps it was a reaction to the failure of 1998. For whatever reason, there was a sense that some necessary act of alchemy did not quite take place.

There have also been some deliberately, numbingly negative and cautious teams who—and you have to love Brazil for this—are always highly controversial at home, simply for playing dull football. The apotheosis of that was the winning 1994 team, whose coach was Carlos Alberto Parreira, now back in charge of the national side. The 1994 team was captained by the sideways-and-backwards midfield enforcer Dunga, whom I for one always sneakily rather liked, in the way you sometimes end up rooting for the baddie in a Western. That team also had the amusing subplot in the overt dislike felt by one of its star strikers, Romario, who'd been born poor, for the other star striker, Bebeto, who'd been born rich. It was sometimes as if Romario couldn't bear to pass the ball to his teammate, and their joint goal celebrations were hilariously strained.

So the chart would look a bit like this (I'm citing here only Brazil sides I've actually watched):

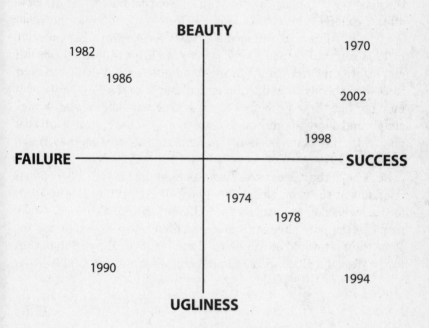

What about the 2006 team? Well, they have the potential to be up there on the top right, no question, with players like Ronaldo and Ronaldinho, Roberto Carlos and Kaka and Robinho and "Emperor" Adriano. The team is at least as talented as the 2002 winners. They charged through the qualifying stages, where Brazil sides sometimes make heavy weather; and great teams, almost by definition, tend to save their best form for the biggest occasions. Their coach has the advantage of already having won the World Cup once, with the grim 1994 side, and the further advantage of job stability, having been in charge for the last four years. Parreira will want to win the World Cup again, but this time with a much more favorable critical response. Ronaldinho is the best soccer player in the world. It could happen.

Will it? Maybe. You never know how a team will react to the pressure—the mind-bending, inconceivable pressure—until they arrive at the World Cup. In a country where there were suicides following the defeat by Uruguay in 1950 (two of them actually at the stadium after the match) this is not a new phenomenon, but it is one that has got worse as financial and media stresses have grown. The pressure in 1998 caused Ronaldo, *O Fenômeno,* to have a still-mysterious fit just before the final against France, and pressures of a different sort caused somebody to make him go out and take the field anyway. It may be that these pressures are now so great—for reasons which simply and depressingly boil down to money—that no team will ever play with the same sense of freedom and adventure that Brazil showed in 1970.

Let's hope that's not true. To do something as if your life depends on it, and at the same time to do it beautifully, as if it mattered only for its own sake, are usually two different things. The great Brazil teams of the past have at times made them seem as if they are the same thing. It would be wonderful if they could do that again in Germany. We could all do with a reminder of what football can be.

World Cup Record

FIFA Ranking: 1
World Cup Appearances: 17
World Cup Champions: 5
Federation Name: Confederação Brasileira
de Futebol
Confederation: CONMEBOL
Founded: 1914
FIFA Affiliation: 1923
Nickname: Os Canarinhos (The Little Canaries);
Selecao (The Selected)
Manager: Carlos Alberto Parreira
Website: www.cbfnews.bol.com.br
Stadium: Maracanã
Home Uniform: yellow/blue/white
Away Uniform: blue/white/white or blue
Provider: Nike

1930: First round exit
1934: First round exit
1938: 3rd place
1950: 2nd place
1954: Quarterfinal exit
1958: CHAMPIONS
1962: CHAMPIONS
1966: First round exit
1970: CHAMPIONS
1974: 4th place
1978: 3rd place
1982: Second round exit
1986: Quarterfinal exit
1990: Second round exit
1994: CHAMPIONS
1998: 2nd place
2002: CHAMPIONS

Matches	Wins	Draws	Losses	GF	GA	GD	Points
87	60	14	13	191	82	+109	194

Brazil is 1st on the all-time World Cup table

Path to Qualification for World Cup 2006

7-Sep-03	Colombia	1	Brazil	2	W
10-Sep-03	Brazil	1	Ecuador	0	W
16-Nov-03	Peru	1	Brazil	1	D
19-Nov-03	Brazil	3	Uruguay	3	D
31-Mar-04	Paraguay	0	Brazil	0	D
2-Jun-04	Brazil	3	Argentina	1	W
6-Jun-04	Chile	1	Brazil	1	D
5-Sep-04	Brazil	3	Bolivia	1	W
9-Oct-04	Venezuela	2	Brazil	5	W
13-Oct-04	Brazil	0	Colombia	0	D
17-Nov-04	Ecuador	1	Brazil	0	L
27-Mar-05	Brazil	1	Peru	0	W
30-Mar-05	Uruguay	1	Brazil	1	D
5-Jun-05	Brazil	4	Paraguay	1	W
8-Jun-05	Argentina	3	Brazil	1	L
4-Sep-05	Brazil	5	Chile	0	W
9-Oct-05	Bolivia	1	Brazil	1	D
12-Oct-05	Brazil	3	Venezuela	0	W

Brazil qualified by finishing in the top four in the South American Zone

Costa Rica

Capital: San Jose
Independence: September 15, 1821
  (from Spain)
Area: 51,100 sq km
Population: 4,016,173
Median Age: 26.0 years
Life Expectancy at Birth: 76.8 years
Ethnic Groups: white (including mestizo) 94%,
  black 3%, Amerindian 1%, Chinese 1%,
  other 1%
Religions: Roman Catholic 76.3%, Evangelical
  13.7%, Jehovah's Witnesses 1.3%, other
  Protestant 0.7%, other 4.8%, none 3.2%
Languages: Spanish (official), English
Suffrage: 18 years of age; universal and
  compulsory
Military Obligation: 18 years of age
GDP Per Capita: $9,600
Budget: $3.094 billion
Military Expenditures: $64.2 million
  (0.4% of GDP)
Agriculture: coffee, pineapples, bananas,
  sugar, corn, rice, beans, potatoes; beef;
  timber
Industries: microprocessors, food processing,
  textiles and clothing, construction
  materials, fertilizer, plastic products
Currency: Costa Rican colon

Source: *CIA World Factbook*

Costa Rica

Matthew Yeomans

Like any self-respecting Latin land, Costa Rica lives football. But unlike, say, Mexico to the north or Argentina and Brazil to the south, Costa Rica's football culture hasn't seeped into every pore of the media and society—or at least it isn't apparent to an outsider like me. Whenever I've been there I've found myself forgetting my own football passions and falling for the place on its merits as, well, paradise. It is a land of surfers and backpackers, of jungle rides, Pacific beach hikes, volcano vistas and tree canopy tours to see exotic toucans and howler monkeys. Tropical rainforest, rolling surf, arid cowboy country and belching volcanoes, all packed into a country about half the size of Ireland.

Costa Ricans pride themselves on living *la pura vida*—the pure life. The Ticos, as Costa Ricans refer to themselves, maintain a relaxed, sunny disposition and make a virtue of respecting nature. Partly this is just a good public relations stunt aimed at wooing stressed-out gringos like me. But some part of la pura vida is a deep-seated outlook that has made a large chunk of Costa Rica into national park and kept the country at peace for decades. While its Central American neighbors self-destructed into civil war, Costa Rica opted not even to have a professional army. And in 1987, Costa Rica's president Oscar Arias Sánchez won the Nobel Peace Prize for his efforts to end conflict in Central America.

Over time I'd come to think of Costa Rica as my perfect tropical escape—an exhilarating yet easy-to-navigate piece of exotica where I felt completely at home. Like many harried city-livers, I dreamed of decamping to a beach retreat—Tamarindo Beach on the Nicoya Peninsula, in my case—a place where life moves slowly, where you're woken by a silent sea breeze instead of by the sounds of fire engines or garbage trucks. My house would have a view of the beach and the vibrant, often wild Pacific Ocean. There would be a wooden verandah where I could drink my organically grown, fairly traded morning coffee and, oh yes, it would also have a broadband hookup so I could continue to earn a living.

All of this came back to me while watching the last World Cup, in 2002. I've always been a sucker for an underdog. At every World Cup some small nation upsets one of the smug superpowers, fighting its way to a surprise draw or at least failing heroically, pushing one of the favorites close while winning the hearts and minds of soft romantics. It started for me with Haiti in 1974, when the impoverished Caribbean island shocked Italy by taking a 1–0 lead in their opening match. Italy recovered to win but, even though I was only eight years old, I found the whiff of an upset against the mighty *Azzurri* intoxicating. In 1978 my heart went for Peru, who hammered an overconfident Scotland 3–1. Since then I've been mesmerized (and slightly horrified) by Cameroon's near humiliation of England in 1990 and enthralled by the flamboyant showing of Nigeria's Super Eagles in 1994. But it wasn't until the summer of 2002 that I discovered true underdog love.

It was a group stage game between Brazil, the four-time winners of the World Cup, and Costa Rica, in only their second appearance in the competition. I had gotten up in the middle of the night to watch the game on TV. In their previous matches the Brazilians were at their swerving, juggling, imperious best, and I was expecting them to weave their usual magic and then some against such lowly opposition. La Roja (the Red), as the Costa Rican team is known, looked like lambs to the slaughter of *o jogo bonito*—the Brazilians' beautiful game. Instead I sat transfixed by the most frenetic, exhilarating match I'd seen in years. Through the first half Costa Rica should have been about three goals up but they were three down by the 37th minute, the last goal an outrageous volley by the Brazilian defender Edmilson. Yet so inspired in attack was the whole Brazil team that they completely forgot to defend and, a minute later, Costa Rica's star forward Paolo Wanchope scored to make it 3–1. Ten minutes into the second half, Costa Rica scored again and Brazil had a potential fright on their hands. Now Costa Rica needed just one more goal to secure a draw and guarantee their place in the second round of the competition. They began to play with almost the same élan as Brazil—but not quite enough. Two late goals sent the Ticos out of the World Cup.

All of Costa Rica may have mourned but for me it didn't matter. The underdog had bitten the favorite's tail once again. What's more, Costa Rica had played in a style that reinforced all my fantasies about their land. Here was a team that played la pura vida. At home in New York, watching Costa Rica made my dream seem, well, possible.

And that, of course, is the problem with fantasies: they rarely have any relation to reality. The likelihood that I could decamp to Costa Rica was pretty slim. The likelihood that my beach idyll would turn out to be as idyllic as I imagined was slimmer still.

Little did I know that the very elements that combined to create my ideal escape—the natural beauty, the simple charms and now the vibrant football—were the same factors that were slowly eroding my idea of la pura vida.

In the late 1980s, Costa Rica found itself caught up in a real-estate boom as thousands of foreigners—many of them American retirees and tourism entrepreneurs, flocked in search of the sort of tropical retreat I could only dream about. It was partly in response to the pressure of this rampant coastal development that the government decided to create an expansive national park network, ruling millions of acres of virgin rainforest, beachline and mountains—some 25 percent of the country—off limits to development. In doing so, Costa Rica not only protected one of the world's greatest concentrations of biodiversity, but it also established the ecotourist playground that would soon attract thousands of tourists. As Costa Rica flourished, money began pouring into domestic football, spurred on by the national team's new prominence.

Throughout its history, Costa Rica's wealth and power has been focused in a narrow corridor through the heart of the country known as the Central Valley, home of Costa Rica's finest coffee plantations and its two largest cities—San José, the capital, and Alajuela, the second city. These two cities have always produced the strongest football teams in Costa Rica, drawing quality players away from the Caribbean and Pacific coasts. San José's Saprissa club, named after a Spanish benefactor who began his association with the team by donating the player's kit, and Alajuelense enjoy a rivalry dating back nearly a century.

Since the foundation of the Costa Rican football league at the turn of the last century, football had been the domain of sporting and fraternal associations and benevolent local tycoons not too bothered about turning a profit. Teams tended to be semipro and often teetered on the brink of bankruptcy. One exception was Alajuelense, which had a long tradition of stable, conservative but solvent administration. Saprissa, its more flamboyant local rival, enjoyed more success on the pitch but was a guaranteed financial rollercoaster off it.

The good showing at the 2002 World Cup in Korea/Japan further stoked interest in Costa Rican football. Galvanized by La Roja's performances, FIFA announced plans to open one of its prestigious Gol football academies in Costa Rica, and Costa Rican national team players became hot commodities for European teams. Some twenty Costa Ricans have now played in foreign leagues. For young players in Costa Rica, the success of stars like Wanchope (who had stints at Manchester City, West Ham United and Malaga) is an inspiration, while the Costa Rican clubs have eagerly embraced the chance to make a mint off their talent.

Costa Rica hasn't just exported its football talent; its own clubs have also become investment toys for wealthy foreign businessmen. In 2003, Mexican vitamin tycoon Jorge Vergara, the owner of Club Deportivo de Guadalajara (Chivas) and later its sister club, Los Angeles–based Chivas of Major League Soccer, bought Saprissa. He soon secured Reebok as a main sponsor, quite a change from the low-level coffee sponsorship most Costa Rican teams had previously enjoyed. He also instituted a policy of buying only native-born or naturalized Costa Rican players, part of a marketing ploy to install Saprissa as "Costa Rica's team." Around the same time, Italian investors bought a Guanacaste club located on the northern Pacific Coast, moved it upland to Escazu in the Central Valley and renamed it Brujas (the Witches). Moving the club to Escazú, one of Costa Rica's most affluent towns, may have been heresy to the Guanacaste fans but it provided the investors with a sounder financial footing to raise Brujas' international profile and create a lucrative farm system for foreign clubs. One local star, Winston Parks, was sold to Italian Serie A club Udinese.

Meanwhile, Saprissa decided to galvanize its fan base. Watching Tico football had always been a low-key pursuit compared to the craziness associated with the Italian or Spanish game. For one thing most of the stadiums were rudimentary, far from the intimidating cauldrons of Milan's San Siro, Real's Bernabau or Boca's Bombonera, and the fans didn't get too worked up. Maybe it was the relaxed Tico spirit or the half a century of footballing underachievement, but Costa Rican football fans lacked a little something in attitude. In what must surely be the first instance of a club recruiting hooligan consultants, Saprissa brought in the hardcore fans of Chile's Universidad Católica to develop a local *fanatico* culture. The result was La Ultra, a superfan clique that looked to mirror the rabid commitment of the best-organized *barrabravas*. Fan chants were scripted, La Ultra congregated en masse and dressed all in purple and smoke bombs began to appear on the terraces. Alajuelense soon followed suit, launching its own hardcore fan based known as La Doce ("the twelfth man").

The results of this investment in fanaticism were quick and spectacular. A gang culture tied to La Ultra and La Doce quickly took root, fueled by a growing sense among poor Ticos that the burgeoning national economy was leaving them behind. With it came a startling increase in fan violence at football matches. The traditional animosity of the regular "Clasico" between Saprissa and Alajuelense took on new venom.

Fan violence became such a problem that, by the early 2000s, both Saprissa and Alajuelense took steps to bring La Ultra and La Doce under control. The outright crime subsided but the underlying mood of fan anger ignited by the *barrabravas* remains. Just last March, national team fans rioted during a qualifying round defeat to Mexico. Costa Rica had to play their next home qualifying game without fans.

Occasionally, as I gaze at Costa Rica from afar, dipping into Guanacaste surfing websites to grab a view of the Pacific or scanning the headlines in the online editions of *La Nacion* or *AM Costa Rica,* I can't help but wonder if my personal paradise will endure long enough for me to taste it. Crime, both petty and violent, is on the rise throughout the country and available real estate is being snapped up in a speculative frenzy. These are hardly Costa Rica's woes alone— it's part of a development pattern that is changing society the world over. And what right do I have to fret over a land I only daydream about, anyway? Still, if you can't protect your daydreams, what else does a dreamer have left?

Recently, excited to see that Costa Rica had qualified once more for the World Cup finals, I called Matias, a friend in Costa Rica, to check on the pulse of Tico football.

He still follows Alajuelense with weekly dedication, he said, but is no longer a regular at the games. "I used to have season tickets for myself and my family but I gave them up," Matias said. "Now when you go to a game there is a whole area taken over by an organized fan base. Some even come into the ground armed."

World Cup Record

FIFA Ranking: 21
World Cup Appearances: 2
World Cup Champions: 0
Federation Name: Federación Costarricense de Fútbol
Confederation: CONMEBOL
Founded: 1921
FIFA Affiliation: 1927
Nickname: Los Ticos
Manager: Alexandre Guimaraes
Website: www.fedefutbol.com
Stadium: Estadio Ricardo Saprissa, San José
Home Uniform: red/blue/white
Away Uniform: white/blue/red
Provider: Joma

1930:	Did not enter
1934:	Did not enter
1938:	Did not participate
1950:	Did not participate
1954:	Did not participate
1958:	Did not qualify
1962:	Did not qualify
1966:	Did not qualify
1970:	Did not qualify
1974:	Did not qualify
1978:	Did not qualify
1982:	Did not qualify
1986:	Did not qualify
1990:	Second round exit
1994:	Did not qualify
1998:	Did not qualify
2002:	First round exit

Matches	Wins	Draws	Losses	GF	GA	GD	Points
7	3	1	3	9	12	-3	10

Costa Rica is 37th on the all-time World Cup table

Path to Qualification for World Cup 2006

Date	Home		Away		Result
12-Jun-04	Cuba	2	Costa Rica	2	D
20-Jun-04	Costa Rica	1	Cuba	1	D
18-Aug-04	Costa Rica	2	Honduras	5	L
5-Sep-04	Guatemala	2	Costa Rica	1	L
8-Sep-04	Costa Rica	1	Canada	0	W
9-Oct-04	Costa Rica	5	Guatemala	0	W
13-Oct-04	Canada	1	Costa Rica	3	W
17-Nov-04	Honduras	0	Costa Rica	0	D
9-Feb-05	Costa Rica	1	Mexico	2	L
26-Mar-05	Costa Rica	2	Panama	1	W
30-Mar-05	Trinidad	0	Costa Rica	0	D
4-Jun-05	United States	3	Costa Rica	0	L
8-Jun-05	Costa Rica	3	Guatemala	2	W
17-Aug-05	Mexico	2	Costa Rica	0	L
3-Sep-05	Panama	1	Costa Rica	3	W
7-Sep-05	Costa Rica	2	Trinidad	0	W
8-Oct-05	Costa Rica	3	United States	0	W
12-Oct-05	Guatemala	3	Costa Rica	1	L

Costa Rica qualified by finishing in the top three in the Concacaf Zone

Côte d'Ivoire

Capital: Yamoussoukro
Independence: August 7, 1960
(from France)
Area: 322,460 sq km
Population: 17,298,040
Median Age: 19.1 years
Life Expectancy at Birth: 48.6 years
Ethnic Groups: Akan 42.1%, Voltaiques
or Gur 17.6%, Northern Mandes 16.5%,
Krous 11%, Southern Mandes 10%,
other 2.8% (includes 130,000 Lebanese
and 14,000 French)
Religions: Christian 20–30%, Muslim 35–40%,
indigenous 25–40%
Languages: French (official), 60 dialects with
Dioula the most widely spoken
Suffrage: 18 years of age; universal
Military Obligation: 18 years of age for
compulsory and voluntary military service;
18 months conscript service obligation
GDP Per Capita: $1,500
Budget: $2.767 billion
Military Expenditures: $180.2 million
(1.2% of GDP)
Agriculture: coffee, cocoa beans, bananas, palm
kernels, corn, rice, manioc (tapioca), sweet
potatoes, sugar, cotton, rubber; timber
Industries: foodstuffs, beverages; wood
products, oil refining, truck and bus
assembly, textiles, fertilizer, building
materials, electricity, ship construction
and repair
Currency: Communaute Financiere Africaine franc

Source: *CIA World Factbook*

Côte d'Ivoire

Paul Laity

He who follows the elephant is not touched by the dew.
—Baule proverb

The party began at ten to six. A last-gasp Cameroon penalty struck a post in Yaoundé, and Côte d'Ivoire had qualified for the World Cup— for the first time ever. In an instant, the city of Abidjan was full of people and noise. Fans in tangerine and green poured onto the streets, drivers hooted their horns; loud fast-paced *zouglou* music was playing and pots and pans were joyously banged. The partygoers danced a new dance, the "Drogbacite," named in honor of the team's star striker, Didier Drogba: to the beat, they mimed his feints, turns and the unleashing of unstoppable shots. Others tried out the *fouka-fouka,* Drogba's trademark celebratory hip-swivel—a little piece of Ivoirian culture known to soccer fans everywhere. The *maquis*— open-air cafés, bars and mini-nightclubs—stayed open all night serving "Drogbas": bottles of local beer, so called because of their considerable size and potency. A number of the drinkers had "Les Elephants" painted on their chests, the nickname of the national side: elephants represent power, and are said to be lucky, too— protected by a spell. The team has suffered its share of disappointments; now, finally, the name seems appropriate.

There was rejoicing all around this war-torn country. In Bouake, the second city and capital of the rebel-held north, shots were fired into the air. Street parties were held in the east and the west. In Abidjan, the festivities lasted all night; and in the morning, a crowd of fans heedless of fatigue headed off to the airport where the players were due to return from their winning game in the Sudan. (A 3–1 victory in Omdurman had secured qualification, thanks to Cameroon's penalty miss against Egypt.) Drogba, Bonaventure Kalou, Kolo Toure and the others were rushed and surrounded and embraced. As the players were paraded on trucks through the districts of Port-Bouët, Koumassi, Marcory and Treichville, excited fans announced that soccer had done more than any politician to put an end to the war; the time for reconciliation had come.

Over the past decade, the southern-based regime has fomented hatred of immigrants, Muslims and northerners, yet many of Côte d'Ivoire's best soccer players are from Muslim and immigrant families, so that the national side has become an irresistible symbol of unity. At the end of the Abidjan victory parade, the head of the Ivory Coast Football Federation addressed a plea to President Laurent Gbagbo: "the players have asked me to tell you that what they most want now is for our country to become one again. They want this victory to act as a catalyst for peace in Côte d'Ivoire, to put an end to the conflict and to reunite its people. This success must bring us together." The party on the streets lasted another whole day.

President Gbagbo did his best to be identified with the conquering team. He talked of a rejuvenated nation and gave each of the players the equivalent of a knighthood and a swanky villa. Côte d'Ivoire matches any African country in its enthusiasm for soccer: fans organize prayer groups weeks before a crucial game, and, on the day, congregate at dawn to begin their clamor of encouragement. But the mix of soccer and politics can get ugly. In 2000, General Robert Guei, who had just engineered the country's first military coup, held the national side in detention for two days at an army base, as punishment for being knocked out of the African Nations Cup in the first round. He stripped the players of their passports and cell phones, publicly denounced them and suggested they should learn some barracks discipline. "I asked that you be taken there so you could reflect a while," Guei said, "You should have spared us the shame." Now that World Cup qualification has been achieved, there is, for the time being, no shame, and the summer of 2006 promises to remind Ivoirians, however fleetingly, of a national life beyond politics.

The story of Côte d'Ivoire in recent years is about the brightest of successes fading and dying. For most Ivoirians the world has gone dark. *Tristes tropiques*. Last July, the United States Fund for Peace declared it to be the most dangerous country in the world; the British Foreign and Commonwealth Office advises against all travel there. On one checkpoint gate on the northern outskirts of Abidjan, a scrawl of graffiti insists that "Côte d'Ivoire is neither Rwanda nor the Congo," but the denial is itself a recognition that an ethnic war is being fought in Côte d'Ivoire by young men with machetes and AK-47s, and the tone of desperation reveals how badly things have gone wrong.

For decades after it achieved independence in 1960, Côte d'Ivoire was a model of prosperity. Abidjan grew into a city of gleaming skyscrapers and superhighways, banks and corporations, elegant shops and high-class restaurants: it was sophisticated and cosmopolitan, the "Paris of Africa." The sumptuous Hotel Ivoire, an air-conditioned pleasure palace, had an underground ice rink kept glassy whatever the temperature outside. Félix Houphouët-Boigny, the nation's first president and benevolent dictator for thirty years, transformed his home village of Yamoussoukro, a small settlement in the middle of the bush, into a grand capital with boulevards and parks. His presidential palace there was an African Versailles; he also built, at extraordinary expense, a full-size replica of St. Peter's, which was blessed by Pope John Paul II.

When boom went to bust, "H-B" remained as the tottering guarantee of national unity. In the early 1980s, V. S. Naipaul traveled to Côte d'Ivoire in search of the glamor and sophistication of "France in Africa." Characteristically enough, he discovered an older country of tribal lore and magic and shadows. The palace at Yamoussoukro was impressively modern but, every day, live chickens were fed to sacred crocodiles in the lake. This ritual was "part of the night, ceaselessly undoing the reality of the day." Which, he wondered, was the more enduring: the Africa of the night or the skyscrapers? Ten years after Naipaul published his reflections in an essay entitled "The Crocodiles of Yamoussoukro," Houphouet-Boigny died. One Ivoirian was so upset he threw himself to the palace crocodiles; crowds watched for two days as his ravaged body kept resurfacing before being dragged underwater again. It was a fitting coda to Naipaul's essay—an anticipation of self-destruction, of a community surrendering, or being urged to surrender, to old ethnic loyalties and more brutal habits.

Following Houphouet-Boigny's death, politics became centered on the concept of *ivoirité,* or "Ivoirianness." The new regime embarked on its anti-northern and anti-immigrant policies, and it began to matter who were the original settlers in villages and who had moved in. Politicians from the wrong ethnicity were denied a chance to run for office; there were disputes over land. In September 2002, rebel soldiers from the largely Muslim north mutinied against the government, and civil war began.

But there is another element to the conflict: a resurgent rebellion against French influence in Côte d'Ivoire. President Gbagbo sees France's continued military presence and its political mediations in the war as distastefully pro-northern. When France destroyed the Ivoirian airforce (two old jets and a few helicopters) in November 2004, his generously financed militia, the Jeunes Patriotes, whipped up anti-French feeling in Abidjan and orchestrated riots—the notorious "hunt for the whites"—which drove more than eight thousand French citizens out of the country. Gbagbo argues that France is naturally losing its grip over Côte d'Ivoire. He told *Le Figaro* that while his own generation would happily sing "La Marseillaise" on July 14, the Ivoirian young—and 70 percent of the population is under thirty—don't care for such things: the language of protest and of aspiration is English, and fresh-faced rebels look to America for role models. Soldiers on both sides of the war favor the pimp-roll and wear gold chains and tracksuits. They listen to the Bastards, a *zouglou* rap band; a favorite song is "Sacrificed Generation."

France declared Côte d'Ivoire a colony in 1893; it was already systematically exploiting the region's resources and would carry on doing so. A young Henri Cartier-Bresson journeyed to the country in 1931 and sent shocking letters home about the practices of imperialism: Africans fleeing recruitment drives for soldiers and road-builders; black woodcutters beaten to death by site foremen. Cartier-Bresson was on a search for experience rather than profit; in his luggage was an edition of Rimbaud and a second-hand Krauss camera, on which he took his first photographs. To earn a living, he hunted hippos and crocodiles—by night, with an acetylene lamp fixed to his forehead. One day his piss turned black and he spent his remaining months in Côte d'Ivoire recovering from bilharzia. On his way home he read *Heart of Darkness*. Only a few of his photographs survived the mildew: one is of a black dockworker, broad-chested and framed against the geometric lines of a ship's hull; an iron anchor chain and massed coils of rope speak of trade and sweat and the long history of the French presence in Africa.

Henri Michel, the French manager of the Ivoirian soccer team, was a notable absentee from the celebration dinner held at President Gbagbo's residence after the Sudan match last October. He was, presumably, an awkward reminder of the neocolonial legacy. Yet the official sponsors of anti-French thinking in today's Côte d'Ivoire face a difficulty when it comes to football. Of the first-choice players in the current national team, eight or nine play in France, and a number of others have lived most of their lives there: Drogba left Côte d'Ivoire at the age of five to stay with an uncle who turned out for minor French sides. He tells of a childhood watching European soccer on TV and messing around on pitches in Dunkerque and Abbeville; eventually he made his name as a muscular, mercurial striker in the colors of Marseille.

Several of the national team are products of the youth academy founded on behalf of the Abidjan club ASEC by Jean-Marc Guillou, who played for France alongside Michel Platini. Guillou combed Côte d'Ivoire for soccer prodigies and offered them high-tech facilities— manicured pitches, a medical clinic and gym. In an Ivoirian squad which sparkles with attacking talent, one of the most promising forwards is Bakari Koné, or "Baky": "One day," Guillou says, "I was passing through the Williamsville district and some kids stopped me. They kept saying 'We've got Pelé living here, you've got to take a look at him.' " Guillou watched for ten minutes, then signed Kone up to the academy. He's now one of the star performers at Nice.

But even this Franco-Ivoirian relationship has turned sour. In 2002 Guillou left ASEC to set up his own soccer school, and took thirty of his protégés with him. It became clear that his main purpose was to sell young players on the European market. Soon almost all of Côte d'Ivoire's soccer talent was being sucked out of the country: groomed for export, the most skillful teenagers went to Europe before local fans had even seen them play. European clubs have recently been barred from signing non-European players under eighteen, but not before Guillou became the chief villain in what was known as the new ivory trade.

Gbagbo may choose to ignore the continuing importance of France to Ivoirian soccer as long as Côte d'Ivoire keeps winning, and he has loudly publicized the extent to which his government has financed the national team. He is likely to distance himself from another form of assistance, however. In 1992, when Côte d'Ivoire played in the final of the African Nations Cup, the sports minister enlisted a battalion of *fétisheurs*—juju men—to give the Ivoirian side a supernatural advantage against Ghana (it worked). The story goes that, despite the victory, the minister then reneged on promises to pay the *fétisheurs,* so they put a hex on the team, which duly suffered a ten-year-run of disappointing results. In April 2002, defense minister Moïse Lida Kouassi eventually approached the witch doctors to make amends, offering them bottles of gin and large sums of money. The hex was lifted and presto: World Cup qualification.

Witch doctors might scatter charms on the field or smear their team's goalposts with magic ointments to keep the ball out. In 1984, no fewer than 150 *fétisheurs* stayed with the Ivoirian national side at their hotel before a crunch game in the African Nations Cup: each player took a bath in water treated with various potions, before being invited to make a wish in the ear of a pigeon. ASEC was taken to court by its rival Africa Sports in 1998, when, following a decisive league match in Bouake, its players admitted to drinking a concoction prepared by a juju man (the case was dismissed). Soccer's governing body in Africa is aware of the PR damage done by juju stories, and has now banned "team advisers" from being part of a squad's official entourage. But superstition, of one kind or another, has always played a large part in sport, and fetishism is sure to continue in Ivoirian football. (Before last September's crucial World Cup qualifier against Cameroon, the gutters of Abidjan ran red with chicken blood.) For better or worse this is Naipaul's Africa: a place of magic and the mysteries of the village, now also on display at the many roadblocks in the north and west of the country, where soldiers are convinced that the amulets they wear around their necks will ward off bullets. War, too, encourages superstition.

The *Jeunes Patriotes* organized a big rally to salute qualification: President Gbagbo, while it's in his interests, will heed the proverb and follow the Elephants. And it seems everybody—on both sides of the civil war—is willing the team to do well in Germany. But there is likely to be anger if things go badly: when the Ivoirians lost for the second time to Cameroon in the qualifiers, and it was believed their chance had gone, Drogba—who had played brilliantly in the match, and scored two goals—received threats and menacing messages from fans, and was worried enough to consider giving up his international career. Too many hopes were riding on him. By itself, soccer will never bring about national reconciliation. (Think of France's World Cup winning team—so very *immigré,* so much the symbol of a transracial unity that has never come good.)

But it can lift spirits—and offer moments of truce and sociability. In his autobiographical novel, *Climbié,* Bernard Dadié, who was imprisoned for anticolonial activities in Côte d'Ivoire in the late 1940s and later became minister for culture in the days of the "Ivoirian miracle," writes of a soccer match between Grand-Bassam and Bouake, attended by both whites and blacks. Antagonisms are forgotten in the excitement of watching the game:

> The ball whistled, roared, squealed under the kicks of the players hurrying wildly to score goals. All breathing stopped. All eyes followed the ball in its trajectory, urging it on or anxiously holding it back. Some people, with their elbows, helped the ball to fly faster; some clapped their hands to encourage it, others to frighten it . . . Europeans and Africans, in a sporting mood, tapped one another on the shoulder and spoke familiarly:
>
> "You see, my friend, we're beating Bouake."
>
> "Nonsense . . . we'll beat you."
>
> All distance between them was abolished. And Climbié, standing near an orange-seller, who was expertly peeling her fruit, looked at the people in the stands, the people on the green . . . and he said to himself: "Ah, if this harmony, this open cordiality, could last!"

World Cup Record

FIFA Ranking: 42
World Cup Appearances: 0
World Cup Champions: 0
Federation Name: Fédération Ivoirienne de
    Football
Confederation: CAF
Founded: 1960
FIFA Affiliation: 1960
Nickname: The Elephants
Manager: Henri Michel
Website: www.fif.ci
Stadium: Houphouët-Boigny Stadium, Abidjan
Home Uniform: orange/orange and
    white/green
Away Uniform: green/green/white
Provider: Puma

1930:	Did not enter
1934:	Did not enter
1938:	Did not enter
1950:	Did not enter
1954:	Did not enter
1958:	Did not enter
1962:	Did not enter
1966:	Did not enter
1970:	Did not enter
1974:	Did not qualify
1978:	Did not qualify
1982:	Did not enter
1986:	Did not qualify
1990:	Did not qualify
1994:	Did not qualify
1998:	Did not qualify
2002:	Did not qualify

Matches	Wins	Draws	Losses	GF	GA	GD	Points
0	0	0	0	0	0	0	0

Côte d'Ivoire is appearing in the World Cup for the first time

Path to Qualification for World Cup 2006

6-Jun-04	Côte d'Ivoire	2	Libya	0		**W**
20-Jun-04	Egypt	1	Côte d'Ivoire	2		**W**
4-Jul-04	Cameroon	2	Côte d'Ivoire	0		**L**
5-Sep-04	Côte d'Ivoire	5	Sudan	0		**W**
10-Oct-04	Benin	0	Côte d'Ivoire	1		**W**
27-Mar-05	Côte d'Ivoire	3	Benin	0		**W**
3-Jun-05	Libya	0	Côte d'Ivoire	0		**D**
19-Jun-05	Côte d'Ivoire	2	Egypt	0		**W**
4-Sep-05	Côte d'Ivoire	2	Cameroon	3		**L**
8-Oct-05	Sudan	1	Côte d'Ivoire	3		**W**

Côte d'Ivoire qualified by finishing first in Group 3 of the African Zone

Croatia

Capital: Zagreb
Independence: June 25, 1991 (from Yugoslavia)
Area: 56,542 sq km
Population: 4,495,904
Median Age: 40.0 years
Life Expectancy at Birth: 74.5 years
Ethnic Groups: Croat 89.6%, Serb 4.5%, other 5.9%
    (Bosniak, Hungarian, Slovene, Czech and Roma)
Religions: Roman Catholic 87.8%, Orthodox 4.4%,
    other Christian 0.4%, Muslim 1.3%, other and
    unspecified 0.9%, none 5.2%
Languages: Croatian 96.1%, Serbian 1%, other and
    undesignated 2.9% (including Italian,
    Hungarian, Czech, Slovak and German)
Suffrage: 18 years of age; universal
    (16 years of age, if employed)
Military Obligation: 18 years of age for
    compulsory military service, with 6-month
    service obligation; 16 years of age with consent
    for voluntary service

GDP Per Capita: $11,200
Budget: $15.65 billion
Military Expenditures: $620 million (2.4% of GDP)
Agriculture: wheat, corn, sugar beets, sunflower
    seed, barley, alfalfa, clover, olives, citrus, grapes,
    soybeans, potatoes; livestock, dairy products
Industries: chemicals and plastics, machine tools,
    fabricated metal, electronics, pig iron and
    rolled steel products, aluminum, paper, wood
    products, construction materials, textiles,
    shipbuilding, petroleum and petroleum
    refining, food and beverages; tourism
Currency: kuna

Source: *CIA World Factbook*

Croatia

Courtney Angela Brkic

For several years since the end of the war in Yugoslavia, the Croatian Ministry of Tourism has searched for a slogan that encapsulates both the country's geography and its ethos. "A Small Country for a Great Holiday" was catchy but vague. "Croatia: Heaven on Earth" was thought overly boastful, potentially off-putting to the tourists who are the life-blood of the country's economy. "The Mediterranean as It Once Was" seemed to favor Croatia's seacoast over its northern and eastern regions entirely. Settling on a slogan has been tougher than one might suppose.

Unlike the slick mass tourism so common in other corners of the Mediterranean, Croatia takes pride in its rough edges—the fast-talking vendors hawking fruit in outdoor marketplaces, the lambs turning slowly on spits at roadside restaurants, the men who sell brandy on seafront promenades. Older generations are unlikely to speak much English and passports must still be surrendered to the local police wherever you spend the night. And then there is the challenge of summarizing Croatia's diversity in a single phrase. In the northeast, Slavonia's rich plains yield vast fields of sunflowers, corn and wheat. In the autumn, the air is sweet with the smell of plumbrandy being brewed in every village. To the west, creeks and rivers crisscross the hills of Zagorje, where Zagreb is surrounded by hundreds of picturesque villages. In the west, Istria is the largest peninsula in the Adriatic Sea with a landscape that has been likened to Tuscany. Hilltop villages and stone farmhouses abound and its truffles are world-renowned. To the south, Dalmatia's limestone is bright next to the blue-green Adriatic, and hundreds of islands dot the sea. And at the country's southernmost tip is the walled city of Dubrovnik, described by Lord Byron as "the pearl of the Adriatic," and by George Bernard Shaw as the place for "those who seek paradise on Earth." How to convey such variety in a single phrase?

Soccer has long served as an expression of regional pride. Today, Croatia's main club rivalry is between Split's Hajduk and Zagreb's Dinamo and when the two teams play each other the regions' differences are often made to seem more pronounced than their similarities. There is language (Zagreb's *kajkavski* employs some German words, Split's *čakavski* Italian ones) and food (Zagreb's cuisine is more Central European and Split's typically Mediterranean). Each club's fans tap into cultural archetypes that are as long-standing as they are inaccurate: Zagreb's *Bad Blue Boys* shout that *Splićani* are lazy, Split's *Torcida* that *Zagrepćani* are effeminate.

When Croatia was still part of Yugoslavia, the main rivalries were between republics. Football was an expression of ethnicity, of political orientation, of self. Many feel that a 1990 match between Zagreb's Dinamo and Belgrade's Red Star marked the beginning of Croatia's war for independence. The game had not even begun when fans from both sides clashed in the stands and on the field. The Serb-dominated police beat Croatian fans while allowing Serb fans to run amok, and the events caused the already-bubbling frustrations with Yugoslavia to boil over. Even the players were not immune. Upon witnessing a policeman beating a fallen Dinamo fan, world-renowned midfielder Zvonimir Boban leaped into action and karate-kicked him, becoming a hero of the growing independence movement.

The war that followed was long and brutal. More than ten thousand people were killed between 1991 and 1995, and more than one thousand are still missing today. Old Town Dubrovnik sustained two thousand artillery hits, despite the fact that it had no strategic military value. And the Yugoslav People's Army and paramilitaries laid waste to village after village, town after town. At one time, a third of Croatian territory was under occupation, and any hope of a speedy conversion to a market economy and of foreign investment floundered for as long as hostilities lasted. Not surprisingly, tourists stopped visiting the Adriatic Sea and the region became associated mainly with suffering. Those four years were marred not just by destruction and casualty figures, but also by a horrible stasis, which continued for several years after hostilities ended. For a country so rich in potential, so enthusiastic about what it could achieve now that it was on its own, being classified simply as a *war-zone* or *former Yugoslav republic* was a blow.

• • •

Though Croatia's independence was recognized in 1992, it wasn't until the 1998 World Cup that Croatia earned widespread recognition for something besides warfare and hardship. Elation began to sweep the country when Croatia beat Germany in the quarterfinals. "Is it really possible?" people seemed to be asking one another, unable to contain the optimism that touched my twenty-four-year-old brother, my eighty-one-year-old great-aunts and everyone else. After that match, the rock band Baruni wrote a song that began, *There is a small country that everyone has now heard of . . . what Brazil used to be, that's what Croatia has become.* The chorus goes: *If you don't like it . . . tough! Croatia is world champion.* Although Croatia's hopes for winning the title were shattered when it lost to France in the semifinals, the song became a national sensation. It was played and sung in bars, at weddings, at sporting events large and small for months afterward.

At the time, I was working in Zagreb. Large screen televisions were set up on the city squares so that people could watch the Croatia–Netherlands third-place match outside in raucous groups. It was a Saturday and I watched the match in my apartment with friends, going onto the balcony at several points to listen to the excited conversations and shouts coming from the six floors and cafés below. The sound of cheers filled the air when Croatia scored. It was like the city was one gigantic living room, everyone's eyes on a single television set. Traffic all but stopped and the street below my apartment was empty. When the game finished with Croatia the winner, the people flooded the streets, ranging from men of my father's age who could remember playing soccer in streets with cloth-filled balls to a new generation of children whose parents bought them only FIFA-approved soccer gear. Huge numbers were dressed in Croatian checkerboard jerseys and the streets swam in red and white. They filled the main square and that night, all night, we heard happy, drunken voices singing.

Coming only three years after the war ended, it was an emotional moment in a young country's history and people in every town and city took joyfully to the streets. That night on television reporters interviewed grown men who could not stop themselves from weeping. The country had not seen such unified celebration since its declaration of independence and the general consensus was that now no one could deny Croatia its place on the map.

That December a friend and her husband organized a St. Nicholas party at the SOS Children's Village in Lekenik, and Baruni provided the entertainment. Austrian-founded SOS set up Lekenik in 1996 to care for children whose parents had been killed or had disappeared during the war. The children, ranging from babies to teenagers, were from Croatia and from Bosnia-Herzegovina. Some came from families that had celebrated St. Nicholas in earlier, happier years, others did not. Some of the cases were cut-and-dried: parents and extended family members were dead, and there was no one left who could care for them. In other cases parents were missing, or in transit, or separated from their children by wartime circumstances.

St. Nicholas, the Central European version of Santa Claus or Father Christmas, comes on December 6 to well-behaved children, filling their shoes with fruit and nuts, and leaving other presents besides. Naughty children fear the *krampus,* the devil who shakes his chains at them and leaves nothing but coal and switches in his wake, although even the naughtiest children are usually able to evade him with the promise of future good behavior. The holiday, and others like it, bore special significance for children who were separated from their families. The smallest wondered how St. Nicholas would find them, removed as they were from their homes and villages. Older children, who knew perfectly well that their parents used to fill their shoes with oranges and walnuts, faced the holidays alone.

I had visited the village several months after it was founded, and was impressed by the organization's straightforward yet radical approach. Unlike institutional workers in shelters or orphanages, an SOS mother (a woman screened both for her qualifications and to ensure that her commitment to the tightly knit community is long-term) cares for several children in an actual home. Siblings are kept together and the village is not a holding cell for future adoption, but a viable alternative to state-run orphanages as well as standard family placements. The goal is to provide as normal a living situation as is possible, and a mother organizes all aspects of her children's daily life, from cooking and cleaning to helping with schoolwork.

The third-place World Cup finish had been proof to many (including residents of the SOS village) that times were changing, that the war, while it could never be forgotten, was over and that the country was moving on to better things. And, most important, that people outside Croatia's borders were realizing this fact. Tourists had already started returning to the Adriatic and each season was proving better than the one before it. Magazines began to do articles about the pristine beauty of the country's sea, the possibilities for hikers and divers, the cultural offerings including the Dubrovnik summer festival, the Motovun film festival and an Animation Festival in Zagreb. Another lyric from Baruni's song says, *They brought empty fishing nets and we filled them.* In other words, *We defied all expectations.*

The families attending the St. Nicholas party in Lekenik included children of all ages. After Baruni finished its first set they asked for audience requests. The rock band had already played "Croatia is World Champion" and a number of their other popular songs. Every time they finished playing a song, the children roared for their favorite. The adults tried to convince them to request other songs, to give it a rest. But the children would not be swayed. They only wanted to hear "Croatia is World Champion," over and over and over again.

World Cup Record

FIFA Ranking: 20
World Cup Appearances: 2
World Cup Champions: 0
Federation Name: Hrvatski Nogometni Savez
Confederation: UEFA
Founded: 1912
FIFA Affiliation: 1992
Nickname: Vatreni (Fiery)
Manager: Zlatko Kranjcar
Website: www.hns-cff.hr
Stadium: various
Home Uniform: red white/blue/white
Away Uniform: blue/white/blue
Provider: Nike

1930: Did not participate
1934: Did not participate
1938: Did not participate
1950: Did not participate
1954: Did not participate
1958: Did not participate
1962: Did not participate
1966: Did not participate
1970: Did not participate
1974: Did not participate
1978: Did not participate
1982: Did not participate
1986: Did not participate
1990: Did not participate
1994: Did not participate
1998: 3rd place
2002: First round exit

Matches	Wins	Draws	Losses	GF	GA	GD	Points
10	6	0	4	13	8	+5	18

Croatia is 28th on the all-time World Cup table

Path to Qualification for World Cup 2006

4-Sep-04	Croatia	3	Hungary	0		W
8-Sep-04	Sweden	0	Croatia	1		W
9-Oct-04	Croatia	2	Bulgaria	2		D
26-Mar-05	Croatia	4	Iceland	0		W
30-Mar-05	Croatia	3	Malta	0		W
4-Jun-05	Bulgaria	1	Croatia	3		W
3-Sep-05	Iceland	1	Croatia	3		W
7-Sep-05	Malta	1	Croatia	1		D
8-Oct-05	Croatia	1	Sweden	0		W
12-Oct-05	Hungary	0	Croatia	0		D

Croatia qualified by finishing first in Group 8 of the European Zone

Czech Republic

Capital: Prague
Independence: January 1, 1993
    (Czechoslovakia split into the
    Czech Republic and Slovakia)
Area: 78,866 sq km
Population: 10,241,138
Median Age: 39.0 years
Life Expectancy at Birth: 76.0 years
Ethnic Groups: Czech 90.4%, Moravian 3.7%,
    Slovak 1.9%, other 4%
Religions: Roman Catholic 26.8%,
    Protestant 2.1%, other 3.3%,
    unspecified 8.8%, unaffiliated 59%
Languages: Czech
Suffrage: 18 years of age; universal
Military Obligation: 18–50 years of age for
    voluntary military service
GDP Per Capita: $16,800
Budget: $45.8 billion
Military Expenditures: $2.17 billion (1.8% of GDP)
Agriculture: wheat, potatoes, sugar beets, hops,
    fruit; pigs, poultry
Industries: metallurgy, machinery and equipment,
    motor vehicles, glass, armaments
Currency: Czech koruna

Source: *CIA World Factbook*

Czech Republic

Tim Adams

Some countries have a place in your head long before you visit them. The idea of their football team is enough to take you back there. For me, the Czech Republic is in that place that means possibility, and all that follows from it. It begins, this place, with typewritten pages chugging slowly from a fax machine. It's after midnight, it's been a long day and the pages are coming slowly: as if the fax machine is reading them word by word, running a finger under each line, before they emerge.

The fax machine itself still seems to me dazzlingly high tech. This is long before email, and though people have computers, they still use them like typewriters. It is November 1989, and I'm in Cambridge, in the office of *Granta,* the literary magazine where I have been working for a year or so, above a hairdresser's salon. It's cold enough in the office to see your breath and no else is around, but I don't mind. I'm twenty-three and it's about the first time I've felt even distantly part of something more important than myself. The pages are stuttering through painstakingly from Prague, bringing news of a revolution made in a theater called the Magic Lantern.

I'm not sure the events in the Czech capital were being called the Velvet Revolution yet but in my head that's how it already seems. The name arose from the stealth with which a group of writers and dissidents took political power. But the velvet I'm imagining in the *Granta* office, next to the fax machine, is the velvet of the Magic Lantern's seats, in my mind purple and shadowed and rising into the dark, while the future of Europe is being recast into the night on a lamplit stage.

The fax that is coming through is one of a series that has been emerging all day, rolls and curls of copy in languages that none of us in the office understand—neither Bill, our editor, or the rest of us, Ursula and Angus and me—but about which all of us are unusually—uniquely—heady and uncynical. We have been trawling for translators, wondering how typesetters will cope with all those diacritics, watching deadlines come and go, listening to the news on the office transistor radio and changing our stories hour by hour. On any little magazine moments of genuine excitement are infrequent, perhaps quarterly, if you are lucky; but for a few days now such moments have been coming thick and fast.

The faxes have arrived in response to desperate letters and phone calls first to Berlin and Warsaw, now to Budapest and Bucharest and Prague. The letters had asked simple questions, the only ones we had been able to think of in that month when the news was delivered breathlessly by foreign correspondents, and you thought anything at all might happen: What does it look like? And, um, how does it feel? And, do you think you might find time to tell us (today, please, or sooner if possible, in one thousand faxable words)?

They had all been sent, these begging letters, by Bill and Ursula and Angus and me, to addresses that seemed either too long or too short, or to writers on fax numbers we didn't quite believe. They were sent mostly to novelists who had been imprisoned, poets who had lived whole lives under surveillance, short story writers who had been exiled or worked as nightwatchmen and streetsweepers and milkmen and gravediggers. The letters had gone out more in hope than expectation. There was, after all, a lot going on. The Berlin Wall had fallen and within a week or two, successive greatcoated governments had melted into air.

There were, no doubt, that night in Prague, constitutions to be written, powers to be shared, hopes to be raised, toasts to be drunk. But even so, a few of those who had watched all of this first hand, who had scripted it even, took the time to respond to our magazine above a hairdresser's salon. That, I was telling myself then, keeping vigil for that latest fax, was at these moments exactly what real writers did (and I was very keen, then, to know all about what real writers did, would have wanted to witness one of those moments myself, write about it even, though I would probably never have mentioned that particular ambition to anyone).

As a child, I had not thought it was odd that Europe was cut in two, and that the other part was unknowable, and out of reach. Born in 1965, in England, I could barely imagine anything different. The facts of that separation seemed then as distant as the war that my parents, and other impossibly old people, talked about as if it were yesterday.

But the split had an effect; it seemed so irrational and so permanent. These countries less than a day's drive away were, it appeared, as cold and distant as Greenland or Siberia. I learned to group them easily together, a bloc, PolandHungaryYugoslaviaCzechoslovakia on the blue globe on my bedside table.

They all had footballers who looked like soldiers with sharp knees and elbows and when I saw games that long-haired English teams played against them the television cameras would scan across the watching crowd of pale-looking people in big coats and hats who clapped gloved hands together and made hardly a sound. Their policemen had dogs. Their breath went up in clouds in the cold night air. I spent probably rather too much of my spare time back then playing endless homemade European Cups in the back of school exercise books, with dice and blunt pencils and bendable rules. I would painstakingly copy out team sheets full of Olegs and Milans; then always make sure that the Spartas and the Partisans and the Lokomotivs went out early on.

Czechoslovakia, as it was, seemed to me a lot like its football teams: at the very least no fun; or worse, lifeless and sinister. Those footballers came from behind an "iron curtain," you were told in commentaries, a phrase that always triggered in me as a small boy, and still triggers now, the thought of those concertina grilles in old elevators, that if you were not careful could snap shut and trap you inside and rumble you to an unknown floor of a department store or a hospital, and thereby separate you from your Mum and Dad and everyone you knew forever.

I was in my teens when those particular ideas about Czechoslovakia started to change. It was then that I began to read some of those writers who risked their liberty to whisper and shout and laugh through that iron grille and explain that the place where they lived was not in itself at all cruel and cold—that was just the people who tried to keep it all in check, who organized the tanks and the secret policemen, and who did not want any of their subjects to publish books or write poems or perform plays or make jokes or fall in love.

Underneath this structure of power, in spite of it, these whispering, brilliant voices said, the necessity of doing those things, of "living in truth" as Václav Havel declared, was in fact worth risking everything for. Even better, the lightness and absurdity and sex and fantasy that was produced as a result was far more real than anything you came across growing up in suburban England.

I started, as many of my friends at that time seemed to start, backward, with the exile Milan Kundera, read his tales of laughter and forgetting, and the great comic seductions set in his homeland with its "surplus of poets." I went on to Ivan Klíma, the direct bleak comedy of life under Soviet rule, and Havel, his extraordinary letters to his wife Olga written on smuggled scraps of paper from prison. I graduated from there to Bohumil Hrabal, read and reread his wonderful anecdotal novels of Prague, great discursive yarns that sounded as if they had been overheard before closing time (which was in fact often the case). And from there to *The Good Soldier Svejk*, Hrabal's model for his Czech heroes, and Kafka, read how in his native city it was not possible, in 1984, of all years, to celebrate the centenary of his birth. This was, I couldn't help thinking, exactly as he would have wanted it.

In this way, I suppose, I built in my head an image of a country, and in particular a city, Prague, which became as real to me as if I was wandering its streets. I had by that time decided to place all my faith in words, and solemnly believed that the world could be understood with the techniques of practical criticism; Czechoslovakia, it seemed to me, was a place where words counted for everything, where authority could be undone with irony, where poets were, from the outside at least, the most important people in society. (I had been reading a lot of Shakespeare.)

I only went to Czechoslovakia once before the revolution. I had become on leaving university a sort of travel writer, not quite the poet that I imagined, and I was invited on one occasion on a curious press trip along the Danube on a flat-bottomed gin-palace of a cruiser. Our flash boat set off from Vienna and moored at one point in Slovakian Bratislava. We were shown around for a couple of days by a young couple who had somehow invested in an antique charabanc; he drove and she talked. Our guide was very proud of her blue jeans, but when we asked her any questions about her life she was struck dumb and gestured around the bus, as if it might be bugged. When she sat us down to eat she stiffened visibly if we said anything that might be considered critical of her country, and glanced nervously around the room. She seemed by the end both relieved to be rid of us and desperately sad that we were going.

I didn't write about any of that. The brief was hotels and restaurants and I quickly stopped being a sort of travel writer soon afterward. At least, later, I could half convince myself, working at *Granta,* that I shared some vague common cause with those writers who worked against such fears. We published a few of them for a start, Kundera and Havel and Klíma, and we stayed up late cutting and pasting, literally then, sentences and paragraphs together, our own entirely safe and commercial version of samizdat, the carbon-copied stories and essays and poems that Czech writers circulated in the evenings. By the time 1989 came around I was hanging on these writers' every word.

A year or so after Havel had become president, in that most theatrical of denouements (like the return of the Duke in *As You Like It*) that had him skateboarding through the corridors of Kafka's *Castle* in a sweater and jeans, I went to a conference where I met some of those samizdat editors and writers. The conference was organized by the financier George Soros and was aimed at finding a way of sustaining the little magazines now that their purpose had disappeared, and their words no longer quite mattered. These men and women with pamphlets that they'd published as if their lives depended on it were now out of a job. I remember talking to them a bit about mailing lists and subscriptions and serialization deals, all the things that kept *Granta* going. They could not quite understand that in the new Czechoslovakia truth might not be enough, and would have to be replaced by marketing. Or, at least, they could see the irony of it all. Inevitably, we ended up talking football in place of ideas.

Not long after that I had lunch with the novelist Ivan Klíma at a smart west-London restaurant. He insisted on eating only a bread roll and some soup and while I gabbled about the importance of his writing and how it must feel to have triumphed, to be free, he talked bleakly of sacrifices endured. He differentiated sharply between the writers who had left, Kundera in Paris, and those that had stayed, gestured wearily toward the years his generation had lost. When his books were not available, he said, everyone had wanted to read them, but now they were in the shops.

When I eventually went to visit Prague I'd like to have believed it would be like meeting a lifelong pen pal for the first time. I was sent there for a couple of weeks to write a literary sort of guide to the city for the newspaper I then worked for (I was still trying to be a real writer, or to find a subject that counted, but realizing too, that such things don't come along very often and that all of life was anyway not contained in sentences and paragraphs). I began that tour at the Slavia café where Havel had courted his wife Olga and I sat among earnest Czech men with booming laughs and old ladies in raffish hats and scarves and lovers meeting in the afternoon and students deep in conversation (just like the old days except that now there was only me at the next table eavesdropping and taking notes).

I made my way around the city in the coming days in search of the place I had in my head, always imagining I might find Bohumil Hrabal sitting in a corner telling tales. The city had quickly been colonized by weekend visitors and American students and British stag nighters. It was January and sensationally cold, and every other bar had strippers in it, sliding down poles as proof of liberation. I drank a good deal of perfect pilsener and I came to realize that Kafka was the author of the greatest of all hangover tales: "As Gregor Samsa awoke one morning from uneasy dreams he found himself transformed in his bed into a gigantic insect . . ."

In my mind, Prague had lived through its writers, and I wanted to convince myself in those first few years after the revolution that it had been recreated by them. I did my best to relive Kafka's notion of Prague as a place of "People who cross dark bridges passing saints, with faint candles/Clouds that parade across gray skies, passing churches with darkening towers." Walking through the castle at night I rarely saw a nonuniformed soul in its chill, gray arcades. But every evening of that first stay I took to wandering past the couples snogging by the carved saints on Charles Bridge and on up to Kafka's tiny old house to watch the stars begin to move over the city.

It couldn't survive. But on subsequent visits to Prague, I thought I could see it in the faces of old men and young women: that Czech mix of solemnity and devilment. And I sensed it too in the way the football team began to play, with great theater, never for a moment forgetting it is all a game. I loved the fact that the greatest of all Czech players, Pavel Nedved, came of age in 1989, and joined the first Sparta Prague team that stopped looking like soldiers. He had his hair long. He has played for all the years since, for his country and for Juventus, with what looks to me like the authentic spirit of the velvet revolution in his boots: deft and strong; mischievous and quietly powerful.

For most of that time, in theme bars of Prague and in the new Starbucks, you would hear men talk of the style and substance of the Czech finalists in Euro '96, the team of the young Karel Poborský and Patrik Berger, and the untouchable Nedved. That is when the same men were not grumbling of how Havel was outstaying his welcome, how he had his head in the clouds, that the Czech Republic was a modern European country now and you could not just keep harking back to 1989.

Havel, himself, it seemed to me, having had once to make up the country as he went along, never forgot the staging of it all. I loved the story of how just before he left the castle in 2004 he hosted President Bush and Donald Rumsfeld at a NATO summit. He choreographed an evening's entertainment that included a rococo dance (full of be-wigged courtiers and simulated sex) as well as a top-volume rap version of "La Marseillaise" and John Lennon's "Power to the People." ("It may," he conceded afterward, "have been on the verge of what Mr. Rumsfeld and certain others could tolerate.")

In a valedictory speech Havel looked back on the events of his extraordinary life and the revolution, and answered once and for all that old faxed request of how it felt to him in November 1989. "At the very deepest core of it there was," he suggested, "ultimately, a sensation of the absurd: what Sisyphus might have felt if one fine day his boulder stopped, rested on the hilltop, and failed to roll back down." It's almost ancient history now, of course, but as anyone who has ever wanted to be a writer—or anyone who has ever lined up for a football match—knows, it takes a long time to forget those first teetering moments when anything at all seems possible, and all you have in front of you is a blank page, and no words have yet been set down to spoil it.

World Cup Record

FIFA Ranking: 2
World Cup Appearances: 8
World Cup Champions: 0
Federation Name: Ceskomoravsk Fotbalov Svaz
Confederation: UEFA
Founded: 1901
FIFA Affiliation: 1907
Nickname: Locomotive
Manager: Karel Bruckner
Website: www.fotbal.cz
Stadium: Evzena Rosickeho
Home Uniform: red/white/blue
Away Uniform: all white
Provider: Puma

1930: Did not participate
1934: 2nd place
1938: Second round exit
1950: Did not participate
1954: First round exit
1958: First round exit
1962: 2nd place
1966: Did not qualify
1970: First round exit
1974: Did not qualify
1978: Did not qualify
1982: First round exit
1986: Did not qualify
1990: Quarterfinal exit
1994: Did not qualify
1998: Did not qualify
2002: Did not qualify

Matches	Wins	Draws	Losses	GF	GA	GD	Points
30	11	5	14	44	45	-1	38

Czech Republic is 18th on the all-time World Cup table
Note: Played as Czechoslovakia until 1998

Path to Qualification for World Cup 2006

8-Sep-04	Netherlands	2	Czech Republic	0	**L**
9-Oct-04	Czech Republic	1	Romania	0	**W**
13-Oct-04	Armenia	0	Czech Republic	3	**W**
17-Nov-04	FYR Macedonia	0	Czech Republic	2	**W**
26-Mar-05	Czech Republic	4	Finland	3	**W**
30-Mar-05	Andorra	0	Czech Republic	4	**W**
4-Jun-05	Czech Republic	8	Andorra	1	**W**
8-Jun-05	Czech Republic	6	FYR Macedonia	1	**W**
3-Sep-05	Romania	2	Czech Republic	0	**L**
7-Sep-05	Czech Republic	4	Armenia	1	**W**
8-Oct-05	Czech Republic	0	Netherlands	2	**L**
12-Oct-05	Finland	0	Czech Republic	3	**W**
12-Nov-05	Norway	0	Czech Republic	1	**W**
16-Nov-05	Czech Republic	1	Norway	0	**W**

Czech Republic qualified by finishing second in Group 1 of the European Zone and beating Norway in a home-away playoff

Ecuador

Capital: Quito
Independence: May 24, 1822 (from Spain)
Area: 283,560 sq km
Population: 13,363,593
Median Age: 23.3 years
Life Expectancy at Birth: 76.2 years
Ethnic Groups: mestizo (mixed Amerindian and white) 65%, Amerindian 25%, Spanish and others 7%, black 3%
Religions: Roman Catholic 95%, other 5%
Languages: Spanish (official), Amerindian languages (especially Quechua)
Suffrage: 18 years of age; universal, compulsory for literate persons ages 18–65, optional for other eligible voters
Military Obligation: 20 years of age for conscript military service; 12-month service obligation
GDP Per Capita: $3,700
Budget: $7.3 billion
Military Expenditures: $655 million (2.2% of GDP)
Agriculture: bananas, coffee, cocoa, rice, potatoes, manioc (tapioca), plantains, sugarcane; cattle, sheep, pigs, beef, pork, dairy products; balsa wood; fish, shrimp
Industries: petroleum, food processing, textiles, wood products, chemicals
Currency: US dollar

Source: *CIA World Factbook*

Ecuador

Jake Silverstein

Marisol had given me a book of poems called *El Armador de Relojes*. She said her uncle had written the poems. I couldn't understand the title.

"The *armer* of clocks?" I asked, hopelessly pantomiming.

"No," she said, "the *armor* of clocks."

That didn't make any sense either. Her English was as untrustworthy as my Spanish. Once, when I had not seen her waiting at a bar, she said it was because she was "invincible." All day long I pored over the book, trying to wring from its pages some fundamental insights into Ecuador. "A shadow walks along the pier," went one line, "looking for a place to get drunk." I was living in the Hostal Belmont. The roof had a laundry sink and a nice view. The poet was from Atuntaqui, a village in the Imbabura province near the Colombian border. He had studied theater in Quito. With a pocket dictionary, I waded through the stanzas.

> *I understand the loneliness of the Andean villages*
> *When the snow invades them*
> *And the dogs are seized by silence.*
> *The solitude of those who dream of tomorrow's achievements,*
> *Sleeping in front of a television that glows*
> > *With an astronaut, returning to earth*
> *To confirm that God does not exist . . .*

It was August 1996 and a new president was ready to be inaugurated. Abdalá Bucaram, the former mayor of Guyaquil, had defeated Jaime Nebot by twenty thousand votes. The strange campaign had riveted the nation for months. All four frontrunners, including Bucaram and Nebot, were descendants of Lebanese immigrants, which reflects not the quantity of Levantines in Ecuador, but their disproportionate flourish. Among them, Bucaram stood out. His slogan was "First the Poor!" Since every citizen in the country was required by law to cast a vote, and since more than 65 percent of them lived in poverty, this was a wise calculation. But Bucaram was a madman. His nickname was "The Madman." Throughout the campaign, he'd appeared at rallies as the front man for Los Iracundos (The Irascibles), an Uruguayan rock band. (They later released an album together, *A Madman in Love,* featuring a rambunctious cover of "Jailhouse Rock.") He'd shaved his moustache on television and auctioned the shavings for charity. At rallies, he'd handed out cartons of his very own brand of milk, *Abdaleche.* He'd dismissed previous presidents as "donkeys." He'd torn off his shirt and guzzled beer. He'd railed against the rich. He'd mugged for the camera wearing thick gold chains. He'd cavorted with the scantily clad.

Now he was the president of Ecuador. We congregated in some plaza to hear him speak. It was the evening of the day of his inauguration. Huge posters of him and Rosalia, his running mate and frequent dance partner, hung from the lampposts. Los Iracundos played an up-tempo set to warm the crowd. Hundreds of toy paratroopers filled the sky. Someone must have been giving them out to the kids. Thrown high in the air, they fell fast enough to inflate the small plastic parachutes attached by string to their small plastic chests. Then they drifted lazily over the crowd. The troopers were red and the chutes were white. Having spent the day plunged in the moody imagery of *The Armor of Clocks,* I was inclined to see as much significance in this childish diversion as in the hoopla onstage. Kids roamed blindly through the crowd, knocking into legs and kicking over beers as they tracked the falls of their men. Sometimes a chute wouldn't open and the man would plummet straight down and everyone would laugh.

The Madman mounted the stage and shouted some boilerplate about *"la sistema"* and *"los pobres."* It was the first time I'd seen him in action. In his youth, he'd been an Olympic sprinter, and though he had lost the sprinter's build, some of that twitchy, high-strung athleticism persisted in his public demeanor. Pacing to and fro, he roused the crowd with vague generalities. He was already toning down the full-scale attacks on the country's oligarchs, whom he'd vowed to destroy *a un solo toque* (with a single blow). *A un solo toque,* a phrase borrowed from the soccer world, had been a rallying cry during the campaign, part of the Madman's particular brand of populism, a kind of sports populism. He was always playing soccer, and talking about soccer, and challenging his opponent to name as many soccer players on the Barcelona club as he could. He compared the presidential campaign to a soccer game, and called for a debate to be held in Atahualpa Stadium in Quito.

All this despite the fact that in the athletic history of his country there was little to celebrate. At the time of the Madman's campaign, Ecuador had never qualified for the World Cup. Few Ecuadorian athletes had done much to distinguish themselves on the international stage. No Olympic medals, no Copa America triumphs. The Madman himself hadn't done anything. In 1972, at the Munich Olympic Games, an injury had prevented him from even competing. It was staggering to think what sort of campaign Ecuador would have had to endure had he actually sprinted and won a medal. The constant brandishing of the trophy. The donning of the laurel crown. Why not just have a footrace for the presidency? A nation's first champion on the international sports stage is probably worth three of that nation's presidents. The Madman was not too mad to grasp this, so it was with tremendous excitement and fanfare that he called up to the stage none other than Jefferson Pérez.

Jefferson Pérez: The summer's other big story. Two weeks earlier, I'd been in Cuenca, Pérez's hometown. I was living in Hostal La Ramada, a noisy place with little to recommend it other than the room rate. One morning, I was standing in a bookstore reading through *Time*'s Twenty-Five Most Influential Americans article. Jim Clark, the founder of Netscape, ranked number one. Other winners were Sandra Day O'Connor, Jerry Seinfeld, Louis Farrakhan, Courtney Love and Stephen Covey, who wrote *The Seven Habits of Highly Effective People*. He was so effective that he'd become influential. Or maybe it was his influence that gave him his effectiveness. In any case, it would be interesting to know how many of these Americans shared the seven mystical habits. All of them? None? Suddenly, I noticed a distant bedlam in the streets. Shouting could be heard from restaurants. Small clots of Cuencans stood on the sidewalks, talking excitedly. Had the Madman finally snapped, kicking into some hideous Black Sabbath covers with Los Iracundos? Maybe biting off the head of a Galapagos turtle? I ducked into a bar.

The bar was unusually full and amazingly tense. It took a moment or two to figure out why. Moaning and groaning, the patrons sloshed their drinks at the television, goading along a twenty-two-year-old Ecuadorian speedwalker who hustled around a track in Atlanta, closing in on that tantalizing first Olympic medal. Not only that, he was in position to make it a gold.

"¡Jefferson!" a woman screamed, as he strode past a German on the homestretch, his hips swaying from side to side and his fists thrusting forward.

Soon the finish line hove into view, only it wasn't a finish line. It was the threshold of a new historical epoch. The bar froze with concentration. Seconds were centuries beneath his feet, to borrow a phrase from *The Armor of Clocks*. I had the feeling that throughout the entire country, only brute animals and airplanes were moving at all. With one step, *a un solo toque,* Pérez plunged the country through to the other side. Up went a delirious cry. Flags were frantically waved. Outside the horns of cars began to blare incessantly. The revelry had a serious edge. This was not just some brainless catharsis or vain display of strength. This was History. Hands were shaken instead of slapped. The man in front of me turned around and smashed his beer stein against mine. I asked him how he felt.

"Ecuador is now . . ." he gravely proclaimed, pausing to think about it for a moment. *"Ecuador!"* he concluded.

Perez immediately became a national hero. He was granted a stamp in his honor and a government pension worth 200 million sucres ($62,705 USD in 1996; $8,044 four years later). A TV station gave him a new Mazda and Toni Yogurt arranged for him to have a lifetime supply of their product. Speedwalking was suddenly trendy. Out on the highways, people strode back and forth, elbows swinging. Musicians performed Jefferson Pérez numbers, and a poet named Washington Medina wrote him an ode entitled "Glory and Honor." Some said he should run for president.

Mounting the stage now in Quito to his customary ovation, Pérez looked every bit the athlete statesman. He grasped Bucaram's hand, and the two of them turned to stare out at the hundreds of red and white paratroopers drifting over the crowd. The Speedwalker and the Madman. The Ecuadorians I'd come with were friends of Marisol, art students mostly. The guy next to me poured some beer on the ground. He sighed deeply. "This man is a . . ." he speedwalked in place to give me the idea. I said I knew.

"What does it mean that our first Olympic medal comes from this?" He speedwalked in place some more.

This was years ago. Bucaram turned out to be the greatest scoundrel president in the history of Ecuador, installing his relatives in key posts and his mistresses in swanky apartments, even as he announced withering austerity measures to please foreign lenders. If he'd hung around a little longer he might even have had an outside chance at Greatest Scoundrel President in the History of Latin America, which is saying something. But only six months after his inauguration, the congress declared him "mentally unfit to rule." A strong case could be made that he'd tried to warn them. His presidency was short and scandalous. One of the highlights was when he received infamous amputationist Lorena Bobbitt, a native Ecuadorian, to dine with him in lavish ceremony. Another was when he looted an estimated $100 million from the nation's coffers, even going so far as to pull paintings off the walls of the Presidential Palace. He finally fled into exile on February 11, 1997, accused of the Misuse of State Funds and, because a good case could be built around it, the Irregular Purchase of School Backpacks.

But Bucaram was not through with Ecuador. Four years later, as the national soccer team was heading into the World Cup qualifying rounds under the guidance of manager Hernán Dario Gómez, he allegedly had Gómez pistol-whipped and shot three times. Apparently, the coach had passed over Bucaram's son for the national junior squad. Gómez faxed in his resignation from his hospital bed, only to dramatically return, leading the team to a thrilling qualifying round victory over Brazil, and at long last, a trip to the World Cup. Talk about *Gloria y Honor!* All the yogurt in Quito wouldn't have covered it. Though they didn't make it past the group stage in 2002, the team immediately supplanted Jefferson Pérez as the focus of the country's athletico-nationalistic hopes and dreams.

Bucaram laid low for a while, but during the run-up to the 2006 World Cup, he made what many pray will be his final foray into Ecuadorian politics. Last April, with the blessing of then-president Lucio Gutiérrez, a former crony, Bucaram dropped into the country by helicopter, mounted a horse and galloped away, screaming to the gathered throng of reporters that once Gutiérrez' term was up, he would reclaim the literal reins of power. As political theater, it was right in line with the kinds of performances that had captivated the nation and got him elected in 1996, but Ecuador was now nine years older and wiser, and the prospect was so horrifying that it touched off days of rioting and bloodshed. When it was all over, Gutiérrez had been deposed and Bucaram was back in Panama, stewing in his own juices.

The malfeasance of these corrupt politicos played in counterpoint throughout the summer and fall to the building momentum of the national soccer team, a polyphony familiar to longtime fans in the South American Zone. In October, the same week that a goalless draw with Uruguay secured the Ecuadorians a spot in Germany, Gutiérrez was locked away in a maximum security prison, still muttering about his rightful claim to the presidency. "I thank all my players," said new manager Luis Suárez, "who have made the people of Ecuador happy again."

El Armador de Relojes. As the crowd broke up and the last paratrooper floated down on its tiny billowing chute, Marisol explained the title to me once more. It didn't mean the *armer* of clocks, or the *armor* of clocks. It meant the *assembly* of clocks—the guts, the parts and pieces, the gears. The things that made time run. I still have the book. The title poem is a parable about a people who accidentally destroy some sort of totemic clock. This causes them to lose faith in their gods, at which point their entire world starts to grow smaller. Their village is reduced to a single house, their language is reduced to a single word and their population is reduced to a single man. This man is pretty confused. He gets into bed. He has only one arm, one leg, one finger and one eye. In time he pulls himself together. He roams around the world, collecting clock parts. Back home he begins to assemble the parts. Finally, the second hand springs to life, and the "tic-tac" sound "shakes the foundations of the house." Murmuring can be heard in the halls. Outside, children begin to play.

What do you think they are playing?

World Cup Record

FIFA Ranking: 38
World Cup Appearances: 1
World Cup Champions: 0
Federation Name: Federación Ecuatoriana de Fútbol
Confederation: CONMEBOL
Founded: 1925
FIFA Affiliation: 1926
Nickname: La Tri (color)
Manager: Luis Suárez
Website: www.ecuafutbol.com
Stadium: Casa Blanca, Quito
Home Uniform: yellow/blue/red
Away Uniform: blue/white/blue
Provider: Marathon

1930:	Did not enter
1934:	Did not enter
1938:	Did not enter
1950:	Withdrew
1954:	Did not enter
1958:	Did not enter
1962:	Did not qualify
1966:	Did not qualify
1970:	Did not qualify
1974:	Did not qualify
1978:	Did not qualify
1982:	Did not qualify
1986:	Did not qualify
1990:	Did not qualify
1994:	Did not qualify
1998:	Did not qualify
2002:	First round exit

Matches	Wins	Draws	Losses	GF	GA	GD	Points
3	1	0	2	2	4	-2	3

Ecuador is 51st on the all-time World Cup table

Path to Qualification for World Cup 2006

Date	Home		Away		Result
6-Sep-03	Ecuador	2	Venezuela	0	W
10-Sep-03	Brazil	1	Ecuador	0	L
15-Nov-03	Paraguay	2	Ecuador	1	L
19-Nov-03	Ecuador	0	Peru	0	D
30-Mar-04	Argentina	1	Ecuador	0	L
2-Jun-04	Ecuador	2	Colombia	1	W
5-Jun-04	Ecuador	3	Bolivia	2	W
5-Sep-04	Uruguay	1	Ecuador	0	L
10-Oct-04	Ecuador	2	Chile	0	W
14-Oct-04	Venezuela	3	Ecuador	1	L
17-Nov-04	Ecuador	1	Brazil	0	W
27-Mar-05	Ecuador	5	Paraguay	2	W
30-Mar-05	Peru	2	Ecuador	2	D
4-Jun-05	Ecuador	2	Argentina	0	W
8-Jun-05	Colombia	3	Ecuador	0	L
3-Sep-05	Bolivia	1	Ecuador	2	W
8-Oct-05	Ecuador	0	Uruguay	0	D
12-Oct-05	Chile	0	Ecuador	0	D

Ecuador qualified by finishing among the top four in the South American Zone

England

Capital: London

Independence: England has existed as a unified entity since the 10th century

Area: 130,357 sq km

Population: 49,138,000

Median Age: 39.0 years

Life Expectancy at Birth: 78.4 years

Ethnic Groups: white 92.1%, black 2%, Indian 1.8%, Pakistani 1.3%, mixed 1.2%, other 1.6%

Religions: Christian (Anglican, Roman Catholic, Presbyterian, Methodist) 71.6%, Muslim 2.7%, Hindu 1%, other 1.6%, unspecified or none 23.1%

Languages: English

Suffrage: 18 years of age; universal

Military Obligation: 16 years of age for voluntary military service

GDP Per Capita: $29,600

Budget: $896.7 billion

Military Expenditures: $42,836.5 million (2.4% of GDP)

Agriculture: cereals, oilseed, potatoes, vegetables; cattle, sheep, poultry; fish

Industries: machine tools, electric power equipment, automation equipment, railroad equipment, shipbuilding, aircraft, motor vehicles and parts, electronics and communications equipment, metals, chemicals, coal, petroleum, paper and paper products, food processing, textiles, clothing

Currency: British pound

Source: *CIA World Factbook*

Note: Economic data is for the United Kingdom

England

Nick Hornby

It was all so straightforward back in the 1960s, when I started to watch football. England had just won the 1966 World Cup, and, therefore, unarguably, was the best team in the world: fact, period, end of story. It's true that the winning goal in the final shouldn't have counted; true, too, that the Brazilians and Pelé were systematically beaten up in the '66 tournament, Pelé to the extent that he was carried off on a stretcher after the umpteenth brutal foul. But still, eh? The best! Probably! And we were the second-best team in 1970, clearly, although one has to be a little more creative with the evidence. Yes, England was knocked out in the quarterfinals. But they really shouldn't have been—they were 2–0 up against the Germans with twenty minutes left, and contrived to lose the game 3–2. Brazil won the 1970 World Cup, easily, but they only just beat us in the group stage of the tournament, 1–0. And Jeff Astle missed a sitter toward the end, so that game should have ended 1–1. Brazil thumped everybody else. So, to recap: easily the best team in 1966, and pretty much the best team—let's give the Brazilians some credit, and we'll settle on equal best—in 1970.

And then everything went wrong, pretty much forever. For a start, I became a grown-up, and became much more troubled about what it meant to belong to a country; meanwhile England's football team was hopeless. The equal-best team in the world didn't even qualify for the World Cup finals of 1974 and 1978; the world-class players we'd been blessed with during the 1960s had gone, and anyway, by the 1980s, the whole subject of patriotism and football had become much more complicated. In the mind's eye now, England games during that decade were frequently only just visible through a cloud of tear gas, used by European police to disperse our rioting hooligans. England fans were fast becoming a pretty sinister bunch; and though our club games were frequently plagued by riots, it never felt as though the yobs were setting the tone. If you went to see England play at Wembley, as I still did, once in a while, you could observe people around you making the Nazi salute during the national anthem, and abuse of black players—even the black players playing for the home team—was commonplace.

In those days, Wembley held 92,000 people; neatly, there were (and still are) ninety-two professional football clubs in England. Sometimes it seemed as though the thousand worst scumbag fans from every single league club were gathered at Wembley so that they could make monkey noises and sing anti-IRA songs. It was these people who helped create the commonplace fear and loathing of our two national flags. If you saw someone coming toward you in a T-shirt sporting either the Cross of St. George or the Union Jack, you'd have been best advised to cross the street. The T-shirt was a graphic alternative to a slogan which might say something like, "I'm a racist but I hate you no matter what color you are"—or, as a piece of graffiti captured by the Philadelphia photographer Zoe Strauss read, FUCK YOU IF YOU READING THIS. And if he didn't get you, his pit bull terrier would.

And so, perhaps understandably, some football fans started to feel a little conflicted about the national team. In 1990, when England played Cameroon in the quarterfinals of the World Cup, it wasn't hard to find people in England—middle-class, liberal people, admittedly, but people nonetheless—who wanted Cameroon to win. I watched that game with some of them, and when England went 2–1 down (they eventually won 3–2 in extra time), these people cheered. I understood why, but I couldn't cheer with them, much to my surprise. Those drunk, racist thugs draped in the national colors. . . . they were, it turned out, my people, not (as I'd previously thought), the nice liberal friends I was watching the game with, and England was my national football team. I mean, you can't choose stuff like that, right? The 1990 World Cup turned out to be something of a turning point. The team wasn't embarrassing—not after the opening games, anyway. The fans weren't embarrassing either, apart from the odd skirmish. And in the end England lost, narrowly and bravely, to Germany, on penalties, in the semifinal. (England, incidentally, has been sent home in four of the last six World Cups by either Germany or Argentina, two countries we have had Issues with in the past. Those familiar with the bellicose nature of English tabloid newspapers can imagine that these misfortunes have done little for the cause of world peace.) After a horrendous couple of decades, the national team, and the national game, were once again basking in the warmth of the nation's affections.

The rebirth lasted about five minutes. There was a disastrous managerial appointment, which resulted in yet another failure to qualify. And by 1998, football was a different game. France won the 1998 World Cup, but only a couple of their team played their football in France. Their key men, Zidane and Desailly and Deschamps, played in Italy; the rest played in Spain or England or Germany. Meanwhile, the big stars in English football were Zola of Italy, Bergkamp of Holland, Schmeichel of Denmark. Manchester United, the biggest club in England, had retained a core of young English players, including David Beckham; but Arsenal, my team, had comfortably won the championship with a mixture of English grit and Franco-Dutch flair. Foreign players were, for the most part, better, fitter and cheaper, and they didn't drink much, either. (People like Bergkamp and the brilliant French striker Thierry Henry clearly regard abstinence as the price you have to pay for a career as an athlete, but this attitude was viewed as something akin to cheating by a lot of English footballers.) Before long, the majority of the players in our top division came from outside the British Isles.

The globalization of the transfer market was beginning to rob international football of much of its point. In the old days, you used to look at the best players playing in the club teams and think, What would they be like if they played together? And the answer was that they looked like the national team—that was the idea, anyway, even if in reality the national team, especially the English national team, was often an undercoached and ill-fitting mess. Now, Chelsea, Manchester United, Real Madrid, Juventus, the Milans and Barcelona have replaced the national sides as fantasy football teams. If your national team doesn't contain players from those clubs, it's because those clubs don't want them, which means your national team is no good. Over the last few years, England have even been reduced on occasions to choosing players who are not automatic starting choices for their club sides, an indication of how it's all changed. In the old days, an international-class footballer would have been first on any club's team-sheet. Now, it depends—on the quality of the club, and the quality of the country.

There's no doubt, however, that the foreign imports have dragged the cream of the English players, sometimes reluctantly, toward something approaching competence. We used to be very game, and very limited (and by "we," I may be referring to every single inhabitant of the country); we didn't have to worry about other countries much, because we only played them every couple of years anyway. Now the English players play with or against the best in the world every single week, and they've had to learn very quickly just to stay in the game, and in the profession. Even sane people are beginning to argue that the England team contains some of the best players in the world. Wayne Rooney was a teenager during the 2004 European Championships, but when he limped off injured in the game against Portugal, the team fell apart. He's very strong, incredibly skillful, and as likely to get a red card, possibly for swearing, as he is to score one of the best goals you've ever seen. (In a game against Arsenal last season, Rooney was estimated to have told the referee to fuck off more than twenty times in sixty seconds. As "foul and abusive language" is supposed to be a yellow-card offense, one can only presume that there are some really *really* bad words, words worse than the f-word and the c-word, that footballers know and we don't.) Frank Lampard and John Terry are Chelsea's most important players, which in the current economic climate means that they are two of Europe's most important players; if they weren't, they would have been sent to the salt mines by now. Ashley Cole is perhaps the world's best left-back, which means that he won't be playing for my team, Arsenal, for much longer. At least half of this England team is seriously good, so when they are beaten in the quarterfinals, as is their custom, there will be pointless anger rather than weary resignation.

Toward the end of their uninspiring 2006 World Cup qualifying campaign, England contrived to lose 1–0 to Northern Ireland, most of whose players come from Britain's tinier club teams; during the game, you could almost see the England stars thinking, What the fuck am I doing here, in this dump, playing against these losers? (The fact that the losers were winning seemed of only marginal interest to them.) It was hard to see the ideal of international football lasting the whole ninety minutes, let alone until the World Cup finals and beyond. And then, a few short weeks later, after a meaningless but enthralling last-minute win over Argentina, we all decided that England was going to win the World Cup. This represents progress of sorts: usually, national self-confidence would have been boosted by a narrow win over the hapless Irish, and demolished by a proper team. Now we have a group of cosmopolitan sophisticates (or blinged-up prima donnas, depending on your worldview, age and newspaper of choice) who can't be bothered, unless the occasion warrants it.

Sixteen years ago, England played out a goalless draw against Sweden, a result that helped ensure qualification for the World Cup in 1990. The enduring image of that game is of the England captain, Terry Butcher, swathed in bandages, his white England shirt and shorts covered in blood that had pumped steadily out of a head wound throughout the duration of the game. "Off the pitch I was always an ordinary, mild-mannered bloke," said Butcher in an interview years later. "But put me in a football shirt and it was tin hats and fixed bayonets. Death or glory." That was the old England: the war imagery, the crucial nil-nil draw against modest opposition, the unavoidable replacement of style and talent with blood and graft. Those who loathe David Beckham, the current England captain, and everything he stands for would claim that he will wear a tin hat and bandages only when tin hats and bandages become de rigueur in some ludicrously fashionable European nightclub. That's not fair, because despite his looks and his cash, he too has worked surprisingly hard to compensate for the things that he lacks as a player, notably pace. But there's no doubt that he is brilliantly illustrative of a new kind of English sportsman: professional, media-aware, occasionally petulant and very, very rich. The England fans who went to the friendly match against Argentina (played, as is the way of these things now, in Geneva, for reasons that remain obscure) were still singing their "No Surrender to the IRA" song, and there's more than a suspicion that they'd rather watch Terry Butcher and his fixed bayonets than

David Beckham, a man who, after all, has been photographed wearing a sarong. But then, that's England all over at the moment. We'd still prefer to be bombing the Germans; but after sixty years, there's a slowly dawning suspicion that those days aren't coming back any time soon, and in the meantime, we must rely on sarong-wearing, multimillionaire pretty boys to kick the Argies for us. We're not happy about it, but what can we do?

My most thrilling moment of the 1998 World Cup came when Vieira of Arsenal slid the ball through to Petit of Arsenal for France's third goal in their 3–0 win over Brazil in the final: I was on my feet. (The following morning, the *Daily Mirror,* then edited by an Arsenal season ticket holder, had a front-page headline that said ARSENAL WIN THE WORLD CUP. I had the cover framed.) These were definitely my people: I spend much of the year hating most of the England players anyway, and if any of those Manchester United or Chelsea bastards are in direct competition with any of my beautiful, talented French boys, then there's no agonizing to be done. It turns out that you can choose these things after all. *Allez, Les Bleus.*

World Cup Record

FIFA Ranking: 9
World Cup Appearances: 11
World Cup Champions: 1
Federation Name: The Football Association
Confederation: UEFA
Founded: 1863
FIFA Affiliation: 1905
Nickname: The Three Lions
Manager: Sven-Goran Eriksson
Website: www.the-fa.org
Stadium: Wembley
Home Uniform: white/navy blue/white
Away Uniform: red/white/red
Provider: Umbro

1930:	Did not enter
1934:	Did not enter
1938:	Did not enter
1950:	First round exit
1954:	Quarterfinal exit
1958:	First round exit
1962:	Quarterfinal exit
1966:	CHAMPIONS
1970:	Quarterfinal exit
1974:	Did not qualify
1978:	Did not qualify
1982:	Second round exit
1986:	Quarterfinal exit
1990:	4th place
1994:	Did not qualify
1998:	Second round exit
2002:	Quarterfinal exit

Matches	Wins	Draws	Losses	GF	GA	GD	Points
50	22	15	13	68	45	+23	81

England is 5th on the all-time World Cup table

Path to Qualification for World Cup 2006

4-Sep-04	Austria	2	England	2	**D**
8-Sep-04	Poland	1	England	2	**W**
9-Oct-04	England	2	Wales	0	**W**
13-Oct-04	Azerbaijan	0	England	1	**W**
26-Mar-05	England	4	Northern Ireland	0	**W**
30-Mar-05	England	2	Azerbaijan	0	**W**
3-Sep-05	Wales	0	England	1	**W**
7-Sep-05	Northern Ireland	1	England	0	**L**
8-Oct-05	England	1	Austria	0	**W**
12-Oct-05	England	2	Poland	1	**W**

England qualified by finishing first in Group 6 of the European Zone

France

Capital: Paris
Independence: 486 (unified by Clovis)
Area: 547,030 sq km
Population: 60,656,178
Median Age: 38.9 years
Life Expectancy at Birth: 79.6 years
Ethnic Groups: Celtic and Latin with Teutonic,
    Slavic, North African, Indochinese, Basque
    minorities
Religions: Roman Catholic 83–88%, Protestant 2%,
    Jewish 1%, Muslim 5–10%, unaffiliated 4%
Languages: French 100%, rapidly declining
    regional dialects and languages
    (Provencal, Breton, Alsatian, Corsican,
    Catalan, Basque, Flemish)
Suffrage: 18 years of age; universal
Military Obligation: 17 years of age with consent
    for voluntary military service
GDP Per Capita: $28,700
Budget: $1.08 trillion
Military Expenditures: $45 billion (2.6% of GDP)
Agriculture: wheat, cereals, sugar
    beets, potatoes, wine grapes; beef, dairy
    products; fish
Industries: machinery, chemicals, automobiles,
    metallurgy, aircraft, electronics; textiles, food
    processing; tourism
Currency: euro

Source: *CIA World Factbook*

France

Aleksandar Hemon

Throughout the 1982 World Cup I was in love, which is to say that I suffered through a painful conflict of interests. I was a high school senior and an unwilling virgin. My girlfriend—let her be known as Renata—had just graduated and was studying for a medical school entrance exam. Under the pretense of helping her prepare for it, I spent a lot of time at her home, which she shared with her father and schizophrenic brother. In her room I recited mock test questions, mainly biology related, until, slowly, hotly, we moved from theory to the practical questions of adolescent biology: Where does the heat in our heads come from? What should we do with these hormone-driven, tinderbox bodies? The biology textbook tossed away, we practically dared her father or brother to barge in and catch us locked in a feral clinch, engaged in biological research by way of petting each other very, very heavily. Sometimes the room was so infested with arousal that we had to open the windows to share some with the birds and bees of Sarajevo.

Sex and soccer do not mix well. In the evenings, when Renata's father and brother would go for a long walk, we would be left alone—which allowed for all kinds of fantastic possibilities—but I had to balance my soccer obsession and our biology. I regret to say that I missed a few games. Some I perceived with just half of my brain, the other half given over to biological research. Only for the semi-finals did I find enough gumption and hormone control to forgo the heavy petting and risk indefinite deflowerment deferral: I demanded to watch in peace—no biological experiments, please. Renata put away her books and pencils and we lay on the living room sofa facing the TV. Her father and brother were away, France–West Germany was on, and I knew it wasn't going to be easy.

I was rooting for France. Although the French were laughably unimpressive in Argentina in 1978, I liked the 1982 team: after a slow start in Round 1 (losing to England, a draw with Czechoslovakia, finally beating Kuwait) *Les Bleus* picked it up in the round two group stage. They beat Austria with Bernard Genghini's superb free kick, while Northern Ireland was dispatched mercilessly: Michel Platini danced past their entire defense before passing the ball to puny Alain Giresse, who scored the first goal; Domenique Rocheteau ran with the ball all the way from the half line to beat Pat Jenkins at the near post; Giresse and Rocheteau scored another goal each. It was an impressive performance, but they did it all with a certain charming ease, which somehow recalled for me the relaxed atmosphere of Parisian cafés. When I remember Platini from 1982, I see a full head of uncombed Rimbaudian hair, indecently short shorts and a big smile—a *copain* having loads of fun.

You could imagine Platini or Jean Tigana coming up, kicking a deflated ball on the street with other boys, rehearsing the magic with which they would dazzle the world. The ease and flair they played with was different only in degree but not in kind from the soccer I played with my mates—in the French game, much as in the Brazilian one, there is a joy of playing rooted in the purity of the street game. In contrast, no one could ever accuse Germans of enjoying themselves, and no one could ever imagine them playing on the street—those men were always at work, and enjoying it would've run counter to their work ethic. On the parking lots where I played soccer, a German was the boy who brought you down on the concrete, someone who would run a lot because he couldn't do shit with the ball. Victory in soccer, I believed, should never be a consequence of hard work—rather, it should be a kind of epiphany, an act of supreme magic, unlearnable and inexplicable. That is why I had always hated German soccer: the mechanical discipline and the maddening, unmagical ability never to give up made the classic German soccer philosophy my main ideological enemy. Thus the 1982 semifinal was a great battle in the philosophical war between work and magic, between the (stereotypical) Teutonic rationality and (equally stereotypical) Gallic passion. So it was set up to be a great game.

And a great game it was. Though I had trouble seeing it, for Renata, liberated from the shackles of biological theory, was all over me—despite her promise to let me watch—and I was, I confess, helplessly responsive. I struggled to peek over her shoulder as she was working on a collection of flaming hickeys; I listened closely to the exhilarated game commentators, as she alternately whispered into and licked my ear; I leapt out of concupiscent clinches to see the goals (Pierre Littbarski for Germany, Platini, from a penalty, for France) repeatedly replayed; I sped to take us to consummation at half time, but didn't quite make it. Then, in the 60th minute, my erection was deflated by the brutal goalkeeper with the Teutonic name—Harald Schumacher—mauling the gentle Patrick Battiston, sending him to the hospital without so much as a foul or a yellow card given. It seemed that Schumacher's hard work was being rewarded by the Dutch referee, and the familiar sense of philosophical injustice overwhelmed me. When the regulation time ended in a 1–1 draw and the game went into overtime, I accepted the possibility of a break-up and turned exclusively to the French–German battle.

At this point, Renata vanishes in my memory. I suppose she worked too hard, and could not match the excitement and magic Platini and his *copains* provided. I am fully aware this is an awful thing to say and hereby admit that any man who spurns a woman's love for a soccer game is an idiot and nothing but an idiot.

But what a game it was. In overtime, the French played beautifully, scoring two quick goals: a gorgeous volley by Tresor; Giresse's precise shot from the edge of the box, and looked set for the finals. But when Karl-Heinz Rummenigge, previously injured, came in as a sub and scored a goal with his first shot, I knew, once again, that hard work would pay off and the Germans would come back from behind. Rationality and discipline would overcome magic and passion. And so it was: Klaus Fischer tied the game with an overhead kick to Horst Hrubesch's header; it went to penalties; Diego Bosis missed his shot in sudden death and the French buckled; Renata was pissed. I was philosophically fucked and biologically unfucked. I would not lose my virginity for another few months.

Those long months included a few weeks in Africa. My father worked in Kinshasa, Zaire, where we (my mother, sister, myself) went to visit him. My remorse at sacrificing, for soccer, those beautiful summer evenings in Renata's arms, was alleviated by daily trips to the

French Cultural Center, which I stumbled upon while roaming the streets of Kinshasa. In a dark, air-conditioned room, the French World Cup games were replayed, most often the one against West Germany, and I relived the great match; I cried foul; I bemoaned all the wasted chances; I thought of Renata; I became part-time French. Nothing feeds patriotism like the sense of victimhood, so I rose to my feet with my fellow Frenchmen to shout abuse at the Germans; with them I recalled 1940 and any number of unintelligible injustices. I did not speak French, but in the smoky room there was a mass of Frenchness, and I merged right in. I don't remember any individual faces, but somehow, strangely, I imagine Giresse being there with us, hollering at the screen. It was from him (or whoever it really was) that I learned my first—and last—words of French: *"Merde! Putain!"*

So it was hardly surprising that I rooted for France in the 1986 World Cup in Mexico. They certainly were among the favorites: the team that had beautifully congealed around the genius of Platini had become European Champions. Platini was at the top of his game: the European Player of the Year for three years running, and the World Player of the Year in '84 and '85. So the French sailed through the group stage; they beat the World Champions, Italy, handily, and reached the quarterfinals to play Brazil, another favorite, who had not conceded a goal in the previous four games. For this game there were, (un)fortunately, no girlfriends to distract me.

Pelé famously said that the 1986 World Cup quarterfinal in Guadalajara, between Brazil and France, was the greatest game he had ever seen. It is certainly one of the greatest games I have ever seen. Socrates, the lanky, chain-smoking genius, had one of the best matches of his career, superbly orchestrating the Brazilian midfield, visibly enjoying the whole thing. Giresse and Platini, my old *copains,* ruled the French game. Passes flowed, the ball moved swiftly from box to box, shots bounced off posts, at any given moment a goal was in the air. Only two were scored, however, even after overtime: the scoreline was 1–1. France went to the penalties again and the shadow of the disaster with West Germany loomed darkly over *Les*

Bleus—and it got darker when Platini smacked the ball over the bar. But all the other Frenchmen scored, while the Brazilians missed twice (Socrates, Julio Cesar). The French were in the semifinals, where they were to meet West Germany again.

For the second successive World Cup it was 1940 *and* 1982 all over again—and my part-time French patriotism was rekindled. Alas, in a typically clinical manner, the West Germans disposed of my team: the French goalkeeper, Bats, fumbled Brehme's shot early on, and the Germans defended with infuriating discipline, then scored another goal in injury time. The French had their chances but missed them all: Bosis (who had blown his penalty in Spain) failed to score—*twice*—facing an open goal. It was the last World Cup game of a great generation of French players, Platini the greatest of them all. One shudders with unattained pleasure at the thought of a final in which Argentina's Maradona—who, in Mexico, had been playing like nobody else before or after him—faced the magic of Platini, instead of a hardworking German called Wolfgang Rolff.

The French missed the next two World Cups, both times losing their crucial qualifying games: in 1990 they failed to beat lowly Cyprus, and lost to Yugoslavia and Scotland as well; they did not reach the United States in 1994, because they lost at home to Israel and Bulgaria. But they came back in 1998. A whole new generation, much different from Platini's, had come of age. Unlike the home-based players in the '82 and '86 teams, the French of 1998 consisted of international stars (Zidane, Henry, Deschamps) who played in prime European clubs. After going through the group stage half-asleep, they beat sturdy Paraguay with a golden goal, withstood the challenge of Italy to beat them on penalties, brushed aside feisty Croatia, and crushed Brazil in the final, thereby becoming only the seventh nation to win the World Cup.

A great deal was made of the diversity of the team. It reflected a France that gave nightmares to the right-wing, racist patriots—French-born players united with those born in former colonies; white and black Frenchmen playing as one. They never faltered under pressure, doubtless spurred on by the support of the entire soccer-mad country, which recognized an exciting future for the Republic, and the national soccer team that stood for it.

They did become European Champions in 2000, in an amazing final against Italy. But in the 2002 World Cup, they lost the opening game to Senegal—all of whose starters played in the French league—and never got out of the group stage, failing even to score a single goal. This was largely the same team that had impressed in 1998 and Euro 2000—so the downfall was most ignominious, inexplicable and undeserving of the great tradition. I was married then, on my way to divorce, so I watched every lousy game alone.

It is hard to predict what France can do in Germany in 2006. They qualified with no problems and there is no shortage of good, experienced players: Henry, Viera, Trezeguet, Makelele. But all of them will have had a long, competitive season behind them, by virtue of playing for the best European clubs. The good news is that they cannot meet Germany before the semifinal. If they do, the 2006 World Cup will be an occasion for remembering all the chances we—France and I—have missed together.

World Cup Record

FIFA Ranking: 5
World Cup Appearances: 11
World Cup Champions: 1
Federation Name: Fédération Française de
  Football
Confederation: UEFA
Founded: 1919
FIFA Affiliation: 1904
Nickname: Les Bleus (Blues)
Manager: Raymond Domenech
Website: www.fff.fr
Stadium: Stade de France, Paris
Home Uniform: blue/white/red
Away Uniform: white/blue/white
Provider: Adidas

1930: First round exit
1934: First round exit
1938: Second round exit
1950: Did not qualify
1954: First round exit
1958: 3rd place
1962: Did not qualify
1966: First round exit
1970: Did not qualify
1974: Did not qualify
1978: First round exit
1982: 4th place
1986: 3rd place
1990: Did not qualify
1994: Did not qualify
1998: CHAMPIONS
2002: First round exit

Matches	Wins	Draws	Losses	GF	GA	GD	Points
44	21	7	16	86	61	+25	70

France is 6th on the all-time World Cup table

Path to Qualification for World Cup 2006

4-Sep-04	France	0	Israel	0	D
8-Sep-04	Faroe Islands	0	France	2	W
9-Oct-04	France	0	Ireland	0	D
13-Oct-04	Cyprus	0	France	2	W
26-Mar-05	France	0	Switzerland	0	D
30-Mar-05	Israel	1	France	1	D
3-Sep-05	France	3	Faroe Islands	0	W
7-Sep-05	Ireland	0	France	1	W
8-Oct-05	Switzerland	1	France	1	D
12-Oct-05	France	4	Cyprus	0	W

France qualified by finishing first in Group 4 of the European Zone

Germany

Capital: Berlin
Independence: January 18, 1871 (German Empire unification); October 3, 1990 (unification of West Germany and East Germany)
Area: 357,021 sq km
Population: 82,431,390
Median Age: 42.2 years
Life Expectancy at Birth: 78.7 years
Ethnic Groups: German 91.5%, Turkish 2.4%, other 6.1% (made up largely of Greek, Italian, Polish, Russian, Serbo-Croatian, Spanish)
Religions: Protestant 34%, Roman Catholic 34%, Muslim 3.7%, unaffiliated or other 28.3%
Languages: German
Suffrage: 18 years of age; universal
Military Obligation: 18 years of age (conscripts serve a 9-month tour of compulsory military service)
GDP Per Capita: $28,700
Budget: $1.3 trillion
Military Expenditures: $35.063 billion (1.5% of GDP)
Agriculture: potatoes, wheat, barley, sugar beets, fruit, cabbages; cattle, pigs, poultry
Industries: among the world's largest and most technologically advanced producers of iron, steel, coal, cement, chemicals, machinery, vehicles, machine tools, electronics, food and beverages; shipbuilding; textiles
Currency: euro

Source: *CIA World Factbook*

Germany

Alexander Osang

Shortly before Germany played in the quarterfinals of the 2002 World Cup, Fritz Walter, former captain of the national team, died at home in Rheinland-Phalz. I got the news in the Korean Baseball Hall of Fame, on the island of Cheju, where the German team, having just defeated Paraguay 1–0, was holding its daily World Cup press conference. The speaker of the football federation took the stage and said: "Germany's *Ehrenspielführer* Fritz Walter is dead." It sounded as if we had just then definitively lost the war. He asked us to stand for a minute of silence. I was one of approximately fifty journalists in the German press center. Many of us wore shorts and flip-flops, as it was humid in South Korea, and, obviously, no one had expected to be taking part in a moment of silence. We stood up like spa guests going to pool aerobics. Through the open door I saw an orderly carefully stocking a glass refrigerator with bottles of Bitburger beer, the German World Cup sponsor.

Distinguished Sports Champion—*Ehrenspielführer*—echoed in my head.

In 1954 Fritz Walter, leader of the team that invented the German soccer virtues, took the national side to its first World Cup, in Switzerland. In the final Walter beat the magical Hungarians, the best team in the world, 3–2, despite the fact that the Germans had already lost to Hungary in the preliminary round, 8–3, and had to come back from 2–0 down. It was raining, the ground was sodden, but they never gave up. Walter's West Germany overpowered the Hungarians just as they would go on to beat all the other teams who played beautiful soccer: Hungary in '54, England in '70, Holland in '74, France in '82—the German national team always rose again. Walter was responsible for Germany's reputation as a tournament team, a team that was never beautiful, but always the best, and the most determined when the game depended on it. Walter gave a little self-confidence back to Germany for the first time after the war. A famous photo shows him on the shoulders of his teammates, dark, wet hair falling in his face, exhausted but redeemed. Germany could win after all.

In *The Miracle of Bern,* a hit movie in Germany a few years ago, Walter and his team, playing in the '54 final, look into the Swiss sky and hope that the clouds will darken. We're only happy when it rains.

German chancellor Gerhard Schröder was supposed to have cried when he saw the film.

I did not cry.

Fritz Walter wasn't my *Ehrenspielführer.* I stood in the pavilion of the South Korean baseball federation and hoped that my cell phone wouldn't start to ring. It was a long, torturous minute of silence. I felt like an East German soccer player who had lined up for the West German national anthem. I was at the wrong funeral.

For me the most important World Cup wasn't in 1954, but 1974. It was the first to be held on German soil, but this meant nothing to me. I was twelve years old and lived in East Germany—Hamburg, Frankfurt and Munich lay on the other side of the wall, as inaccessible to me as Rio de Janeiro. But my country, the smaller Germany, the German Democratic Republic, for the first and only time, had qualified. *This* was my German team. We played against Chile, Australia, and then, in Hamburg, the Federal Republic of Germany, the big Germany. It was the key game of my life.

The GDR won 1–0 with a goal in the 78th minute by the Magdeburger forward Jürgen Sparwasser. I jumped around on the dark brown linoleum of my newly built East German flat and screamed as I've never screamed again. I can still see the smoky living room curtains, the black and white television on top of a thin steel stand in the corner, outside the still, East German world, my father away somewhere in it, and I see myself in a victory leap. It is a moment that captures my childhood.

I was born in East Berlin, in 1962, a year after the wall was built. When it fell, in 1989, I was twenty-seven. I became an adult in that small, narrow country, a man who always felt like he was wearing the wrong shoes, an insecure man; in short, a very German man. In the middle of this twenty-seven-year span, at its high point, came the East German goal. Of course our swimmers, oarswomen and bobsled drivers won all the gold medals in the world, but no Berliner youth wants to become a bobsledder. I wanted to be a soccer player, and the most famous German soccer players lived on the other side of the wall.

At ten I wrote postcards to two of them, Franz Beckenbauer and Gerd Müller, whose fan addresses I found in a friend's well-thumbed West German magazine. Beckenbauer was the sweeper of the West German team, Müller its center-forward. They played for FC Bavaria Munich. I explained my situation behind the Iron Curtain, and asked for an autographed picture. Then, while I waited, I imagined how their reply would change my life. I owned a trading sticker of Müller in flight, legs scissoring the air, scoring against England in the 1970 quarterfinal. I had a picture of Uwe Seeler trading his jersey with Gianni Rivera. And I had a photograph of the rock band Uriah Heep. With an autographed photo of Müller and Beckenbauer, I would have been a new man in East Germany. They never wrote back.

So begin lifelong enmities.

After that I found it hard not to notice certain things: When FC Bavaria Munich came to Dresden or Magdeburg for a European Cup game, they brought their own cook, because they didn't trust our cooks. They laughed at us. They had the bigger country, the better cars, the better chocolate, the better chewing gum, the better sneakers, and, of course, better national team jerseys. (The numbers on ours always looked as if they had been sewn on by hand.) But on that summer evening in 1974, in Hamburg, we beat them.

I beat them.

It was a victory from which I have not recovered. Neither did the GDR soccer team. It dropped out in the intermediate round and never qualified for an international tournament again. Later even the goalscorer, Jürgen Sparwasser, fled to the West. The big Germany went on to become world champions for the second time that year, beating Holland 2–1 in the final. The Dutch and the English— both regularly defeated by Germany—represented my interests in the tournaments of the eighties and nineties. Holland was a small country and England was an island. My world was small and island-like, too.

With reunification there was an opportunity for change—no more GDR and no more GDR national team—but I couldn't let go of the past.

I watched the 1990 World Cup semifinal, between Germany and England, on a big screen in the Berlin Lustgarten, with thousands of people. England's Paul Gascoigne cried, and I cried too when Germany won. I stood among rejoicing German fans, very alone. I couldn't watch the final against Argentina. I simply couldn't bear it. I drove my seventeen-year-old Polski Fiat, a gift from my brother-in-law before he fled to the West, to a residential area in Berlin and parked there for ninety minutes. I sat in the stillness of the city and waited. When I heard the screams and the fireworks, I knew that it was over. Germany had won and I had lost again. Later I learned that the game had been decided by a penalty kick, taken by Andreas Brehme, a blond defender; a typical German goal. After winning the championship, Franz Beckenbauer, who'd coached the team, predicted that a reunified soccer-Germany would be undefeated for years.

In 1999 I moved to New York to leave it all behind. I didn't have a soccer team anymore—why not live in a country that didn't care about soccer? Things went well. I only encountered the game in the tiny tables at the back of the *New York Times* sports section. Or sometimes, watching my son play in Prospect Park, when another father made a friendly reference to the great German soccer tradition, and I'd nod, smiling. Some things you can't explain.

In the summer of 2002, *Der Spiegel* sent me to Japan and Korea to cover the World Cup, and everything rose up in me again. It would be the second most important World Cup of my life.

Fritz Walter's German virtues carried the national team through the easy preliminary round. They advanced into the last eight with the 1–0 win over Paraguay; and in the quarterfinal the players wore black armbands and defeated the U. S. In the second half, there was a seemingly clear hand-ball by midfielder Torsten Frings, but the referee didn't call it. The Americans were the better team, but the Germans won 1–0. Everything happened like it always did. The teams who played beautiful soccer were tired or haughty: Holland hadn't even managed to qualify for the tournament; Portugal, Italy and Spain lost to the pumped-up South Koreans; France to Senegal; Argentina to England; England to Brazil. But Germany was happy and effective throughout: the perfect tournament team.

After the quarterfinal I met Franz Beckenbauer, the man who started my German soccer crisis. Though he had not responded to my autograph request thirty years before, Beckenbauer was personable, not at all the arrogant figure I'd come to expect. For three days we traveled together through Japan, a country as foreign to him as it was to me; but I found that he was at home everywhere, boarding the Japanese Shinkansen-Express as if it were a German InterCity train. Though he'd lived in New York, he could still barely order a dish off an English menu, but he experienced and grasped things intuitively. It was this quality that had helped him secure the 2006 World Cup for Germany. As a soccer goodwill ambassador, he traveled around the globe for two years, stood in the dusk on hotel terraces in African cities, cities whose names he could no longer remember, drinking red wine, smoking cigars and feeling perfectly at home.

As both a soccer player and a coach, Beckenbauer was a World Cup champion; now, as an organizer and diplomat, he has brought home the entire tournament. He triumphs and triumphs, but he is not a man who loves the sodden field and the rain. A sweeper, he has a light touch in sport and in life. One evening we stood together in a bar in Tokyo, drank beer and watched England play Nigeria. His comments were sporadic—"Sheringham is a blind man"—and I wrote them down. We were a strange pair. Because "Osang" sounded somehow Asian to him, he called me the "half-Chinese from the *Spiegel*," and I was flattered.

I never told him about the postcard. But I began to suspect that he'd never received it. Perhaps everything was a misunderstanding.

Great enmities often begin with misunderstandings. (A year later, in Munich, I met Beckenbauer's teammate, Gerd Müller, the man with the record for most German World Cup goals, and the other recipient of a postcard from East Germany. A friend introduced us during the halftime break of a league game. Müller was a small man in sweats and oversized glasses. He looked like a janitor. The friend who introduced us took a picture in which I look like the champion.)

In the 2002 semifinal Germany met South Korea in Seoul. The Koreans had exceeded all expectations, playing six unbelievably fast, dogged, inexhaustible matches, and transporting the entire country into a state of theretofore unknown euphoria. Before the semifinal, the government had given an entire island in the Yellow Sea to their Dutch coach, Guus Hiddink, as a thank you gift. They were content just to be semifinalists. But Germany wasn't. Germany wouldn't give up until everything was over. And in the 75th minute they scored, South Korea failed to equalize, and the game ended 1–0, of course.

I stood in the stadium, filled with seventy thousand South Korean fans in identical crimson T-shirts, emblazoned with the word "Reds," feeling like I was caught in a cultural revolution. Fortunately, they were in good spirits, despite their loss. Strangely enough, I wasn't in bad spirits either. Like the Koreans in the stadium, I had also conceded to German superiority. I'd been in Japan and Korea for three weeks, running to distant stadiums that emerged out of the haze of tea plantations, and sleeping on a round bed covered with oilcloth in a hotel room usually rented by the hour. I was homesick. And the men down there on the turf in Seoul were the closest thing to my native country. My father in Berlin was a fan of the German team and so was my son in New York. On that humid summer night in Seoul I made my peace with the national team.

I looked at the turf, at the exhausted men with their angular German faces. My defense fell apart. I didn't rejoice—I relaxed. I took the road home.

The German team met its first real opposition in the final, and they lost. Oliver Kahn, the German captain and goalie, the most perfect, grimmest player on the team, made the game-deciding error. It was a fitting end to a bizarre World Cup. I sat in the huge concrete bowl of Yokohama Stadium and groaned as Ronaldo approached with fast, strong steps and poked Kahn's fumble into the German goal. Brazil was the world champion, and the German players celebrated second place in a windowless Yokohama banquet hall, along with the chancellor, who had rushed over for the occasion.

Outside the rainy season began.

It reminded me of the minute of silence for the *Ehrenspielführer*. I felt that something was coming to an end. Germany's two most important politicians, Gerhard Schröder and Edmund Stoiber, were photographed with the German players in their warm-up suits. There was a cold buffet, a roast, potatoes and Bitburger beer. Oliver Kahn had a thick bandage on the hand that hadn't been able to hold onto the ball. The bandage signified that he had given everything. A German pop band named PUR stood on a stage and sang the national soccer song: "There's only one Rudi Völler."

Coach Völler smiled bravely. As a player he had been a world champion, and now, as a coach, he was runner up to the world champions. But he didn't look like a winner, he looked like a man of days past.

I left the party early and took a taxi back to Tokyo in the black, ceaseless rain. Fritz Walter was dead. The German virtues weren't enough anymore. I didn't know that Gerhard Schröder and Rudi Völler would step down, but I sensed it. Things wouldn't continue the way they had in the past.

Before leaving I bought a silver-gray German jersey in a Tokyo sports shop, and brought it back to New York for my son. I bought the Italian jersey for myself. It just looked better.

Four years later, in Frankfurt, the new German national team jerseys were presented. They are red. They remind me of the jerseys England wore in 1966, when they became the world champions. And jerseys aren't the only thing to have changed in my country.

We now have a new coach and a new chancellor. The coach is Jürgen Klinsmann, the son of a baker from Swabia who broke out into the big wide world. The chancellor is Angela Merkel, the daughter of a pastor from Uckermarck who broke out into the big wide world. Both have picked their fights with the old West German system and won. In Michael Ballack, Klinsmann has made an East German player into team captain. Angela Merkel has defeated Helmut Kohl and Gerhard Schröder, the biggest big men of West German politics. Klinsmann has played in Italy, England and Monaco, and now lives in California, where he sometimes plays under a false name for a semi-pro team in Orange County. Angela Merkel is a physicist, a cool Protestant in the excitable man's world of career politicians. She speaks Russian. Both have broken the German defense.

Red jerseys, not bad.

Klinsmann lives in America like me. Angela Merkel comes from East Germay like me. Maybe, in the end, I really will win.

Translated from the German by Annie Falk

World Cup Record

FIFA Ranking: 17
World Cup Appearances: 15
World Cup Champions: 3
Federation Name: Deutscher Fussball-Bund
Confederation: UEFA
Founded: 1900
FIFA Affiliation: 1904
Nickname: die Mannschaft (The Team)
Manager: Jürgen Klinsmann
Website: www.dfb.de
Stadium: Olympia-stadion
Home Uniform: white/black/white
Away Uniform: black and red/white/red
Provider: Adidas

1930: Did not enter
1934: 3rd place
1938: First round exit
1950: Did not enter
1954: CHAMPIONS
1958: 4th place
1962: Quarterfinal exit
1966: 2nd place
1970: 3rd place
1974: CHAMPIONS
1978: Second phase exit
1982: 2nd place
1986: 2nd place
1990: CHAMPIONS
1994: Quarterfinal exit
1998: Quarterfinal exit
2002: 2nd place

Matches	Wins	Draws	Losses	GF	GA	GD	Points
85	50	18	17	176	106	+70	168

Germany is 2nd on the all-time World Cup table
Note: As West Germany from 1950 to 1994

Path to Qualification for World Cup 2006

Germany qualified as the host nation

Ghana

Capital: Accra
Independence: March 6, 1957
(from the UK)
Area: 239,460 sq km
Population: 21,029,853
Median Age: 20.5 years
Life Expectancy at Birth: 58.5 years
Ethnic Groups: black African 98.5%
(major tribes: Akan 44%,
Moshi-Dagomba 16%, Ewe 13%,
Ga 8%, Gurma 3%, Yoruba 1%),
European and other 1.5%
Religions: Christian 63%, Muslim 16%,
indigenous beliefs 21%
Languages: English (official), African
languages (including Akan,
Moshi-Dagomba, Ewe and Ga)
Suffrage: 18 years of age; universal
Military Obligation: 18 years of age for
compulsory and volunteer military
service
GDP Per Capita: $2,300
Budget: $3.5 billion
Military Expenditures: $49.2 million
(0.6% of GDP)
Agriculture: cocoa, rice, coffee, cassava (tapioca),
peanuts, corn, shea nuts, bananas; timber
Industries: mining, lumbering, light
manufacturing, aluminum smelting, food
processing, cement, small commercial ship
building
Currency: cedi

Source: *CIA World Factbook*

Ghana

Caryl Phillips

In August 2005 I sat on a crowded British Airways jet that was flying from London to Accra. Seated all around me were the players and coaches of the Black Stars—the Ghanaian national football team— who, the previous evening, had drawn 1–1 in a friendly match with Senegal that had been played in London at the ground of Brentford Football Club. The players were polite, relatively quiet, and displayed good manners and behavior of a type that one would never expect from an equivalent group of English players. An hour into the flight one player tapped me on the shoulder and politely asked if he might "borrow" my iPod, while another player eyed my newspaper until I folded it in half and offered it to him. It appeared that these young men did not have much in the way of material possessions; in fact, I had seen better kitted-out high school teams, and the mind boggled when one realized that by contrast with their own seemingly modest lifestyles, one of their teammates, Michael Essien, had just been transferred from Lyon to Chelsea for $40 million and was earning more than $75,000 per week. In fact, he probably earned enough in one half-hour stretching session in the gym to equip all of his teammates with iPods. Of course, Michael Essien was not on the flight. He had remained behind in London, but as I somewhat self-consciously listened to my music I wondered just what kind of a cohesive team spirit could possibly be engendered in a squad of players where First and Third World values clashed so crudely.

Three months later, Ghana qualified for its first-ever World Cup appearance. A surprising weekend in early October 2005 saw the traditional giants of African football, Nigeria, Cameroon and South Africa—all of whom were, to some extent, disorganized, casual and a little overconfident—fail to qualify, while relative minnows, Togo, Côte d'Ivoire, Angola and Ghana all secured their places for Germany '06. Of these newcomers, Ghana possesses by far the most impressive pedigree. They have won the African Nations Cup four times, twice they have triumphed in the World Under-17 Championships, and twice they have been runner-up at the World Youth

Championships, but despite their obvious talent and proven ability, the Ghanaian players have never, until now, had the chance to display their talent at the final stages of the game's biggest tournament.

I first visited Ghana during the 1990 World Cup, and I discovered a nation that was crazy about football. The whole country seemed to grind to a halt whenever near-neighbors, Cameroon—who were enjoying a remarkable run of success—took to the field. I watched the Cameroon–England quarterfinal at the home of my department head at the University of Ghana. Having grown up in England as a staunch football fan, I thought I possessed unimpeachable loyalties when it came to supporting "my" national team. However, within minutes of the kickoff I found myself swept up in the hysteria of African football and responding loudly and vocally to the skills of *both* teams. I wanted England to win, but I marveled at the exuberance of the Cameroonians. I soon learned to appreciate ostentatious displays of individual skill that rose up above the team effort, and I became familiar with acrobatic modes of celebrating goals that I didn't believe could possibly exist outside of the circus tent.

Of all the African newcomers to the 2006 World Cup, Ghana has the finest grassroots infrastructure and commitment to the game. National investment in the sport remains high, the league system is highly organized and sponsorship—both state and commercial—is generous. Spectators turn up in great numbers, and local rivalries abound. In fact, the current president of the country is also president of the club side in the second city of Kumasi. By contrast, the situation in neighboring Sierra Leone is somewhat different for their recent history of civil war has seriously depleted most of the resources in the country. There are other, much more pressing areas that are crying out for investment before one would even think about spending money on sport. On a recent trip to Sierra Leone, I was disturbed to see how quickly interest in the local game has been replaced by crowds of youths packed into the most rudimentary bars on weekends to watch English Premier League matches on satellite television. In Ghana the interest in the English game is also strong, but in no way can it compete for interest with local football rivalries.

In the late eighties, my club team—Leeds United—signed a Ghanaian player, Tony Yeboah. He was, at the time, one of the most feared strikers in Europe. Captain of the German team, Eintracht Frankfurt, he immediately became a cult figure at Elland Road. Nothing warmed my heart more than traveling to Ghana and seeing Ghanaian men and boys sporting Leeds United shirts bearing the name of "Yeboah" on the back. However, Tony Yeboah was not a man who was unsure of his value, and if he felt slighted he would let you know. His differences with the Leeds United manager eventually led to his premature departure from the club, but at the national level there were also problems. Tony Yeboah did not see eye to eye with the other outstanding Ghanaian star of the period, the French-based Abédi Ayew Pelé who, in the early nineties, was three times named African Player of the Year. From different tribes, and possessing different temperaments, both men saw themselves as leaders of the national team, and during the nineties their squabbling and infighting contributed to the almost chronic underachievement of what, on paper at least, should have been an internationally successful team.

At the start of the World Cup 2006 qualifying campaign, these same problems of temperament looked as though they might once again defeat the Black Stars. Sammy Kuffour, a Ghanaian defender with Roma in Italy's Serie A, and one of the team's handful of European-based players, decided that his own needs and demands were more important than those of the national side. Ghanaian fans began once more to fear that they might have to witness another potentially successful campaign being hijacked by disharmony and squabbling. In recent years most African national teams have struggled to come to terms with the problem of how to blend their overseas-based elite players (with their huge salaries and often self-serving demands) with the more modestly rewarded local players. The key to resolving this problem has always been strong leadership from the manager that has to be backed up by the national governing body. In November 2004 the Ghanaian Football Association appointed the Serbian Ratomir Dujkovic as coach of the national side, and his first task was to suspend the "superstar," Kuffor, informing him that if he had no desire to be a team player then he could stay in Rome. This no-

nonsense approach did not please everybody, but the new manager was confident that the Black Stars could qualify for their first World Cup finals if they trained, played and thought as a team. On October 8, 2005, in their last World Cup qualifying match with the Cape Verde Islands, Dujkovic was proved right when a 4–0 victory ensured that Ghana finished top of their group and therefore qualified for Germany '06.

Three months earlier, as my plane began its descent into Accra's Kotoka Airport, the player who had borrowed my newspaper leaned over to hand it back to me. "Do you think you'll qualify for the World Cup?" I asked him. He smiled, then laughed nervously. "If we stay together then we will qualify," he said. "If we stay together then it is possible that we can achieve anything." I was, I admit, skeptical. Michael Essien had stayed behind in London with his club side, Chelsea, and even as we spoke the Ghanaian captain, Stephen Appiah was traveling to Turkey where he now plays his football for Fenerbahce following a $10 million transfer from Juventus. Even more disturbingly, the player who *should* represent their "future," the young Ghanaian Fredua Koranteng Adu, who was born in the fishing port of Tema some twenty miles outside of the capital city of Accra, is now known to the world as Freddy Adu. He has embraced both American citizenship and a huge contract from Nike, and will most likely never play for the country of his birth. However, three months later the player who handed me back my newspaper was, like his manager, proved right.

The trend of continually exporting home-grown African talent to countries that not only welcome them into their richly funded and well-rewarded league systems but—as in the case of Freddy Adu—even absorb them into their national sides, may well destroy the chances of any African country actually ever winning the World Cup. Pelé once claimed that in the first decade of the twenty-first century an African nation would win the World Cup. However, the realities of the marketplace, and increasingly flexible national affiliations, seem likely to continue to have a detrimental effect on the ability of African nations to produce resolute and focused national teams.

Ghana's Black Stars may have finally got it right under Dujkovic, but by 2010 football will be even more subject to the influence of money and sponsorship, and top African players—like the best players everywhere—will continue to be little more than money-making celebrities. Germany '06 will be the first, and probably the best, chance for a united Ghanaian team to show the international world what they have been missing for the past twenty years. Their arrival has been long overdue, but finally the dynamic Black Stars have a chance to shine on football's biggest stage.

World Cup Record

FIFA Ranking: 50
World Cup Appearances: 0
World Cup Champions: 0
Federation Name: Ghana Football Association
Confederation: CAF
Founded: 1957
FIFA Affiliation: 1958
Nickname: Black Stars
Manager: Ratomir Dujkovic
Website: NA
Stadium: Accra Stadium
Home Uniform: yellow/yellow/yellow
Away Uniform: white/black/black
Provider: NA

1930:	Did not enter
1934:	Did not enter
1938:	Did not enter
1950:	Did not enter
1954:	Did not enter
1958:	Did not enter
1962:	Did not qualify
1966:	Withdrew
1970:	Did not qualify
1974:	Did not qualify
1978:	Did not qualify
1982:	Withdrew
1986:	Did not qualify
1990:	Did not qualify
1994:	Did not qualify
1998:	Did not qualify
2002:	Did not qualify

Matches	Wins	Draws	Losses	GF	GA	GD	Points
0	0	0	0	0	0	0	0

Ghana is appearing in the World Cup for the first time

Path to Qualification for World Cup 2006

Date	Home		Away		Result
16-Nov-03	Somalia	0	Ghana	5	W
19-Nov-03	Ghana	2	Somalia	0	W
5-Jun-04	Burkina Faso	1	Ghana	0	L
20-Jun-04	Ghana	3	South Africa	0	W
3-Jul-04	Uganda	1	Ghana	1	D
5-Sep-04	Ghana	2	Cape Verde	0	W
10-Oct-04	Ghana	0	Congo DR	0	D
27-Mar-05	Congo DR	1	Ghana	1	D
5-Jun-05	Ghana	2	Burkina Faso	1	W
18-Jun-05	South Africa	0	Ghana	2	W
4-Sep-05	Ghana	2	Uganda	0	W
8-Oct-05	Cape Verde	0	Ghana	4	W

Ghana qualified by finishing first in Group 2 of the African Zone

Iran

Capital: Tehran
Independence: April 1, 1979
    (Islamic Republic of Iran proclaimed)
Area: 1.648 million sq km
Population: 68,017,860
Median Age: 24.2 years
Life Expectancy at Birth: 70.0 years
Ethnic Groups: Persian 51%, Azeri 24%,
    Gilaki and Mazandarani 8%, Kurd 7%,
    Arab 3%, Lur 2%, Baloch 2%, Turkmen 2%,
    other 1%
Religions: Shi'a Muslim 89%, Sunni Muslim 9%,
    Zoroastrian, Jewish, Christian and Baha'i 2%
Languages: Persian and Persian dialects 58%,
    Turkic and Turkic dialects 26%, Kurdish 9%,
    Luri 2%, Balochi 1%, Arabic 1%, Turkish 1%,
    other 2%
Suffrage: 15 years of age; universal
Military Obligation: 18 years of age for
    compulsory military service; 16 years of age for
    volunteers; 18-month service obligation
GDP Per Capita: $7,700
Budget: $47.7 billion
Military Expenditures: $4.3 billion (3.3% of GDP)
Agriculture: wheat, rice, other grains, sugar beets,
    fruits, nuts, cotton; dairy products, wool; caviar
Industries: petroleum, petrochemicals, textiles,
    cement and other construction materials, food
    processing (particularly sugar refining and
    vegetable oil production), metal fabrication,
    armaments
Currency: Iranian rial

Source: *CIA World Factbook*

Iran

Saïd Sayrafiezadeh

In the summer of 1998, as Iran and the U.S. were preparing to play each other in the first round of the World Cup, I decided to examine my own Iranian roots a little more closely. This was not a simple matter. For starters, my father was Iranian and my mother was Jewish American, leaving me somewhere in between, in a kind of ethnic no-man's-land. Then there was the messy business of my father abandoning me as a baby and my mother raising me without any knowledge of Iranian language, culture and history. The result: at age twenty-nine I found myself an American in every regard except for a certain thirteen-letter unpronounceable last name. I was a composite of two halves that were irreconcilable strangers to each other.

None of this personal complexity was evident, however, in the lead-up to the World Cup match between my two sides. In fact, the pre-game was surprisingly cordial despite the history between the two countries. Iran hadn't been to the World Cup since before the 1979 revolution and the United States was hobbling along with a short, pathetic history in the sport. The whole thing was being billed as a just-happy-to-be-here competition.

It also happened that in the months leading up to the World Cup relations between Iran and the United States were markedly improving. The recently elected president Mohammed Khatami appeared on CNN delicately presenting his "felicitations to all the followers of Jesus Christ, to all human beings, and particularly to the American people." Bill Clinton said that he sincerely hoped the two nations could find a way to end their long estrangement, and Madeleine Albright found it in herself to thank the Iranian government for helping to bring peace to Afghanistan. Nineteen years of enmity was finally being laid to rest, said the *New York Times*.

That figure, nineteen years, was derived by counting forward from the day Iranian students stormed the American Embassy in Tehran in 1979, and proceeded to hold fifty-two Americans hostage for four hundred and forty-four days. Another way to calculate the duration of Persian-American ill will would be to start from the CIA's over-throw of the democratically elected prime minister Mohammed Mossadegh in 1953 and the re-installation of the shah to his throne. That would make forty-five years of enmity to finally bury. But the people who mattered when it came to these things were saying let bygones be bygones.

I was disappointed by this happy turn of events. First of all, I hap-pened to agree that 1979 was the genesis for enmity, because it was most certainly the genesis for *my* enmity. In 1979 I was a father-less ten-year-old living in Pittsburgh and being labeled by my sixth-grade classmates as a co-conspirator of those Iranian hostage takers. These classmates had great fun mispronouncing my name (first and last), speculating on whether my father had ever engaged in sexual intercourse with a camel, and describing my mother as having a dot on her forehead and terrible body odor. If given the chance at age ten I would have cashed in all of my Iranian heritage for the most middle of the road American identity and never looked back. But nineteen years later, what need did I have for reconciliation? I had become fully acclimated to my deep sense of exile and was looking forward to seeing Iran beat the shit out of the U.S.

I fidgeted through the cloying pre-game exchange of gifts and the happy group photograph, Iranians and Americans, arms about shoulders. This discomfort was quickly balanced, though, by the pleasure I took in examining the bodies of the Iranian players: thick thighs and calves, broad shoulders, firm buttocks. I contrasted this with my skinny half-Iranian body and my father's potbellied intel-lectual one. The players, with their black hair, big noses and hairy legs seemed to be virile, godlike versions of my father and me. Even their blood-red uniforms excited me. And then there were the names, names as preposterous as my own: Ahmadreza Abedzadeh, Khodadad Azizi, Mehdi Mahdavikia.

At the opposite end of the field were the very ideals of American beauty, clothed in white. None were more handsome than the U.S. goalkeeper Kasey Keller, a West Coast blonde with a strong jaw and thick forearms. I had spent my entire childhood envying boys who looked like Kasey Keller and wishing I could trade my face for theirs.

I longed to see those physical attributes vanquished once and for all. And in the 40th minute of the game Hamid Estili headed the ball past a flailing, impotent Keller to give Iran a 1–0 lead.

If I was antagonized by the American side of myself, I was equally antagonized by the Iranian side: my father. We do not speak often, but when we do it is full of that false familiarity and outsized exuberance that characterizes two people who are trying to ignore thirty years of unspoken rage and sadness. When I was about twenty-five I summoned the courage to ask my father why he had left my mother and me.

"This is a big question," he said gently, "we should wait until we can give it the attention it deserves."

I remember that we were standing in his kitchen and I was so pleased by his candor, so impressed by his readiness to make a full disclosure, that it was literally years before I realized the question continued to go unanswered.

But in the summer of 1998, with the Clinton-Khatami détente in the air, I was willing to let my own bygones be bygones. I found myself reasoning that while it was certainly true, yes, my father was entirely absent for my childhood, it was also true that he was the best of all possible entirely absent fathers. Furthermore, I was lucky to have a father who came from such a rich, exotic land. A land that was mine by birthright. I was sure those sixth-grade classmates of mine were now wishing to have a little depth in their Pittsburgh lives. And in the spirit of trying to understand my father and myself more fully, I decided to undertake the most daunting of all adventures: a trip to Iran. If ever there was a time to go, the time was now, what with the felicitations and the thank-yous flowing both ways. I decided I had better take full advantage of the thaw.

This was a daring proposition. Every so often I would run into an Iranian expat who would tell me a horror story about some clueless Iranian visiting Iran for the first time and being tossed into jail without a trial, or being forced to serve in the military—military duty being mandatory for all able-bodied men. Not to mention the ever present U.S. State Department edicts: "The Department of State continues to warn U.S. citizens to carefully consider the risks of travel to Iran." I was not to be dissuaded. I imagined my father meeting me at JFK upon my return from Iran, clapping me proudly on my back, admitting how oblivious he had been to my interest in my Iranian heritage, apologizing for his lapse of fatherhood and saying, "Now about that question you asked." Tears would be shed.

I began by purchasing a travel book at the gorgeous, monumental Barnes & Noble at Union Square. The building dates from 1880 and seemed a fittingly grandiose place to begin my voyage into the past. I chose *The Lonely Planet Guide to Iran*. The cover advertised, "Features on trekking, carpets and architecture." There was no mention of nineteen years of enmity. It cost $17.95. I bought it with the intention of devouring it and transforming myself overnight into an expert on the country. I was so overwhelmed, however, by the scope of history—beginning with the Achaemenians and moving on to the Seleucids and the Sassanians—and, frankly, bored that I decided on around page fourteen that this was a pedantic way to prepare to visit a foreign country. I put the book on my bookshelf, prominently displayed, so that guests would see the title and be prompted to engage me in conversation about my travel plans.

My father had once told me that traveling to Iran was like traveling to a neighborhood like Bedford-Stuyvesant. You would not be catered to in Iran the way you would in, say, Turkey. Iranians did not know English, period. If you could not speak Farsi you would, quite simply, not speak. I imagined driving along a deserted road, trying to make sense of the signs, asking someone for help in English, and winding up in the Iranian Army. No. I would need to learn the language. I knew precisely one word: "googosh." Which I was taught meant penis. When I was little my mother would refer to my penis as "googosh." "Did you make sure to wash your googosh?" she would say. The psychological implications that the one word of Farsi I learned from my absent father was the word for penis, and moreover that it was conveyed via my Jewish mother, are far too complicated to attempt in an essay on the World Cup.

Suffice it to say I was in need of a Farsi lesson. I returned once more to the monumental Barnes & Noble and bought the Language/30

Farsi cassette tape. "Start speaking today," it promised on the box. $16.95. A friend cautioned me that no one ever learns how to speak a foreign language from a tape. Nonsense, I thought, this language is part of my heritage. I put the tape in and pressed play. It began with an American man intoning dryly: "The Farsi alphabet." This was followed by another man—sounding a lot like my father—enunciating the Farsi alphabet. I repeated as best I could. Then the American voice said, "Sounds of the Farsi language: diphthongs." And then my father appeared again and began speaking. I tried to repeat after him, but he moved on too quickly and I was forced to stop and rewind the tape, press play, try to repeat it again, stop, rewind . . . This was no way to master a language. A language was a living thing that could only be learned by speaking with a real human being.

The Berlitz Language Center in Rockefeller Center is billed as the largest in the world. "Effective, Intense, FAST!" Their advertisement reads: "When you're ready to learn a new language, we're ready to help!"

The place for me. I was greeted warmly by an older, doctorly man who ushered me into a brilliantly clean room that had a table and two chairs. I half expected to see tongue depressors and a stethoscope. I felt suddenly like a crippled Iranian who was hoping to find a miracle cure.

"Let's start by understanding your needs," he said with a deep look of concern.

"Well," I started, "I'm American, but my father's Iranian."

"Of course," he said, "and you'd like to communicate with your father."

The irony was rich.

I continued, "I'm planning on traveling to Iran soon and I'd like to know enough Persian to get by."

"Farsi," he said, "is not a popular language so we do not offer group classes." I was embarrassed that I had used the wrong word for Persian. "We do, however, have individual Farsi classes. These are all one-on-one with a native-speaking teacher who uses a Berlitz method that was designed by studying the way children learn to speak. From the moment you enter the classroom you and your teacher will speak only Farsi. There is no translation ever. We use flash cards to aid the learning process. The teacher will hold up a picture of a pen, for instance, and then say the word for pen . . ."

He mimed holding up a flashcard and hesitated as if I might fill in the word for pen. I assumed he thought that I knew at least that much. I imagined him holding up a flash card of a penis.

"We offer four levels," he went on, "each level has fifteen classes. The basic level does not concern itself with grammar or conjugation, but by the end of it you will be able to shop and order food in a restaurant. The intermediate level builds on that and so on and so forth. By the end of the advanced level you would be fluent."

"Sixty classes and I would be fluent in Farsi?" I asked.

"Yes." He was a great doctor and I was ready to be his patient. "Let's start with the basic level," he said. "When would you like to begin?"

"Right away," I said.

"Great," he said, "the price will be $2,475."

I did not begin. The next day I picked up a schedule at NYU and signed up for Persian I. Eight classes for $460. I would learn the basics. Plus there would be instruction in grammar and conjugation—what was so wrong with learning grammar and conjugation? I would also learn how to write, which Berlitz did not offer in their basic course. There were two texts for the class: *Persian Vocabulary* went for $50, and *Elementary Persian Grammar* for $31.99. The latter contained various sentences for translation. Sentences like: "The Safavid dynasty was founded by Shah Esma'il, who ascended the royal throne in 907 A.H." I purchased both at the NYU bookstore. We were also required to bring a calligraphic pen, which I found at a local drugstore for $1.54.

The class was to meet every Saturday from one to four. It was summer and not an ideal time to be indoors, but I felt good sacrificing for such personal enlightenment. I arrived on time with all of my supplies, including a spiral notebook and several pens. The professor was a small Iranian man with an impish smile and chalk stains on his ass. We began by introducing ourselves and explaining why we were interested in learning the language.

"I'm interested in learning Farsi," I began, "because I'm planning to travel to Iran." Being the only student of Iranian descent I imagined that this would impress everyone. But instead the professor said:

"Using the word Farsi makes no sense. Farsi is the Persian word for Persian."

I laughed a self-effacing laugh. The professor did not laugh.

"That would be like saying 'I speak *español*.' Would you say that?"

"No," I said. "I wouldn't."

"Of course you wouldn't," he said. "You would say, 'I speak Spanish.' " This was obviously a contentious issue for him and he continued on long after the point had been made, using other examples to illustrate the illogic of using the Persian word for Persian while speaking English—"Would you say, 'I speak *russo*?' "

Next on the agenda was whether any of us knew any Persian words. On this I kept silent. "Spinach," the professor declaimed, "comes from Persian." For some reason this made me proud. Then he went on to give an overview of the alphabet, its basic sounds, its grammatical structure. Being Iranian I'd imagined having a head start over everyone else, like those children in my school who earned high marks, say, at math because their parents were mathematicians. The opposite, however, seemed to be the case. By the end of the first class I felt a bit lost, and by the end of the second class I was well behind. The rest of the semester I watched as my non-Iranian classmates excelled while I retained nothing. I was incapable of forming the letters with the calligraphic pen or of pronouncing even the most rudimentary words.

"Don't clear yourself out so much," the professor would say to me when I had tried my best to mimic his back-of-the-throat pronunciation. "This isn't French."

In fact, the only phrase I learned to say with some mastery was *"Man khanoomha e sabok dost daram"* (which translates roughly to "I like bad women"). The Monica Lewinsky affair was on the front page almost everyday, and the subject of some titillation for the professor, who found ways to use it to illustrate various linguistic subtleties.

I had already paid for the classes so I continued to go, but I spent most of the time sitting in the back of the room, hoping the professor would not call on me.

It was time to apply for a visa. I started by contacting the Iranian Embassy in Washington D.C. The first thing I learned is that there is no Iranian Embassy in Washington D.C. Technically, the two countries do not have diplomatic relations. There is, however, something called an Interests Sections of the Islamic Republic of Iran, housed within the Pakistani Embassy. I sent away for the materials and three weeks later I received a visa application. The stationery was printed with the headline "In the Name of the Almighty" and beneath that it read, "Dear applicant, Listed below please find the procedures for processing an entry and/or transit visa." I quickly got everything together: a copy of my passport, a $60 money order, and a letter explaining why I wanted to travel to Iran, which I wrote in the voice of an elementary school student, thinking that it would assure them that I was no threat to their revolution. It began, "Dear Interests Sections of the Islamic Republic of Iran, I have always wanted to travel to Iran. My father is Iranian. I think the culture is very beautiful . . ."

A month later the phone rang.

"I'm calling for Mr. Sayrafiezadeh," said a voice that sounded strangely reminiscent of my father's voice.

"This is Mr. Sayrafiezadeh," I said.

"Mr. Sayrafiezadeh, this is the Ministry of Foreign Affairs for the Islamic Republic of Iran. I am calling to inform you that you I am returning your visa application. You are not eligible for a visa."

"Did I forget to provide you with something?"

"No, Mr. Sayrafiezadeh, you don't understand. You do not need a visa because you are an Iranian citizen."

I pictured the clerk crammed into a small storage room that the Pakistani Embassy had grudgingly cleaned out for him. "I only need a place to crash for a few days," says Iran. A few days had turned into a few years, which had turned into nineteen years, and now, here was this official squashed against his desk, a small window facing out toward the Capitol, his paper bag lunch sitting atop a mountain of papers.

"There must be a misunderstanding," I said. "I was born in the United States."

"If your father is Iranian then you are also Iranian."

"But I'm an American."

"No, Mr. Sayrafiezadeh," he said, "you are both."

A filmstrip ran though my head, narrated by one of those expats I had met, showing my plane touching down in Iran and the authorities immediately conscripting me into the military.

"Thank you all the same," I said, trying not to hurt his feelings, "but I'd rather travel to Iran on a visa."

"If you are an Iranian citizen the only way you can enter Iran is with a passport. Send me a copy of your Iranian birth certificate and I will process your papers for citizenship."

"I don't have an Iranian birth certificate," I said.

"You don't have an Iranian birth certificate?" the man sounded flummoxed. "But why didn't your father apply for an Iranian birth certificate when you were born?" There was a heavy, shameful pause on my end. "It will be very difficult for you to get one now at your age." And then he added dramatically, "But it is the only way you will be able to travel to Iran, so you must try."

I had no recourse now but to enlist the person who had started it all: my father. He had just separated from his second wife, an Iranian woman twenty years his junior, and was living in a rundown two-bedroom apartment in Brooklyn with a mattress on the bedroom floor, a dead spider plant and a roommate.

When he answered the phone I tried to impress him by saying, *"Man khanoomha e sabok dost daram."*

"What?" he said.

I tried again. My throat filling with snot.

"What? Who is this?"

"It's me, Pop," I said, "it's me."

"What are you saying to me?"

"Nothing," I said, "forget it." And then I proceeded to tell him the whole story of my desire to go to Iran, beginning with the language classes and ending with Iranian citizenship and the birth certificate.

"You want to go to Iran!" he said with outsized exuberance. "This is momentous!"

"The birth certificate, Pop," I said.

"Yes, yes. I will take care of it," he said.

A week passed, two weeks passed, then a month. My Persian classes came to an end. Fall arrived. I called my father again.

What was it he was supposed to do? Oh, that's right. He will look into it. First thing. Not to worry. This is momentous!

Another month passed. Nothing. November came. I called again and left a message on his answering machine reminding him. The next day he called me back saying that it was not a good idea to leave messages concerning Iran on his answering machine.

Why this was he did not offer and I did not ask. He said it so matter-of-factly that I assumed the reasoning must be sound and I was simply naïve for not having been cognizant.

Another week passed, two weeks. My enthusiasm dwindled. Then, in late December, I received a package with my father's return address. Could this be it? I opened the envelope carefully and withdrew a book entitled *Ali and Nino: A Love Story.* It was written by someone named Kurban Saïd. "A vividly unique vision of colliding cultures and enduring love," read the cover, which had a photograph of a turbaned young man embracing a woman, and beneath them an illustration of a desperate and bloody battle scene. The whole thing was reminiscent of a Harlequin romance. There was nothing else in the envelope.

The next day I took *Ali and Nino* back to that same Barnes & Noble at Union Square, this time trying to ignore its grandeur and history. I told them I had lost the receipt for the book and received $13.60 in store credit. *The Lonely Planet Guide to Iran,* the Persian grammar books, the language tape, the calligraphic pen, the defunct visa application and everything else I placed in a shoe box and put on a high shelf in my closet.

That was 1998. My father never applied for my birth certificate. I never went to Iran. I never learned to speak Persian. Relations between Iran and the United States went bad, and then went worse. But in the 83rd minute of that World Cup game, Mehdi Mahdavikia stroked the ball past Kasey Keller and beat the U.S. 2–1.

World Cup Record

FIFA Ranking: 19
World Cup Appearances: 2
World Cup Champions: 0
Federation Name: IR Iran Football Association
Confederation: AFC
Founded: 1920
FIFA Affiliation: 1945
Nickname: Team Melli (phonetic for "National Team" in Persian)
Manager: Branko Ivankovic
Website: NA
Stadium: Azadi Stadium, Tehran
Home Uniform: all white
Away Uniform: all red
Provider: NA

1930:	Did not enter
1934:	Did not enter
1938:	Did not enter
1950:	Did not enter
1954:	Did not enter
1958:	Did not enter
1962:	Did not enter
1966:	Did not enter
1970:	Did not enter
1974:	Did not qualify
1978:	First round exit
1982:	Withdrew
1986:	Did not qualify
1990:	Did not qualify
1994:	Did not qualify
1998:	First round exit
2002:	Did not qualify

Matches	Wins	Draws	Losses	GF	GA	GD	Points
6	1	1	4	4	12	-8	4

Iran is 48th on the all-time World Cup table

Path to Qualification for World Cup 2006

18-Feb-04	Iran	3	Qatar	1		W
31-Mar-04	Laos	0	Iran	7		W
9-Jun-04	Iran	0	Jordan	1		L
8-Sep-04	Jordan	0	Iran	2		W
13-Oct-04	Qatar	2	Iran	3		W
17-Nov-04	Iran	7	Laos	0		W
9-Feb-05	Bahrain	0	Iran	0		D
25-Mar-05	Iran	2	Japan	1		W
30-Mar-05	North Korea	0	Iran	2		W
3-Jun-05	Iran	1	North Korea	0		W
8-Jun-05	Iran	1	Bahrain	0		W
17-Aug-05	Japan	2	Iran	1		L

Iran qualified by finishing in the top two in Group B of the Asian Zone

Italy

Capital: Rome
Independence: March 17, 1861
  (Kingdom of Italy proclaimed;
  Italy was not finally unified until 1870)
Area: 301,230 sq km
Population: 58,103,033
Median Age: 41.8 years
Life Expectancy at Birth: 79.7 years
Ethnic Groups: Italian (includes clusters of
  German-, French-, and Slovene-Italians in the
  north and Albanian-Italians and Greek-Italians
  in the south)
Religions: predominately Roman Catholic with
  mature Protestant and Jewish communities
  and a growing Muslim immigrant community
Languages: Italian (official), German, French,
  Slovene
Suffrage: 18 years of age; universal
  (except in senatorial elections,
  where minimum age is 25)
Military Obligation: 18 years of age
GDP Per Capita: $27,700
Budget: $820.1 billion
Military Expenditures: $28,182.8 million
  (1.8% of GDP)
Agriculture: fruits, vegetables, grapes, potatoes,
  sugar beets, soybeans, grain, olives; beef, dairy
  products; fish
Industries: tourism, machinery, iron and steel,
  chemicals, food processing, textiles, motor
  vehicles, clothing, footwear, ceramics
Currency: euro

Source: *CIA World Factbook*

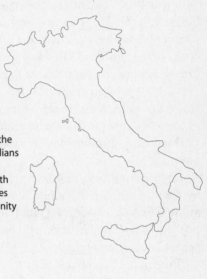

Italy

Tim Parks

In 1994, during the World Cup, my father-in-law, Adelmo, pointed out graffiti that had appeared on the parapet along the seafront at Pescara on the Adriatic coast of Italy. The letters were almost a meter high so that the message stretched out its wicked red paint for quite some way.

It was early morning and we were walking the children to the beach. It is hard to cross the busy seafront road at Pescara. There are plenty of crossings, but no one will stop until you actually step off the curb, and even then the cars brake unwillingly, swervingly, skiddingly. Acts of faith are a must here. *Cretino!* is a common cry.

Once allowed to cross, the kids—Michele, Stefania—dash, palm tree after palm tree under brilliant sunshine, along the unending promenade toward the bathing station where we have a sunshade, La Medusa. "Take a look at that," my father-in-law nods to the parapet.

Adelmo is a short, fat man, with a big bald freckled head, protected by a white hat. He has a handkerchief too. He lifts his battered hat an inch or two, inserts the handkerchief, mops and returns it to the pockets of his Boy Scout shorts that bear the brand name, in English across both rolling buttocks, Old Dog.

"Funny, no?" he chuckles.

I have to step back a couple of paces to read the whole thing. Someone has worked hard with their spray-can to give us this one. It says: *I PELI DELLA FREGNA ISTUPIDISCANO LA GENTE.*

I'm not familiar with *fregna,* I tell him laughing. It must be a dialect word.

"Dead right." Adelmo is a local, Abbruzzese born and bred. In his warm, gravelly voice, he says: "But you can guess what it means."

I can indeed: "THE HAIRS ON THE . . . FREGNA . . . STUPEFY PEOPLE."

"Drive us crazy," the old man growls in the English he learned in prison camp. My father-in-law is perhaps the only man with whom I have ever walked arm in arm. He encourages a dangerously conspiratorial male solidarity: day by day, he seems to be saying, one way or another, we are all stupefied and driven crazy by the other sex. He might have written the graffiti himself.

"Not to mention football," I suggest. *"La palla rotonda istupidisce la gente!"*

The night before Italy had beaten Norway 1–0. The whole world was glued to the television, then swarmed out into the streets to honk horns and let off fireworks into the early hours. We have not slept well.

"And wine of course!" Adelmo goes on.

"With this difference," I object. "The wine sets you up for the footie or the *fregna,* or helps you to celebrate or drown sorrows afterwards, but it's not in itself the thing that enchants. You don't dream of wine. You don't get obsessed by it."

"I do," my father-in-law protests, "especially when accompanied by a mountain of grilled fish."

Adelmo is a glutton and gluttons in these Adriatic parts love to speak of a *gran grigliata di pesce* as the ne plus ultra of hedonism. It's a dish I find hard to think of at eight in the morning.

We turn into the terrace bar of the Medusa, order a cappuccino and croissant and sit in the sunshine. The world is a dazzle of color here, of oleander and fleshy hibiscus, of row upon row of blue-and-white sunshades that seem to hover over the pale Adriatic sand in the bright morning's intense stillness.

"Let's add the sunshine," I propose: *"Fregna,* footie, booze and sunshine, four great gifts that stupefy us all."

"But the greatest of these . . ." Adelmo begins blasphemously. He is watching a pretty young mother who is dragging a little boy across the terrace to the jukebox. It is disturbing how much attention my seventy-year-old father-in-law pays to young women.

"The greatest of these . . ." She wears sharp high heels and a yellow sash of flimsy crepe wrapped round her tight bikini bottom.

"Is footie," I tell him firmly. "Let's grab the *Gazzetta.*"

We come to the beach so early because this is the moment, popular wisdom has it, when the air and iodine is good for the children, and the sun not too scorchingly high. You can breathe and move and think. If Italians drive aggressively and don't always obey the rules on the streets or playing fields, they nevertheless live their lives by well-tried routines and are admirably aware of health matters. The best air for children is in the early morning and the best month for the sea is June, before the sun gets too hot and the water too dirty.

For all the years my children have been growing up, June for me has meant Pescara, where my in-laws live, and sunshine, and wine and mountains of grilled fish and *fre* . . . my wife that is . . . and once every four years, of course, the World Cup, which always starts in June and which I cannot imagine unfolding in any other setting. For me the host country of the world's greatest sporting event is always and only the seaside town of Pescara, or to be precise, a ground floor sitting room in the shabby block of four concrete flats my father-in-law built as a young man and never got round to putting a proper roof on. The "prison" people call it. Back from the war, Adelmo married, built this ugly structure in a sandy wasteland barely a hundred yards from the beach, then hurried abroad before it was finished to make his fortune, he imagined, as a building-site manager in the furthest outposts of the developing world. When, thirty years later and not much wealthier, he retired home, it was to find that thanks to seaside tourism and the sixties boom the real fortunes had been amassed in his absence all around his backyard. Today the "prison" is hemmed in, dwarfed and shamed by larger, well-stuccoed *palazzi* flaunting Californian roofs and expensive remote-controlled gates.

Like many educated Italians, and almost all who have lived abroad, my father-in-law may one minute speak with great contempt of his country and compatriots, their crippling provincialism, their corruption, their general small-mindedness and lack of civic sense, almost as if he would sign up for American citizenship tomorrow morning if given half the chance, and then only seconds later he will be assuring you that in all his travels—and whatever Third World country makes it to the World Cup my father-in-law has always built a hospital there, or a textiles factory, or a sewage farm—in all his epic travels he never saw a country as beautiful as Italy, where the young mothers and the wine and the grilled fish are so seductively stupefying, and of course the football the best in the world, though to my knowledge my father-in-law never kicked a ball competitively or attended a single match inside Italy or out in all his born days.

We grab the bar's copy of the pink *Gazzetta dello Sport* and read the regular mix of triumphalism, indignation and injury alarms. Meanwhile, the young mother has found the song she wants on the jukebox. Every summer there is a song that sets the mood of the beach experience. Inevitably it sings of love and sultry longing. There will be a hoarse male voice, straining to strain—oh these torrid Mediterranean afternoons are so sad and long without his woman—or a languid *signorina* crooning her regret: "Not here not here, your smell this year." The underlying emotion, shared no doubt by the listeners as they open their deck chairs and slip on designer swimwear, is a profound complacency in the humanity of their suffering, which is not unlike the complacency of the *Gazzetta*'s journalists, who are pretending that Norway really was a tough team to beat.

Our young mother begins to dance, alone with her eyes closed, her arms gently writhing at eight-fifteen in the morning on the near-empty terrace of the Medusa. Her four-year-old boy wants to run straight into the sea, but she won't let him. It's not warm enough yet. Only 25 degrees. "You'll catch cold." She dances. One look at her lithe waist and you can see why the *Gazzetta* is adamant that the players' wives must not be allowed to accompany their husbands in their World Cup retreat. The enchantments of *fregna* and football are not compatible.

The boy kicks his ball angrily against the terrace wall. He runs after it among the chairs. At last Mamma wakes up to the danger. "Alberto! Don't sweat! You'll catch cold." The boy is obliged to fret away his time pushing buttons on the bar's video games while his mother returns to her profound self-absorption, eyes closed under the pergola, moving to this sultry song. "Interesting," I attempt to distract my father-in-law "to think that at some time or other every Italian footballer has been warned not to sweat. Don't you think? Mamma's voice could come back to them perhaps at crucial moments of the game, slow them down." I know Adelmo loves to refer to the

Azzurri as spoiled and pampered brats, while exulting over every goal they score and spoiling his grandchildren rotten with pizzas and Cokes and an endless supply of small change for the video games. And sure enough, here are the kids running onto the terrace to demand attention. "Papà, Nonno, come and play!"

If the World Cup ideally announces the equality of all peoples, the reality when we get down to the beach to build our daily sandcastle is that black, Asian and Arab hawkers drift humbly through the maze of rented sunshades while the well-creamed whites, who have paid through the nose for their patch of protection, finger cheap towels, or try on contraband sunglasses and shake their heads and shout at their children not to throw sand and go back to discussing the relative merits of 4–4–2 and 4–3–3 and whether Baggio should be played as a straightforward midfielder or in a more advanced position beside Signori and which is the best bathing station for an aperitif.

I love all this. I love the lazy domesticated eroticism of it all, the complete lack of that perverse English pride in braving inclement weather. In Pescara you don't swim if the sea is not warm and if a cloud should cross the sun the red flag that forbids reckless bathing is run up at once, though only the few who've been inexplicably slow to depart will ever see it. It's the shameless contentedness of it all that's so enticing.

But there is definitely a difference in World Cup years. Normally, for miles along the beach, the twenty yards between sunshades and tepid sea is a back and forth of leisurely sauntering flesh taking the air at the exact point where—all the magazines insist—the salutary iodine content is highest. There are even those who paddle along in the shallows, perhaps for the length of four or five bathing stations, to get the greater benefit and enjoy a cigarette along the way.

But in World Cup years this promenade of humanity is threatened by a string of football games along the seashore. We must mimic the national triumphs and this is the only place to do it, where the modest ebb and flow of the Adriatic tide makes the sand hard enough to play on. So the kids' early morning sandcastle is soon flattened by flying feet. My daughter Stefi is upset. And so are the promenaders who suddenly find themselves walking right into an offside trap, or a diving header. There are shouts and complaints. But the bathing-station officials don't ask the players to stop as they normally would. In these heady World Cup weeks the game invades every space, mental and physical. You can't breathe for football.

It's curious, I notice, fooling in the shallows with the kids, how these seaside games are divided into regional groups. You can tell by the accents as they shriek for a pass or celebrate a goal. The Lombards are playing the Lombards, the Veneti the Veneti, the locals the locals. Italians like to go on holiday in groups, groups that may have formed as long ago as primary school. And once away from home they stick together. United as a nation usually only by their indignant reaction to foreign criticism, Italians enjoy the World Cup as a rare moment of positive collective pride, but to be rehearsed, re-played and gloated over in the safety of their exclusive regional groups. Certainly we are light years away from the racial-mix pieties of TV advertising where blond Vikings exchange rapid one-twos with swarthy Turks and grinning Koreans. A tall African sweating under a heap of rugs to sell and with five sombreros on his head has to duck a wayward volley. He smiles at the goalkeeper who has dived in the sand, but is not invited to join in.

We swim with the kids. We dig holes in the sand and bury each other. We have pizzettas and beer on our way home for lunch. But really the whole day is a long hot wind-up for the evening's game, and, taken together, the next three or four days will be a longer and even more torrid wind-up for the moment when Italy takes the field again. So in World Cup years these usually languid Pescara days are given an urgent direction. A powerful tide is running. Watching other teams play, of course, is no more than entertaining. There's always the hope that Germany or Argentina or Brazil will be swept away to threaten no more. But watching your own boys perform is nerve-biting. The moment approaches like a first date with a pretty woman. Much is at stake. Men sit in the Medusa, studying the *Gazzetta,* petrified. Even the women are on edge. And the kids have sensed it of course. They clamor for the attention hemorrhaging off toward football.

Zia Maria drops by. All my wife's many relatives know where our sunshade is and visit at least once a day. Childless and recently widowed, stout Zia Maria knows every player in every Italian side in every sport. Televised competitions fill her long retirement. If there was a World Cup in marbles or tiddledywinks, Zia Maria would know the Italian team and all their gossip and be an anxious expert on broken fingernails and repetitive flick syndrome. As it is, she's concerned today about someone's pubalgia. Will it heal before the clash with Mexico? It's an odd fact about the World Cup that it seems to have the greatest effect on those who rarely or never go to a game. For three weeks vast reserves of idle emotion can be invested in the notion of national community, individualism submerged in the embattled belonging of us against the world: the only downside being that, nine times out of ten, at some point you crash out. In 1994 it almost ended for Italy against Mexico, and then again even more embarrassingly against Nigeria. I shall always remember that evening as the first time my son declared a fierce allegiance to his Italian nationality.

Although hosted at 6 P.M. in my in-law's gloomy sitting room, much was made in the media of the idea that the game was actually being played under the midday sun in Boston, something that would surely be, the *Gazzetta* alerted its readers, to the advantage of the Africans. As if the Italians didn't have their *solleone*. To prepare for the occasion, after the usual stupefying morning at the Medusa, we had eaten heavily, taken a long siesta and then killed a scorching afternoon hour or two pestering lizards with water pistols. At 5:30 my father-in-law was already in front of the box with a cheap two-liter bottle of unlabelled Lambrusco. Nonna Maria provided large tumblers.

Around the television, the room was furnished with 1950s armchairs on a bare stone floor (pleasantly cool) and decorated, so to speak, with trophies and totems brought back from the family's Third World travels: a Peruvian wall hanging, an ebony statuette with a large phallus, a pretty set of desert roses. These travels had not, it turned out, included Nigeria, though Adelmo spoke fondly now about his difficulties twenty years ago in getting Africans to obey the safety rules on building sites, a remark that prompted

Nonna Maria to pull out an album full of photographs of herself smiling broadly beside Saharan nomads, South American Indians and other picturesque peoples, usually in full traditional regalia. Six-year-old Stefi oohed and ahhed over these, but the older Michele glared gloomily at the team lists now scrolling up the screen. At nine he was already one of those people who find the tension of a big game unbearable.

With wonderful condescension the commentator begins to talk about the *simpatici nigeriani,* a clear sign that the game is seen as a must win for the Italians. Other teams always described as *simpatici* are the Scots, Luxembourg, the Finns. Then there was the usual indignation about the fact that hardly any of the Italian players wanted to sing their national anthem, as if Italian national unity were such a fragile thing that it entirely depended on a few wired-up athletes remembering to belt out *"Fratelli d'Italia."*

There is a sort of exquisite pleasure for the outsider at moments like these. For myself I mean. Everybody around you is in a state of great anxiety. Your adopted country's foibles and paranoia are on full display. Already the commentator is complaining about the refereeing. But what is really at stake, you wonder? Nothing. My wife, in many ways an epitome of Italianness, won't even bother to watch a moment of this game. Strangely immune, she is more concerned about whether the salad for dinner is clean and the mozzarella fresh. Or then again, everything: Zia Maria will weep bitter tears if the *Azzurri* lose this one. Adelmo will walk the seafront, perhaps as far as the town center, perhaps even the harbor, and smoke a whole packet of cigarettes pushing his blood pressure to the limit.

Pescara is a noisy place. Since hardly anyone bothers with air-conditioning, which is known to be unhealthy, everybody's windows are left open. You can hear the traffic. You can hear the PA systems of the bathing stations calling out the names of lost children, you can hear your neighbors' interminable Ping-Pong under the shade of their pergolas. But now it's all gone quiet. Or rather, a single grating voice dominates the general hush, wafts in and out of every window: *"NON È POSSIBILE!"* the commentator cries. In the 28th minute Nigeria have scored. *"Cretini!"* Adelmo declares.

This is a terrible blow. For more than half an hour now Adelmo and Nonna Maria repeat over and over at the expense of the *Azzurri* the things they have been saying all week about their own children and grandchildren and indeed Italians in general, especially those who built the big *palazzi* that now overshadow Adelmo's "prison": that they're all hopelessly spoiled; that they've been given too much, too much money of course, that they think everything's due to them, that they don't try, they don't *sweat,* for God's sake: that everybody in Italy has got too rich since the war, so rich and so spoiled that now they can't even beat the Africans.

Halftime comes and goes. Another two-liter bottle of Lambrusco appears. Michele pours himself a glass. I'll have to keep an eye on this. Still the *Azzurri* don't score. Unforgivably smug (after all, England didn't even make it to the World Cup that year). I try to distract my in-laws with some linguistic reflections: "Notice how the commentator always says *intervento regolare*—fair tackle—when an Italian makes a dubious tackle that the ref lets by, and then *intervento giudicato regolare*—judged fair—when the Nigerians do the same. Or again: *intervento falloso* when a foul is given against the Nigerians, or *giudicato falloso* when given against the Italians. Isn't it wonderfully symmetrical? But with the obvious subtext . . ."

Nobody wants to listen. Can you blame them? For still Italy hasn't scored. It's nail-biting. It's unbelievable. The *Azzurri* are going out. To Nigeria! Michele starts to get angry with me because I don't care enough, because I probably *want* Italy to go out. "You're not Italian!" he yells, "But I am. I'm Italian and I want Italy to win." He's in tears. I feel guilty. I've never seen him care like this before. I start to insist that I do want Italy to win, though the truth is that if there's one thing the ex-pat holds back from his beloved adopted country, perhaps because in the end it is so meaningless, it is support for their football team. I'm finding it all very funny.

More sensibly, little Stefi has lost interest in the game and is trying to stand on her head on the couch, perhaps to show off her pretty pink knickers. And about every ten seconds she asks, "Has anybody scored yet? Has anybody scored?" Which only drives Michele even crazier.

For still Italy hasn't scored. It's as if, despite that daily act of faith, stepping off the curb of the seafront road, one morning the traffic just refused to stop. The green shirts of the Africans just won't give way. We've got a serious accident on our hands. Then Zola who has only just come on is sent off for a single foul. Now it's perfectly clear to everyone that the Mexican referee is biased, that someone doesn't want Italy to win the World Cup. "And that Zola is a *cretino*," Adelmo shouts. *"Cretino!"* The foul was indeed a bad one.

With five minutes to go the commentator starts talking about the *Azzurri* as *them* rather than *us*. This is most ominous. And now he uses the word *Caporetto!* Yes, there it is, that fateful name. A lost game of football is being likened to a military defeat that cost thousands upon thousands of lives. Catastrophe, disaster, shame. Beaten by the Africans, by the immigrants, the beach hawkers! Nonno and Nonna are silent, staring. The whole of Italy is silent.

Until, *"Gol GOL!"* Baggio has scored. Baggio the *maestro*. No, *we* have scored. I *nostri ragazzi* have scored. *Bravissimi. Bravissimi Azzurri!* The TV explodes, the room explodes. Nonna Maria crosses herself, and Stefi too, upside down on the couch. My son throws himself on me and hugs me tight. *"Papà!"* What can I do but choose to be happy.

Later, when Italy won the game with a penalty in off the post in extra time, it would be horns honking into the early hours and fireworks again and a largely sleepless and stifling night on the lumpy old wool mattress beneath Christ's bleeding heart in the guest room. My wife slept through it all as she always does, beautifully unstirred, secure in the knowledge, as all women are in the end, and priests too, that football is only an intermittent enchantment. But toward dawn I was still listening to the mosquitoes whining in the darkness, waiting for the morning, the Medusa, the *Gazzetta,* another stupefying day on the beach, blissfully unaware that this would be, alas, as it turned out, my last World Cup beside my father-in-law. He wouldn't make it to see the penalty shootout with France in 1998, the Korean disaster of 2002. Years later, every time one of the *Azzurri* is sent off, I still miss his gravelly voice pronouncing, *Cretino!*

World Cup Record

FIFA Ranking: 12
World Cup Appearances: 15
World Cup Champions: 3
Federation Name: Federazione Italiana
 Giuoco Calcio
Confederation: UEFA
Founded: 1898
FIFA Affiliation: 1905
Nickname: la Squadra Azzurra (Blues)
Manager: Marcello Lippi
Website: www.figc.it
Stadium: Olimpico
Home Uniform: blue/white/blue
Away Uniform: white/blue/white
Provider: Kappa

1930: Did not participate
1934: CHAMPIONS
1938: CHAMPIONS
1950: First round exit
1954: First round exit
1958: Did not qualify
1962: First round exit
1966: First round exit
1970: 2nd place
1974: First round exit
1978: 4th place
1982: CHAMPIONS
1986: Second round exit
1990: 3rd place
1994: 2nd place
1998: Quarterfinal exit
2002: Second round exit

Matches	Wins	Draws	Losses	GF	GA	GD	Points
70	39	17	14	110	67	+43	134

Italy is 3rd on the all-time World Cup table

Path to Qualification for World Cup 2006

4-Sep-04	Italy	2	Norway	1	W
8-Sep-04	Moldova	0	Italy	1	W
9-Oct-04	Slovenia	1	Italy	0	L
13-Oct-04	Italy	4	Belarus	3	W
26-Mar-05	Italy	2	Scotland	0	W
4-Jun-05	Norway	0	Italy	0	D
3-Sep-05	Scotland	1	Italy	1	D
7-Sep-05	Belarus	1	Italy	4	W
8-Oct-05	Italy	1	Slovenia	0	W
12-Oct-05	Italy	2	Moldova	1	W

Italy qualified by finishing first in Group 5 of the European Zone

Japan

Capital: Tokyo
Independence: 660 BC
  (traditional founding by Emperor Jimmu)
Area: 377,835 sq km
Population: 127,417,244
Median Age: 42.6 years
Life Expectancy at Birth: 81.2 years
Ethnic Groups: Japanese 99%, other 1%
Religions: observe both Shinto and
  Buddhist 84%, other 16%
Languages: Japanese
Suffrage: 20 years of age; universal
Military Obligation: 18 years of age for
  voluntary military service
GDP Per Capita: $29,400
Budget: $1.748 trillion
Military Expenditures: $45.841 billion
  (1.0% of GDP)
Agriculture: rice, sugar beets,
  vegetables, fruit, pork, poultry,
  dairy products, eggs, fish
Industries: among world's largest and
  technologically advanced producers of motor
  vehicles, electronic equipment, machine tools,
  steel and nonferrous metals, ships, chemicals,
  textiles, processed foods
Currency: yen

Source: *CIA World Factbook*

Japan

Jim Frederick

In Japan, you can get a pizza topped with fish roe and sea urchin, a green-tea latte and a shrimp burger at the local hamburger joint. Voters head to the polls at regular intervals, as they do in democracies all over the globe, but always return the same party to power (the Liberal Democratic Party, which incidentally is neither liberal nor particularly democratic). And while the traditional squat toilet is all but extinct, the sit-down, Western-style toilets that superceded them not only flush, they bathe you clean with a jet of warm water and dry you off with a blast of hot air. (Anyone who contends that these toilets are not a quantum improvement has not tried one.) To a great degree, the history of modern Japan is the assimilation of foreign influences on its own terms: there is always a little *Yamato damashi*—"Japanese spirit"—added to the mix.

This tendency toward chaotic culture sampling is one of the reasons that Japanese soccer is so much fun. It's a mad mish-mash of traditions, styles and conventions from all over the globe. Just take the names of teams playing in J. League, the Japanese professional soccer federation started in 1993. Amalgams of obscure local references and often misused foreign words, the double and triple meanings embedded in these names can be as ingenious as a folded paper crane or a bonsai tree. League champion Gamba Osaka, for example, is named after the Italian word for "leg" but it is also a homophone for a form of the Japanese verb "to try hard." Sanfrecce Hiroshima is a pairing of the Japanese word for "three" and the Italian word for "arrows." It's a reference to a lesson Motonari Mori, a legendary sixteenth-century samurai who ruled the region, is said to have given his three sons to encourage them to stick together: a single arrow can easily be broken, but three arrows bound together are almost impossible to break. Kyoto Purple Sanga combines the English word for Japan's royal color (in honor of the city's status as Japan's former imperial capital) with *sanga*, which in Sanskrit means "group" (its Buddhist overtones appropriate to Kyoto's role as one of

Japan's spiritual centers) and in Japanese means "mountains and rivers" (of which Kyoto has many).

Japan's eagerness to sample and season to taste whatever is on offer from the global cultural buffet—whether soccer or shrimp burgers—stems from at least the sixth century, when Prince Shotoku declared that Buddhism, the new religion recently arrived from the West, was not the total refutation of native Shinto beliefs that it plainly appeared to be but . . . a complement. Such dilettantish syncretism continues to this day. Many Japanese follow Shinto ceremonies at birth, get married like Christians and are buried as Buddhists. But Japan's fascination with foreign modernity began in 1853, when American Commodore Matthew Perry arrived in Tokyo Bay with four black-hulled gunships and an order that Japan open up to foreign trade. After more than two centuries of almost complete isolation (for a long time, attempting even to leave the country was a capital offense), Japan's leaders had little choice but to acquiesce to Perry's superior firepower.

Once the doors were flung open, they would never be shut. In 1868, a coterie of proto-technocrats overthrew the shogunate that had ruled Japan since the seventeenth century and re-installed the emperor as the nation's supreme ruler. Effectively governing on the emperor's behalf, modern Japan's founders believed they needed drastic measures to avoid being conquered by a western power. They embarked upon a massive campaign to catch up to the West, dispatching ambassadors and fact-finding teams throughout Europe and North America with instructions to return with the very best systems of government, education, commerce and technology. From Prussia, Japan adopted its legal system, corporate structure, army and educational system—to this day, boys from many Japanese private schools still wear high-collared blue jackets with gold buttons like so many nineteenth-century Germanic military cadets. From England, Japan took its parliamentary system and navy. From France, Japan adopted a powerful bureaucracy, and the United States was the inspiration for its banking system and the theory (if not the practice) of governmental checks and balances.

But through it all *Wakon yosai!*—"Japanese spirit, Western learning!" —was the rallying cry. In all matters, the Japanese applied a strict code of samurai ethics, a literal worship of the emperor and an adherence to the belief that even foreign technologies were best used in the service of becoming more Japanese. In the 1930s a German economist at Tokyo Imperial University named Kurt Singer pinpointed Japan's combination of "plasticity" and "endurance" as the nation's defining characteristic, its ability to absorb foreign influence while never sacrificing its unique cultural essence.

Until recently, baseball has been the most popular sporting import in Japan—and a perfect example of Japan's expertise at cultural absorption. The Japanese have played baseball since 1873, the country fielded its first professional league in 1936, and since the American occupation at the end of the Second World War, it has overwhelmingly been the country's favorite sport. Baseball may be an American game but the Japanese have transformed it into something completely their own. After playing for the Yakult Swallows in 1987, American Bob Horner said, "I don't know whether the Japanese system is good or not. I just don't understand it." The fundamental disconnect Horner and other Westerners attempting to play in Japan have grappled with is this: sport in Japan has never really been about having fun. It has always been a tool for education and cultural indoctrination. According to Suishu Tobita, the early twentieth-century godfather of Japanese baseball, "Baseball is more than just a game. It has eternal value. Through it, one learns the beautiful and noble spirit of Japan." Japanese baseball is no mere pastime to waste away lazy summer afternoons; it's a method of learning and expressing perseverance, self-discipline and other national virtues.

With militarism outlawed after the Second World War, baseball became a crucial part of Japan's postwar reconstruction. It was the best available means for teaching youngsters Bushido—the way of the warrior. In practice sessions, coaches still emphasize samurai virtues of loyalty and selflessness, obedience and respect for elders, self-control and stoicism. High school, minor league and even

Japan's top-level professional teams undergo punishing workout schedules, subscribing to the belief that strength is forged only through extreme suffering.

Baseball's militarism-by-other-means proved ideal training for young men destined to join the suit-and-tie ranks responsible for Japan's economic miracle. Filled with a sense of mission, Japan's top postwar university graduates headed straight for government bureaucracies, big banks and export manufacturers to become the foot soldiers in the nation's economic reconstruction. The sacrifices they made were tremendous. Every day, middle managers at the Ministry of Finance, Mitsubishi Heavy, Sumitomo Trading and thousands of similar concerns would awake at dawn in their tiny suburban homes and ride the train to work for an hour or an hour and a half. Once there, they would sing the company song, do the company exercises and put in a ten- or twelve-hour day in fluorescent-lit offices where the desks were crammed side by side, from wall to wall. After work, they would drink late into the night with their coworkers, catch the last train home at midnight, and get a few hours sleep before waking up at dawn to do it all over again. In return, Japan's blue-suited *sararimen,* as they are still known, were guaranteed lifetime employment, annual raises, a comfortable pension and the prestige of being a member of the most efficient economic engine the world has ever seen. And for a long time, that was enough.

On weekends and evenings, the salaryman was expected to root for one of the nation's twelve professional baseball teams. Often he would join one of his favorite team's *oendan,* or cheering groups. At first sight, *oendan* are impressive for their seemingly unbridled displays of enthusiasm and highly coordinated cheers, songs and bleacher dances. But they can also be stultifyingly regimented: there are leaders and lieutenants, seating is ordered by rank and seniority, dress codes are enforced and tardiness is punished. On the field, meanwhile, the salaryman sees a person not so different from himself since Japanese ballplayers are not much more than salarymen themselves. Japanese teams are owned by giant corporations, as major sports teams are throughout the rest of the world. But in

Japan, baseball clubs are not expected to make money. They serve primarily as advertising and publicity vehicles. For that reason, teams like the Giants are generally named not after their hometowns (in this case, Tokyo) but for their owner (Yomiuri, Japan's largest newspaper). Other teams include the Orix Buffaloes (financial services), the Hanshin Tigers (railways), the Yakult Swallows (beverages) and the Nippon Ham Fighters (meat packers).

Japanese ballplayers, meanwhile, have to deal with a level of corporate interference in their lives that would be unimaginable in a major league sport elsewhere. Players are not paid well and free agency and salary arbitration are still frowned upon as uppity and ungrateful. Players are subject not just to punishing workouts and abusive coaches but to dress codes, curfews, haircut regulations, drinking prohibitions and limits on outside promotional contracts, ads or endorsements. It looks and feels like work for everyone involved.

But something horrible happened on Japan's way to the twenty-first-century global economic domination. After decades of world-leading growth, the Japanese money engine slowed to a sputter in the early 1990s. Stock prices plummeted and property values cratered. The Japan Bubble didn't so much deflate as explode and then vanish into thin air. The country is only now emerging from fifteen years of economic stagnation, its stock market remains more than 50 percent off its all-time high, its government bonds are less creditworthy than Botswana's, and the lifetime employment that was once considered a Japanese birthright has been replaced by routine layoffs and chronic job uncertainty.

Founding a new professional sports league at a time like this, especially a sport with no real roots in the country, might seem like folly. But the establishment of J. League during one of Japan's darkest periods may well go down as a masterstroke of timing. Soccer is well on its way to becoming a sign of a rejuvenated and dynamic Japan—a symbol for the new as potent as baseball is for the increasingly old and tired way of Japan, Inc.—for an era that's a lot more uncertain and plenty scary, but also far looser, more creative and a lot more fun.

In the early 1990s, top-tier soccer was virtually nonexistent in Japan. There was a corporate amateur league and there were barely remembered stories about a heroic 1968 squad that won a bronze medal at the Mexico City Olympics, but that was about it. Youth soccer was popular, but there was nothing for adolescent players to aspire to and Japan's national team had never qualified for the World Cup. But one member of Japan's national team of the 1960s, Saburo Kawabuchi, had never forgotten a training trip the team once took to Germany. As Sebastian Moffett describes in a history of Japanese soccer called *Japanese Rules,* Kawabuchi was amazed at how deeply entwined the game was with German communities. Parents coached their children's teams, played in adult leagues themselves after work, and on weekends, three and four generations of families would head to the stadium or the nearest TV to watch professional matches. Soccer wasn't just recreation, youth development or entertainment—it was all three, and it was a fundamental part of German life. In Japan, sport was part of being a corporate drone. In Germany, sport was a part of being human.

After years of effort, Kawabuchi finally achieved a critical momentum to get a professional league off the ground in the early 1990s. No doubt Japan's instinctive competitiveness with South Korea, whose national team had become a global up-and-comer in the 1980s, had something to do with it. Japan's increasing awareness that globalism meant more than just friendship with the United States, and that excelling at the world game would improve its international profile, probably helped as well. Once the money was collected and the go-aheads given, the league founders did what the Japanese have always done in such situations: They dispatched committees all over the globe to find the best practices, and then they whipped it together into something uniquely Japanese.

From all over Europe and South America, they adopted the basic league structure. From the International Olympic Committee, they learned how to develop corporate sponsorships. From the American football and basketball leagues, they learned marketing, television licensing, clothing sales and other team-related merchandizing. Following the fashions of the times, most teams adopted either a Brazilian style of play or a German one. Since Japan had no native soccer stars at the time, the league imported legendary players from abroad who were only a few years past their peak—Brazil's Zico, England's Gary Lineker, Germany's Pierre Littbarski—to boost box office sales, to ensure on-field excitement, and to serve as unofficial player-coaches.

Not surprisingly, the quality of J. League was abysmal at first. Playing in 1994 for Jubilo Iwata, Salvatore Schillaci told an Italian paper, "Japanese players couldn't keep up with my dribbling. It is much less tiring than Serie A, but it was quite mentally tiring having to fit in with the low level of the game." True to many clichés about Japanese will and determination, however, Japanese soccer has made huge strides; it may not yet come close to the European and South American leagues, but overall play is not bad and it's getting better all the time. And while baseball remains the more popular sport, it is in persistent decline, while average attendance at J. League matches is now 18,000 a game (up from 11,000 in 1996), more than four hundred games are televised each year, and Japan's national team has qualified for the last three World Cups in a row.

For proof that something different is happening in Japan, however, you need to go to one of the games. In contrast to the oppressive feel of Japanese baseball, Japanese soccer is freewheeling, unburdened, even joyous. The play is loose, expressionistic, wide open. Since soccer is more fluid than the routine stop-and-start of baseball, coaches encourage players to make decisions on their own, to adapt and improvise, to develop their own creativity and individuality. And while practices are rigorous, they are usually devoid of the growth-through-pain samurai histrionics that damages more rising baseball talent than it helps. For all these reasons, Japanese players look and act like they are from a different planet than the automatons playing pro baseball. Shaggy-maned soccer stars argue with the refs, celebrate with abandon, develop signature post-goal victory dances and sulk after a bad play. Hidetoshi Nakata, Japan's top soccer talent is emblematic of this trend. Nakata is a quick-thinking midfielder with an innate gift for knowing where he is in relation to opponents, teammates and the ball. He has said he keeps an aerial view of the action in his head. Brash and independent (but distrustful of the press) Nakata demonstrates a kind of take-it-or-leave-it arrogance that is rare among Japanese athletes. He routinely criticizes the rigidity of Japanese society. "It's a vertical society," he has said. "You must constantly pay respect to the person above you. From the time I was a boy, I didn't feel like this. I felt a freedom from this." Shunsuke Nakamura and Shinji Ono fill out Japan's starting midfield, the team's greatest hope for World Cup glory. Ono is a patient tactician and a devastatingly accurate setup man, renowned for the expert placement of long passes and crosses. Nakamura, meanwhile, is the quiet, introverted artist of the threesome. He often seems oblivious to the world, absolutely lost in concentration before he unleashes one of the bending free kicks for which he is famous.

Japanese soccer fans, meanwhile, are uninhibited and passionate. Soccer has official cheering sections just like baseball does, but they are a lot more spontaneous. While Japanese fans will likely never approach true hooliganism, they frequently demonstrate a degree of naughty behavior unthinkable elsewhere. They boo players. Sometimes, they even boo their own players. For Japan, this is borderline transgressive behavior. Japanese fans have clearly studied the habits of soccer fans around the world and are bafflingly international in their choices of cheers and songs; at any given game, the roiling, hopping die-hard fan section will sing Liverpool's anthem "You'll Never Walk Alone," Spanish-speaking teams' chants of *"¡Campeones, campeones! ¡Olé, Olé, Olé!"* and the classic Japanese exhortation to *"Gam-ba-tte."*

World Cup Record

FIFA Ranking: 15
World Cup Appearances: 2
World Cup Champions: 0
Federation Name: Japan Football Association
Confederation: AFC
Founded: 1921
FIFA Affiliation: 1929
Nickname: Blues
Manager: Zico
Website: www.jfa.or.jp
Stadium: National Stadium
Home Uniform: blue/white/blue
Away Uniform: white/blue/white
Provider: Adidas

1930: Did not enter
1934: Did not enter
1938: Withdrew
1950: Did not enter
1954: Did not qualify
1958: Did not enter
1962: Did not qualify
1966: Did not enter
1970: Did not qualify
1974: Did not qualify
1978: Did not qualify
1982: Did not qualify
1986: Did not qualify
1990: Did not qualify
1994: Did not qualify
1998: First round exit
2002: Second round exit

Matches	Wins	Draws	Losses	GF	GA	GD	Points
7	2	1	4	6	7	-1	7

Japan is 42nd on the all-time World Cup table

Path to Qualification for World Cup 2006

31-Mar-04	Singapore	1	Japan	2	W
9-Jun-04	Japan	7	Indonesia	0	W
8-Sep-04	Indonesia	0	Japan	4	W
13-Oct-04	Oman	0	Japan	1	W
17-Nov-04	Japan	1	Singapore	0	W
9-Feb-05	Japan	2	North Korea	1	W
25-Mar-05	Iran	2	Japan	1	L
30-Mar-05	Japan	1	Bahrain	0	W
3-Jun-05	Bahrain	0	Japan	1	W
8-Jun-05	North Korea	0	Japan	2	W
17-Aug-05	Japan	2	Iran	1	W

Japan qualified by finishing in the top two in Group B of the Asian Zone

Mexico

Capital: Mexico City
Independence: September 16, 1810
(from Spain)
Area: 1,972,550 sq km
Population: 106,202,903
Median Age: 24.9 years
Life Expectancy at Birth: 75.2 years
Ethnic Groups: mestizo (Amerindian-Spanish)
60%, Amerindian or predominantly
Amerindian 30%, white 9%, other 1%
Religions: nominally Roman Catholic 89%,
Protestant 6%, other 5%
Languages: Spanish, various Mayan, Nahuatl,
and other regional indigenous languages
Suffrage: 18 years of age; universal and
compulsory (but not enforced)
Military Obligation: 18 years of age
for compulsory military service,
12-month conscript service obligation;
16 years of age with consent for
voluntary enlistment
GDP Per Capita: $9,600
Budget: $158 billion
Military Expenditures: $6.043 billion
(0.9% of GDP)
Agriculture: corn, wheat, soybeans, rice, beans,
cotton, coffee, fruit, tomatoes; beef, poultry,
dairy products; wood products
Industries: food and beverages, tobacco,
chemicals, iron and steel, petroleum, mining,
textiles, clothing, motor vehicles, consumer
durables, tourism
Currency: Mexican peso

Source: *CIA World Factbook*

Mexico

Jorge G. Castañeda

It has often been said that Mexico takes its prickly individualism to extremes: Mexicans excel at individual sports (boxing, long-distance walking and running, tennis) and perform with mediocrity—at best—in collective ones: baseball and, most important, football. Like every generalization about a country or a people, this one is partly false: Mexico's successes in tennis, boxing and the marathon (except for women, who continue to shine) are every day further in the past, and conversely, our World Cup teams have often distinguished themselves, if not in their results, at least in their teamwork and effort. The home-team advantage helped our 1970 and 1986 national squads reach the quarterfinals; and millions of Mexicans recall Luis Hernández's prowess in France in 1998. Still, our teams reflect our soul, as with so many other countries: somehow we never quite make it to the top, and we are never quite up to our potential.

Yet we rarely abandon our optimism. I remember shamefacedly how our government was so sure in 2002 that we would beat the U.S. during the World Cup in Korea/Japan that, as foreign minister at the time, I called Secretary of State Colin Powell, my colleague in Washington, to suggest that presidents Vicente Fox and George Bush watch the game together at the U.S.-Mexico border. Our aides advised caution: What we would we do if we lost? But Fox and I dismissed their warnings. Inconceivable, we responded; the 2002 team was one of our best ever, and Americans don't play what they call football. For practical reasons, the get-together didn't take place; good thing, as we lost 2–0, provoking a national display of hand-wringing and self-pity.

This year Mexico will be simultaneously watching the World Cup and democratically electing a new president, for only the second or third time in its history. Like elsewhere, the country is much more interested in the former activity than in the latter, but the importance of this year's vote cannot be underestimated. For Mexico is running out of time, and 2006 may be one of its last chances both to do well in the World Cup and to emerge from the lethargy, poverty and disappointment that have plagued it for decades. While it is now perhaps the richest of the poor countries, it is still not, like Taiwan or South Korea, among the poorest of the rich countries. It has proved unable to climb out of the ranks of what years ago was known as the Third World, or underdevelopment; nor has it recovered economic growth rates similar to the ones it achieved between 1940 and 1980, or that countries such as China, India or Chile have experienced over the past fifteen or twenty years.

Thus Mexico today is a nation where half of the population of nearly 110 million lives in extreme or relative poverty (defined as one or two dollars per day in income); where approximately four hundred thousand young men and women leave the country each year seeking opportunities in the United States; where joblessness, delinquency and the absence of the rule of law contribute to poverty, insecurity and a lack of competitiveness; and where nearly a quarter of a century of stagnation and fits and starts have generated a collective frustration alleviated only by individual solutions, as in boxing versus football.

There have been moments of great expectation and excitement. One was during the administration of former president Carlos Salinas de Gortari (1988–1994), particularly when the North American Free Trade Agreement (NAFTA) was signed by Mexico, the United States and Canada, and when Mexico joined the so-called "rich countries club," the OECD. It seemed then that the country was poised for take-off, as the economists' expression goes, and that it was only a matter of time before it would eradicate extreme poverty, establish the rule of law, adopt a political system of a full-fledged representative democracy and open up to the world. By 1994, those hopes were dashed: there were political assasinations, there was the Zapatista uprising in Chiapas, and the economy collapsed at the end of that year. The nation's inhabitants were all the more enraged and disappointed because they had truly believed that Mexico had left many of its travails behind it.

Another episode of hope sprang up in 2000, when after seventy years of virtual one-party rule, the country finally achieved something like the rotation of parties in office, clean elections and a true separation of powers. Vicente Fox became president, the traditional PRI ruling party was swept out of office and the future seemed within reach. It was not to be: mediocre economic growth for six years, legislative paralysis, the breakdown of law and order and the impossibility of reaching any agreement with an American president obsessed with Iraq left Mexico once again mired in frustration and introspection. Also, this year's presidential elections have awakened hopes that Mexico will finally fulfill its enormous potential.

That potential is remarkable. Its mainstay, the diversity and extraordinary creativity of Mexican society and culture, is stronger than ever. A deep sense of national identity, together with the proximity to the world's largest market and wealthiest economy, the depth of pre-Columbian roots along with the cosmopolitan reach of an extensive intellectual and business elite, the political and social stability of a nation where power has been transferred in an orderly and peaceful—if not always democratic—fashion for three quarters of a century: all of this should allow Mexico to at last prosper and enter an age of modernity.

Mexican culture and the creativity of its people in all walks of life are more notable than ever today. The country's artists and architects, its poets and stars, its music and cuisine, its movie directors in Hollywood and its businessmen in Brazil and Spain—are enjoying greater and more widespread fame and fortune than before. Mexico's beaches, archeological ruins and colonial cities attract more visitors than ever, and its exports of creative industries, from recordings to telenovelas, are booming. With a political system that allows for dissent and opposition, an open economy and free trade agreements with myriad nations, increasing respect for human rights and freedom of the media, huge oil reserves (and the highest crude prices in decades), abundant remittances sent home every year by more than 10 million expatriates working in the United States, Mexico has just about everything it needs to break through and become a thriving country. Why hasn't it?

There is nothing more dangerous than pop-anthropology or sidewalk-psychoanalysis when tying to explain why a given country is faring well or poorly. And this is not the place to suggest definitive and complex answers to questions that have left scholars perplexed for many years. So all we can attempt here is to suggest a couple of ideas that may explain why, in an increasingly competitive, interdependent and collective world, Mexico, despite its strengths, continues to disappoint itself.

The first idea has to do with individual solutions. Every society, particularly open and modern ones, allow and even promote individual effort, enterprise, achievement and success. But mostly, this encouragement and realization of individual endeavor occurs *within* those societies; it then contributes to the well-being of that society, of all its members, however unequally. Mexico is different. Perhaps because it is the only poor nation in the world to share a border with a rich one; maybe because family ties are so strong that no other loyalty or solidarity exists except at times of major catastrophy; possibly because all collective intents in the past (the War for Independence, the reforms of the mid-nineteenth century, the Mexican Revolution early in the twentieth century) seemed to have failed: the fact is that in Mexico today individual solutions overpower attempts to work as a collective, as a community, as a nation. Mexicans, of course, take advantage of those individual ways out because they can: because those options exist.

The most expedient way out is obviously emigration. One in every ten Mexican citizens lives in the United States: one of the highest rates of emigration in the world. A quarter to a fifth of all Mexican households receive remittances from abroad, and nearly 40 percent of all Mexicans say they have family north of the border. While the trend used to be concentrated in a few regions, in the countryside and among young males, it has spread to the entire nation, to the cities, and now includes young women as well as older men. More than twelve hundred Mexicans leave their country every day; although many of them are fully committed to returning, few actually do. It can be surmised that despite the unquestionable economic and social benefits of mass emigration, as long as so many Mexicans can hope to solve their problems by leaving, they will not come to grips with them at home.

This situation is not totally uncommon in the world. What could be unique is that Mexico is on the verge of becoming one of the first countries in modern times to export both labor and capital, the latter not simply as portfolio investments, called "flight capital," but in the form of foreign direct investment (FDI) by huge Mexican conglomerates. In 2004 and 2005, investments by Mexican companies abroad almost equaled total FDI in Mexico; and yet more than four hundred thousand emigrants left the country. Why are firms like Telmex, Cemex, Femsa, Televisa, Azteca, Comex, Alpha, Hylsa, Maseca and Bimbo investing abroad? Because it is better business for them individually than to do so only in their country of origin, that is, in their collectivity. In the long term this is probably good for Mexico; in the short run, the fact that Cemex, the world's second or third largest cement company, now produces 60 percent of its output abroad inevitably makes it less concerned about what happens at home. While the Mexican rich and famous have been taking their money out of the country for years and buying up real estate in San Diego, Vail, San Antonio, Houston and now Miami, the corporate and much more profound economic trend is relatively new. It is part of the Mexican search for individual solutions to collective problems.

This is also the case for a growing number of well-trained, talented and successful Mexican professionals: doctors, lawyers, architects, economists, accountants and small entrepreneurs who have expatriated themselves in recent years and are doing better abroad than at home. They miss Mexico, return on occasion, and may misjudge whether they really live better outside their country of birth. But they have that choice, they are taking advantage of it, and that benefit is Mexico's loss: not only of their talent and enterprise but also of the loss of their potential contribution back home.

A second idea involves the Mexican penchant for belief in magic, or more forthrightly, wishful thinking. It is an inclination deeply rooted in impotence and adversity: from the barren hostile environment of the central plateaus where many of the region's inhabitants lived before the Spanish arrived, to the conquest and colonial period itself, and ending with seventy years of largely benign but always oppressive and overpowering authoritarian rule. Out of impotence comes inaction; out of inaction stems the hope that somehow, some way, things will come out all right, but that little can be done in order to achieve that desirable outcome.

This mentality leads to a passive wait-and-see attitude, where strategic thinking, preemptive or preventive action and anticipating events or consequences, are simply nonexistent. On the one hand, destiny decides; on the other hand, luck, the Virgin of Guadalupe or serendipity will make things work out in the end. There is thus no need to plan or to act ahead of time; nothing is inevitable, but nothing can be changed that is already ordained.

In a highly competitive world, in an increasingly complex society, in a democratic political system, this view of life is more and more unsustainable. Getting a head start on the future, avoiding devil's alternatives before they present themselves, knowing that Murphy's Law is in place among and within nations—these are not simply feel-good exhortations from self-help books, but invaluable precepts for economic policy and international affairs. In their absence, it is almost impossible for Mexico to overcome the immense challenges it faces today.

So as it enters World Cup competition in Germany, Mexico faces the clamor of ever-more demanding football fans and of a more impatient society than before. It can disappoint its fans, once again, but shouldn't let down its people.

World Cup Record

FIFA Ranking: 7
World Cup Appearances: 12
World Cup Champions: 0
Federation Name: Federación
Mexicana de Fútbol Asociación A.C.
Confederation: CONCACAF
Founded: 1927
FIFA Affiliation: 1929
Nickname: El Tri (color)
Manager: Ricardo La Volpe
Website: www.femexfut.org.mx
Stadium: Azteca
Home Uniform: green/white/red
Away Uniform: all white
Provider: Nike

1930: First round exit
1934: Did not qualify
1938: Did not participate
1950: First round exit
1954: First round exit
1958: First round exit
1962: First round exit
1966: First round exit
1970: Quarterfinal exit
1974: Did not qualify
1978: First round exit
1982: Did not qualify
1986: Quarterfinal exit
1990: Did not participate
1994: Second round exit
1998: Second round exit
2002: Second round exit

Matches	Wins	Draws	Losses	GF	GA	GD	Points
41	10	11	20	43	79	-36	41

Mexico is 15th on the all-time World Cup table

Path to Qualification for World Cup 2006

19-Jun-04	Dominica	0	Mexico	10		W
27-Jun-04	Mexico	8	Dominica	0		W
8-Sep-04	Trinidad	1	Mexico	3		W
6-Oct-04	Mexico	7	St. Vincent	0		W
10-Oct-04	St. Vincent	0	Mexico	1		W
13-Oct-04	Mexico	3	Trinidad	0		W
13-Nov-04	St. Kitts and Nevis	0	Mexico	5		W
17-Nov-04	Mexico	8	St. Kitts and Nevis	0		W
9-Feb-05	Costa Rica	1	Mexico	2		W
27-Mar-05	Mexico	2	United States	1		W
30-Mar-05	Panama	1	Mexico	1		D
4-Jun-05	Guatemala	0	Mexico	2		W
8-Jun-05	Mexico	2	Trinidad	0		W
17-Aug-05	Mexico	2	Costa Rica	0		W
3-Sep-05	United States	2	Mexico	0		L
7-Sep-05	Mexico	5	Panama	0		W
8-Oct-05	Mexico	5	Guatemala	2		W
12-Oct-05	Trinidad	2	Mexico	1		L

Mexico qualified by finishing in the top three in the CONCACAF Zone

Netherlands

Capital: Amsterdam; The Hague is the seat
of government
Independence: January 23, 1579 (from Spain)
Area: 41,526 sq km
Population: 16,407,491
Median Age: 39.0 years
Life Expectancy at Birth: 78.8 years
Ethnic Groups: Dutch 83%, other 17%
(of which 9% are non-Western origin
mainly Turks, Moroccans, Antilleans,
Surinamese and Indonesians)
Religions: Roman Catholic 31%,
Dutch Reformed 13%, Calvinist 7%,
Muslim 5.5%, other 2.5%, none 41%
Languages: Dutch (official), Frisian (official)
Suffrage: 18 years of age; universal
Military Obligation: 20 years of age for an all-
volunteer force
GDP Per Capita: $29,500
Budget: $274.4 billion
Military Expenditures: $9.408 billion
(1.6% of GDP)
Agriculture: grains, potatoes, sugar beets, fruits,
vegetables; livestock
Industries: agroindustries, metal and engineering
products, electrical machinery and equipment,
chemicals, petroleum, construction,
microelectronics, fishing
Currency: euro

Source: *CIA World Factbook*

Netherlands

Tom Vanderbilt

When a pair of U.S. defense strategists suggested in the *Armed Forces Journal* in 2003 that soccer, with its "dispersed and decentralized leadership" and "autonomous units capable of individual acts," and not the more formulaic and rigid American football, was the paradigm for twenty-first-century warfighting, they might have had Dutch football in mind. The Dutch penchant for managing space and for creating space where none existed before, as David Winner noted in his book *Brilliant Orange,* is renowned. "Dutch football also is about measuring space very precisely," a museum curator tells him. One does not have to explore this metaphor too deeply—the observer of the Dutch landscape will sit on a train, watching the geometrically perfect fields flicker by, intersected by irrigation canals and bounded by low, expansive sky. After a while, the sense of familiarity that had troubled the edge of his consciousness will come into light: This looks like a nation of football pitches.

These thoughts filled my head when, last November, I flew to the Netherlands to spend a few weeks researching traffic. It did not take long to see that traffic in the Netherlands is unlike traffic anywhere else. I took the train one afternoon to the small, charming city of Culemborg—prim church spires, cobblestone plaza with fish market, the ceaseless sounding of the carillon—to speak with Joost Vahl, the retired traffic engineer who invented the speed bump in the late 1960s. He met me at the train station on his bicycle, and proceeded to take my luggage in a set of enormous panniers hanging from the back wheel. Is there another country in the world in which a traffic engineer would arrive by bike? As if to reinforce the point, we spent the rest of the drizzling afternoon examining local traffic schemes—on two wheels.

We weren't alone. The Dutch take nearly a third of their trips by bicycle; no other nation of comparative affluence comes close (the United States manages a paltry 1 percent, the United Kingdom, 8 percent). Outside train stations in cities like Groningen, the ne plus

198

ultra of Dutch cycling, there are sprawling double-decker bicycle parking structures. In the Grachtengordel, the storied district of café intellectuals and primly opulent townhomes in Amsterdam, the streets fill with mothers atop their bikes taking their children to school. Bundled on the front, the back or both, the children seem oblivious to the chill. In the evening rush hour, well-dressed office girls pedal into the night on black Batavias and Gazelles, clusters of yellow tulips wrapped in white paper peeping from the back racks.

For the foreign visitor who considers cycling a hazardous activity, the Netherlands can be a revelation. Bike commuters in America are sweaty, intrepid souls with pant-leg clips and insectoid helmets; the Dutch ride calmly, erect and almost beatific in the seat, and refuse to wear bicycle helmets. In many countries, this puts one in the category of imminent organ donor. But in the Netherlands, where there are more bicycles than cars or people, I was presented with the argument that the avoidance of the helmet is in itself a safety strategy— that to begin wearing helmets would be a capitulation to cars, a subtle message, both internal and external, that cycling is somehow a dangerous activity.

This kind of logic—which is borne out by statistics (one study found the United Kingdom had five times more bicycle fatalities per kilometer cycled than the Netherlands)—seemed emblematic of what I began to take as a kind of Dutch singularity, the idea that I was having a particularly "Dutch moment." These were random as rain. In Amsterdam, for example, I walked into a tobacconist in the hope of buying aspirin for my wife. The proprietor told me, in the fluent English of a diplomat, that he did not sell it but he would gladly give us some of his own. "It's a law, you have to keep a first-aid kit for the employees." Politeness, frankness—very Dutch. In a small town in Friesland I saw a butterfly net of some sort on a pole, flapping in the breeze by the side of the road. "It's a *blikvanger*," my companion said, "so drivers can throw out their cans for recycling." The word *blik* means "can," but somehow *blikvanger* also means something like "eye-catcher." Novel, even whimsical, solutions to social and environmental problems? Very Dutch. Another time, a man told me he had made an effort to visit all the Hollands in America; upon arriving in Holland, Michigan, he informed the oblivious owner of a replica windmill that the position of his vanes indicated he was in mourning. He was promptly feted by the town. Well-traveled and jocular? Very Dutch. Then there was my afternoon in Delft, whose small quaint streets were overwhelmed with packs of parents and children celebrating the arrival of *sinterklaas,* or Saint Nicholas. It all seemed very quaint: The market with sturdy wheels of orange cheese, men milling in the cold eating strips of herring—even the children wearing *sinterklaas* crowns decorated with a familiar set of golden arches, bearing the McDonald's advertising slogan "I'm Lovin' It"—could not sabotage the scene. Then I began to notice the abundance of men, and children, in blackface—*Zwarte Pieten* or "Black Petes," after Saint Nick's capricious helpers, who are said to be based on everything ranging from medieval chimney sweeps to Moorish servants. A potentially fractious (if not fully understood) tradition carried on through sheer force of not getting particularly worked up about things? Very Dutch.

There is nothing more tiresome than the visitor to some country bellowing on with sanctimonious authority about the unique customs of the place—"it's not very *Italian* to order cappuccino after lunch, my dear," or, "in Mexico they just have a less *complex* view of life." And yet, against my own resistance, as I made my way across this small country, I found I could entirely repress the feeling that the Dutch really *are* different from you and me.

The Dutch are the world's tallest people living on the world's flattest land. Actually, the world's second-flattest land (the Maldives, barring any recent tectonic stirrings, still claims the topographical cellar), but this does not deter from the essential point: that the Netherlands, contrary to appearances and reputation, is a place of extremes.

The most famous of these, of course, is population density. The Netherlands, one hears with unnerving regularity, is among the world's most densely populated places. It is usually said in a way to suggest a Boschian panorama of terminal overcrowding, a Malthusian clustering whose inhabitants must surely be pressed to the very edge of the North Sea—which is on the verge of subsuming them.

And yet this place, so teeming with people, is also one of the world's most successful agricultural exporters—some 70 percent of its land is reserved for agriculture. One can, within minutes from Amsterdam, be on what is essentially a quiet country road, looking in vain for those 395 souls that are meant to reside in that square kilometer.

What the Netherlands has been able to do, perhaps better than anyone, is work within its limits, to quietly sublimate those extremes—to do the most with what little it has. It is striking, for example, to note in how many categories, sundry and profound, in which the Dutch lead or are near the top on a per capita basis. The Dutch, for example, have the highest concentration of museums in the world. They have the highest home-birth rate. The most naturists. The highest water quality standards in the world. The most Greenpeace supporters per capita. The highest concentration of Muslim immigrants in the European Union. The most bookshops per capita. The continent's highest rate of broadband penetration. The highest rate of male sterilization in the world. The highest-density populations of pigs in the world. The most energetic consumption of nuts in the European Union. The highest density of international highways in the European Union. The most bicycles per capita in the world and the most cycle trips in the Western hemisphere. The most bicycle thefts. The most theme parks per square kilometer in the world. The highest concentration of psychologists (outside the United States, of course).

Whatever form it takes, Dutch exceptionalism is not new. During its seventeenth-century Golden Age, historian Geert Mak notes, the Dutch had more ships at sea than the English, Scottish and French combined. The English scholar William Aglionby observed of the Netherlands, "In the conversations of wise men, almost no topic features so frequently as the wondrous ascent of this small State, which has risen within no more than a hundred years, to a height which does not only infinitely exceed the standing of all the old Greek republics, but in some ways is not even shamed by the greatest monarchies of our times."

Somehow the Netherlands, with 16 million people, has an unerring ability to find itself the exemplar of some condition, good or bad, with a frequency that far exceeds its size. Perhaps this is because of the way the country often seems some kind of laboratory for social and political innovation (which itself might be the dynamic product of a nation constantly managing physical extremes), so willing to do things differently, which is admirable or confounding depending upon one's point of view, but which often leaves one with the impression that some aspect of national life could only happen here: "Well, it works for the Dutch, but . . ." Perhaps the most prosaic example is the Dutch toilet, the legendary "shallow flusher." I at first took it to be some kind of hydrologic necessity, given the country's high water table. But it seems the result of late-nineteenth-century progressive Dutch health practices—a diligent customs officer viewing one's exports. In which case, why does this device seem to exist only here?

One could not talk of modern Dutch exceptionalism without invoking the country's celebrated tolerance. This may signify much more to the people who visit the Netherlands (its sex and soft-drug emporiums are as touristy as clogs and windmills, a point driven home to me in a head-shop window: a pipe in the form of a wooden shoe, decorated in the style of Delft pottery) than the Dutch themselves. "The Dutch are not that tolerant," a Dutch historian told me one night over a plate of *wurst* speared by little blue EU flags (with outdated numbers of stars) at an European Union function in Germany. "It's just good business." He might have been a *rentier* capitalist talking to me at a seventeenth-century Amsterdam café. "Tolerance was in this town not a mere principle but a practical necessity," writes Geert Mak. "The open merchant city, being the meeting place of all sorts of different cultures, could not allow itself to indulge in the large scale prosecution of those adhering to different beliefs."

It is difficult to imagine the Dutch suddenly becoming like anxious Americans, plastering Dutch flags and "Proud to Be a Netherlander!" stickers on their bike fenders. Such overt national chauvinism just does not seem very Dutch. This might just be "good business," the discovery that a trading nation does better when it checks its sense of national superiority at the door. But this ability to handle problems with seeming sangfroid is not to suggest that the Dutch are immune to the greater problems of Europe, that there is not trouble on the low Netherlands horizon. Statistics tell a striking story: more people left the Netherlands last year than at any previous time since the 1950s.

In football, Dutch exceptionalism is on full display—in attention-getting orange. No country has as many coaches helming national teams in this World Cup as the Dutch, the level of talent the Netherlands produces per capita is staggering (although one might argue Dutch football is only sustainable by imports from Surinam), and it has managed to produce its own technically brilliant model style of play that seems quintessentially Dutch. Melding a German-like organizational prowess with touches of Brazilian flair, Dutch football has for the past few decades strove to perform like a self-organizing system, "total football," in which each highly functioning component part acts independently to achieve a spontaneous network of "organized complexity."

For all its promise, its "embarrassment of riches," the Dutch national team seems to perennially underwhelm in the World Cup. Winner cites political scientists and psychologists who trace this mystery to some deeply seated trait in the Dutch personality, perhaps linked to Calvinism, perhaps a side-effect of keeping national-ism quiet, that winning is ugly, that it is morally wrong to parade one's national triumphalism, the bizarre Cruyffian logic that playing better is better than winning. There is a discernible dearth of monu-ments and statues in the Netherlands, which would seem to speak toward a discomfort with putting people on pedestals (the average Dutchman is taller than the statue in Delft of William of Orange, one of the nation's few heroes). Is it any wonder that *Big Brother,* the show that peered in on a group of noncelebrities living in claustro-phobic proximity, was invented in the Netherlands? Whenever the Netherlands plays in the World Cup, they are on the shortlist of favorites. This year they are ranked third in the world. The question, however, that occurred to me as I cycled by the Ajax stadium one afternoon and watched a warm-up session at the club's De Toekomst ("The Future") youth training facility, is not so much whether the world is ready for the Netherlands to win the World Cup this year, as whether the Dutch are.

World Cup Record

FIFA Ranking: 3
World Cup Appearances: 7
World Cup Champions: 0
Federation Name: Koninklijke Nederlandse
   Voetbalbond
Confederation: UEFA
Founded: 1889
FIFA Affiliation: 1904
Nickname: Oranje (Orange)
Manager: Marco van Basten
Website: www.knvb.nl
Stadium: Amsterdam Arena
Home Uniform: orange/black/orange
Away Uniform: all black
Provider: Nike

1930: Did not participate
1934: First round exit
1938: First round exit
1950: Did not participate
1954: Did not participate
1958: Did not qualify
1962: Did not qualify
1966: Did not qualify
1970: Did not qualify
1974: 2nd place
1978: 2nd place
1982: Did not qualify
1986: Did not qualify
1990: Second round exit
1994: Quarterfinal exit
1998: 4th place
2002: Did not qualify

Matches	Wins	Draws	Losses	GF	GA	GD	Points
32	14	9	9	56	36	+20	51

Netherlands is 12th on the all-time World Cup table

Path to Qualification for World Cup 2006

Date	Home		Away		Result
8-Sep-04	Netherlands	2	Czech Republic	0	**W**
9-Oct-04	FYR Macedonia	2	Netherlands	2	**D**
13-Oct-04	Netherlands	3	Finland	1	**W**
17-Nov-04	Andorra	0	Netherlands	3	**W**
26-Mar-05	Romania	0	Netherlands	2	**W**
30-Mar-05	Netherlands	2	Armenia	0	**W**
4-Jun-05	Netherlands	2	Romania	0	**W**
8-Jun-05	Finland	0	Netherlands	4	**W**
3-Sep-05	Armenia	0	Netherlands	1	**W**
7-Sep-05	Netherlands	4	Andora	0	**W**
8-Oct-05	Czech Republic	0	Netherlands	2	**W**
12-Oct-05	Netherlands	0	FYR Macedonia	0	**D**

Netherlands qualified by finishing first in Group 1 of the European Zone

Paraguay

Capital: Asuncion
Independence: May 14, 1811 (from Spain)
Area: 406,750 sq km
Population: 6,347,884
Median Age: 21.2 years
Life Expectancy at Birth: 74.8 years
Ethnic Groups: mestizo (mixed Spanish
    and Amerindian) 95%, other 5%
Religions: Roman Catholic 90%, Mennonite
    and other Protestant 10%
Languages: Spanish (official),
    Guarani (official)
Suffrage: 18 years of age; universal and
    compulsory up to age 75
Military Obligation: 18 years of age for
    compulsory and voluntary military
    service; conscript service obligation:
    12 months for army, 24 months
    for navy
GDP Per Capita: $4,800
Budget: $1.129 billion
Military Expenditures: $53.1 million
    (0.9% of GDP)
Agriculture: cotton, sugarcane, soybeans, corn,
    wheat, tobacco, cassava (tapioca), fruits,
    vegetables; beef, pork, eggs, milk; timber
Industries: sugar, cement, textiles, beverages,
    wood products, steel, metallurgic, electric
    power
Currency: guarani

Source: *CIA World Factbook*

Paraguay

Isabel Hilton

The Paraguayan national football team, the Guaranis, is named after the largest group of Paraguay's indigenous peoples, the Guarani Indians. On the pitch, they are said to speak in Guarani, rather than Paraguay's official language, Spanish, to confuse their opposition. Like Paraguay itself, the identity of the national team is not what it seems on the surface.

Paraguay is a country with a long history of tragedy: two-thirds of its adult male population were lost in the catastrophic War of the Triple Alliance (1865–1870), in which Paraguay was completely defeated by Argentina, Brazil and Uruguay. It took fifty years for Paraguay to recover. Then, in the 1930s, came the three-year Chaco War to expel an invading Bolivian army, followed by years of instability until the arrival in power of General Alfredo Stroessner in 1954. Stroessner was to dominate Paraguay with remarkable savagery for thirty-five years, and was the longest serving dictator in the Western Hemisphere when he was overthrown in 1989.

Surrounded by hostile neighbors, Paraguay was isolated both by geography and habit, a nation born of the forced marriage of Spanish and indigenous cultures, where the Indians of the past are sentimentalized but the Indians of the present despised.

Though formal Paraguay rarely stops to measure it, the dominant culture is shot through with the indigenous influence. The most obvious is the language of Guarani which is spoken by 75 percent of the population; the herbal remedies sold on the street are derived from the Indian pharmacopoeia; Paraguayan peasant cooking, with its maize dishes, manioc and palm shoots, dates from pre-Columbian days; Guarani military tactics served in Paraguay's appalling wars.

There are formal facts about Paraguay that are in any reference book: it is bordered by Bolivia, Brazil and Argentina; its economy depends overwhelmingly on trade, legal and illegal, primarily with its giant neighbor, Brazil. There is a constitution, a parliament, a set of laws; the economy is predominantly agricultural, producing soy beans, cotton, cattle; there is a high minimum wage and no child labor.

But the Paraguay of reference books, as any Paraguayan will tell you, bears little resemblance to the real Paraguay. The laws are freely broken, often by those who make them; the jails are full of innocent people and the police force full of criminals; children are working everywhere; the statistics on the formal economy are unreliable and the informal economy—mainly in contraband goods—is huge.

Contraband is Paraguay's real national game—from electronic goods to cars, Scotch whiskey and soy beans, timber and cattle, animal skins, currency and drugs. Formal Paraguay has customs duties. The real Paraguay is a free trade area. In formal Paraguay, border guards and military men are charged with stopping contraband. In real Paraguay, they hold the concessions for it.

"Where," I asked a friend in Asuncion when I was last there, "do I go to see contraband?"

He found the question absurd.

"Where do you not see contraband?" he replied.

I went north, to the border with Brazil, to the town of Pedro Juan Caballero, regarded by Asuncenos as a wild and lawless place where arguments are settled with a gun, though Joe Weaver, a Paraguayan of American descent, had lived in Pedro Juan most of his life, he said, without ever seeing a murder. But he had seen a lot of contraband.

We drove through the center of the town, hunting the border with Brazil.

"That's it," said Joe, pointing to a stone marker by the side of the street. Across the street, two soldiers dozed over their rifles.

"Border guards?" I asked.

"Well, not exactly," he said. "They are guarding the car." The car in question sat on a platform behind them. It was to be a bingo prize the following week, if someone didn't steal it first. We crisscrossed the border at almost every block, partly to see how easy it was, mostly to avoid potholes. I soon lost track of which country I was in. This border was clearly no obstacle to smuggling. There was a customs post, but it was far enough away from the border not to trouble anybody.

Pedro Juan was a crossing point for a variety of contraband: cattle on the hoof, which went either way, depending on the price; uncut timber, from Paraguay to Brazil; Brazilian soya beans, which were packaged as Paraguayan to evade Brazilian export tax; stolen Brazilian cars, popularly known as *mau* cars, after the Kenyan *mau-mau* guerrillas, because they always came in the night. (I had met many exasperated Brazilian officials who had spent years fruitlessly trying to stamp out the car racket. They were up against insuperable odds: the last president, Luis Ángel González Macchi, was found to be riding in an armored BMW, his official car, stolen from Brazil.)

Nobody regarded these items as illegitimate, though cocaine and marijuana were slightly less acceptable. There was also an intermediate category of "semi-legitimate contraband" in prohibited animal skins, many of them from endangered species.

"Social attitudes to that vary," said Joe Weaver. "They used to wrap the smuggled cocaine in animal skins and own up to the skins. Now people are getting more ecologically sensitive."

Occasionally someone takes a stand—usually because contraband is threatening his interests. The Paraguayan Rural Association, the cattle ranchers' lobby, had tried to stop cattle smuggling because, during the previous year's cattle fair, between 1,800 and 2,000 head of cattle, some forty truckloads a day, had come across the border and the price had dropped 40 percent in a few days. The Rural Association monitored the traffic and publicly named the smugglers and the buyers, though they stopped short of naming the soldiers and customs men who were letting them through. They demanded action, but nothing had happened.

There had been more success in suppressing timber smuggling after Fernando Mendoça, one of Pedro Juan's biggest businessmen, had worked out an elegant solution. Realizing that it was a business from which everybody profited, he devised a way of bribing officials the same amount to obey the law as they had previously been bribed to break it.

"I called everybody together," he explained, "the sawmill owners, the transport companies, the army, the local officials, the ministry of agriculture officials. The sawmill owners and the transport companies just wanted to work and didn't mind which side of the border. The transport companies the same. So it was simple."

The sawmill owners were paying 6,000 guaranies in bribes to get a contraband log. A new system of permits was set up, open only to those who traded legally, costing 1,500. An extra 4,500, paid to the sawmill owners' association, was distributed to the officials who previously were taking bribes.

"The Paraguayan state, which previously got nothing, is getting 1,500 per permit and the soldiers and officials, who are paid a miserable salary, are getting their 'bonus.' So if they want to be honest, they can," said Mendonça, beaming with the beauty of it.

But not all of Paraguay's contraband trade is as susceptible to imaginative solutions. The illicit trade in animal skins, for instance, goes to the heart of the uneasy relationship between Paraguay's original inhabitants and the colonizing society. Formal Paraguay signed the Cites Convention in 1975, prohibiting the hunting of any creatures on the Cites endangered list, with the exception of Indians hunting for food.

The ban had little effect. In any one of dozens of shops in the capital, everything from whole jaguar skins to snakeskin boots and crudely made crocodile handbags were offered openly for sale. In tourist hotels, traders left leaflets that boasted of their large collections of skins.

One of the prime victims of this illicit traffic was the *yacare,* the endangered South American crocodile, ostensibly hunted by the Indians for food, but mainly targeted for its skin. For the Indian hunters, the poorly paid work brought both income and exploitation. To buy supplies for the hunt—up to 100 kilos of salt are needed to preserve crocodile skins—they had to mortgage the catch to a middleman who lent them a boat and gave credit to their families while the men were away. The hunters, I was told, were often left in debt for what had become risky work: on the Brazilian side, the police had begun to shoot them.

I set out to find a group of Chamacoco Indian hunters who lived near the Rio Negro, in the Paraguayan wetlands of the Pantanal, on the edge of the Chaco, the huge, harsh plain of western Paraguay. The Chaco is a hot, mosquito-infested land of hardship and heroism, the locus of Paraguay's romantic imagination. Originally Indian land, it has been plundered for its precious timbers and animal skins, deforested by ranchers in the great land grab and settled by pioneering communities. There are still forty thousand Indians in the Chaco, from thirteen distinct ethnic groups, but now they live a precarious existence as a labor pool for the colonizers.

To get to the Chamacoco I first had to get to Bahia Negra—accessible by boat, five days upriver from the capital Asuncion—or on the risky flight run by the military company, TAM. I chose TAM. The plane was an old DC8 that had been toasting on the runway in Asuncion's suffocating heat. Luggage was heaped casually inside the bare metal body, cluttering the access to the passenger benches bolted onto the sides. Passengers who boarded quickly, I discovered too late, got the few seatbelts.

The plane hopped up the map, landing first on tarmac strips, then on bare earth as it worked its way north. On board, an air hostess, a miracle of elegance in black, shiny high-heeled shoes and a straight skirt, picked her way around the luggage, precariously balancing a tray of orange juice. The lavatory door yawned open and banged shut. Passengers threw up, discreetly, into airsick bags. Below us, the great Amazonian forest looked like a moth-eaten hearth rug as the smoke from dozens of illicit clearance fires hung in the heavy air.

We touched down in what had been pioneering settlements, like Puerto Casado, the headquarters of a huge Chaco landowning company set up in the late nineteenth century to exploit quebracho, the ax-breaking tree, and the tannin it yields. Other settlers had come later, like the Mennonites, who had fled from Russia in search of religious freedom and who survived their early hardships to establish prosperous, if controversial, colonies.

Bahia Negra felt like a tropical frontier town. Horses grazed placidly on front lawns. The electricity was intermittent. At night, through the open windows, the blare of television—a Brazilian channel as often as a Paraguayan one—drowned the night-croaking of frogs and the whoopings and whistlings from the fauna of the surrounding jungle. In an open courtyard behind the main street an audience of entranced children were watching *A Man Called Horse* on a giant TV screen. It is one of the few Hollywood movies in which the Indians win.

The town was run by the navy in the person of Captain Balthazar Romero, who had 250 men under his command. He was also the law—and agreed that the area was a hotbed of trafficking of every kind. "Skins, drugs, precious stones—it's virtually impossible to control," he shrugged. "There are big ranches with airstrips. Light planes come and go. They don't report to anybody."

The Chamacoco, I learned, were camped another two hours upriver from Bahia Negra, in a settlement called 14 de Mayo and Captain Romero had a patrol boat going up there the next day. The river seemed endless—wide, fast flowing and the color of brown sugar. Vultures turned lazily in the warm updrafts, herons and kingfishers took off in noisy showers of spray. Colonies of cormorants watched us pass and great heavy swamp turkeys flapped inelegantly across the river as we chugged through drifting islands of water iris.

To call 14 de Mayo a place was a slight exaggeration, though it merited a dot on the map. It was founded by an Italian artist and explorer called Guido Boggiani who had come to Paraguay in 1885. Just over a century later, 14 de Mayo consisted of a rotting plank at the water's edge—the landing stage—and one abandoned house. For the Chamacoco, though, it was the location of their creation myth, and sacred ground.

Groups of Chamacoco were sitting, surrounded by bundles of supplies and bags of clothes, fanning cooking fires. They were returning to their villages after a spell of seasonal work in the white man's Paraguay.

It was late afternoon and I pitched my tent and made some food, then swam, as others were doing, to wash and cool off. As I left the river, I asked some Indian boys what fish they had caught. "Piranha," they replied. I decided there was not going to be a lot more washing.

The sun went down with all trumpets blazing and the little camp was wrapped in a vast tropical night. The men sat in a circle talking—low, drifting conversations about fragments of faraway news, heard on the radio and reinterpreted. Then they talked of the hunt.

For them the hunt was both survival and ritual. They hunted birds with slingshots, fish with bows and arrows, larger game with guns. When white men had arrived in the Chaco, it was the hunt that gave the Indians a currency for trade. Both missionaries and commercial traders supplied them with traps, bullets and sometimes guns. They talked of Paraguay as another country, dominated by the white men, a place with which they negotiated as best they could. Small fair-haired children, scattered among the black-haired majority, testified to generations of contact.

Now the hunt had become dangerous: fourteen men from this handful of villages had been shot by Brazilian law enforcement in the previous two years. But the men here had always hunted and they felt it their right. Clemente Lopez, the sixty-eight-year-old patriarch of the group, complained, "I would like to tell the Brazilian president that the crocodiles do not belong to Brazil or to Paraguay but to the Indians, as they always have."

They would not be shot on the Paraguayan side of the river, which marked the border with Brazil. But the idea of a border had little meaning for a people who believed that you cannot buy or sell air, water, land or the sun.

That night a boat slipped away from the bank carrying a pair of hunters. In the morning, I woke to the smell of the night's kill boiling in a black pot over the fire. Clemente spooned a lump of crocodile meat onto a plate and handed it to me.

I looked at it.

"It needs pepper," he said.

I tasted it, gingerly. The sticky flesh still had the skin clinging to it. What might have made a small handbag was sitting on my plate, evidence that this crocodile had not died for the skin trade. It was not the best breakfast I have ever had, but unlike many of the things I had encountered in Paraguay, it was, at least, legal.

World Cup Record

FIFA Ranking: 30
World Cup Appearances: 6
World Cup Champions: 0
Federation Name: Asociación Paraguaya de Fútbol
Confederation: CONMEBOL
Founded: 1906
FIFA Affiliation: 1921
Nickname: Guarani, Albirroja (White and Red)
Manager: Anibal Ruiz
Website: www.apf.org.py
Stadium: Defensores del Chaco
Home Uniform: red white/blue/blue
Away Uniform: yellow/white/white
Provider: Puma

1930:	First round exit
1934:	Did not participate
1938:	Did not participate
1950:	First round exit
1954:	Did not qualify
1958:	First round exit
1962:	Did not qualify
1966:	Did not qualify
1970:	Did not qualify
1974:	Did not qualify
1978:	Did not qualify
1982:	Did not qualify
1986:	Second round exit
1990:	Did not qualify
1994:	Did not qualify
1998:	Second round exit
2002:	Second round exit

Matches	Wins	Draws	Losses	GF	GA	GD	Points
19	5	7	7	25	34	-9	22

Paraguay is 22nd on the all-time World Cup table

Path to Qualification for World Cup 2006

Date	Home		Away		Result
6-Sep-03	Peru	4	Paraguay	1	L
10-Sep-03	Paraguay	4	Uruguay	1	W
15-Nov-03	Paraguay	2	Ecuador	1	W
18-Nov-03	Chile	0	Paraguay	1	W
31-Mar-04	Paraguay	0	Brazil	0	D
1-Jun-04	Bolivia	2	Paraguay	1	L
6-Jun-04	Argentina	0	Paraguay	0	D
5-Sep-04	Paraguay	1	Venezuela	0	W
9-Oct-04	Colombia	1	Paraguay	1	D
13-Oct-04	Paraguay	1	Peru	1	D
17-Nov-04	Uruguay	1	Paraguay	0	L
27-Mar-05	Ecuador	5	Paraguay	2	L
30-Mar-05	Paraguay	2	Chile	1	W
5-Jun-05	Brazil	4	Paraguay	1	L
8-Jun-05	Paraguay	4	Bolivia	1	W
3-Sep-05	Paraguay	1	Argentina	0	W
8-Oct-05	Venezuela	0	Paraguay	1	W
12-Oct-05	Paraguay	0	Colombia	1	L

Paraguay qualified by finishing among the top four in the South American Zone

Poland

Capital: Warsaw
Independence: November 11, 1918
   (independent republic proclaimed)
Area: 312,685 sq km
Population: 38,635,144
Median Age: 36.4 years
Life Expectancy at Birth: 74.7 years
Ethnic Groups: Polish 96.7%, German 0.4%,
   Belarusian 0.1%, Ukrainian 0.1%, other and
   unspecified 2.7%
Religions: Roman Catholic 89.8%, Eastern
   Orthodox 1.3%, Protestant 0.3%, other 0.3%,
   unspecified 8.3%
Languages: Polish 97.8%, other and
   unspecified 2.2%
Suffrage: 18 years of age; universal
Military Obligation: 17 years of age for
   compulsory military service after
   January 1st of the year of 18th birthday;
   17 years of age for voluntary military
   service
GDP Per Capita: $12,000
Budget: $54.93 billion
Military Expenditures: $3.5 billion
   (1.7% of GDP)
Agriculture: potatoes, fruits, vegetables, wheat;
   poultry, eggs, pork
Industries: machine building, iron and steel, coal
   mining, chemicals, shipbuilding, food
   processing, glass, beverages, textiles
Currency: zloty

Source: *CIA World Factbook*

Poland

James Surowiecki

In 1949, the Communist government in Poland broke ground on a new project just outside of Krakow. The project was called Nowa Huta ("New Steelworks") and it was intended to be the ultimate planned community, a place that would blend home and work into a seamless whole while bringing a Haussmannian sense of rigor and order to urban design. At the heart of Nowa Huta was the Lenin Steelworks (later renamed Sendzimir), a massive integrated complex that at its peak produced 7 million tons of steel a year, employed more than forty thousand workers, and owned the largest blast furnace in Europe. Despite its industrial core, though, Nowa Huta was a garden city of sorts, bedecked with parks and lakes, as well as the obligatory cultural center, movie theaters and soccer stadium. It was known as the town without traffic jams.

The garden city is now the rust belt. Over the years, acid rain from the steelworks wreaked havoc on Nowa Huta's environment, and even etched designs into the buildings of Krakow. And while there is less pollution, that's because the arrival of democracy and free market reforms in 1989 forced Sendzimir Steel to slash its payrolls and shut down its furnaces. Today, the company, which was recently sold to the Indian firm Mittal Steel, employs only a few thousand workers and unemployment in Nowa Huta is above 15 percent. Those who do have jobs hope that Mittal will keep the plant open long enough to allow them to make it to retirement.

Not many miles away in Krakow, things look a bit different. There, Motorola has opened a high-end telecom infrastructure laboratory where it can develop and test software for its latest mobile-phone technology. Down the road, IBM is building a new software development lab, too. And the auto-parts manufacturer Delphi has set up both its national headquarters and a technology center in the city. The workers in these companies are not, as you might expect in a country where the average wage is three dollars an hour, engaged in low-skill labor. Instead, they're working on engineering projects that are little different from those an American or British engineer would be given.

The future, William Gibson famously said, is already here—it's just unevenly distributed. There are few places where that's more true today than Poland. From one angle—the angle that encompasses the IBM labs and the coders at Warsaw University, who are among the best in the world—the country looks a burgeoning economic powerhouse. Since the economy in the mid-1990s came out of the massive recession that accompanied the initial introduction of market reforms, it's grown steadily at an annual rate of almost 4 percent a year. A recent survey ranked it the eighth-best place in the world to do business, while IBM put it in the top ten best destinations for research and development jobs last year. Billions in foreign investment now flood in each year, and a city like Wroclaw, in Lower Silesia, has become home to a small-scale technology boom. Hewlett-Packard has a massive business-process outsourcing center there, and Philips is in the process of building a $400 million flat-screen television factory that will create three thousand jobs. Poland is now a member of the European Union, and is often talked about as a potential major player in Europe's economy in the near future.

Poland's success is not exactly a surprise. It was in an excellent position to make the transition from communism to capitalism, because its people were not just literate but well educated, it had historical experience with market capitalism, and civil society in the country had not (as in Russia) been demolished by the Communist state. Poland embraced the free market in 1990 in a sudden leap, and it ended up making the sharpest and fastest recovery from transition of any Eastern European country. From another angle, though, Poland remains a country stuck very much in the past. Since the early 1990s, the unemployment rate has been in the high teens—today, it's around 18 percent. GDP per capita is just 60 percent of what it is in the Czech Republic, and is lower even than in Slovakia. Poles are remarkably hard workers—the average employee puts in almost two thousand hours a year, more even than workaholic Americans do—but only half of working-age adults are actually in the labor force. Most people remain anxious and unsure about what capitalism has wrought. One typical survey found that while a plurality of people would like to own their own business, and a sizeable chunk would like to work for a state-owned company (of which there are still many), only a small percentage would pick, as their first choice, working for a private boss. And while young Poles (40 percent of the population is under thirty) seem more comfortable in the brave new world of work, massive numbers of them now head abroad in search of better prospects—just as the best Polish soccer players, in the wake of entry into the EU, now do. Most of the starters in this summer's national team, in fact, now play professionally in the United Kingdom.

It would be a mistake to say that either Nowa Huta or Wroclaw is the more genuine example of what life in Poland is like today. Instead, it's the contrast between the two that's so telling. But on a deeper level, Poland does not feel like a country enjoying an economic boom. Instead, it's a country where people are deeply dissatisfied with what's happening, and deeply frustrated that the hopes they had for life after communism have not, for the most part, become real. Eight out of ten Poles say they're unhappy with the current state of affairs, which is why last fall Polish voters tossed out their existing government and replaced it with one headed by Lech Kaczyński, a former Solidarity leader who has morphed into a tough-talking member of the center-right.

If there's a single explanation for that unhappiness, it would be corruption. There is nothing that Poles seem to be more convinced of than the fundamental corruptness of politicians, businessmen and bureaucrats. In the popular imagination, the state is little more than a tool that politicians use to enrich themselves and their friends, ensuring that a few will walk away with much while most people are stuck with little. This explains the paradoxical fact that Poles routinely say they want more social programs and more subsidies but also say that the state is spending too much money and needs to be put on a shorter leash. The more money the state has, the thinking goes, the more will end up in the pockets of the well connected.

The corruption is real, and it extends well beyond the government. Last fall, for instance, the chairman of a lower division club revealed that he had bribed referees and other clubs to fix matches, and that his club had been bribed to do the same, and one newspaper reported that referees had actually set up companies in order to launder the payments. But there's little evidence that corruption is significantly worse in Poland than in any other transition or developing country (or, when it comes to soccer, worse than it is in much of Europe), and there's plenty of evidence that it's much better than in places like Russia or Ukraine. Yet Poles understand corruption as pervasive, and assume that people in power are, almost by nature, sleazy. This attitude is an expression of a much deeper conviction, which is that political participation is an exercise in futility. Such a deep-seated distrust of the political realm is a legacy of the Communist era, when the state rode roughshod over its citizens. As Adam Michnik, the legendary Polish dissident and current editor of the country's most popular newspaper, *Gazeta Wyborcza,* wrote, "We inherited the conviction that wisdom is the same as permanent suspicion."

The absence of trust—or of what economists call social capital—is a problem in many developing countries. But what's distinctive about this Polish sense of distrust is that it is directed so specifically at people in power rather than, for the most part, at ordinary citizens. History again plays an important role here, because although the popular image of totalitarianism was of a society completely dominated by the state, that was never true of Poland. In fact, Poland's postwar years were punctuated by a series of massive public uprisings, and while each of them was eventually quashed, the crackdowns were never as violent (or as successful) as in Hungary in 1956 or Prague in 1968. Even more striking, these uprisings were not just small, cadre-driven events. They were instead genuine mass movements, which collectively created a historical memory of popular struggle against the people in power.

The most important of those movements, of course, was Solidarity, which started in a Gdańsk shipyard in 1980 and within the space of a few months had spread across the entire country. Even now it's hard to grasp just how big and how popular a movement Solidarity was. At its peak, 10 million Poles (a third or so of the population) proclaimed themselves members of the organization. Even more amazing, by the end of the uprising a fifth of all Poles (and a fourth of all Poles who lived in cities) had actually participated in some form of demonstration or strike. And while the arrival of martial law and the outlawing of Solidarity in December 1981 obviously pushed the vast majority of Poles off the streets and, in some sense, back aboveground, Poland's peaceful toppling of the Communist regime in 1989 was clearly rooted in the earlier historical moment.

The triumph of Solidarity was one of the great examples in history of the power of peaceful collective action, an overwhelmingly vivid demonstration of the idea that democracy is in the streets. And yet it may be that the lessons learned during the long struggle against totalitarianism have not served Poland all that well during the transition to democracy and markets. The struggle against communism had a kind of moral clarity, an easy separation of us and them, that's poorly suited to the necessary give-and-take of democratic deliberation, which is designed to balance and respect conflicting interests. And decades of dealing with a government that ignored the public except when it was forced to listen has taught Poles that democracy exists only in the streets, that what happens in parliament or in the president's office is nothing more than a prelude to confrontation. In the years after Solidarity formed its first government, Poles kept mounting demonstrations and collective protests (hundreds of them annually) in order to achieve their political goals.

It's a mistake to fetishize the electoral process, especially since it is so often dominated by special interests and manipulated to frustrate the goals of ordinary voters. And mass mobilization is a valuable tool. But the deep-seated hostility to politics, coupled with the faith in mass action, has led people to think of victories as things that either came quickly or not all, which leave them profoundly impatient. In the fall of 1989, as the transition to democracy was getting under way, 61 percent of voters expressed confidence in the government and in Solidarity. Just a year later, only 21 percent of voters had confidence in either. The Poles wanted the world, and they wanted it now, and when they didn't get it, they wanted someone to be punished. Between 1989 and 1993, Poland had eight different prime ministers, six governments, three parliamentary elections and two presidential ones.

Polish soccer has been beset by the same tendencies. While the Poles had once been strong on the world stage—they finished third in the World Cup in 1974 and 1982—the quality of the game declined sharply in the 1990s, in large part because Polish soccer was run as an authoritarian state. After a player strike, new management led Poland back to the World Cup finals in 2002. But when the team was knocked out in the group stage of the World Cup that year, the manager was immediately fired, and the players were attacked for being more concerned with money than with national pride. The logic of autocracy still shapes the way owners, players and fans see the game.

The real problem, in the end, is that ordinary life—life in a democracy and in a free market economy, and even life in the World Cup—is much messier and more complex than life during an uprising or a revolution. Most of what happens in a free society is outside the government's control, and most of what a government can do to make things better takes time and doesn't always work. This is an idea to which Adam Michnik continually returns, the notion that what Poland needs is to be a "society of ordinary people and ordinary conflicts," which is to say a society in which change takes time and not all solutions are ready to hand. Michnik once wrote that he was the "defender of gray democracy," as opposed to one focused on black-and-white. That motto doesn't have the glamor of the martyred demonstrator, or the immediate appeal of a call for moral transformation. But it is the essence of how things actually get accomplished. As the last decade has shown, Poland's natural strengths—its well-educated population, its ideal geography, its strong civil society—are enough to keep the economy moving. But there are too many people who are being left out of this new world. Acknowledging that gray is beautiful may be the first step to bringing them back in.

World Cup Record

FIFA Ranking: 22
World Cup Appearances: 6
World Cup Champions: 0
Federation Name: Polish Football Association
Confederation: UEFA
Founded: 1919
FIFA Affiliation: 1923
Nickname: The White and Red
Manager: Pawel Janas
Website: www.pzpn.pl
Stadium: Slaski
Home Uniform: white/red/white
Away Uniform: all red
Provider: Puma

1930:	Did not participate
1934:	Did not qualify
1938:	First round exit
1950:	Did not participate
1954:	Did not participate
1958:	Did not qualify
1962:	Did not qualify
1966:	Did not qualify
1970:	Did not qualify
1974:	3rd place
1978:	Second round exit
1982:	3rd place
1986:	Second round exit
1990:	Did not qualify
1994:	Did not qualify
1998:	Did not qualify
2002:	First round exit

Matches	Wins	Draws	Losses	GF	GA	GD	Points
28	14	5	9	42	36	+6	47

Poland is 14th on the all-time World Cup table

Path to Qualification for World Cup 2006

4-Sep-04	Northern Ireland	0	Poland	3	W
8-Sep-04	Poland	1	England	2	L
9-Oct-04	Austria	1	Poland	3	W
13-Oct-04	Wales	2	Poland	3	W
26-Mar-05	Poland	8	Azerbaijan	0	W
30-Mar-05	Poland	1	Northern Ireland	0	W
4-Jun-05	Azerbaijan	0	Poland	3	W
3-Sep-05	Poland	3	Austria	2	W
7-Sep-05	Poland	1	Wales	0	W
12-Oct-05	England	2	Poland	1	L

Poland qualified by finishing as one of the two best second-place finishers of the European Zone

Portugal

Capital: Lisbon
Independence: 1143 (Kingdom of Portugal recognized); October 5, 1910 (independent republic proclaimed)
Area: 92,391 sq km
Population: 10,566,212
Median Age: 38.2 years
Life Expectancy at Birth: 77.5 years
Ethnic Groups: homogeneous Mediterranean stock; citizens of black African descent who immigrated to mainland during decolonization number less than 100,000
Religions: Roman Catholic 94%, Protestant 2%
Languages: Portuguese (official), Mirandese (official, but locally used)
Suffrage: 18 years of age; universal
Military Obligation: 18 years of age for voluntary military service
GDP Per Capita: $17,900
Budget: $79.86 billion
Military Expenditures: $3,497.8 million (2.3% of GDP)
Agriculture: grain, potatoes, olives, grapes; sheep, cattle, goats, poultry, beef, dairy products
Industries: textiles and footwear; wood pulp, paper, and cork; metals and metalworking; oil refining; chemicals; fish canning; rubber and plastic products; ceramics; electronics and communications equipment; rail transportation equipment; aerospace equipment
Currency: euro

Source: *CIA World Factbook*

Portugal

William Finnegan

Every village worth its salt had a *campo de futebol*. Prazeres, up the mountain, had one. Calheta, the next place on the coast to the east, had one. Even low-down, raggedy-ass Paul do Mar had one. Why not Jardim do Mar? This was a hot question when I first started spending time in Jardim, in 1994, and the short answer was topography. Jardim sits on a small, storybook headland in southwestern Madeira, squeezed between the sea and towering cliffs. The village is a dense little patchwork of red-tile-roofed houses, terraced fields and narrow, often stepped, meticulously paved footpaths. There simply wasn't room for a soccer field. There was hardly even any flat ground.

Ah, but look behind the *quinta*—the manor house. There, in a saddle between the lane leading down to the boat ramp and the bottom of the mountain wall, was a surprising amount of land. It was terraced, and thickly planted with bananas, but not steep. It could be cleared and leveled. The land belonged to the *quinta* family, the Vasconcellos, traditional overlords of Jardim do Mar. The family's members all lived in Lisbon now, or Funchal, the capital city, at the far end of the island. But here, as the village council gathers its courage to approach the *quinta* family, or its lawyers, the dense shadow of Madeira's history starts to fall across events. No outsider, no foreigner, could possibly gauge the true weights of grievance, usage, status, entitlement and payback that all participants carried into their negotiations over the soccer-field proposal.

I didn't care, especially, how it came out. I was in Jardim for the surf. When there were waves, it was impossible for me to think about anything else. When there were no waves, all right, I took an interest in the place. And I despised the *quinta* family on principle. The feudal bastards had run the place for centuries. All Madeira had been divided up and handed out, complete with serfs and slaves, to factions and individuals on the lower half of the Portuguese crown's long list of toadies. There were old people in Jardim who remembered when villagers were required to carry priests and rich people up and down the mountains in hammocks. This was before the road was built down from Prazeres, in 1968. There had been a fat priest whose visits were particularly dreaded. And the island's history, the farther you looked back, only got darker.

But I liked Jardim as it was. I liked the dark-green terraces of bananas. I liked the constant light, gulping music of spring water rushing off the mountain—it ran down through the village, through an intricate system of gutters, watering all the fruit and vegetable gardens. I even liked the crumbling pink *quinta* house, with its ornate little private chapel. Did every village really need a soccer field? It would fill the air with dust every time a hard southeasterly blew, which it all too often did. Look at Paul do Mar.

It was actually difficult not to look at Paul. The two villages face each other across a mile of sea, with no other settlements in sight. The shoreline between them is forbidding: a narrow, canted tangle of rocks that can disappear altogether at high tide. Cliffs rise straight from the shore, and huge red jagged boulders lie brutally at their base, some half-submerged. When I first started going to Jardim, I was rebuked by a young village woman for walking under those cliffs—her brother, she said, had been killed by falling rocks there. But a glorious wave broke midway between Jardim and Paul, off a small point known as Ponta Pequena, and I kept making the walk.

There was a fantastic, if fickle, wave at Paul do Mar as well. From Jardim, with binoculars, you could watch it stand up, throw out, and peel ferociously. The drive over the mountain took forty frantic minutes. Everything could change—the wind could come up—during the drive, no matter how fast you took the dozens of hairpin turns. Whatever the waves were doing, when you got to Paul do Mar, you entered a different world.

The village stank, for a start. At the east end, by a small wharf where fishermen pulled their boats up a ramp, it was fish stench. To the west, where the surf was, it was lavatorial—people used the shoreline rocks as an open-air toilet. Paul do Mar was slovenly, semi-industrial. There was primitive worker housing strung along the sea-facing road. Dirty, half-naked children jeered at strange cars. Roughly half the adults in Paul do Mar on any given day seemed to be falling-down drunk.

And yet Paul had a *campo de futebol*. It had the necessary flat acreage. The field sat behind the school, just across from the waves. It had concrete bleachers, a clubhouse, even a small parking lot. There were always kids out there kicking a ball around. The village had a team. In Jardim I had heard plenty about what low-lifes the people of Paul do Mar were. In Paul, as I slowly met a few people, I heard about the snobbery of Jardim folk, in their jewel-like hamlet. The rivalry was apparently deep, centuries old. It wasn't the only reason people in Jardim wanted a soccer field, but it was right up there.

But negotiations with the Vasconcellos did not go well. The *quinta* family was unwilling to give up its land for this, or any, communal use. Shortly after talks came to a halt, someone snuck into the *quinta*'s fields at night and chopped down all the banana trees. The following winter, when I came back to Jardim, the fields had still not been replanted. My landlady, Rosa, smirked when I asked about it. She seemed to believe that replanting would just inspire more vandalism. What I couldn't tell was whether she thought the attack on the bananas was justified peasant revolt or a shameful, destructive act. I have never been able to figure out what people in Jardim really think about anything remotely political.

Rosa's house was on the point. When the surf was big, mist and roar filled the air. Paul do Mar and Ponta Pequena were serious surf spots, but the marquee wave on Madeira was Jardim. On a good day, the lines marched out of the west, bending around the headland into a breathtaking curve. They feathered and bowled and broke at the outermost point of the horseshoe, and then reeled down the point with hypnotic power and beauty. It was a high-performance wave that could, at full fury, humble nearly any surfer in the world. At night, when it was big, there was, at Rosa's place, a general roar—a deep, bass throb that was not the sea but the rocks underneath the point, groaning.

Rosa's husband was in England, working at a fast-food restaurant at Gatwick Airport. Rosa herself had worked at the same place, and it had left her with a vivid dislike of the British. She had two rooms that she let to visiting surfers. Both were tiny and bare, but they looked straight down on the wave at Jardim. The eight dollars a night I paid didn't seem to brighten the family financial picture much. Rosa's mother lived with her, and the two of them would walk up the mountain to Prazeres, a grueling one-hour hike, rather than pay a few escudos for the bus. Like all rural Madeirans, they had formidable legs.

The village gardens were lush, yes—bananas, papayas, avocados, cabbages, mangos, oranges, grenadilla. And virtually every house had its grape vines for wine, as well as flowers in well-tended, subtropical profusion. But never mind the appearance of bounty. The story of Jardim, and of Madeira's peasants generally, is a melancholy fado of poverty, oppression and isolation.

Foreigners often think Madeira's main export must be wine, but it's actually people, labor. The island has been unable to support its own population since the mid-nineteenth century. I remember, when I was a kid, living in Hawaii, there were tough, clannish kids at school whom we called Portagees. Most of them, I later understood, were from Madeira. Their ancestors had come to work in the cane fields. South Africa, the United States, England, Venezuela—every Madeiran seems to have relatives living overseas. When Antonio Salazar, the mid-century Portuguese dictator, tried to export his surplus-peasant problem to his colonies in Angola and Mozambique, a great many Madeirans joined the exodus. Most became farmers (cotton, cashews). Eventually, inevitably, many served as soldiers. Even little Jardim do Mar had, among its few hundred residents, several veterans of the anticolonial wars.

One of these fellows told me that, as hard as the Africans fought to throw out the Europeans, they secretly loved Portuguese culture. Look how closely they still follow Portuguese *futebol,* he said. I've worked as a journalist in Mozambique, and what he said about *futebol* was true, at least in the cities. He and I were watching, at the time, a mainland soccer match on TV in a village bar—a bar owned by a sweet guy named João who, as it happened, lived many years in Africa himself. Both teams seemed to have, I thought, more than their share of African players.

Madeira is to the mainland as Portugal is to Europe—farther south and west and, at least traditionally, poorer. It's Portugal's Portugal. As such, it was in line for a slew of European Union grants after the EU started shoveling money into its "underdeveloped regions" in the 1990s. To the extent that I was paying attention, this enormous transfer, worth hundreds of millions of euros in Madeira alone, was in rare accord with my idea of the benign (perhaps the only benign) face of economic globalization: richer countries helping poorer countries, directly.

But I wasn't paying attention. I was surfing, which meant getting to know small bits of coast as intimately as possible. When there weren't waves, I was reading or writing about distant topics, or swimming in the sea—checking out underwater hazards, trying to stay fit. I sometimes hung out with other visiting surfers. And I spent a lot of time worrying about the secret of Madeira's great waves getting out.

In surf magazines, which are the main bourse of surf gossip, a complex discretion surrounds the identification of newly discovered spots. Stunning photos of Madeira's waves were turning up all over the world, but the American mags, at least, were loath to name the place. The Portuguese mags weren't so shy. They splashed the name across their covers, ran huge articles. They were, oddly, claiming the waves for Portugal. It seemed to be a size thing. Lacking a continental shelf, Madeira, like Hawaii, gets surf bigger than the mainland does, and this fact seemed to fuel the indiscreet, chest-beating jingoism in the Portuguese mags. *They* now had a big-wave spot. The first Madeira poster I saw showed a mainland pro riding a huge green wall at Jardim, which the caption called "the largest wave ever ridden on Portuguese national territory."

But there was another, less dramatic picture in the same magazine that stopped me. It was a wide shot, taken from the mountainside, of Paul do Mar on a day of big, glassy, immaculate waves. There was no one in the water. In the foreground was the soccer field, with two uniformed teams playing and dozens of onlookers, their backs turned to the surf. The caption identified and located Paul in scandalous detail, and asked, "Could it be that some day we will see this soccer field empty and the lineup full?" The editors' attitude was hard to read. They seemed to feel competitive with the popularity of *futebol*. Did they *want* the surf at Paul to get crowded?

Then, one night, the Portuguese national team turned up in Jardim. I wasn't familiar with the concept of a national surfing team. It's not a team sport. But I was impressed by how impressed the villagers were. This was, by God, *the national team*. They surfed *for Portugal*. They wore official windbreakers, like Olympic athletes— or the beloved national *futebol* squad. To me, of course, they were just a bunch of scruffy young rippers.

But I was fascinated by the coach. I never spoke to him. I just watched him climb slowly out of his rental car one morning in the village square. He had his wife with him, and a toddler in a stroller. He wore his official windbreaker, and matching warm-up pants, and he looked bored. Lanky and pale, he did not look like a surfer, or even an ex-surfer. He looked like a sports administrator, or a phys-ed teacher, or maybe a soccer coach. What fascinated me was his ordinariness, his ease. Where I grew up, surfing was a wild thing. You did it with your friends, or you did it alone, but it happened out in the ocean, and could not be socialized. When I first went to Australia, I was shocked by how pervasive and presentable and clubbed-up surfing there was. It *could* be socialized, and here, in cozy, remote Jardim, I was catching a glimpse of my old anchoritic obsession being integrated into Euro-yuppie social-democratic norms. Just a glimpse.

I understood, or thought I did, about feudalism and isolation. The ancient, despotic order of Church and nobles thrived where contact with the outside world was meager. In Jardim the arrival of electricity, of TV, of the paved road from Prazeres—these were each, despite their drawbacks, blasts of spiritual oxygen. On a surfless Sunday morning, I heard a sermon in the village church by a visiting Brazilian priest extolling liberation theology. You would not have heard that when the only way into Jardim was by goat trail or open boat.

The local passion for building a soccer field was, among other things, part of the general yearning to connect the village more firmly to the greater world. At least one young Madeiran, a poor kid from Funchal named Cristiano Ronaldo, had made it big playing for Manchester United. Ronaldo—he was named for Ronald Reagan, of all people—is on the Portuguese national team. He drives a silver Porsche. Every boy in Madeira, according to my sources, wants to be him.

Now surfing was connecting Jardim to the world. My heart sank when I heard that Billabong, the beachwear company, was sponsoring a "big-wave contest" on Madeira. More wanton publicity. I made sure to be home in New York City when the contest happened. People in Jardim seemed happy about it, though. More surfers meant more money coming into the village. Some of the visitors were uncouth, true, and a few village boys were taking up the sport, which was absurdly dangerous, but crowds in the water were of no concern to the villagers. Indeed, most people in Jardim seemed thoroughly bored with surfing.

That wasn't always the case. The first time I surfed Jardim, back in 1994, a crowd gathered on a terrace below the church. I was with my friend Peter. We weren't the first surfers that people in the village had seen, but close. They cheered when one of us caught a wave. They seemed to know a good ride when they saw it. More than that, they knew their patch of ocean exceedingly well, and they soon started whistling us into position. A piercing whistle meant that a big wave was coming and that we needed to paddle farther out. A more piercing whistle meant we needed to paddle faster. A gentler whistle meant we were in the right spot. We surfed till dark, and that evening we ate in a café in the village. We wanted to thank the whistlers, maybe buy them a drink, but people were shy, not used to strangers.

When we left that year, Peter gave his board to a village kid named Orlando. The next year we found Orlando scooting along on the white water that washed through the rocks on small days. He had astonishing balance, and was already learning to turn. More than that, he was fearless. He jumped from boulder to jagged boulder in the

Jardim shallows, often with a board under his arm. I had never seen such feats of tidepool agility. His confidence came in part, no doubt, from having grown up on these rocks, but Orlando, it occurred to me, was also probably a hell of a soccer player.

On days when the surf got very big, and returning to shore without being smashed against the headland became a daunting proposition, villagers came out on the seafront to help us get in. At dusk they brought flashlights, fiercely signalling the best route and the best moment to try. Plenty of people thought we were idiots, of course. Once, after a particularly hairy episode, an old woman berated us for risking our necks, and the happiness of our families, in a sea that had claimed the lives of many local fishermen. Did we have no respect? This was before most Jardineiros got bored with surfing.

Suddenly, one autumn, they were building a tunnel from Jardim to Paul. It was like the setup for an absurdist joke. A highway tunnel, nearly a mile long, through a mountain of rock, to connect two tiny fishing villages that hated each other?

Yes, and work was under way from both ends. In fact, they were building bridges and tunnels all over Madeira, furiously spending EU grants for "transport infrastructure." These projects would produce, according to the EU, "time savings." In the meantime, they were producing jobs for Madeirans and windfall profits for politically connected corporations and local contractors. Graft and corruption were rife—that was what people said. But I saw nothing about it in the papers, where the local strongman and regional governor, Alberto João Jardim (no relation to the village), seemed to preside over a ribbon-cutting on some vast new erection every day. There was a rush to build before the EU admitted Eastern European nations that would then start getting these grants.

Were the rumors of corruption true? It was hard to know. I was a tourist, just here to surf, thanks. There was certainly a form of madness loose on the island. It was a time to make money—in a place where there had been, through the centuries, precious few such opportunities. Plenty of older people seemed stunned, watching the tranquil, terraced hillsides they had known all their lives bulldozed into flyovers for sleek new highways. In Jardim I heard people fret that, once the tunnel was finished, drunken louts from Paul would come streaming through, turning Jardim's quiet square into a reeking hangout. Still, men from Jardim had jobs in the tunnel, and their families were thankful for that. It beat emigrating to Venezuela.

We got bad surf that winter. I spent too much time staring at waveless, wind-torn ocean. At low tide the villagers picked *lapas* (limpets) off the exposed rocks. There was a dwarf, Kiko, who went for *lapas*, but his legs were too short for clambering across big slippery rocks, and his struggles were painful to watch. At high tide, though, Kiko spear-fished off the point, and then he was in his element. His swim-fins and his masked head looked huge, at either end of his muscular, abbreviated body. He would disappear underwater for what seemed like minutes. People said he wriggled fearlessly into crevices where the octopus hid. Born and raised in Jardim, Kiko knew every boulder in the sea off the village. He sold his catch to a local café, the Tar Mar, where his octopus was a house specialty. I often ate it.

Another specialty was *espada*—a sweet-fleshed, monstrous-looking, deep-water fish that was caught offshore. The Madeiran coast is so steep that the water turns blue-black—the color of deep ocean—unusually close to shore. I would study the movements of the small boats working the bank off Jardim. On still nights they would stay out, their yellow lights bravely knitting the blackness under a sheet of stars.

The Portuguese national anthem is "Herois do Mar"—Heroes of the Sea. And "The Lusiads," the sixteenth-century epic poem that enjoys pride of place in the country's literature, is oceanic in both rhythm and subject, celebrating Vasco da Gama's voyage to India in more than a thousand stanzas of ottava rima. The poem is fantastical, and too ornate for most modern tastes, but it is terrific on the sea and ships. Small details come radiantly into focus, just as they do in the architecture of the Portuguese Empire's golden age—the Manueline style, it's called, after King Manoel I. Even in the stone-carving around church doors of the period, the finest details (bits of perfectly rendered coral, shockingly accurate seaweed) are invariably maritime. Henry the Navigator, King John II—the Portuguese Renaissance was brief but rich, and solidly sea-centered. By the time Luis de Camoes, a hard-luck patriot and sailor and the author of "The Lusiads," wrote his masterpiece, the Inquisition was on, of course, and the empire was in terminal decline—already in hock to German bankers.

I sometimes wondered if the keening, nostalgic sadness of the fado, the national folk music, which is itself often sea-themed, came from a pervasive sense of lost grandeur. More likely, I was just hearing the fado's Arabic taproots. Portugal, like Spain, has always been western Europe's interlocutor and borderland with Morocco and Muslim North Africa.

Madeira was discovered in the early days of Portuguese exploration, in 1420. The island was uninhabited, and heavily wooded. The settlers cleared the land by burning the primeval forests. One great fire burned out of control, according to legend, for seven years. Madeira became a center of the sugar trade, and then the slave trade. Later its big export was wine. Everything came and went by sea, and in that sense, too, the island was more Portuguese than Portugal: it was even more thalassic. Madeira's economic mainstay today is tourism.

At night, because there was no roar of surf, I could hear the machines, the blasting, inside the mountain—the work on the tunnel to Paul. Sleepless in my dank room, I imagined Adamastor, a sea-monster made of rock in "The Lusiads," "Scowling from shrunken, hollow eyes / Its complexion earthy and pale, / Its hair grizzled and matted with clay, / Its mouth coal black, teeth yellow with decay."

I got a nasty cold. Rosa's mother, Cecilia, came down with the same thing. She blamed her illness, though, on a fruit seller who had failed to wash the pesticides off a batch of custard apples she bought. We went together, in my car, to a clinic down the coast in Calheta. Cecilia was coughing, her eyes swollen. We kept passing men with big yellow jerry cans strapped to their backs and wandlike nozzles in their hands. These contraptions were pesticide sprayers. Cecilia glared at the men, muttering.

But we each got well in time for Carnival, a local *festa*—nothing to do with the famous blowout in Rio de Janeiro—that's celebrated on Shrove Tuesday. In Jardim people were gathering at the Tar Mar that night. Rosa and Cecilia and Rosa's little niece and nephew were rigging up party costumes. They dressed me in an atrocious lime-green wig and big disco sunglasses. Rosa snickered that I looked like an Englishman, and we all headed over to the café.

At least half the village was at the party. The jukebox was blasting samba, Europop, fados. Most people were in costume—little kids in superhero capes and bunny rabbit outfits, with many adults done up, to my surprise, as ugly, oversexed women with huge breasts, huge pillow-enhanced bottoms, big wigs and rubber masks with deep wrinkles and too much makeup. A certain hysteria surrounded these flamboyant hags, mainly because one really couldn't tell if the person inside the costume was male or female. The painted ladies were dancing and carousing and flirting outrageously, but were careful not to speak. I was no doubt more in the dark than any local about who was actually who, but the giddy confusion and sexy buffoonery were general. And a collective delirium seemed to build through the evening as the wine flowed and the music pounded and laughter broke in great waves against the ceiling. It was a brilliant party and, surrounded by witty disguise, I had never felt closer to the secret, unspoken, communal life of Jardim do Mar.

Derelicts from Paul do Mar did not invade the square. The tunnel was finished by the next winter, amazingly, and it seemed to be scarcely used. Certainly I never saw any drunken pedestrians in there. It was long, dark, musty. It was also stunningly convenient for surfers. The waves in Paul were now five minutes' drive away. Everything in Madeira was getting closer fast. Funchal, which had been a tough three-hour drive from Jardim when I first visited, was now less than an hour. Of course, I dreaded the implications of easier access. It could only mean more surfers. The surfwear companies had now staged two "big-wave contests" at Jardim. An Australian pro had won the first one. A Tahitian power surfer known as Poto—an international surf celebrity—had won the second. Not good. Meanwhile, little Orlando had become an expert surfer, and other Jardim kids were starting to learn. Orlando now had a shed full of boards given to him by visitors.

The waves were still magnificent. That, at least, would not change, I thought. What did I know?

I began to hear rumors that year—this was early 2001—about a "promenade" that the government wanted to build around the Jardim seafront. This made no sense. At high tide, the sea crashed against the cliffs. I talked to a building contractor in the village about the rumors. He said he supported the project. He was vague about what it might entail. He said it would be modest, if it were even built—just a little paved walkway. I said it would be impossible to build. And who would ever use it?

Later that year my daughter was born, and the next winter was for me a blur of life with baby. I didn't make it back to Madeira for two years.

The promenade, in the meantime, had turned into a roadway, and by the time I came back it was under construction.

The project had not been unopposed. A surfer from California named Will Henry, who had been coming to Madeira, organized protests. Environmentalists, geologists, biologists and surfers from both Portugal and abroad met and marched in Funchal and in Jardim. The threat to the great wave at Jardim wasn't the only rallying point—there were other surf spots being buried under other boondoggles, including new marinas, and, it was argued, the EU-driven construction boom was damaging Madeira's coastal ecology as a whole. The protesters revealed that one of the main beneficiaries of the huge new construction contracts was in fact a company owned by the son-in-law of Alberto João Jardim, the regional governor.

Governor Jardim went ballistic. He called the protesters "communists." He said that surfers represented "barefoot tourism," not the type that Medeira wanted. He even mocked their understanding of ocean waves: "Surfers? They're a bunch of fools who must think the waves break from land to sea. So what if the waves break here or fifteen meters further in the water? The waves will always be the same."

The reception that the protesters got in Jardim do Mar was hostile. Local men associated with the ruling party chased them from the village, hurling food and abuse. Even Orlando was run out. Will Henry got hit in the face. Who were these foreigners, these barefoot fools, to think they could stop progress in Madeira? Construction went forward.

I returned to the island in October 2003, having heard about some of this, and decided not to stay in Jardim. My wife and daughter came along, and we stayed up the mountain at an inn in a seventeenth-century *quinta* house. The inn had a small pool that looked out on the ocean. My daughter, not yet two, called the ocean "big pool." Driving down into Jardim with a surfboard on my car, I felt people turning away from me in the square. I imagined they were ashamed. Or maybe they just hated surfers now.

The devastation along the shoreline was hard to comprehend, even while standing beside it. I had said it would be impossible to build a walkway, but that was because I lacked imagination. Vast quantities of rock and dirt had been trucked in and dumped along the waterfront, right around the headland. The job was not complete, but it was clear now that, with enough fill, they could build an eight-lane freeway along the coast if they chose. Huge yellow earthmovers were roaring back and forth on the landfill, which was not yet paved. In a plume extending from Jardim, the ocean was milky-brown with mud. And between the half-built roadway and the water was the most hideous seawall I have ever seen—a gray heap of giant concrete slabs. It was aggressively featureless and yet painful to the eyes. This was the new shoreline. Brown wavelets lapped against the slabs.

Governor Jardim, of course, was wrong. For the descendant of a seagoing race, his ignorance of the sea was impressive. Waves don't move offshore when you bury a reef. They simply smack into whatever is where the reef was. Still, I found it hard, staring at the destruction in Jardim, to grasp its finality. Maybe on a very big day, at low tide . . . Even in the rare circumstances under which surfing here might still be possible, however, an always dangerous spot would have become orders-of-magnitude more dangerous. Meanwhile, the ravishing beauty of the shore as seen from the water—the cliffs and terraced fields of bananas, vegetables, papayas and sugarcane between the point and the cove—had been expunged, replaced by a sinister industrial wall. Accept it: the great wave was gone. Like the tide pools where Jardineiros had harvested shellfish for generations, and the boulders and shallows where Orlando had leapt like a klipspringer and Kiko had speared his octopus, it was now buried under ten thousand tons of crushed rock.

I talked to a few villagers. I heard rationales for the new seawall and roadway. They would help protect the village from the sea. More villagers would be able to drive cars closer to their houses. They represented progress—other villages, after all, had such improvements. Tourists, someone even told me, would come to admire the sea from the new road. These comments were offered sheepishly, or defensively, or belligerently, or halfheartedly. There was some truth to some of them, none to others. The brute fact was, the authorities had decided to build the project for their own reasons, financial and political, and the villagers had had no say in the matter. Joao, the sweet tavernkeeper, was fatalistic. "You think you're living in paradise," he said. "And then . . ." He gave an eloquent shrug—the gestural equivalent of the fado.

Rosa was less diplomatic. Indeed, she was spitting mad. She denounced the whole fiasco, and she named names—who had profited, who had lied. Her rooming-house business had dried up, of course. Talking to Rosa, I realized that I had finally got what I wanted: there were no other surfers around.

There was still surf, though—at Paul do Mar and Ponta Pequena, if not Jardim. We stayed for two weeks and, when there were waves, I surfed, alone. But I was unlucky—it never got good during those two weeks. We hiked in the mountains, along the great system of irrigation canals, known as *levadas,* that striates Madeira. The *levadas,* many of them hand-built by slaves, are falling into disrepair as the economy shifts from agriculture to tourism. Meanwhile, at the refurbished *quinta* house where we stayed, the other guests, who were Danish and German and French, groused about how all the new construction along the coasts was destroying Madeira's charm.

Cristiano Ronaldo didn't seem worried. He had been spotted checking out a palatial new house in Ribeira Brava, not far east of Jardim, looking to buy. Ronaldo is often reported, in the British press, to have grown up in a "tin shack." I sometimes felt like the only person in Madeira who wasn't fascinated by Ronaldo. The regional government even gave him, on World Tourism Day, a Tourism Medal of Merit, explaining that more British tourists were now expected to visit because Ronaldo played in Britain. I hadn't known there was a World Tourism Day.

I remembered that Portuguese surf-mag photo of Paul do Mar, with the soccer field in the foreground. The editors, I decided, really were jealous of the popularity of *futebol*. I didn't grow up with soccer, so the whole thing was hard for me to understand. Certainly I would never grasp even a subconscious wish to see big, clean waves become crowded. Surfers seek a bare canvas, a pure encounter with the ocean, full stop. Besides that, Paul do Mar, when the surf is big, is extremely dangerous. In soccer, as far as I know, nobody dies, or even confronts the possibility.

One morning, after checking the surf (small and bad) at Paul, we got stuck in our car behind a parade. The village had been celebrating the feast of its patron saint for several days. The streets were festooned with blue paper flowers strung from rough striped poles, but everything was fairly dirty and wind-tattered by that point. A school band was going at a slow pace from the boat ramp to the church, blaring gamely, blocking the road. Behind them staggered several dozen men, drunk. My daughter was transfixed by a marching boy who clutched an arsenal of homemade rockets. The rockets were long sticks with their business ends jammed into a hood made of newspaper. Every few paces the boy would slip a rocket from the sheath, take a cigarette from his mouth, light a fuse, and casually, as if flicking away rubbish, point the missile back over his shoulder and, without looking, let fly. It would shoot away with a rising whistle for several seconds and then give a surprisingly loud bang. Nobody but us seemed to jump at the bangs. This, I thought, was real Paul-style merrymaking.

We finally reached the tunnel, zoomed away and emerged at the Jardim end. The tunnel mouth sits slightly above the village, and we stopped there. Jardim do Mar, from that height, looked like it was drowsing in the sun; the sea was mud-brown and waveless. We were directly above the *quinta* house of the Vasconcellos. Its fields, no longer planted, were the main staging area for the construction on the seafront. Bulldozers, cranes, cement mixers, dump trucks were parked at random angles across a broad expanse of scarred dirt. Behind the beautiful old private chapel, more concrete slabs for the seawall were stacked in rows. I wondered how the Vasconcellos, those feudal bastards, felt about this use of their land. It was another one of those things that an outsider could never know. But the chances that the fields of the old manor house might yet become a *campo de futebol* seemed improved.

World Cup Record

FIFA Ranking: 10
World Cup Appearances: 3
World Cup Champions: 0
Federation Name: Federação Portuguesa
de Futebol
Confederation: UEFA
Founded: 1914
FIFA Affiliation: 1923
Nickname: Selecao das Quinas (Team of the
Escutcheons)
Manager: Luiz Felipe Scolari
Website: www.fpf.pt
Stadium: Estádio Nacional
Home Uniform: red/green/red
Away Uniform: white/dark blue/white
Provider: Nike

1930: Did not participate
1934: Did not qualify
1938: Did not qualify
1950: Did not qualify
1954: Did not qualify
1958: Did not qualify
1962: Did not qualify
1966: 3rd place
1970: Did not qualify
1974: Did not qualify
1978: Did not qualify
1982: Did not qualify
1986: First round exit
1990: Did not qualify
1994: Did not qualify
1998: Did not qualify
2002: First round exit

Matches	Wins	Draws	Losses	GF	GA	GD	Points
12	7	0	5	25	16	+9	21

Portugal is 23rd on the all-time World Cup table

Path to Qualification for World Cup 2006

4-Sep-04	Latvia	0	Portugal	2		W
8-Sep-04	Portugal	4	Estonia	0		W
9-Oct-04	Liechtenstein	2	Portugal	2		D
13-Oct-04	Portugal	7	Russia	1		W
17-Nov-04	Luxembourg	0	Portugal	5		W
30-Mar-05	Slovakia	1	Portugal	1		D
4-Jun-05	Portugal	2	Slovakia	0		W
8-Jun-05	Estonia	0	Portugal	1		W
3-Sep-05	Portugal	6	Luxembourg	0		W
7-Sep-05	Russia	0	Portugal	0		D
8-Oct-05	Portugal	2	Liechtenstein	1		W
12-Oct-05	Portugal	3	Latvia	0		W

Portugal qualified by finishing first in Group 3 of the European Zone

Saudi Arabia

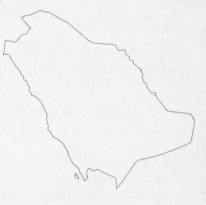

Capital: Riyadh
Independence: September 23, 1932
  (unification of the kingdom)
Area: 1,960,582 sq km
Population: 26,417,599
Median Age: 21.3 years
Life Expectancy at Birth: 75.5 years
Ethnic Groups: Arab 90%, Afro-Asian 10%
Religions: Muslim 100%
Languages: Arabic
Suffrage: adult male citizens aged 21
  or older
Military Obligation: 18 years of age (est.);
  no conscription
GDP Per Capita: $12,000
Budget: $78.66 billion
Military Expenditures: $18 billion
  (10% of GDP)
Agriculture: wheat, barley, tomatoes, melons,
  dates, citrus; mutton, chickens, eggs, milk
Industries: crude oil production, petroleum
  refining, basic petrochemicals, ammonia,
  industrial gases, sodium hydroxide (caustic
  soda), cement, construction, fertilizer,
  plastics, commercial ship repair, commercial
  aircraft repair
Currency: Saudi riyal

Source: *CIA World Factbook*

Saudi Arabia

Sukhdev Sandhu

The fatwa is adamant: "Play in your normal clothing, or in pajamas, but not in colorful shorts and numbered jerseys. Shorts and jerseys are not appropriate clothing for Muslims. They are the clothing of the nonbelievers and of the West, and therefore you must be careful not to wear them." Colorful shorts a crime against Allah? Numbered jerseys an infidel act?

Issued in 2003 by Sheikh 'Abdallah Al-Najdi, and printed by the Saudi newspaper *Al-Watan* in August 2005, the fatwa forbidding soccer—except when played as training for Jihad—lists fifteen prohibitions, including:

> Don't play soccer with four lines [surrounding the field], since this is the way of the nonbelievers.

> One should not use the terminology established by the nonbelievers and the polytheists, like: "foul," "penalty kick," "corner kick," "goal" and "out of bounds." Whoever pronounces these terms should be punished, reprimanded, kicked out of the game and should even be told in public: "You have come to resemble the nonbelievers and the polytheists, and this has been forbidden."

> Do not set the number [of players] according to the number of players used by the nonbelievers, the Jews, the Christians and especially the vile America. In other words, eleven players shall not play together. Make it a larger or a smaller number.

> Do not play in two parts [i.e. halves], but rather in one part or in three parts, so as to be different than the sinful and rebellious, the nonbelievers and the polytheists.

> When you finish playing, be careful not to talk about the game, and not to say "we play better than the opponent," or "so-and-so is a good player." Moreover, you should speak about your

body, its strength and its muscles, and about the fact that you are playing as [a means of] training to run, attack and retreat in preparation for Jihad for Allah's sake.

If one of you inserts the ball between the posts and then starts to run so that his companions will run after him and hug him, like the players in America and France do, you should spit in his face, punish him and reprimand him, for what do joy, hugging and kissing have to do with sports?

It's difficult to take seriously, especially when the fatwa's solution to adjudicating whether certain fouls are worthy of yellow or red cards is not, as Western commentators and talk-radio listeners are always demanding, making more sophisticated camera technology available to referees, but rather the use of shari'a law: "the injured player must testify together with [his tackler] that so-and-so tripped him up intentionally."

Some of these laws sound as if they could be a lot of fun. How wonderful it would be if tripped-up players, rather than shouting "foul!" were compelled to cry something on the lines of "Infamy" or "O egregious turpitude!" How right in an age when onfield scuffles are increasingly subjected to police inquiries that all mid-match spats should be resolved by a theocratic version of justice. How beautiful if those forwards who toe-poke a two-yard sitter and use the occasion to go on to tumble, pirouette and hop-skip-jump across the pitch in carefully choreographed dance formations more suited to cheerleader routines in American football were to find themselves being drenched in a jeroboam of their teammates' phlegm.

It's more sobering to learn, from an earlier story in *Al-Watan*, that three players belonging to the well-known Al-Rashid team had abandoned the game after reading the fatwa, and that one of them, Majid Al-Sawat, was later arrested while planning a suicide bombing attack in Iraq.

Football has always had a strange history in Saudi Arabia. It was banned until 1951, though no one seems to know why. Matches that kick off as late as 8:30 are played in glutinously humid conditions and in temperatures hot enough to make even camels start a go-slow strike. Few European or South American players of any stature have opted to while away their dotage there. Turkish crowds have been known to greet foreign fans at European Championship fixtures by unfurling huge flags bearing the slogan "Welcome to Hell"; Saudi Arabia lacks even that kind of diabolical renown.

Saudi Arabia doesn't need football. Despite the economic downturn of the mid 1980s, it is seen as Bedouin-bling territory, a resort nation whose citizens enjoy the kind of luxurious, boutique lifestyles that are the envy of those who live in other Middle Eastern states and acts as a magnet for the dispossessed of the earth who dream of nabbing service-sector jobs there. Until recently, it was the largest importer of cars, home-entertainment systems, yachts and executive aircraft per capita in the world. Families, accustomed to having foreign servants clean their homes, drive their children to school in huge, oil-guzzling autos, spend their money on designer labels and international produce from upscale supermarkets, and take their holidays abroad (Saudi, despite its small population, ranks among the top ten nations when it comes to splashing out on foreign tourism).

Modern Saudi is a child of the 1950s. The discovery of oil parented it. Immediately, the country went cash crazy, moving from desert wilderness to gleaming metropolis, a backwater lacking schools, hospitals and paved roads into a global financial giant. New industrial cities were established: Jubail, on the Gulf; Yanuba, on the Red Sea. Mega-malls, stadia, airports, highways and hotels replaced the sandy pastoralia of old. Citizens grew up expecting to receive free cradle-to-grave healthcare as well as free education up to doctoral level. They paid minimal taxes, and were able to maintain high standards of living because of the country's vast army of imported labor (as much as 40 percent of its population of 25 million—though that's nothing compared to the United Arab Emirates where it's estimated that only 12 percent of the country is of native stock). These incomers have replaced the Jordanians and Palestinians who were kicked out after the first Gulf War for fear that they would band together to form a massive "enemy within"; the new migrants are drawn from Egypt, South Asia and most of all from the Philippines. Manning the petrol pumps at garages or patrolling hotel lobbies by day, and sleeping twelve to a room at night, their grim and muted lives represent the dark heart of Saudi's new gold dream.

The country's petro-dollar-funded affluence was most gaudily symbolized by the excesses of its five thousand princes; rumors abounded that they routinely arranged for their Cadillacs to be dumped in the desert as soon as the ashtrays were full. Young people in Saudi expressed themselves by shopping rather than by dribbling footballs. Even those who developed a passion for the game had not grown up making do with stones or oranges or tightly wound stockings instead of leather balls. They lacked the hunger, the favela fervor possessed by the ragged and shoeless in other countries. Football was entertainment, optional; it wasn't a cry of freedom, an expression of vernacular creativity. Its players have never pulled off an upset like Algeria's victory over Germany in 1982 or Cameroon's win over Argentina in 1990 or Senegal's anticolonial coup over France in 2002. They've never been seen as ushering in a new era of stylish football such as the one Pelé thought he detected among African national teams. They have injected no note of brio—no samba gaiety, no hip-wriggling sensuality, no athletic back flips.

In a country noted for its secrecy, statistics about the Saudi Arabian team are patchy and hard to get hold of; national officials, caring little about how they are perceived outside their own borders, make getting access to their top performers a tricky business; players routinely amass many dozens of caps without being known to even the most conscientious foreign reporter. Every so often, one hears whispers about a national player not being Saudi at all, but coming from Sudan or from Cameroon. It would be hard to find out if such stories were true, and certainly not in any reporter's self-interest. As such the country has rarely tugged the imagination of even hipster football fans.

Since 1994 when the game was professionalized, only two Saudis have gone abroad (Sami Al Jaber to Wolverhampton in England, and Fahd Al Ghashayan to AZ Alkmaar in Holland). The Saudi Arabian

Football Association apparently fearing that its players might not be ready for the rigors and discipline of foreign leagues, has sought to stop would-be exiles from leaving. The result is a cosseted league system, bankrolled by princes and the state rather than by local entrepreneurs, in which most of the excitement is generated by the rare arrival of European and Latin American expats such as Frank LeBoeuf and Gabriel Batistuta who jog around serenely for a season or two in order to pick up one last big pay packet before they retire or start looking for managerial positions.

Riyadh's Al-Hilal and the Jeddah-based Al-Ittihad supply most of the players for the national side, and even there the standard of play rarely rises above mediocre. Part of the problem is money. Not the lack of it, but its relative abundance. According to the Brazilian Carlos Alberto Parreira who coached them in the run up to the 1998 World Cup (for a tidy sum), Saudi players are only professional inasmuch as they get paid; they lack, however, the necessary attitude: they lack hunger, drive, ambition. Perhaps Saudi is just too rich to be good.

The perception of Saudi's undeserved affluence and delusions of greatness makes its national team detested across the Middle East. They are the Germany of the Gulf states—regarded as a joyless, arrogant and wealthy juggernaut. Everyone seems to want them to get a hiding. They're overdogs, the region's America-affiliated bullyboys whose footballing ethos is widely thought to mirror its cruel social and economic polity. Small wonder that the Iranians, who back in the 1960s were the area's most successful team, hate them: when they play each other the atmosphere is volatile with the clash of competing ideologies—radical Islamism versus U.S.-leaning lackeyism, Shi'ite versus Sunni, insurgent peasantism versus corporate capitalism.

Traditionally the Saudis cleave to a kind of Arab exceptionalism, a defensive mentality that means, no matter how humiliating a defeat or disjointed and witless their display, the players themselves escape censure; it is the coach who cops the flak. As often as not these coaches are imported labor—of the obscenely remunerated type. They come laden with plaudits and personal honors. They are heaped with gifts and goodwill as soon as they touch the airport runway. But they rarely speak Arabic, and when results fail to live up to the exaggerated fantasies of fans and federation officials, they are summarily booted out.

The speed and ruthlessness of these sackings can shock outsiders. In 1998, Carlos Alberto Parreira, who just months earlier had led Saudi to a creditable 0–0 draw against England at Wembley, was told to pack his bags just two games into the World Cup. A couple of years later, former Czech Republic coach Milan Macala was given the elbow after the very first game of the Asian Cup: a 4–1 defeat to Japan. More recently, following losses to Iraq and Iran in the West Asian Football Federation Cup held in Qatar last December, Argentinian Gabriel Calderón was fired. His replacement is Brazilian coach Marcos Paquetá, who up until then managed the high-flying Al-Hilal club side; how long will he last?

What's clear is that here, as on so many other issues, it's the outsider who gets blamed and demonized; never those born in the country itself. The underlying principle—success at an international level cannot be bought off the shelf—seems not to have sunk in. Like Bangladeshi workers cleaning the trash on the country's city streets, these white champs and trophy winners, signed to manufacture instant success, are little more than hired help.

This state of affairs may improve over time. It will have to. In the same month that *Al-Watan* published (to wide consternation) the anti-soccer fatwa, King Fahd, the country's leader since 1975, died of a long illness. The man who had turned the country into the Monaco of the Gulf region had been in poor shape since a major stroke in 1995. Even before that, the Saudi bubble had been slowly deflating: oil prices began falling in the mid-1980s. The population has been rising at a rate of more than 3.5 percent a year, and jobs for graduates have been scarce. The country's poor human rights track record has been attacked by foreign activists. And the decision to allow American troops into the country helped boost Islamist opposition forces.

Fahd's long paralysis seems, in small measure at least, to mirror the condition of the national football team, and his latter-day invisibility opened up a space for pseudo-scholars and agitators to inveigh against a sport they saw as an example of the very modernity and cosmopolitanism they were prepared to plant bombs and subsidize terrorists to vanquish. Success this summer could be just the fillip the nation needs. It might, just might, swell the hearts of young men who would otherwise be tempted to cling to the pristine orthodoxies of local imams. "What do joy, hugging and kissing have to do with sports?" The answer, in Saudi Arabia as everywhere else, is everything.

World Cup Record

FIFA Ranking: 33
World Cup Appearances: 3
World Cup Champions: 0
Federation Name: Saudi Arabian Football
   Association
Confederation: AFC
Founded: 1959
FIFA Affiliation: 1959
Nickname: Sons of the Desert
Manager: Gabriel Humberto Calderon
Website: www.saff.com.sa
Stadium: King Fahd International, Riyadh
Home Uniform: white/green/white
Away Uniform: all green
Provider: NA

1930: Did not enter
1934: Did not enter
1938: Did not enter
1950: Did not enter
1954: Did not enter
1958: Did not enter
1962: Did not enter
1966: Did not enter
1970: Did not enter
1974: Did not enter
1978: Did not qualify
1982: Did not qualify
1986: Did not qualify
1990: Did not qualify
1994: Second round exit
1998: First round exit
2002: First round exit

Matches	Wins	Draws	Losses	GF	GA	GD	Points
10	2	1	7	7	25	-18	7

Saudi Arabia is 42nd on the all-time World Cup table

Path to Qualification for World Cup 2006

18-Feb-04	Saudi Arabia	3	Indonesia	0	W
31-Mar-04	Sri Lanka	0	Saudi Arabia	1	W
9-Jun-04	Saudi Arabia	3	Turkmenistan	0	W
8-Sep-04	Turkmenistan	0	Saudi Arabia	1	W
12-Oct-04	Indonesia	1	Saudi Arabia	3	W
17-Nov-04	Saudi Arabia	3	Sri Lanka	0	W
9-Feb-05	Uzbekistan	1	Saudi Arabia	1	D
25-Mar-05	Saudi Arabia	2	South Korea	0	W
30-Mar-05	Kuwait	0	Saudi Arabia	0	D
3-Jun-05	Saudi Arabia	3	Kuwait	0	W
8-Jun-05	Saudi Arabia	3	Uzbekistan	0	W
17-Aug-05	South Korea	0	Saudi Arabia	1	W

Saudi Arabia qualified by finishing in the top two in Group A of the Asian Zone

Serbia and Montenegro

Capital: Belgrade
Independence: April 27, 1992 (as self-proclaimed successor to the Socialist Federal Republic of Yugoslavia)
Area: 102,350 sq km
Population: 10,829,175
Median Age: 36.8 years
Life Expectancy at Birth: 74.7 years
Ethnic Groups: Serb 62.6%, Albanian 16.5%, Montenegrin 5%, Hungarian 3.3%, other 12.6%
Religions: Orthodox 65%, Muslim 19%, Roman Catholic 4%, Protestant 1%, other 11%
Languages: Serbian 95%, Albanian 5%
Suffrage: 16 years of age, if employed; 18 years of age, universal
Military Obligation: 19 years of age; 9 months compulsory service
GDP Per Capita: $2,400
Budget: $10.46 billion
Military Expenditures: $654 million (% of GDP not available)
Agriculture: cereals, fruits, vegetables, tobacco, olives; cattle, sheep, goats
Industries: machine building (aircraft, trucks, and automobiles; tanks and weapons; electrical equipment; agricultural machinery); metallurgy (steel, aluminum, copper, lead, zinc, chromium, antimony, bismuth, cadmium); mining (coal, bauxite, nonferrous ore, iron ore,
Currency: euro, Yugoslav dinar

Source: *CIA World Factbook*

Serbia and Montenegro

Geoff Dyer

I first went to Serbia, for a seminar organized by the British Council, in 1992, in the middle of the war in Bosnia. There were no flights to Belgrade so I flew to Budapest and drove—more accurately, was driven—the rest of the way, a journey of several hundred miles and frightening speed.

At the seminar I was often asked by Serbian intellectuals—publishers, writers, journalists, academics—what I knew about their country. I replied that on the way back from Greece, in 1978, our bus had broken down and we'd stayed a night at the Hotel Yugoslavia in Belgrade. The ill-fated bus continued breaking down after it was fixed, after we had left Belgrade, and we spent many hours adding verses to "Welcome to the Hotel Yugoslavia," a poignant and apparently interminable version of the Eagles hit. I said that members of the SOE seemed always to be parachuting in here—to the Balkans, at least—during the Second World War. I used the word "partisans," I said "Red Star Belgrade," I said that at home I had a copy of Ivo Andric's *The Bridge Over the Drina,* and that I liked the Turkish coffee that was served during the eleven o'clock break. I did not say that, if we were being completely honest, I was a little hazy about the difference between Serbia, Croatia and Bosnia. And after I left? Then I would have said that if I had not gone to Belgrade I would not have read Rebecca West's *Black Lamb and Grey Falcon* (a book which came to mean as much to me as any I have ever read) and that, like West after her first visit to the region, I longed to return.

I've since gone back several times, most recently in October 2005. The weather was freakishly warm. If it had been like this in London, in June, we would have termed it a heat wave. It was summer, basically, with autumnal foliage thrown in. Leaves were the color of the dust they were already turning into. Everyone was out on the streets, baring arms, demonstrating their support for the weather. Some people were just out strolling, looking at the windows of expensive shops, but I was on a whirlwind tour, what my friend Natasha called an anti-sightseeing tour, featuring damage caused by the NATO bombing in 1999, much of it still unrepaired. It was difficult not to be impressed by the accuracy of the bombing. Whole streets are intact except for the odd building (the army headquarters on Nemanjina Street, for example) which looks, frankly, as if a bomb has hit it. There was a time, about a lifetime ago, when much of Europe looked like this. Now there are just these odd pockets of destruction: monuments, in a way, and warnings. If you sow the wind you must expect to reap the whirlwind—but there's no guaranteeing that that will be the end of it. When you've reaped the whirlwind you dream of sowing a retaliatory hurricane. Everyone wants to have the last word. (One of the reasons the guns kept firing right up until 11 A.M. on November 11, in 1918, is because everyone wanted to be able to say that they had fired the last shot of the Great War.) When it comes to history there is no end in sight—or in sightseeing.

After a while, though, you have to sit down and have a coffee. If Turkish coffee is the anti-cappuccino then several places in Belgrade serve what might be termed the anti-anti-cappuccino—an epic foamy thing aspiring to the condition of a knickerbocker glory. Although everyone speaks English, Natasha did the ordering. I say ordering but that fails to convey the full complexity of what was involved. Suppose we wanted two coffees. This would begin as an exchange of pleasantries, turn into a conversation, before gradually assuming the intensity of a quarrel. To lodge even the simplest request was to enter a volatile series of negotiations. If we wanted something to eat the discussions would drag on and bog down; ordering a starter, main course and dessert would be akin to agreeing the fine print of the Dayton Accord. It often seemed as if these exchanges were on the brink of erupting into a blazing row; then I realized it was actually a form of flirting.

Once we had finalized the ordering we talked of our respective nations. Natasha loved hers. I complained about mine. It was, I said, a land of high prices and breathtaking inefficiency.

"You should have been here in the 1990s," she said. "You wouldn't have lasted two months. Nothing worked."

"Yes, but that's because it was in the process of disintegrating.

What's our excuse? England is one of the richest countries on earth. Relative to its wealth England is not just more inefficient than Serbia; it's actually the most inefficient country on earth."

"You don't understand. I don't just mean a few things didn't work. Nothing would work out. That's an understatement obviously. *Everything* turned out as badly as it possibly could. Or worse."

Natasha said this, I could not help noticing, with a certain pride.

Ordering had been complex, paying was straightforward, brusque, as if the ritual of flirtation were not to be sullied by reference to money. Even so, Natasha had trouble converting the cost of our coffees into euros.

"I'm terrible with numbers," she said.

"I thought you had a postgraduate degree in mathematics."

"Mathematics has nothing to do with numbers," she snapped.

And history, she might have added, has nothing to do with dates. They have no sense of history, the Serbs—not history as we in Britain understand the term. We know that in 1066 there was a Battle at Hastings, that in 1916 the army suffered a disaster at the Somme but we know, also, that these things—especially the former—took place in the past and that the Battle of Hastings took place long before the one at the Somme. Serbs know about all the massacres and battles of the past as though they happened . . . I was going to say yesterday but I mean today, tomorrow even. History is the name given to the wound and the wound is still fresh. If it heals then you are no more than a scab. Surprisingly, this means that Serbs are not burdened by history, it doesn't weight on them, as ours does, like a damp greatcoat. It is not even *in* their blood; it *is* their blood. Faulkner might have had Serbia in mind when he wrote, "The past is never dead. It's not even past."

It happened that this sense of timelessness was in the air when I was in Belgrade. There was no wind. None at all. A shuttlecock dropped from an airplane would have floated straight down to earth. Wind is time, movement, change. The stillness here was like an unending present. Anything that happened now had already happened, everything that had ever happened was happening now. In the evening we walked around the ruined walls of the Kalemegdan fortress, looking across the river, toward the lights and hotels of New Belgrade.

"Belgrade is a city of bridges," I said, in 1992, when we'd first walked here.

"Like most cities."

"But this one has hills too," I said now.

"Other cities have hills too," Natasha said.

"Yes," I said. "But not these hills, and not these bridges."

The Danube and the Sava were there in the darkness, unseen and unmoving. Nothing moved.

Least of all the traffic. The traffic is bad in Belgrade but—as my taxi driver pointed out the next day—the traffic is bad everywhere.

"Show me city where traffic is not bad. You have not shown city at all," he said. Belgrade, by this definition, is certainly city. A good deal of my time there was spent in taxis but a relatively small part of that time was spent in motion. We jumped and lurched, accelerated and braked. We mounted the pavement. We did everything we could to obtain some tiny advantage over the other vehicles which, in turn, were doing everything in their power to creep fractionally ahead of us. All of this places passengers and drivers alike in a state of extreme stress and agitation. It is worth remembering. however, that the relative calm of driving in the United States or Britain—a shared willingness, however reluctant, to abide by the highway code—is actually anomalous. In most countries—even France and Italy— driving is anything but a sedate or organized activity. It is a free-for-all, a life or death scramble which works to the detriment of everyone involved. Here, though, it was difficult to resist the conclusion that something in the Serb soul craves gridlock. (How does this translate into football? Packing the midfield? Playing for a draw and hoping to sneak through in injury time—as the amber turns to red, so to speak—or on penalties?) We had been waiting at a set of traffic lights for several hours. Many changes later we came to the very brink of the intersection. Our light was showing red but we were filled with the pleasant certainty that at the next green we would be moving. Then, just as the lights were about to change, a car sprinted forward a few yards and blocked the junction even though no advantage could be gained from having done so. Our lights changed to green. We did not move. On the other side of the car blocking our way the road was clear. Our light turned to red and then to green again and still we did not budge. The only recourse was to get on the horn, to send out what was intended as a honk of protest and complaint but which, as more and more people joined in, took on a quality of triumph. As everyone on all sides started honking so it seemed that we were noisily celebrating a wedding or the winning goal in a football game.

Exactly *whose* winner is a moot point. I could be wrong, could have been unduly influenced by Rebecca West's belief "that acceptance of tragedy . . . is the basis of Slav life," but it should not be assumed that all teams attending the World Cup actually want to win it. We hear much about the will to win; the idea of choking is taken as a tightening up, a defeat brought about by wanting too badly to win. But there is also a *will to lose*. We English know all about this. Chris Waddle succumbed to it in Italy '90. Something in his English heart—and in ours too—*craved* defeat, shame, the taste of ashes in the mouth. The urge does not usually manifest itself so simply. Ideally one wants to feel wronged, cheated, robbed, betrayed. The Serbs will not win the World Cup but they might achieve their goal: to crash out as a result of some error of their own which is either compounded by or—even better—indistinguishable from a decision by referees or linesmen who have been duped by the cunning of the opposition who are themselves in cahoots with FIFA. "Only part of us is sane," writes Rebecca West, "only part of us loves pleasure and the longer day of happiness, wants to live to our nineties and die in peace, in a house that we built, that shall shelter those who come after us. The other half of us is nearly mad. It prefers the disagreeable to the agreeable, loves pain and its darker night despair, and wants to die in a catastrophe that will set back life to its beginnings and leave nothing of our house save its blackened foundations."

History plays a part in this. No one in England can remember anything about football from before the 1966 World Cup. But in Serbia, I imagine, people remember incidents and talking points from every game since the dawn of time. This also occurs within the context of an individual match. X fouls Y because Y fouled him because he was fouled by X . . . As I understand the Serbian mentality there are always prior offenses to be taken into account. That's why the Serbian writer Vesna Goldsworthy begins *Chernobyl Strawberries,* her memoir of growing up in Belgrade, with an epigraph from Wittgenstein: "It is difficult to find the beginning. Or better; it is difficult to begin at the beginning, and not to try to go further back."

Such thoughts were very much in my mind because of a show at the Museum of Contemporary Art. This was the second exhibition I had seen in Belgrade. The first, which I had also visited with Natasha, back in 1992, was entitled "Crimes against Serbs." It was a collection of photographs of bodies with their brains splattered out, their throats cut. Strangled with wire, beaten, set on fire, shot. Bodies that had been killed three or four times over. The photos of the dead—some from early in the twentieth century, in black-and-white, others from a few years ago, in full-bleed color—were juxtaposed with pictures of the victims when they were just old people or mothers or girlfriends. It was the most nakedly ideological exhibition I have ever seen (perhaps that's ever been mounted): a tacit justification for and distraction from the crimes that the Bosnian Serbs would commit elsewhere. So, thirteen years on, I was eager to see the ironically entitled "On Normality: Art in Serbia 1989–2001." I was also eager to get out of the cold. The sky was the same pure blue it had been the day before but the temperature had plummeted. A freezing wind was blowing from the frozen east, from the icy wastes of Siberia. It had gone from summer to winter overnight.

The first piece in the exhibition, by Mileta Prodanovic, comprised a single big panel on which a number of images of green trees had been pinned. These trees twitched and moved slightly, activated by an unseen mechanical process. The reason for this was made plain by the quotation from *Macbeth* at the bottom of the page: "Till Birnam wood remove to Dunsinane, I cannot taint with fear." This impossibility did actually come to pass when, to Macbeth's astonishment, Malcolm instructed his troops to use the leaves of trees to camouflage their advance. Presumably Milosevic felt a similar sense of astonishment when he found himself being arrested by his own people. I recognized the quote and the quote enabled me to hazard a guess as to whose hands were pictured in a photograph at the center of the panel: Milosevic's, presumably, and his wife, Mirjana Markovic's.

In another room was *Death in Dallas,* a compilation of footage of the Kennedy assassination by Zoran Naskovski. The film was accompanied by a voice singing mournfully and the wailing of a simple stringed instrument called the *gusle.* Natasha explained that voice and gusle was an archaic combination used, traditionally, in Montenegro and Herzegovina, to lament or celebrate epic events in Serbian-Montenegrin history. If you did not understand the words— and I didn't—you could have been hearing something from the fourteenth century, a lament for massacre (of Serbs), or a celebration of massacre (of Turks).

The great man dies. The nation falls into mourning. The voice soars and wails. The gusle sobs.

Translated into a deliberately archaic English, the subtitles told the story of how America's hopes were snuffed out, how Jackie wept for her slain husband. Also flashing up on screen were more recent images showing the cover of Seymour Hersh's book, *The Dark Side of Camelot.* The music was overwhelming. The gusle wailed. It is a limited instrument, the gusle. It can only wail and sob. It is incapable of articulating the emotions that might transform sobbing and wailing into joy. The only solace it finds is the certainty of its being inconsolable. This lent a quality of matchless tragedy to what was being shown on screen.

Later that night, at dinner, I was told that the instrument and form are not quite as archaic as I had been led to believe. Contemporary tapes are available, apparently, in which the praises of Karadzic or Mladic are sung, or the betrayal of Milosevic lamented. Like so much in Serbian mythology, the gusle had been appropriated by or subsumed within an ideological program. That, if you like, is the dark side of the gusle. *Death in Dallas,* however, offered an alternative, more optimistic (though still tragic, of course) way of deploying the form. Made in 2001 the visual content of the piece derived from

1963 while the music harked back to God knows when—but it had also a prophetic quality. When Prime Minister Zoran Djindjic was assassinated in 2003 he quickly attained the mythical status of a Serbian Kennedy. It was hard to imagine a better demonstration of the way that for the Serbs there is no history: that everything exists in an infinitely expanded present.

Discussion at dinner then moved on—as it would in any of the world's capital cities—to complaints about what *wasn't* in the show. As with the Kennedy assassination a conspiracy and cover-up were suspected. Some of the most authentic expressions of the period, people said, were overlooked or deliberately excluded. There were, for example, things made by the Skart group during the leanest of the lean years: little rationing coupons that were distributed when everything was in short supply—except for the certainty that things were going to get worse. Printed on cheap paper of various colors, the coupons were meager; what they could be redeemed for was anything but. A red coupon—much sought after—was good for "One Orgasm," a green coupon (the most sought after of all) promised "A Miracle." Someone showed me one of these coupons, the size and texture of an old-fashioned cinema ticket. At least I thought they were showing it to me but, no, they were *giving* it to me. I was touched but not surprised, for Serbs, as D. H. Lawrence noted of Sardinians, are generous, "as all proud people are." They are also, I understood as I held this little coupon, this neglected work of art, a people who believe in miracles. They believe that they can come back from 4–0 down with only a minute left to play. And vice versa, of course. They know that everything can change, utterly, from one instant to the next.

I fear I have given a misleading impression—I *have* given a misleading impression—of life in Belgrade. So it's worth reiterating the old lesson of travel and of the World Cup: people are pretty much the same the world over. They might wish for their own state, or freedom from some oppressive neighbor (or, come to that, of oppressing a neighbor), they might dream of bringing home the trophy but, in the hopeful meantime, all but the most fanatical make do with . . . Well, let me give you an example. I was not crazy about the food we were eating. It was heavy, stodgy, meaty, a tad medieval in fact. Trying to show an interest and to play the part of visiting diplomat, I enquired about Balkan cuisine. "Are there differences in the cooking in Croatia, Bosnia, Macedonia and here in Serbia?" I asked.

I paused, unsure whether or not to add the spice of a joke to this bland query. Then I did. "Or is it just the same shit everywhere?" There was another pause—followed by the universal miracle that is laughter.

World Cup Record

FIFA Ranking: 47
World Cup Appearances: 9
World Cup Champions: 0
Federation Name: Fudbalski Savez Srbije
   i Crne Gore
Confederation: UEFA
Founded: 1919
FIFA Affiliation: 1919
Nickname: Blue
Manager: Ilija Petkovic
Website: www.fsj.co.yu
Stadium: Red Star Stadium (Marakana), Belgrade
Home Uniform: blue/blue/red
Away Uniform: white/white/white
Provider: Lotto

1930:	4th place
1934:	Did not qualify
1938:	Did not qualify
1950:	First round exit
1954:	Quarterfinal exit
1958:	Quarterfinal exit
1962:	4th place
1966:	Did not qualify
1970:	Did not qualify
1974:	Second round exit
1978:	Did not qualify
1982:	First round exit
1986:	Did not qualify
1990:	Quarterfinal exit
1994:	Did not participate
1998:	Second round exit
2002:	Did not qualify

Matches	Wins	Draws	Losses	GF	GA	GD	Points
37	16	8	13	60	46	+14	56

Serbia and Montenegro is 9th on the all-time World Cup table
Note: Played as Yugoslavia until 1998

Path to Qualification for World Cup 2006

4-Sep-04	San Marino	0	Serbia & Mont.	3	**W**
9-Oct-04	Bosnia-Herz.	0	Serbia & Mont.	0	**D**
13-Oct-04	Serbia & Mont.	5	San Marino	0	**W**
17-Nov-04	Belgium	0	Serbia & Mont.	2	**W**
30-Mar-05	Serbia & Mont.	0	Spain	0	**D**
4-Jun-05	Serbia & Mont.	0	Belgium	0	**D**
3-Sep-05	Serbia & Mont.	2	Lithuania	0	**W**
7-Sep-05	Spain	1	Serbia & Mont.	1	**D**
8-Oct-05	Lithuania	0	Serbia & Mont.	2	**W**
12-Oct-05	Serbia & Mont.	1	Bosnia-Herz.	0	**W**

Serbia and Montenegro qualified by finishing first in Group 7 of the European Zone

South Korea

Capital: Seoul
Independence: August 15, 1945
(from Japan)
Area: 98,480 sq km
Population: 48,422,644
Median Age: 34.5 years
Life Expectancy at Birth: 76.9 years
Ethnic Groups: homogeneous (except for
about 20,000 Chinese)
Religions: no affiliation 46%, Christian 26%,
Buddhist 26%, Confucianist 1%,
other 1%
Languages: Korean, English widely taught
in junior high and high school
Suffrage: 20 years of age; universal
Military Obligation: 20–30 years of age
for compulsory military service;
24–28 months conscript service
obligation, depending on the military
branch involved; 18 years of age for
voluntary military service
GDP Per Capita: $19,200
Budget: $155.8 billion
Military Expenditures: $20 billion
(2.5% of GDP)
Agriculture: rice, root crops, barley, vegetables,
fruit; cattle, pigs, chickens, milk, eggs; fish
Industries: electronics, telecommunications,
automobile production, chemicals,
shipbuilding, steel
Currency: South Korean won

Source: *CIA World Factbook*

South Korea

Peter Ho Davies

It's one of the queasy realities of World Cups, that at some point the discussion of national teams always begins to turn into a discussion of national or ethnic stereotypes. Germans are efficient, Italians operatic, the French cultured, Spaniards temperamental, Brazilians flamboyant, and the English . . . (bull)dogged. Many reasons could be advanced for this phenomena. Its roots might lie in the colonial past which is so responsible for making football the world game. Perhaps, too, there's a sense that a football team—more than any of the individual competitors in, say, Olympic sports—can somehow embody a national character. But I'd like to suggest that the real culprit for this kind of thinking is the football panel, that hotbed of mispronunciation and half-truth offered as generality, that transforms one man's opinion of a nation or people, into received wisdom. Yet, while stereotypes are reductive, inaccurate, patronizing, implicitly self-regarding, perhaps the one thing worse than being stereotyped is *not* being stereotyped. Stereotypes, as much as they help others to see us, may also allow us to see ourselves. We define ourselves by our own stereotypes, in opposition to those we hold of others, and perhaps those national images that endure longest endure in part because they're shared by the stereotypers and the stereotyped. Regardless of how accurately or narrowly national characters are revealed in World Cups, those events are how many of us the world over first form impressions of other nations. We recognize each other by our footballers; in many cases, they're the first or only people from that country we know. So what does it say when the Asian stereotype is . . . not playing football very well.

When I was growing up, playing football in England in the 1970s no one passed to you if you were Asian. If you played at all, it was in defense (and this at an age when the fatties and four-eyed, the thickos, spackers and benders were stuck at the back); more often than not you were the sub (unused).

This would have been grim for any kid, but it was especially so since one of my classmates was a fellow called Jamie Hill, son of

Jimmy Hill, the iconic TV football pundit, and inventor, so some say, of the football panel. Hill (Sr.) is something of an ironic taste now, his appeal a little retro, but back in the 1970s he was the straight face of BBC football, the presenter of its flagship program *Match of the Day,* the only place to regularly see football (just highlights at that) on British TV—which was the *only* place to see it at all, if your parents, like mine, thought you'd be in danger going to see games in person because of the color of your skin.

Every Saturday night of the season at 10 P.M., the jaunty fanfare of the theme music would start up over a title sequence that included, among other things, a shot of thousands of school kids in a stadium holding up cards to make a giant picture of Jimmy's face (fully half of which appeared to consist of a chin, as sharp and pronounced as most people's elbows, which in later years Jimmy was to highlight with a series of increasingly reckless bow ties). *Match of the Day,* if you need further proof of its seminal place in my life, was the first program I was allowed to stay up late to watch. Jimmy Hill, massive chin and all, loomed over my weekends like one of those huge stone heads on Easter Island.

I didn't know Jamie half as well. We weren't in the same classes and when I saw him in the corridors, or on the football pitch, he seemed cool and aloof. He must have had friends, but my sense is that most of us gave him a respectfully wide berth, as if we were at school with one of the royal princes. Still, his mere presence among us left open the thrilling possibility that one day his father might appear, picking him up at four o'clock, attending a sports day, leaning over the fence watching us play football. A contract, an apprenticeship, a word to the right scout, an invitation to the studio at the least, couldn't be far behind, we thought. But not if no one ever passed you the ball, not if you were stuck in defense with the odds and sods, or worse, on the touchline carrying a linesman's flag (we all knew how Jimmy felt about linesmen, the petty bureaucrats of the beautiful game).

My problem was that if you didn't look like a footballer—British, circa 1975—you couldn't be one. Half of the pleasure of playing football was the pleasure of pretend, of make believe. Kids didn't play football as much as they played their heroes—Keegan or Toshack, Bremner or Lorimer, Souness or Rush—in their own breathless commentary. The roles were as much acting as sporting. Pulling on a replica team shirt was like tying a towel round your neck and pretending to be Superman. But it was easier to believe you could fly than to suspend disbelief and be Kevin Keegan if you looked Asian. And my mother's sporadic Olympic enthusiasm for Chinese table-tennis players, or Malaysian badminton medalists, wasn't much of a consolation.

There were no Asian players in the English leagues throughout my childhood—black players were still a novelty (patronized at best, showered with bananas at worst) and foreign imports were rare. Outside of European competitions, the only place to see foreign players, and in particular the only place to see nonwhite players, was the World Cup. But between 1966, when the North Koreans got to the last eight in England, and 1986, when South Korea went to Mexico, no Asian team qualified for the World Cup finals. Since I was still in my mother's womb in the summer of '66, I was almost twenty before I—or anyone of my generation growing up in England—saw an Asian kick a ball in anger.

I was at university in Manchester by 1986, starting to follow Man United's fortunes seriously (they weren't yet the powerhouse of the 1990s, more a star-studded soap opera) though also just beginning to fancy being Ted Hughes rather than Mark Hughes. The 1986 World Cup is remembered now for Maradona, and especially his goals against England in the quarterfinals, the one magical, the other sleight of hand, but it's South Korea's first-round game against then holders Italy that stays with me.

I was living alone, then, my roommate having gone home for the summer, spending my days checking the marking of the national O and A Level school exams. It was stultifying work—some lucky souls got to read essays, or look at the painting and drawing from art exams, but I was stuck verifying the scoring of multiple choice science tests. We were in essence double-checking the computers, looking for those students who scored improbably low, lower than they should have even if they'd guessed every answer, which could be a sign that they'd filled out the grid incorrectly, in ink, say, rather than #2 pencil. I always looked those files up with the exaggerated hope—born of my own boredom—of rescuing some poor kid's grade, but more often than not these checks only revealed the dismayingly dogged ignorance of candidates who were both obtuse *and* unlucky.

The World Cup that year was—not surprisingly—the highlight of my summer (the England squad of '86, I read with some relief, boasted fewer than a dozen O Levels between them), and I watched as many matches as I could: England games at the flat of my best friend and his girlfriend; the rest alone, on the tiny black-and-white TV back at my railroad apartment (this being before the advent of a big screen TV in every pub).

South Korea started poorly against the eventual champions, Argentina, 2–0 down within twenty minutes, 3–0 down a minute after halftime, losing eventually 3–1, and I remember having the sinking feeling that *this* was why I'd never seen an Asian team in the finals. Back in the studio, I seem to recall, Jimmy helpfully pointing out that this was actually an improvement on South Korea's only prior appearance in the World Cup, in 1954, in Switzerland, when they'd lost 9–0 and 7–0 to Hungary and Turkey respectively. Those were the kind of improbable scores that I'd been trained to be suspicious of at work, but in fact they were quite right (though it's worth noting that the South Koreans of '54 played their first game ten hours after getting off the plane, and that getting to the finals at all was a small triumph. To qualify they had to beat Japan—their former occupiers—twice, on Japanese soil, after the South Korean government refused to allow the Japanese team to enter the country.)

The Argentina game had been so predictable, and almost immediately no contest, that when South Korea gave up a goal to Bulgaria ten minutes into the next match it seemed as if history was in danger of repeating itself. And that, I swear, is when I remember someone—not Jimmy, surely, this wasn't a marquee game, and it must have been covered by the second-string commentary team—chuckle dryly: "They eat underdogs, don't they?"

In retrospect, I can barely believe I heard it myself, half hope my memory's faulty, that I've conflated the moment with another, a crack overheard later in a pub, maybe. And yet, whenever I heard it, whoever said it, it's lodged in my mind at that moment, when the Korean team seemed on the verge of crumbling. But then, somehow, almost as if they'd heard the line themselves, they simply refused to, throwing themselves around the pitch in a flailing blur of energy that would have looked silly—charging after hopeless long balls, diving into tackles, their thick black mops of hair flopping with effort—if it hadn't seemed so desperate.

That was the game that caught my imagination. I'm not Korean, had never been to Korea then or since, but I had that haircut and more important that desperation. It ended 1–1, the equalizer the kind of goal that seems forced over the line by sheer willpower, ensuring that South Korea entered the next game, the one against Italy, with at least the mathematical chance of advancing to the quarterfinals if they won.

They didn't, of course, but after shipping yet another early goal (what *was* their manager telling them in his team talk?), they stiffened again, clung on and equalized midway through the second half. For about ten teetering minutes it was just possible to imagine them winning, and then Alessandro Altobelli made it 2–1 and a little later an own-goal sealed it, though the Koreans still clawed back a late goal and played out a furious but futile last few minutes. A defeat then, but a gallant one, a defiant one, the kind from which stereotypes spring.

"Plucky," someone on the panel said afterward. "Never say die," another expert offered. "They'll be back," a third opined, an uncharacteristically accurate prophesy, since South Korea has appeared in each World Cup since, most recently taking their revenge on Italy en route to a semifinal appearance in 2002. But such then-unimaginable successes, (including the signing of a Korean, Park Ji-Sung, by Man United) haven't overshadowed that game in Mexico.

What remains most vivid in my mind is that the scorer of the first Korean goal was Choi Soon Ho, and that somewhere in the coverage, the commentator or someone back in the studio got his name confused in a typical and trivial error, and called him Ho, instead of by his family name, Choi. I can't be sure who it was, but in my memory, of course, it's Jimmy Hill, Jimmy Hill saying my name, albeit by mistake, Jimmy Hill saying, "The lad Ho looks useful, the boy Ho can play." I can see him now, nodding and smiling, his huge chin seemingly gift-wrapped in one of those bright bow ties.

World Cup Record

FIFA Ranking: 29
World Cup Appearances: 6
World Cup Champions: 0
Federation Name: Korea Football Association
Confederation: AFC
Founded: 1928; 1945
FIFA Affiliation: 1948
Nickname: Taeguk Warriors
Manager: Dick Advocaat
Website: www.kfa.or.kr
Stadium: Seoul World Cup Stadium
Home Uniform: red/blue/red
Away Uniform: white/red/white
Provider: Nike

1930:	Did not participate
1934:	Did not participate
1938:	Did not participate
1950:	Did not participate
1954:	First round exit
1958:	Did not enter
1962:	Did not qualify
1966:	Did not qualify
1970:	Did not qualify
1974:	Did not qualify
1978:	Did not qualify
1982:	Did not qualify
1986:	First round exit
1990:	First round exit
1994:	First round exit
1998:	First round exit
2002:	4th place

Matches	Wins	Draws	Losses	GF	GA	GD	Points
21	3	6	12	19	49	-30	15

South Korea is 31st on the all-time World Cup table

Path to Qualification for World Cup 2006

18-Feb-04	South Korea	2	Lebanon	0	**W**
31-Mar-04	Maldives	0	South Korea	0	**D**
9-Jun-04	South Korea	2	Vietnam	0	**W**
8-Sep-04	Vietnam	1	South Korea	2	**W**
13-Oct-04	Lebanon	1	South Korea	1	**D**
17-Nov-04	South Korea	2	Maldives	0	**W**
9-Feb-05	South Korea	2	Kuwait	0	**W**
25-Mar-05	Saudi Arabia	2	South Korea	0	**L**
30-Mar-05	South Korea	2	Uzbekistan	1	**W**
3-Jun-05	Uzbekistan	1	South Korea	1	**D**
8-Jun-05	Kuwait	0	South Korea	4	**W**
17-Aug-05	South Korea	0	Saudi Arabia	1	**L**

South Korea qualified by finishing in the top two in Group 1 of the Asian Zone

Spain

Capital: Madrid
Independence: 1492 (unification)
Area: 504,782 sq km
Population: 40,341,462
Median Age: 39.5 years
Life Expectancy at Birth: 79.5 years
Ethnic Groups: composite of
  Mediterranean and Nordic types
Religions: Roman Catholic 94%, other 6%
Languages: Castilian Spanish 74%,
  Catalan 17%, Galician 7%, Basque 2%;
  note: Castilian is the official language
  nationwide; the other languages are
  official regionally
Suffrage: 18 years of age; universal
Military Obligation: Voluntary
GDP Per Capita: $23,300
Budget: $386.4 billion
Military Expenditures: $9,906.5 million
  (1.2% of GDP)
Agriculture: grain, vegetables, olives, wine
  grapes, sugar beets, citrus; beef, pork, poultry,
  dairy products; fish
Industries: textiles and apparel (including
  footwear), food and beverages, metals
  and metal manufactures, chemicals,
  shipbuilding, automobiles, machine tools,
  tourism, clay and refractory products,
  footwear, pharmaceuticals, medical
  equipment
Currency: euro

Source: *CIA World Factbook*

Spain

Robert Coover

Spain, the summer of '82, hottest of the century. The smog cap over Barcelona was like the lid of a pressure cooker, ablaze with refracted sunlight, and up on the top tier of the little Sarriá soccer stadium, known popularly as the *Bombonera,* the Candybox, they seemed to have sold ten tickets for every square foot of space. We had to go an hour and a half early just to squeeze in at all. No way to sit, no chance to go for drinks, by the time the matches started it was even hard to breathe. My teenaged son spent one entire game hanging over an exit from a stair railing. Each day we said: if it's not bloody sensational, we'll go to a bar somewhere and watch it on TV, this is crazy. And each day we stayed.

We'd been here before. The other time, in 1977, it was raining and nighttime and turning cold. We stayed that time, too, huddled under an umbrella high up on the roof under the floodlights in the blustery winds and pouring rain in the only available seats, and happy to have them. That night we were watching a late-autumn Spanish league match between the two archrivals of this city, FC (Fútbol Club) Barcelona and Real Club Deportivo Espanyol (the Spanish Royal Sports Club), whose home field this was, a match that was far more than a mere athletic event.

In 1982 it was the setting for the second round of the World Cup and the teams were the national sides of Italy, Brazil and Argentina, all former World Champions—playing each other in a round-robin mini-league for a place in the semifinals (Argentina–Italy, Argentina–Brazil and Brazil–Italy, in that order). The games transcended the quotidian as war may be said to transcend debate.

These are, it sometimes seems to me, our only two universal games, war and soccer. They are to be found, both together, in all but a few rare and remote subcultures of the world (in Melanesia, for example, or here and there in North America) and always at the heart of the national experience. War is perhaps closer to the realm of fantasy, soccer to that of the real, but both share this ubiquity and centrality, as though arising, each, from some collective libidinous source, primary and intuitive. Perhaps they are simply variations of the same game, modern industrial era ritualizations of some common activity from the Dreamtime of the species, back when both used the same players and the same pitch—which is to say, all the men of the tribe and all of nature. Still today, they often fade into each other. Soccer managers "declare war," generals apply soccer tactics and terminology in their campaigns, warlike violence invades the soccer pitch, spreads into the stands and out into the communities (as when border tensions and the passions of World Cup qualifying matches blurred into the notorious and bloody "Soccer War" in 1969 between Honduras and El Salvador—ironically, two of the 1982 finalists, and yet again—or still—shooting at each other back home), soldiers wear their team colors into battle like guerdons or play the enemy in no-man's-land during temporary ceasefires, fan clubs are known as "armies."

In this inextricable commingling of battles on the pitches and the pitched battles elsewhere of war and rebellion, the World Cup twenty-four years later in 2006 could see such match-ups as Iran against the U.S.A. or England, or the Serbs against the Croatians, but in the summer of 1982 the war-of-the-day was between Argentina and England over a barren pitch known respectively as the Malvinas and the Falkland Islands, and both of them had teams at the 1982 World Cup. It was this war that overshadowed Argentina's defense of its 1978 championship, keeping their fans at home, draining their resources, demoralizing team and nation alike as the casualty figures mounted and their hopes for any kind of face-saving exit dwindled. Nevertheless, on the eve of the World Cup inaugural match between the reigning world champions and Belgium, the Argentine junta, facing imminent and catastrophic defeat, decided to keep the war going one more day, making every effort meanwhile to get live TV transmission of the game to the troops holding the islands, hoping for a miracle. Instead, as though to make the world share their sadness, they only lost a few more countrymen. Their world champions had courage on the day maybe, but no bullets, Belgium scoring the only goal of a crunching, cautious, somewhat tedious game. Whereupon, within hours, Argentina surrendered to

Great Britain, the troops switched off the TV sets and returned to the mainland like disillusioned fans (a few citizens protested: they disappeared), and junta leader General Leopoldo Galtieri, presaging the fate of a lot of national team managers before the World Cup came to an end, "resigned." With a straight face, the London *Times* reported that, among senior military officers in the Falklands campaign, commando commander Brigadier Julian Thompson had been nominated "man of the match."

After their opening embarrassment, Argentina did manage to win a couple of games to qualify for the second round, and so recovered a certain respect. Brazil was the big favorite going into the round-robin—indeed, the favorite of the whole 1982 World Cup— and the game between these legendary rivals was touted as the "Latin American Final," with the winner favored to go all the way. Less was expected of Italy, who had gotten through to this round with three dismal draws against unrated teams, but they were a dour defensive squad and could always be a spoiler. Which is how the first game, which the Argentines lost to the Italians 2–1, was read: a reliance on hard men, craft above beauty, an upset victory for "negative" football. The press complained afterward of Italian ruthlessness and brutality. "Anti-football," they called it, "something between defense and homicide," though later their memory of this match would be more generous (as with life, only the past is open-ended). Certainly the tenacity and commitment of the Italian players in the blistering heat was awesome, the crushed pride of the Argentines almost palpable.

It is perhaps this passionate commitment, together with that peculiar but universal tendency of a people to identify its national interest with the success or failure of its soccer team, that most reminded us of the last time we were sitting up here, in the wind and rain, watching that night game that was more than a game between the *Culés,* or "Big Arses" of Barcelona (so called because in the old days the fans sat on open-backed bleachers, which presented to passersby this now-commemorated view celebrated by generations of cartoonists) and the "Parakeets" of Espanyol. This was 1977—or Year 1

A.F. (After Franco) by the new Catalan calendar—that euphoric year of the *destape* (the popping of the cork, the lifting of the lid) which saw the almost instantaneous nationwide demolition of the structures of Francoism, broad political amnesty, the legalization of the Communist Party, free trade unions, the publishing explosion and the Pornographic Revolution, the first general elections since the days of the Republic, and in Catalunya the new cultural *renaixença,* sardana-dancing in the streets, and the restoration of the autonomous Catalan parliament, the *Generalitat.* This body had been operating in exile since the end of the Civil War, and one of the high moments of the autumn of '77 was the welcoming home from almost forty years of exile of its president Josep Tarradellas. This took place at the airport, in the streets and plazas of Barcelona (soon to recover their old pre-Franco Catalan names as though to erase from the communal memory the shame of the Castillian—which is to say, foreign—occupation), and finally at FC Barcelona's Camp Nou, that holy temple of Catalanism across town where the tribe had gathered on alternate Sundays throughout the Franco era in symbolic—and vociferous—resistance.

Mes que un club—"More than a club"—is the Barça motto, and it was easy to grasp its meaning, standing there in that massive soccer stadium (the second largest in the world with a supporters' club of 120,000 paying members and a waiting list years long; for the 1982 team photo alone, to be taken just after the World Cup, some fifty thousand people—more than you could even pack into the antiquated little stadium of Espanyol—would turn up just to watch the clicking of the cameras) alive that day with the fluttering red-and-yellow stripes of the heretofore-outlawed Catalan *senyeres,* interwoven with the claret-and-blue stripes of the club flags, listening to the thunderous roar go up when Tarradellas stepped into the president's box to exchange prolonged embraces with the almost tearful directorate. Then, after an emotional introduction, Tarradellas recalled in a quavering voice for all present his days as a Barça fan in the 1920s and 1930s, concluding with a throaty *"Visca el Barça! Visca Catalunya!"* ("Long live the Barcelona Football Club! Long live Catalunya!"). Whereupon everyone rose to sing, en masse, "Els

Segadors," the long-suppressed Catalan hymn. Tarradellas, accepting the invitation, had said he'd come only if the club, playing Las Palmas of the Canary Islands that day, promised to win. For forty-five minutes it looked as though he might be disappointed, as the two teams slogged along in a 0–0 draw, but then, about a quarter of an hour into the second half, the old fellow looking like he was starting to doze a bit, Barcelona was amazingly awarded, not one, but two penalties in a row, and they then went on to defeat an understandably demoralized Las Palmas, 5–0. *Benvingut, President!*

I'd been something of a follower of the Barcelona football club since my father-in-law, the team doctor for lower-division Gimnàstic of Tarragona and a fervid Barça supporter, introduced me to the game in the late 1950s. To tell the truth, it was probably the astonishing intensity of the emotions aroused each year by the clearly political Barcelona–Real Madrid matches that first drew my attention, rather than the game itself. The left often objects to soccer (indeed to all spectator sports) as a bourgeois manipulation and exploitation of the working classes, deflecting their passions from the other-directed struggle for freedom and justice to the inner-directed mock-sufferings and satisfactions of team support—from the real, that is, to the artificial, the merely symbolic—and turning a quick buck or two while they do it. This may be so, but virtually all the young Catalans who joined the clandestine socialist and communist parties during the Franco era were also dyed-in-the-wool Barça fanatics, a paradox (if it is one) they had to learn, there being no release from such fandom, to live with.

"It's strange," one of them, a communist writer friend, told me at lunch, a couple of hours before the Argentina–Brazil match. "Things dissolve. All our grand ideas are filled with ambiguities when we try to make realities out of them. Under Franco, it was all much clearer. Against Franco, we like to say, we lived better. Perhaps it is because the world itself seems more fragile, the universe now more familiar but also more unfriendly. That astronaut of yours did not know what he was doing when he played golf on the moon. And what you keep coming back to at such times is your family, your village, your culture. Your football club."

"And the World Cup?" I asked. "Has it been a good thing?"

"For Spain," he shrugged, "it is a complete disaster. We are like children. We think the world is full of millionaires who want to come here and give us their money. Then, even if we rob them and cheat them, we think they will still love us. We are still mystics, you see. We expect miracles. And we still love to be punished." He glanced at his watch. "Two hours before kickoff," he said with a rueful smile. Yes, already it was time to go, else ticket or no ticket there would be no way to see the game: out into the sweltering heat, grab a bus till it's forced to a crawl, push into the incredible pack-up around the stadium of Sarriá.

La Bombonera was never Barça's Camp Nou, nothing like it. Over there the Belgians, Russians and Poles were fighting it out to decide who would play the winner of this group in the semifinals, and in that great stadium with its 120,000 capacity, there was ample space for the 819 carefully screened Polish fans permitted to attend (and half of these were said to have defected already somewhere between Spain and Poland), about as many Belgians, and as far as anyone knew, no Russians at all. Years later, after the Barcelona Olympics, Espanyol would inherit the Olympic Stadium, but in '82 the Candy-box was what they had. There had been tremendous pressure, of course, both international and local, to effect a switch: it would have meant at least three times as many ticket sales, not to mention the more generous aspect of giving the fans what they wanted. But there was too much pride at RCD Espanyol: this was one of the greatest moments in the club's history, and they were not going to surrender it. One of the directors, moreover, happened to be the president of the Spanish Football Association. It was a dead issue from the start.

It is important to grasp the historic difference between these two clubs. Barcelona, always Spain's major commercial and industrial center, was a principal beneficiary of the boom years of the *apertura,* the campaign by the new technocrats during Franco's enfeebled final decade to "open up" Spain. Tourism, industry, banking, business all came Barcelona's way. And the richer it got, the more it grew. By 1977 it had nearly 2 million inhabitants and the highest total income of the fifty provinces of Spain. Most of the new arrivals were not Catalans of course, but migrants from poorer regions come north to get a piece of the new prosperity, mostly as unskilled workers in the building trades. When they arrived, they were not made to feel all that welcome. *Xarnegos,* they were called. They formed a whole new bottom class, elevating the Catalan poor to the status of petit-bourgeoisie just by being there. They found that the Catalans tended to use their local language (a crude barking noise, it seemed to them) as a weapon against them, a secret code. It was difficult to get into a Barcelona game, and when they did go, they felt like foreigners. Besides, it was very expensive. So they started drifting over to Espanyol. It had a friendly name, it included everybody. People spoke Christian there. They called the club *"Ayth-pan-YO,"* which made folks feel at home. The management was said to be pro-centrist, anti-Catalan. It was a smaller stadium, a bit tacky and rundown, they didn't get lost there. And it was cheaper. Thus an old rivalry between two Catalan clubs took on a new dimension. Barcelona became the club of Catalanism, of anti-Francoism, of the intellectuals, the tribal elite, the rich; Espanyol the club of nationalism, the old hierarchies, the working class, migrants, the poor. The local derby between these two teams during the highly emotional autumn of 1977, just a couple of weeks after the return of Tarradellas, could not be missed.

Any more than 1982's sensational match-up between the two greatest Latin American teams of the prior decades. The little stadium was more impossibly oversold than ever. General admission tickets such as we had were said to be going on the street for hundreds of dollars, but we didn't even listen to the hawkers' offers to buy, pushing excitedly through the turnstiles with our brightly printed pieces of paper treasure. By then almost everyone in Spain, their own national team fading into ignominy, was a Brazilian fan, and the Sarriá stadium was packed solid with their gold-and-green colors. A flag the size of a basketball court tented an entire section at one end of the field, kites flew, balloons rose, a multitude of drums beat out a restless samba rhythm. It was like a home game for them. No team since the great Hungarian side of 1954 had been such a unanimous favorite for the championship, not just because they were the only team left at this stage of the tournament with a perfect record, but because they were so beautiful. The Peruvian novelist Mario Vargas Llosa, in one of his daily newspaper columns in Spain before Brazil's opening-round victory over the Soviet Union, likened the football pitch (am I mistaken? perhaps the only two universal games are sex and soccer . . .) to a vast pubic patch covered with an "inciting greenish furriness," and a goal to "an orgasm by which a player, a team, a stadium, a country, all of humanity suddenly discharges its vital energy." If each country "plays soccer according to its sexual idiosyncrasies," he speculated, then the Brazilian "is unhurried and titillating, he caresses the ball tenderly before kicking it, it is difficult for him to separate himself from it, and instead of putting the ball in the goal, he prefers to put himself into the goal with the ball. The Russian footballer, contrarily, is sad, melancholy, and violent, given to unpredictable and self-contradictory outbursts, and his relations with the ball are reminiscent of those of the Slavic lover with his sweetheart in those verses and laments that end always in bursts of pistol-fire."

Even the Brazilian pre-match warm-up was exciting. Watching them was like sinking into some sweet sensuous fantasy. It was wonderful, a nonstop *carnaval,* and we all wanted to be part of it. We all wanted to wear the yellow shirts and carry the silky flags and beat the drums. Above all, we wanted to run around on the field with Junior and Eder and Falcao and Zico. It looked so easy. The ball seemed to glide, whispering, between their feet like the marker on a Ouija board, as though it had a spirit of its own, aroused and guided by the transcendent consciousness of the team as a whole (this seemed to radiate from the black shaggy head of their larger-than-life captain Socrates, moving softly, serenely, through the midfield, a head or two taller than anyone around him)—yet released now and then for inspired individual runs, improvisational flights of fancy. The Argentines put all their heart into countering this Brazilian magic with a show of their own, but to no avail. The goals were credited to Zico, Serginho and Junior, but were so communal they might as well have been given to the goalkeeper. Ramón Díaz scored a late consolation goal for Argentina, and then the great Brazilian festival moved out into the streets and around the world. In Brazil, actually, they over-did it a bit: there were two deaths and six thousand injuries attrib-uted to the all-night celebrations.

So Italy and Brazil were going into their decisive match with a vic-tory each over Argentina, but with Brazil ahead on goal-difference: they needed only a draw to reach the semifinals. Though still the overwhelming favorites, the Brazilians no longer had the stadium to themselves: all week long Italian supporters had poured across the border and down the coast into this little highrise neighborhood, compounding the terrible congestion, trying to prove yet again that there's always room for one more angel on the head of that pin. Some had quit their jobs, others had closed down their businesses, walked out on family holidays: nothing was moving, they said, in all of Italy, and perhaps because there was no one around to take his place, the government of Prime Minister Giovanni Spadolini, threatened with collapse during the disastrous first-round ties, with the recent good news seemed stable again.

Indeed, the way the game began, he might have even made Caesar, as Italy, through Paolo Rossi, scored first. But Brazil had been a goal down before—against both Russia and Scotland in the first round—and still won the game. It was almost a pattern: as though they might be too considerate at heart to invade another's privacy with-out provocation. Provoked, Socrates set up Serginho with two or three brilliant opportunities, but the big forward, who just wasn't in the same class with most of his teammates, missed them all. Finally, about five minutes after Rossi's goal, the tall bearded Brazilian cap-tain decided to take matters into his own hands, or feet rather; he drifted in from the midfield as though out for an evening stroll, and, after an exquisite exchange with Zico, which left the Italian defender Claudio ("The Black Beast") Gentile floundering, evened the score with a ball slipped neatly between the flying goalkeeper's out-stretched fingers and the near post. The game settled down then into a pitched battle for the midfield, with a lot of to-ing and fro-ing, some of it spectacular to watch, some of it (as when Gentile revenged him-self by chopping down the clever Zico and got booked for it) not so. Then, about midway through the first half, one of the Brazilian defenders, apparently not even seeing Rossi, casually thumped the ball squarely to another defender: Rossi intercepted it and beat the Brazilian goalkeeper with a cleanly struck shot from the edge of the area. This was the goal that set Rossi on his way to being the 1982 World Cup's top scorer and voted the best player of the tournament, yet ironically (I can live with irony and that's good, because it runs deep in soccer) it seemed to me at the time that the only reason he was hanging back there was due to his lack of fitness: it was hot, he hadn't played for two years (the famous *"Bambino d'Oro"* was caught in a bribery and game-fixing scandal and banned until just a few weeks before), he'd been thrown cold into a tough series with a game every three days, he was just too bushed to move his ass. If the Brazilian defense had pushed up a bit, they'd have left him offside, and the Italian manager might even have decided to give up on him and pull him off. Instead, Italy had a new national hero. The half ended with the Italians 2–1 up, and the favorites in a lot of trouble.

Around us, the ecstatic Italian supporters, stripped to their shorts in the blazing midafternoon heat, then toga'd in red-white-and-green flags and decked out in scarves and funny hats, were shouting, singing, howling, seemingly transported to some other realm. Indeed, there is something oddly otherworldly about the hardcore soccer fan. Invested with his team or national colors, making strange aggressive noises with airhorns, whistles, trumpets, drums and firecrackers, crying out the holy name ("EE-TAHL-*YA!* EE-TAHL-*YA!*") or singing repetitive liturgical chants, falling out of historical time and geographical space into a kind of ceremonial trance, timeless and centripetal, he does not seem a spectator so much as a participant in a sacramental rite (soccer and religion? or is it that war and sex and religion are the only universal games, soccer something more serious?)—indeed, in his despair or ecstasy, he often fails to *see* the game at all, experiencing it rather at a level that is blind, irrational, profound, innocent. Technique, philosophy, the merits of the opposition, peculiarities of the match are of little interest to him. He has come, not to reflect or spectate or be entertained, but to participate, to surrender, to suffer. (There is a lot of pain involved in keeping the faith, as any true supporter will tell you. "Football would be a happy thing," someone has said, "if it weren't for the games.") He absorbs the ceremony into himself, experiencing it as an inner conflict, feeling the movements of the teams, the ever-changing patterns, as one feels health and disease, becoming one with the game, the pitch, the players.

The explanations advanced for soccer's intense mysterious power, the trancelike quality of great matches, its worldwide domination over all other sports, have been many, some finding in it a vivid reenactment of the prehistoric ritual hunt, others echoes of the matriarchal dream, initiation rites, pastoral dreams of a lost golden age. There is, akin to these, the game's inherent theatricality—not the razzamatazz of an American halftime, but the inner dramas of sin and redemption, the testing of virtue, the pursuit of pattern and cohesion, the collision of paradoxical forces: soccer has often been compared to Greek tragedy, or seen as a kind of open-ended morality play. Perhaps the difficulty in scoring (and thus the usual narrowness of margins of victory, even between teams of markedly unequal ability, the everpresent danger of a sudden reversal of fortune) intensifies this sense of theater, causing the denouement—or the collective catharsis—to be withheld almost always until the final whistle. Nor, until that whistle, is there relief from the tyranny of time's ceaseless flow: once you've fallen into a game, there is no getting out. The player must stay with that flow, maintain the rhythm, press for advantage, preserving all his skills, his mind locked into the shifting patterns, and the spectator, though less arduously, shares this experience.

Which in turn suggests another of the game's dreamlike qualities: its ahistoricity. One is left at the end, not with data, but with impressionistic images of bodies in motion. Nothing of importance can be statistically recorded about a match except corners, shots, goals and saves (the American effort to record assists is admirable but—since it's sometimes a complete mystery, even with TV replays, who's *scored* the goal—a bit desperate), and these will tell you almost nothing about the game itself. The player who actually wins the game may be the one who moves into space at the opposite side of the field, drawing a defender, forcing a new configuration upon the defense and making virtually inevitable a goal which was before impossible, but no one—not even he—may be aware of this. It's all narrative, and thus subjective: no two match reports are ever alike, even the goal-scorers are often different from newspaper to newspaper. Each is a story, a sequence of ambivalent metaphors, a personal revelation couched in the idiom of the faith. No game I know of is so dependent upon such flowing intangibles as "pattern" and "rhythm" and "vision" and "understanding." Which may all be illusions. And at the same time it is also a very simple game: like dreams, almost childlike.

It was cold, blustery, on that autumnal night of '77, the rain sheeting down past the floodlights, the night vaulting closely over us like a second umbrella. But we weren't alone in feeling the extraordinary pull of this game, the little stadium was packed out, full of the blue-and-white flags of Espanyol, but also of Catalan *senyeres*. "SEÑOR TARRADELLAS: WE ARE CATALANS, TOO!" declared a huge sign at one end, and the message was repeated, even more eloquently, over the loudspeakers before the game: it was clear that feelings had been badly hurt. Though recently adopted by the Castillian occupying army and then by the southern migrants, Espanyol was originally created by Catalan university students in 1900, only a few months after the founding of FC Barcelona, as the first all-national team, including Catalans, most other teams in that early era of the sport being made up largely of foreigners who had brought the game to Spain.

The sides were not equal. Barcelona, with their expensive Dutch mercenaries Johan Neeskens and the world-renowned Johan Cruyff, were fighting for the championship, just three points behind the leaders and bitter rivals Real Madrid, while Espanyol, at the bottom, were struggling to avoid relegation to the second division. Barcelona, in enemy territory, wanted—needed—both points. So did Espanyol. For Barcelona it was a chance for glory; for Espanyol, a matter of survival. The referee Pes Pérez was young, one of the "New Wave," as they were called, a socialist active in the effort to professionalize the refereeing trade.

Pes Pérez wasted no time in putting his stamp on the game. Espanyol had a controversial black Brazilian up front named Jeremías, who had an unpleasant way of niggling defenders when the ref wasn't looking to make them lose their cool when he was. Pes Pérez caught him at it and started to book him, but Juanjo, the aggrieved Barcelona defender and longtime enemy of Jeremías, had already had enough: he gave a lunging kick at the Brazilian and Pes Pérez threw him out of the game. Which was not even ten minutes old yet. Passions started running high. The Espanyol home fans, inured to suffering, suddenly tasted blood and it tasted sweet: *revolution!* They were on their feet. But, though Barcelona was down a man, Espanyol seemed to lack the conviction to attack. Old habits. Or perhaps there was too much at stake for them. Relegation to the lower divisions is a kind of death, and the fear of it seemed to paralyze them momentarily. Instead, it was Cruyff who ruled. Johan the Great. His midfield moves, even in the heavy rain, were graceful, lucid, surprising. He was in rare form, magnificent; it was maybe his best game of the season. The defenders, unable to stay with him, had no choice but to take him down. They got booked for it by Pes Pérez. One of them got a second booking about a half hour into the game and so had to leave it: the sides were even again at ten men each. Cruyff, understandably, began to find more room. Barcelona now dominated, and only brilliant goalkeeping kept the game scoreless till halftime.

After the interval, the storm worsened. Sometimes you could hardly see the field from our rooftop perch. But we stayed, the crowd stayed. There was an excitement building up, and something like fury. *Ca' Rabia* or the House of Fury, was the stadium's other nickname, and it was living up to it. Time was massing up in here like a cold wet wind out of the past. Down on the field, in spite of the referee's firmness, there was still a lot of pushing and kicking, egged on by shouts from the crowd in high *xarnego* accents with Catalan retorts: "Take the whores down! Let them eat your boots!" The ground was heavy, making deft moves difficult, a lot of players fell on their faces trying, but Cruyff appeared not to notice—only a few minutes into the second half he shook off his defenders (he seemed almost to float through the muck, they seemed knee-deep) and unloosed a cannonball of a shot that brought a spectacular save out of the Espanyol goalkeeper. Before the game was over, he'd make another dozen like it (someone explained: it's easier for a goalie in the rain—it takes the pace off the ball), augmenting Espanyol's anxiety, Barcelona's frustration. Jeremías jabbed and niggled, Johann Neeskens and others retaliated, but Pes Pérez only had one pair of eyes. Even so, he saw plenty, and there were more bookings—ten altogether in the match. "Assassins!" the crowd screamed, whenever a Barça man made a move. "Pigs! Animals!" The scoreless draw was finally broken about fifteen minutes from the end when Neeskens of Barcelona rose unmarked through the pouring rain to head in a powerful goal from a corner. The Big Arses raised a din of *"Visca el Barça!"* but they were drowned out by the home crowd, drenched and embittered Parakeets now, squawking for blood. When Cruyff lashed back after an Espanyol defender, fouling him, ripped his pants off (both players were booked), they yelled: "Kill the dirty bastard! We want his leg! *Bring us Cruyff's leg!*" Four minutes from the end, Neeskens was booked for dangerous play near his own penalty area. There were more appeals for capital punishment from the stands and on the field the momentary threat of scuffles—the Espanyol players were clearly getting pretty pissed off at Neeskens—but Pes Pérez was able to keep it under control. The free kick was taken, the Barcelona goalkeeper punched it away, an Espanyol striker took it on the half-volley and scored the equalizer: 1–1. The place was going wild. The fans were all on their feet, throwing their cigars in the air, demanding miracles, umbrellas bobbing up and down as though being pumped. Both teams were scrambling now for the winning goal, especially Barcelona who all along had dominated the game, and now felt robbed. The players were caked in mud, soaked through, bruised and battered, but playing as though their lives depended on it, and the crowd, by their cries, suggested this might be so. Neeskens, bony elbows out, went galloping through the mud toward goal, and one of the Espanyol players, taking the cries of the fans literally, had a serious go at breaking his legs—and then, while he was still tumbling in pain over by the sidelines out of play, Jeremías also got the boot in. This was too much. Juanjo, the

Barcelona player who had been sent to the showers at the start of the game but hadn't gone, jumped up off the bench where he'd been hiding and went for Jeremías. Soon both teams, trainers and all, were into a fullfledged knock-down drag-out brawl. In the heavy rain, it was like mud wrestling. The fans were trying to climb the wire fence that separated them from the pitch to join in. It was a very joyous occasion, and when it was finally over, Pes Pérez decided he'd handed out enough bookings, he'd let the whole thing pass. "Didn't see it," he smiled and let the game go on. It ended two minutes later in a 1–1 draw. Almost no one left the stands until the field was completely empty. It was hard to believe it was over. It was almost like waking up from a wonderful dream.

Below us, the Brazilian and Italian teams were already back on the field after their halftime break, their gold and blue patterns, now familiar, flashing and shifting on the sunlit pitch like moving diagrams on a green blackboard, the ball chalking out the only possible connections. The Italians used a kind of fluid wedge with Rossi alone at the tip, the rest pulled back into a pulsing wall, fused and organic, essentially stable, with only the occasional speculative sprint up the wing like an escaped particle. The Brazilians embraced this creature, wove patterns through it, retreated, searching out the entire space of the field as though they'd lost something on it. Their fans were edgy but, even as throughout the halftime interval, the steady samba beat went on: ceremonial, insistent, yet somehow soothing. It did not seem meant to incite the team so much, as to remind them of the constancy of their followers: it was a love murmur, and only its interruption needed to be feared. Responding to it, the Brazilians devised scheme after scheme to pierce the Italian defense. Many of them were spectacularly successful, but the forty-one-year-old Italian goalie Dino Zoff was in equally spectacular form, parrying shot after shot. He was finally beaten about halfway into the second half by a splendid individual goal by Falcao, Brazil's man of the match, and one of the most exciting players at the World Cup. This 2–2 draw, of course, was all the Brazilians needed to go through to the semifinal against Poland, but instead of settling back into a negative defensive formation (only Socrates drifted back a step or two, that seemed enough), they kept up the pressure on the Italian goal. It wouldn't have been fun otherwise. Consequently, fifteen minutes from the end, they fell victim to yet another Italian counterattack, giving up a corner kick this time, the Italians' (this is an amazing statistic) only corner of the game. They made the best possible use of it: two or three people got a touch of the ball as it came into the box before Rossi deftly deflected it into goal for his hat trick. The Brazilians then put everything into attack, Socrates moving up into the box, Junior into the midfield, but all to no avail: the party was over. It was the Italians who would go on to beat Poland and West Germany to win the 1982 World Cup. In Brazil there were suicides, burials of the manager in effigy, widespread mourning, death threats to the players' wives. But in the end everyone was forgiven: theirs was the greatest team at the 1982 World Cup and they knew it. One has to learn to live with tragedy.

World Cup Record

FIFA Ranking: 5
World Cup Appearances: 11
World Cup Champions: 0
Federation Name: Real Federación
  Española de Fútbol
Confederation: UEFA
Founded: 1913
FIFA Affiliation: 1904
Nickname: Furia Roja (Red Fury)
Manager: Luis Aragones
Website: www.futvol.com
Stadium: various
Home Uniform: red/dark blue/dark blue
Away Uniform: all white
Provider: Adidas

1930:	Did not participate
1934:	Second round exit
1938:	Did not participate
1950:	4th place
1954:	Did not qualify
1958:	Did not qualify
1962:	First round exit
1966:	First round exit
1970:	Did not qualify
1974:	Did not qualify
1978:	First round exit
1982:	Second round exit
1986:	Quarterfinal exit
1990:	Second round exit
1994:	Quarterfinal exit
1998:	First round exit
2002:	Quarterfinal exit

Matches	Wins	Draws	Losses	GF	GA	GD	Points
45	19	12	14	71	53	+18	69

Spain is 7th on the all-time World Cup table

Path to Qualification for World Cup 2006

Date	Home		Away		Result
8-Sep-04	Bosnia-Herz.	1	Spain	1	D
9-Oct-04	Spain	2	Belgium	0	W
13-Oct-04	Lithuania	0	Spain	0	D
9-Feb-05	Spain	5	San Marino	0	W
30-Mar-05	Serbia & Mont.	0	Spain	0	D
4-Jun-05	Spain	1	Lithuania	0	W
8-Jun-05	Spain	1	Bosnia-Herz.	1	D
7-Sep-05	Spain	1	Serbia & Mont.	1	D
8-Oct-05	Belgium	0	Spain	2	W
12-Oct-05	San Marino	0	Spain	6	W
12-Nov-05	Spain	5	Slovakia	1	W
16-Nov-05	Slovakia	1	Spain	1	D

Spain qualified by finishing second in Group 7 of the European Zone and beating Slovakia in a home-away playoff

Sweden

Capital: Stockholm
Independence: June 6, 1523
(Gustav Vasa elected king)
Area: 449,964 sq km
Population: 9,001,774
Median Age: 40.6 years
Life Expectancy at Birth: 80.4 years
Ethnic Groups: Swedes; Finnish and Sami
minorities; Finns, Yugoslavs, Danes,
Norwegians, Greeks, Turks
Religions: Lutheran 87%, Roman Catholic,
Orthodox, Baptist, Muslim, Jewish, Buddhist
Languages: Swedish, small Sami- and Finnish-
speaking minorities
Suffrage: 18 years of age; universal
Military Obligation: 19 years of age for
compulsory military service; conscript
service obligation: 7–17 months; after
completing initial service soldiers have a
reserve commitment until the age of 47
GDP Per Capita: $28,400
Budget: $199.6 billion
Military Expenditures: $5.729 billion
(1.7% of GDP)
Agriculture: barley, wheat, sugar beets;
meat, milk
Industries: iron and steel, precision equipment
(bearings, radio and telephone parts,
armaments), wood pulp and paper
products, processed foods, motor vehicles
Currency: Swedish krona

Source: *CIA World Factbook*

Sweden

Eric Schlosser

"The degree of civilization in a society," Fyodor Dostoyevsky wrote, "can be judged by entering its prisons." With that idea in mind, during the fall of 2000, I decided to write a book about the American prison system. The United States was in the midst of an unprecedented prison-building spree. Nobody in human history had ever put so many people behind bars. No other society had been rich enough to do it. Communist China had fewer inmates, among other reasons, because it often punished drug dealers inexpensively, with a bullet to the base of the skull. In the United States pot dealers were serving life without parole. I had already visited quite a few American prisons, had seen the overcrowding, had seen how white inmates were always outnumbered by people of color, had spoken to inmates and officers about the gangs and violence and rape, about the rampant drug use and mental illness. Before starting the book, I wanted to find a system that was different in every conceivable way. And I figured the best place to look would be Sweden.

Hall Prison is located on the outskirts of Sodertalje, a port city about half an hour southwest of Stockholm. The day I visited, it was cold, a light rain was falling, and the sky and the sea were the same dark gray. Built in 1940, Hall is a Level 1 facility, maximum security, and unlike most Swedish facilities it is surrounded by a wall and a chain-link fence topped by razor wire. It is reserved for some of Sweden's worst criminals. Like the rest of Sweden's prisons, it's relatively small. At most it can hold fewer than three hundred inmates; maximum security prisons in the United States sometimes contain more than three thousand. One of California's maximum security prisons, CSP Corcoran, houses roughly the same number of inmates (4,900) as all fifty-five of Sweden's prisons combined.

The corrections officer who greeted me at the front gate didn't look like the sort of guard you see in Hollywood prison films, the sadist with bad attitude and well-polished boots. "Karl," as I'll call him here, was tall and burly, but he looked more like a roadie for the Grateful Dead than a fearsome symbol of authority. He had longish hair and a beard. His sense of humor was dry and ironic; his manner laid back. He had the feel of a man who'd seen it all and been left slightly amused. Karl had worked at Hall for years. As we headed down the corridor, I noticed that Karl was wearing clogs.

One of the unusual correctional practices at Hall Prison is the use of underground tunnels to move inmates from one building to another. The tunnels offer protection from bad weather and some control over who goes where. The brightly colored murals on the walls of these subterranean passages try to make them seem less grim. There's only so much you can do, however, to cheer up a concrete tunnel with locked doors at either end. The cell blocks at Hall are far more pleasant. Groups of inmates share a common area with a sitting room and a kitchen. Each inmate has his own cell, which comes with a color television, as well as a matching bed, desk and chair in light Scandinavian pine. The doors are kept open for most of the day, and inmates can stroll in and out. The cells reminded me of rooms I'd seen at a midwestern college dorm.

The officers at Hall constantly interact with inmates, and their dialogue isn't what you'd hear at an American maximum security prison. "When I'm pissed at a guard," one inmate said, after being asked his feelings about the staff, "I just tell him to fuck off." And sometimes they do. Karl allowed me to speak with inmates, unsupervised. They said that fights were rare, and nobody could recall a single rape at the facility during the previous ten years. Once or twice a week, inmates are allowed to enjoy conjugal visits with their wives or partners at a couple of private apartments inside the walls. The prison supplies condoms. A short and stocky Kurd, nearing his release date after spending fifteen years at Hall for murder, spoke fondly of the place. "I've been in Turkish prisons—and I prefer Swedish ones," he said.

One of the basic goals of the Swedish correctional system is to keep people out of prison. "In other countries, you might get ten years in prison for stealing a car," a high-ranking Swedish official told me. "In Sweden you have to get caught ten times stealing a car before you'll go to prison." Most convicted offenders are fined, placed on probation, given suspended sentences, placed in drug treatment, required to perform community service or kept under house arrest. Criminals are put behind bars if they repeatedly break the law or commit a particularly serious crime. Swedish prison sentences are brief: about 30 percent extend for a month or less; 27 percent, for two to six months; and just 7 percent, for two years or more. And you only have to serve two-thirds of the sentence. Nobody has been executed in Sweden since 1910, and a life sentence for murder usually means spending fifteen years in prison. Sweden also lets inmates leave prison for the weekend to see family and friends. During the 1960s, about 10 percent of the inmates given one of these leaves used the opportunity to escape. Today the proportion is less than 1 percent. Even maximum security inmates at Hall are granted leaves. For a few hours every six months, they can visit a nearby town, accompanied by corrections officers.

I wasn't permitted to tour the B Unit at Hall, where eight inmates considered especially dangerous and unruly were being held. Such inmates are given fewer privileges. Everyone else enjoys a remarkable degree of freedom within the facility. The wide assortment of bank robbers, drug dealers, murderers and thieves at Hall can earn money working at the commercial laundry. They can attend classes, join a rock band, play indoor badminton, tennis, Ping-Pong and billiards. The prison has its own tanning bed and masseuse. It has a large, well-stocked library; the most popular book when I visited was Bret Easton Ellis's *American Psycho*.

Many of the inmates at Hall have committed brutal crimes. But what was the point, Karl asked me, of being brutal to them? He thought that prisons shouldn't stoop to the level of the criminals they imprison. His penal philosophy was just what I expected to hear, a point of view at odds with so much of the correctional thinking back home. In countless ways this Swedish maximum security prison was different from anything you'd see in the United States. I was totally unprepared, however, to find that one important thing was the same: the majority of the inmates at Hall weren't white. They were African and Turkish and Middle Eastern, and their skin was much darker than that of the officers watching over them. The sight of all these immigrants and children of immigrants behind bars suggested that something in Sweden had gone wrong.

According to just about every quantifiable measure, Swedish society is a success. The United Nations Human Development Index ranks Sweden as the world's second most "liveable" country, after Norway. The World Economic Forum has named Sweden the second most environmentally responsible country, after New Zealand. The average life expectancy in Sweden is longer than anywhere else besides Japan. The Swedes have some of the highest tax rates in the world, and yet their economy is now considered one of the most innovative, competitive and entrepreneurial. The unemployment rate is relatively low. The rate of spending on research and development is extraordinarily high—perhaps the highest in the world. A recent survey by Transparency International found Sweden to be one of the world's least corrupt nations. A larger proportion of women are in the workforce and in government than anywhere else. Health care, day care and education from kindergarten through university are basically free. The gap between rich and poor is smaller than just about anywhere else. And for a country of only 9 million, Sweden records a lot of popular music—only the United States and Great Britain export more.

And yet, in the nineteenth century, Sweden was one of the poorest countries in Europe, and about one out every seven Swedes emigrated to the United States. The Swedish welfare state wasn't created through class warfare, battles between labor and capital or revolutionary confiscations of private property. In the 1930s the Social Democratic Party avoided all that by creating strong links between labor unions and industrialists, by stressing the interdependent economic needs of every Swedish citizen and by putting forth a vision of the *Folkhem,* the "People's Home," founded upon common values and a common ancestry. Per Albin Hansson, the second Social Democratic prime minister and the leading proponent of the *Folkhem,* outlined its central idea: "Sweden for the Swedes— the Swedes for Sweden!" In his compelling book about racism, *Even in Sweden* (2000), Allan Preed describes how the logical, rational, planning-obsessed social democracy that emerged in Sweden was capable of tremendous compassion, egalitarianism—and discrimination. During the Second World War, Sweden remained neutral, profited from trade with Germany and was slow to accept Jewish refugees. Under a eugenics program begun in 1935, Sweden sterilized more women without their consent than any other nation besides Nazi Germany. Created to prevent deviants and the mentally incompetent from breeding, the program wasn't discontinued until 1975.

Sweden's stunning economic growth after the Second World War was made possible not only by the spirit of the *Folkhem* but also by the fact that the nation's cities were never invaded and its factories were never bombed. A dedication to pacifism, neutrality and social justice later inspired the Swedish goal of becoming a "moral superpower," a worldwide leader in charitable works and opposition to war. Sweden's refugee policy was reformed, and the country soon welcomed victims of foreign oppression: Hungarians fleeing the uprising of 1956; students escaping Czechoslovakia in 1968; Allende supporters leaving Chile in 1973. Those immigrants, along with thousands of Finnish and Italian laborers, were assimilated into Swedish society. The next wave of immigrants presented more of a problem. They looked a lot different and arrived at an unfortunate time.

For much of the postwar era, Swedish foreign policy tried to help solve some of the major problems of the world—the war in Vietnam, apartheid in South Africa, dictatorships throughout Latin America. During the late 1970s the world and its problems started flowing into Sweden, refugees from Lebanon, Iran and Iraq, Turkey, Afghanistan, Bosnia, Serbia and Somalia. Almost three hundred thousand refugees arrived in the decade or so after 1989. The flow hit its peak right as the Swedish economy began to falter. In 1990 the unemployment rate was less than 2 percent; within a few years it reached 12 percent. Impoverished, often illiterate refugees were no longer eagerly welcomed. Anti-immigrant sentiment rose, along with neo-Nazi activity. National identity became a subject for debate, along with the limits of tolerance. A social democracy founded with a homogenous white, Lutheran population had become home to a new type of citizen. For the first time in more than a century, a fundamental question arose: What does it mean to be Swedish?

Today perhaps one-fifth of the population in Sweden are immigrants or the children of immigrants. Perhaps 10 percent have a non-European background. Sweden has become a largely segregated society, with poor immigrants relegated to high-rise housing estates and suburban ghettoes like Tensta, Alby, Rinkeby and Rosengard. Despite the nation's booming high-tech economy, the unemployment rate in some of these communities now exceeds 50 percent. Poverty, racism and a sense of cultural dislocation have created a generation of angry, alienated young men. Robbery and petty theft, drug-dealing, immigrant smuggling and sex trafficking have become lucrative sources of income for some of these outsiders. A recent study by Sweden's National Council for Crime Prevention found that in almost half of all criminal cases, the suspects either were foreign born or had at least one foreign-born parent. Immigrants were four times more likely than native-born Swedes to be suspects in crimes of lethal violence and robbery. The study also noted that the overwhelming majority of immigrants never committed any crimes. That sort of finding, however, was unlikely to appear as a headline in Swedish newspapers, which routinely reported the latest mugging, robbery or rape committed by someone who didn't look Swedish. The inmates that I saw at Hall, with their dark eyes and dark skin, were the people whom Swedish society now feared.

Regardless of skin color or ethnic background, the behavior of Swedish inmates has changed a great deal in recent years, largely due to foreign influences. Soccer used to be by far the most popular sport in Sweden, inside and outside of prison. The social democratic movement considered soccer an invaluable part of the *Folkhem,* promoting it as a healthy form of physical activity and teamwork. Watching a match wasn't enough; you were supposed to play in one. "Soccer was considered an edifying pastime for the working class," says Mattias Göransson, co-editor of *Offside Fotbollsmagasinet,* "and if you were good, you were supposed to be a role model." The sport wasn't viewed as a way to make money. It was a way to unite society. Professional soccer leagues were formed in Great Britain during the late nineteenth century, and in Italy and Spain during the early years of the twentieth—but Sweden didn't allow its players to get paid until 1968. Most of the teams in the highest division remained amateur until the 1990s. Nevertheless Sweden produced some of the best players in the world after the Second World War, possibly, among other reasons, because so many players from other European countries had been killed in battle. A distinctive Swedish style of play evolved, well-organized and defensive, like the nation's military strategy.

Most Swedish prisons used to have their own soccer teams—not to play against each other in a prison league, but to play against teams from local amateur leagues. The prison teams always had the advantage of being the home team, for understandable reasons, and visiting players had to think twice about committing a foul. Today many of those prison teams have been disbanded. Bodybuilding has become far more popular than soccer in prison, and Swedish inmates are beginning to resemble their American counterparts, favoring baggy pants, bandanas and elaborate tattoos. Thanks to television, the prison culture of the United States is altering that of Sweden. A blue-eyed, blond-haired bank robber that I met at Hall said he'd learned about American prison life by watching the Discovery Channel in his cell. Global cultures now blend and collide in unpredictable ways. Today the inmates in Sweden's prisons are more likely than ever to be violent, to be substance abusers, to be members of American-style gangs like the Hell's Angels, the Bandidos, the Original Gangsters and the International Evil Minds. And they are less likely to appreciate the comforts of a Swedish prison.

In July 2004 four inmates escaped from Hall, using a cell phone and handgun that had been smuggled into the facility. After taking an officer hostage, the four sped off in a Saab that had been waiting outside the prison gates. A week later, three inmates escaped from Norrtaelje, another high security prison. Using smuggled cell phones, they kept in touch with accomplices who drove a van through the front gate and threatened its guards with automatic weapons. Six weeks later two inmates at Mariefred Prison used a knife to take an officer hostage, stole a van from the prison parking lot and escaped.

Although all of these inmates were eventually caught, three dramatic escapes in such a brief period of time created a public furor in Sweden and suggested that security could be improved at the nation's prisons. According to one newspaper account, thirty-four cell phones had been confiscated at Norrtaelje in the months prior to the escape. None of Sweden's prisons required visitors to pass through a metal detector. The Swedish Prison and Probation Service resisted demands that officers be issued weapons—but agreed, for the first time, to install a metal detector at Hall. The head of the prison service resigned not long after the escape from Mariefred. The Swedish minister of justice, Thomas Bodström, bore ultimate responsibility for managing the prison system, but his popularity helped him ride out the storm. According to one recent poll, Swedish women rank Bodström number two on the list of men with whom they would most like to have a child. Before becoming justice minister he'd gained attention not only as a flamboyant young defense attorney but also as the first defender for a Swedish professional soccer team to gain high office. During his three years playing for AIK Stockholm, Bodström had been one of the more frequently carded players in the league.

It remains to be seen whether Swedish society can adjust its nationalism to embrace a wider mix of citizens—and whether some of its immigrants are willing to abandon customs that Swedes find unacceptable (such as the "honor killing" of young women). Thus far Sweden has avoided the rioting and angry right-wing politics now spreading through other western European societies. And the huge popularity of Sweden's two biggest soccer stars, Henrik Larsson and Zlatan Ibrahimovic, may help broaden the definition of who can be a Swede. Larsson has a white Swedish mother and a black father, originally from Cape Verde. Ibrahimovic was raised in Rosengard, an immigrant suburb of Malmö, by parents who'd emigrated from Bosnia. His father is Muslim, his mother is Catholic and his style of play is strongly individualistic. He represents a new type.

The tattoo on one of Ibrahimovic's arms—"Only God Can Judge Me"—was inspired by an inmate tattoo he'd seen on a television show called "Jail."

By the end of my time at Hall, it was dark outside. The rain was still falling, and I was ready to go. The best part of every prison visit is leaving. The sound of the gate closing sounds different when you're walking out. Despite the tanning bed and the tennis court and the color TV in every cell, the openness and the earnestness and the desire to help, the conjugal visits and free condoms, Hall is not a place where you would choose to spend the night. It brings to mind failure, mistakes and imperfectability. Walking to the car, I looked back at the administration building and the prison wall, all lit up in the darkness. My host knew exactly what I was thinking. "It's still a prison," he said.

World Cup Record

FIFA Ranking: 14
World Cup Appearances: 10
World Cup Champions: 0
Federation Name: Svenska Fotbollförbundet
Confederation: UEFA
Founded: 1904
FIFA Affiliation: 1904
Nickname: Blågult (Blue and Yellow)
Manager: Lars Lagerback
Website: www.svenskfotboll.se
Stadium: Rasunda
Home Uniform: yellow/blue/yellow
Away Uniform: all blue
Provider: Adidas

1930:	Did not participate
1934:	Second round exit
1938:	4th place
1950:	3rd place
1954:	Did not qualify
1958:	2nd place
1962:	Did not qualify
1966:	Did not qualify
1970:	First round exit
1974:	Second round exit
1978:	First round exit
1982:	Did not qualify
1986:	Did not qualify
1990:	First round exit
1994:	3rd place
1998:	Did not qualify
2002:	Second round exit

Matches	Wins	Draws	Losses	GF	GA	GD	Points
42	15	11	16	71	65	+6	56

Sweden is 9th on the all-time World Cup table

Path to Qualification for World Cup 2006

4-Sep-04	Malta	0	Sweden	7	**W**
8-Sep-04	Sweden	0	Croatia	1	**L**
9-Oct-04	Sweden	3	Hungary	0	**W**
13-Oct-04	Iceland	1	Sweden	4	**W**
26-Mar-05	Bulgaria	0	Sweden	3	**W**
4-Jun-05	Sweden	6	Malta	0	**W**
3-Sep-05	Sweden	3	Bulgaria	0	**W**
7-Sep-05	Hungary	0	Sweden	1	**W**
8-Oct-05	Croatia	1	Sweden	0	**L**
12-Oct-05	Sweden	3	Iceland	1	**W**

Sweden qualified by finishing as one of the two best second-place finishers of the European Zone

Switzerland

Capital: Bern
Independence: August 1, 1291
   (founding of the Swiss Confederation)
Area: 41,290 sq km
Population: 7,489,370
Median Age: 39.8 years
Life Expectancy at Birth: 80.4 years
Ethnic Groups: German 65%,
   French 18%, Italian 10%,
   Romansch 1%, other 6%
Religions: Roman Catholic 41.8%,
   Protestant 35.3%, Orthodox 1.8%,
   other Christian 0.4%, Muslim 4.3%,
   other 1%, unspecified 4.3%, none 11.1%
Languages: German (official) 63.7%, French
   (official) 20.4%, Italian (official) 6.5%, Serbo-
   Croatian 1.5%, Albanian 1.3%, Portuguese
   1.2%, Spanish 1.1%, English 1%, Romansch
   0.5%, other 2.8%
Suffrage: 18 years of age; universal
Military Obligation: every Swiss male has to
   serve for at least 260 days in the armed
   forces; 19 years of age for compulsory
   military service; 17 years of age for
   voluntary military service
GDP Per Capita: $33,800
Budget: $140.4 billion
Military Expenditures: $2.548 billion
   (1.0% of GDP)
Agriculture: grains, fruits, vegetables; meat,
   eggs
Industries: machinery, chemicals, watches,
   textiles, precision instruments
Currency: Swiss franc

Source: *CIA World Factbook*

Switzerland

Peter Stamm

If I'm right, I've only ever once sat down to watch the whole of a football game, and that was the 1986 World Cup final between West Germany and Argentina. It was an exciting match, and it might easily have marked the beginning of a passion for the game. But then I got very busy for twenty years, and that one-night stand was all there ever was.

I had no particular intention of changing this when, a few months ago, Switzerland played Turkey in the second leg of the World Cup qualification playoff. As the game began, we were just sitting down to supper. I was doing the dishes listening to the radio when I heard on the news that Turkey was leading 3–1. Switzerland had won the first leg 2–0; if Turkey scored one more goal, it would mean elimination for Switzerland. I strolled as calmly as I could into the living room, and turned on the TV.

For several days, the newspapers had been full of little else. And for days to come people discussed the game and the violence that followed. About 1.2 million Swiss, just over a sixth of the population, had watched the game on TV. At first I was impressed by the numbers, then I got to wondering what the remaining five-sixths had done with their Wednesday evening. For all the talk of the huge viewing figures, the nonviewing figures were much larger: that great majority of people who form no part of the viewing public, whether it's a world championship or the burial of a princess. If the press claimed Switzerland was in the grip of World Cup fever, then only a small minority of the population were actually suffering. The others, a disturbingly large majority, had normal temperatures.

It's the same thing with elections: it's still the majority of the minority that goes to vote. The true majority doesn't vote, it has no vote or doesn't want to have one. This majority has fascinated me from childhood. When I wandered about on summer afternoons through the deserted Swiss village I grew up in, when I looked around in bars and discotheques later on, I would ask myself where were all the people who allegedly lived and worked and procreated in this country. Even in big crowds, in open-air concerts or on packed ski slopes I was preoccupied with the idea of those missing millions who weren't participating, who weren't there. I imagined my fellow Swiss scattered across the countryside, at home, working in their gardens, walking in the woods and knowing as little about me as I did about them. When I said goodbye to my classmates on our last day of school, I had the sense that my world was exploding, that everything was falling apart and would never be reassembled.

Most nations are artificial creations, more or less arbitrarily defined spaces in which people live, often not connected by anything more than the frontier that was drawn around them while their attention happened to be elsewhere. It's particularly true of Switzerland. Much of it may have so-called natural borders, in the shape of rivers, mountains and lakes, but neither mountains nor water have ever been able to keep people apart, or to contain them in their inborn urge to move. By and large, Switzerland falls away toward its borders, and so everything that's subject to gravity makes its way out of the country. Many of the big rivers of Europe rise in Switzerland— the Rhine, the Rhone, important tributaries of the Danube and the Po—only to leave it as quickly as they can. Physics is against us. We need to hang on to one another, so as not to lose one another. The only thing that keeps us together is willpower and common interests. Our unity exists only in our heads. And not always there either.

Conceived or tolerated as a buffer state between bigger countries, Switzerland has always struggled not so much for its existence as for its identity. It's a land without qualities, and we do all we can to hide the fact. In 1992, one year after the nation had celebrated the 700th anniversary of its existence, there was a huge commotion throughout the country. In the World's Fair in Seville, the artist Ben Vaultier had put up a sign with a single sentence on it: *"La Suisse n'existe pas."* Switzerland does not exist. It's hard to think of a work of art that has provoked as much discussion, as much furor in our country as this. The shocking thing about the statement was that it was true, and basically everyone knew it. Yes, there is a nation called "Switzerland" which issues passports to its citizens proclaiming them to be Swiss, prints banknotes with which they are paid and pay others, has a government and an army and a football team. But however well defined its frontiers, this nation remains a collage, a muddle of different peoples who at some stage or other came here and didn't leave. Switzerland is a transitory country. It always has been. The peculiarity of the country has a lot to do with language. Switzerland has no language, it has many languages, and not just the four official languages. We have the highest percentage of resident foreigners of any European state—around 20 percent. Six other languages are more widely used than our fourth "official language," the slowly dying out Romansch: namely Serbo-Croat, Albanian, Portuguese, Spanish, English and Turkish. Nor are the Swiss the polyglot people they are often held to be. The respective language areas are almost completely homogeneous. The proportion of French speakers in German-speaking Switzerland is between 0 and 2 percent, depending on the canton, and the other way about it's more or less the same. In reality, it's probably slightly lower than that. Even in the bilingual centers, German- and French-speaking Swiss tend to live more alongside than with each other. In Switzerland it's mainly the foreigners who are polyglot.

We are a nation of travelers and of emigrants. More than 600,000 Swiss, almost a tenth of the population, live scattered over the globe. But within the confines of their own country they don't like to move around. A consequence of federalism, of the near-autonomy of individual cantons (districts), is that not only is there a different system of taxation and of schools every few miles, but also that our loyalties tend to be local rather than national. You may feel Swiss when you're abroad, but at home you're from Basel or Zurich or the Valais or Ticino. Most of the members of my family have worked abroad at some stage of their lives, but today we're all living around Lake Constance, within a radius of forty miles. A region that, in turn, is hardly distinguishable from the other side of the fence.

At the time of my birth, Lake Constance was frozen over, and you could walk across it into Germany. The hospital was situated on the shore of the lake, and the first thing I got to see in my country was this frozen lake, this border that suddenly had been made passable. Streams of people apparently crossed the lake at the time, on foot, on skates, in horse-drawn carts, even in automobiles. But even when the lake wasn't frozen over, the south of Germany felt much closer to us than the South or West of Switzerland. The nearest city was Constance, we would go there to do our shopping, or to see a film or a play. The letter boxes and police cars might look different than ours, but culturally we were and are barely distinguishable. Even the dialect across the border is barely different. The only difference really is the passports, which identify some people as Germans, and others as Swiss. Perhaps that's what makes the Swiss so image-obsessed, because we're constantly at risk of being taken for Italians, Germans, Austrians or French. Neither the people nor the landscape has a unity, so a myth must be created to keep the country together. It is the myth of an autochthonous people, doughty but neutral, hardworking but modest as it lives and cultivates the steep Alpine slopes, making cheese and chocolate and expensive watches. It annoys the Swiss if this image, this myth is questioned. The latest revelations and controversies are typical: the role of the Swiss in the Second World War, contacts to South Africa persisting during apartheid and the embargo period, the role of the Swiss in the slave trade, and time and time again, the business ties between Swiss banks and all sorts of international villains.

Switzerland hasn't behaved much worse in the past than other European countries. But the self-critical Swiss are adamant that Switzerland remains a special case, either the best country in the world, or the worst, they haven't quite decided. Switzerland as a country like any other, only smaller and wealthier than most of the others—that's something that a lot of Swiss find impossible to swallow. The image we have of ourselves is almost as naïve as the image that foreigners have of us. Instead of being proud of Rousseau and Le Corbusier and Godard, we hold up Heidi and William Tell—both of whom are fictional. Our pride is vested not in exceptional men and women, but in these icons of averageness. Instead of seeing ourselves as the modern, cosmopolitan industrial and service economy that we are, we cultivate the image of a peasant mountain democracy. And yet the Alps, our trademark, are very sparsely inhabited, and barely used for anything except skiing and hiking. The greater part of the population lives in cities and towns in the flat land. More than 70 percent of the working population is in the service sector. Agriculture employs about 4 percent. (There are about as many unemployed as there are farmers.) It's curious that this blatant clash between self-image and reality appears not to bother the Swiss, that they seem hardly even to be aware of it. The image has become autonomous, it no longer depends on any reality. One of our wealthiest industrialists plays the shirt-sleeved peasant in the corridors of power. The worst fate than can befall a Swiss politician is that he might be taken for urbane and intelligent. Even intellectuals are careful not to speak in accentless High German. And yet Switzerland is a modern and enlightened country, as witness the fact that a year ago plebiscites were carried, legalizing same-sex partnerships and opening the labor market to the new members of the EU. Since the Second World War, the frontiers of Switzerland have become increasingly open. We may not yet be formal members of the EU, but thanks to a series of bilateral agreements, we are firmly integrated in that community of states. The distinctiveness of our regions and inhabitants has not been adversely affected.

Seeing oneself clearly is never easy. Some things are so ingrained, one is barely even aware of them. It's much easier to recognize the exotic than the familiar. A German friend recently described her childhood memories of Switzerland to me. She wrote about how she was forever having to greet people, and how she had never gone to anyone's house without calling first.

> Six o'clock is dinner time, and you never disturb anyone then. In fact, the people all eat at exactly the same time, lunch and dinner anyway. Then, you mustn't remind the Swiss that they weren't actively involved in the Second World War. If you do, then you'll be told about the one or two bombs that fell on Basel, as if that were something to be proud of. The women put on makeup before going to the shops, not to be glamorous but smart at least. If you do sports, it's important that you have the right gear. And the people do quite a bit of sport, and take it very seriously. If someone else's shopping trolley blocks the aisle in a supermarket, and you move it out of the way, then you'll get

dirty looks from people. That's not nice. You don't meddle in other people's business. But as far as scenery goes, Switzerland is very very beautiful.

I myself have often viewed Switzerland from outside. When I was living abroad, I sometimes felt homesick for Switzerland. But it wasn't the neutrality I was missing, or the watch industry or the football team. I felt homesick for people, for my family, my friends and neighbors. I missed the pragmatism of the Swiss, their uncomplicated way of dealing with one another, their dependability. And not least of all I missed the very very beautiful scenery.

In the case of books or paintings I like, I generally make a point of knowing what country the artist or writer comes from. But that has little to do with my liking for their work. When I give readings abroad, the listeners are usually told I come from Switzerland, but I don't think that makes them like my books any better. Nationality is becoming less and less of an issue, and that's something I applaud. The last bastions of our national identity are the army and sport. Skiers win medals not for their canton or region, but for the whole of Switzerland. And the fact that the national team is doing battle on behalf of all of us is betrayed by its German designation, *"Fussball-nationalmannschaft."*

The fact that I sat down and watched the end of the game between Turkey and Switzerland had less to do with any national sentiment on my part than that it was a good game, and the football was of a high standard. I was simply fascinated by the skill and agility of the players, as I am whenever someone is good at their job, or is a master of their craft. Even the many fouls didn't bother me. When the Swiss scored a second goal in the 84th minute, to reduce the deficit to 3–2, a loud "Yeah!" escaped me. My girlfriend, who had come to sit down beside me looked up in some surprise, and with an ironic smile. The Swiss went on to lose 4–2, but it was good enough to qualify. If I'd read the scoreline in the papers the following day, I would just have shrugged. The result only mattered in the context of the game. For the half an hour or so that I watched it, I had become a Swiss, I was playing at being Swiss.

In the same way, I briefly become Swiss when the national anthem is played on August 1, our national holiday. My national feeling just about lasts for the first verse of the anthem. I don't know the second; I think hardly anyone does. The people organizing the various celebrations have cottoned to the fact. By now the text of the anthem is printed on the back of the program in many places. But the climax of the festivities is not the speeches or the singing of the rather undistinguished anthem, but the fires that are lit on the mountain tops to indicate the true frontiers of Switzerland. All that you can see is home.

Translated from the German by Michael Hofmann

World Cup Record

FIFA Ranking: 36
World Cup Appearances: 7
World Cup Champions: 0
Federation Name: Schweizerischer Fussball-Verband
Confederation: UEFA
Founded: 1895
FIFA Affiliation: 1904
Nickname: Die Eidgenosse (Oath Comrades)
Manager: Jakob Kuhn
Website: www.football.ch
Stadium: various
Home Uniform: red/white/red
Away Uniform: white/red/white
Provider: Puma

1930:	Did not participate
1934:	Second round exit
1938:	Second round exit
1950:	First round exit
1954:	Quarterfinal exit
1958:	Did not qualify
1962:	First round exit
1966:	First round exit
1970:	Did not qualify
1974:	Did not qualify
1978:	Did not qualify
1982:	Did not qualify
1986:	Did not qualify
1990:	Did not qualify
1994:	Second round exit
1998:	Did not qualify
2002:	Did not qualify

Matches	Wins	Draws	Losses	GF	GA	GD	Points
22	6	3	13	33	51	-18	21

Switzerland is 23rd on the all-time World Cup table

Path to Qualification for World Cup 2006

4-Sep-04	Switzerland	6	Faroe Islands	0	**W**
8-Sep-04	Switzerland	1	Ireland	1	**D**
9-Oct-04	Israel	2	Switzerland	2	**D**
26-Mar-05	France	0	Switzerland	0	**D**
30-Mar-05	Switzerland	1	Cyprus	0	**W**
4-Jun-05	Faroe Islands	1	Switzerland	3	**W**
3-Sep-05	Switzerland	1	Israel	1	**D**
7-Sep-05	Cyprus	1	Switzerland	3	**W**
8-Oct-05	Switzerland	1	France	1	**D**
12-Oct-05	Ireland	0	Switzerland	0	**D**
12-Nov-05	Switzerland	2	Turkey	0	**W**
16-Nov-05	Turkey	4	Switzerland	2	**L**

Switzerland qualified by finishing second in Group 4 of the European Zone and beating Turkey (by scoring more away goals) in a home-away playoff

Togo

Capital: Lomé
Independence: April 27, 1960 (from French-administered UN trusteeship)
Area: 56,785 sq km
Population: 5,681,519
Median Age: 17.8 years
Life Expectancy at Birth: 57.0 years
Ethnic Groups: black African (37 tribes; largest and most important are Ewe, Mina and Kabre) 99%, European and Syrian-Lebanese less than 1%
Religions: indigenous beliefs 51%, Christian 29%, Muslim 20%
Languages: French (official and the language of commerce), Ewe and Mina (the two major African languages in the south), Kabye and Dagomba (the two major African languages in the north)
Suffrage: NA years of age; universal adult
Military Obligation: 18 years of age for voluntary and compulsory military service
GDP Per Capita: $1,600
Budget: $273.3 million
Military Expenditures: $35.5 million (1.9% of GDP)
Agriculture: coffee, cocoa, cotton, yams, cassava (tapioca), corn, beans, rice, millet, sorghum; livestock; fish
Industries: phosphate mining, agricultural processing, cement; handicrafts, textiles, beverages
Currency: Communaute Financiere Africaine franc (XOF); note: responsible authority is the Central Bank of the West African States

Source: *CIA World Factbook*

Togo

Binyavanga Wainaina

Since gaining independence from France in 1960, Togo's World Cup campaigns have been a litany of abject failure. 1962–1970: Did not enter. 1974–1982: Did not qualify. 1986: Withdrew. 1990: Withdrew. 1994: Did not qualify, lost all their qualifying matches. 1998: Did not qualify, finished bottom of their qualifying pool. 2002: Did not qualify, finished second from last in their pool. When the qualification campaign for the 2006 World Cup began, Togo was ranked 96th in the world.

The campaign began predictably. Togo lost to lowly Equatorial Guinea, and followed this with a loss to Zambia. But then they went on a seven-game unbeaten run, including a win and a draw against mighty Senegal (who had not only made it to the World Cup finals in 2002, but had beaten defending champions France in the opening match). They beat Congo 3–2 in a thriller of a last match to finish top of their qualifying group, with super-striker Emmanuel Sheyi Adebayor scoring eleven goals in twelve games, the most in Africa. (After starring for AS Monaco in France for the past two years, Adebayor signed with Arsenal in January 2006.) The giant teams of West Africa were in shock. The Togolese danced in the streets for days, and the Togolese yellow jersey was said to be flapping over the capital, Lomé, like a new flag.

Watching at home in Kenya, I decided to pay a visit.

In December I set off to Togo by way of Accra, just over the border in Ghana, where I sought out a guide. I found Hubert, a twenty-one-year-old Togolese football player, among a group of fat-free and heavily pectoraled young men in tracksuits and shorts and muscle shirts, sitting by the side of the road near the Togo-Ghana border. People cross over easily; many Ghanaians are Togolese, and many Togolese are Ghanaians. Both nations have qualified for the World Cup. I wondered to myself how many footballers in the Togo team are players who did not make it into the Ghanaian team.

Hubert and his teammates looked boneless and postcoital after a vigorous exercise session at the beach, a swim and a shower. He was much smaller than the others, but he is the star of his team and is due to go to South Africa to try out for a major side there. His coach has high hopes for him.

"Aren't you afraid of these giant Ghanaian players?" I asked, nodding at his hulking friends. He just smiled. He is the one with the international offers.

We crossed the border at Aflao and headed into dry and dusty Lomé. People looked dispirited and the city was rusty and peeling and bleached from an excess of brine and sun and rough times. Hubert pointed out a tourist hotel to me. It looked like it had been closed for years, but the weather here can deteriorate things rapidly. Perhaps it had only been a matter of months; the tourist industry collapsed after pro-democracy riots in early 2005. Hubert grabbed my bags as we made our way through the crowd of people carrying produce and bright and shiny Taiwan trinkets.

The Ewe, who are the largest ethnic group in both Ghana and Togo, settled in the Lomé area in the early seventeenth century. The area had plenty of trees that provided fragrant and healthful chewing sticks, traditional toothbrushes. So it is said they called the place Alo Mé, meaning "among chewing sticks." For two hundred years, the coastal region was a major raiding center for Europeans in search of slaves. To Europeans, what is now Togo was known as "The Slave Coast."

We took a taxi into town and drove around looking for a bureau to change my dollars to CFA francs. One was closed. The next one had the characterless look of a government office and smelled of old damp cardboard. They told us we'd have to wait an hour to change any money.

In the center of the city, buildings were imposing, unfriendly and impractical. Faded paint, plastic fittings looking bleached and brittle. I had seen buildings like this before—in South African homeland capitals, in Chad and Budapest—the kind of buildings that international contractors build for countries eager to show how "modern" they are. They are usually described as "ultramodern." When new, they shine like the mirrored sunglasses of a presidential bodyguard; within months they rust and peel and crumble.

In Accra, signs had been warm and humorous: HAPPY DAY SHOP, DO LIFE YOURSELF, DIPLOMATIC HAIRCUT. Not in Lomé. I saw one called Centre des Cheques Postaux, another Centre National de Perfecionnement Professional. There were International Bureaus of Many Incredibly Important things, and Centres International of Even More Important Things. I counted fourteen buildings with the word "Developement" on their walls.

For lunch, Hubert led me to a small plot of land surrounded on three sides by concrete walls. A group of women were stirring large pots near one wall; across the way, there were couches and a huge television under a makeshift thatch shade. A fat man who looked like the owner was watching *Octopussy* on satellite television. There was a fading mural on the wall of stiff white people waltzing, noses facing the sky. A hand-drawn arrow pointed to a violin, and another arrow pointed to a champagne bottle. An ad for a hotel: *L'Hotel Climon. 12 chambres. Entièrement Climatisées. Non loin du Lycée Française.*

Inside, a topless woman with spectacular breasts served brochettes and a large fish on a larger platter. A chef grinned at us with sparkling cheeks. Everyone was eating, drinking, laughing. Not Hubert—as an athlete he was very finicky about his diet. I ordered the fish.

We made our way out and looked for a taxi. There were more taxis than private cars on the road. Hubert and the taxi driver soon fell into a heated discussion about the price, and we left the taxi in a huff. Hubert was furious. I remained silent—the price he quoted seemed reasonable to me, but Nairobi taxis are very expensive.

"He is trying to cheat us because you are a foreigner."

I assumed the taxi driver was angry because Hubert did not want to be a good citizen and conspire with him to overcharge me. We got another taxi, and drove past more grim-looking buildings. There were lots of warning signs: *Interdit de . . . Interdit de . . .*

And there were several hand-painted advertisements of women serving one thing or another, topless, with the same spectacular breasts. Were they all by the same artist? Most Ghanaian hand-painted murals were either barbershop signs or hair salon signs. In Togo, breasts rule. Is this a Francophone thing? There is no way naked breasts could be publicly displayed in any former English colony I know.

We drove past the suburb where all the villas are, and all the embassies. Nearby there was a dual carriageway, in sober charcoal gray, better than any road I had seen so far. It cut through bushes and gardens and vanished in the distance. This was the road to the presidential palace of the former dictator, Gnassingbé Eyadéma. It was surrounded by lush parkland.

"The presidential family have a zoo in the compound," Hubert said.

Everything else looked beaten. Since the troubles that scared donors and tourists away, there have not been any new buildings built to make the fading old ones less conspicuous. The licks of paint, the gleaming automobiles of a political elite, the fluttering flags on the streets, the pink and blue tourist hotels, the pink and blue bikini-clad tourists on the beach sipping pink and blue cocktails. The illusions of progress no longer need to be maintained. The dictator who needed them is dead.

Dictators always sell the myth that they are all-powerful. The legendary Zairean dictator Mobutu had palaces all over his country. The palaces were huge, full of gold taps and antiques, studded with gems and the seemingly artisanal efforts of the finest European craftsmen. The moment his government fell it became clear that the taps were chrome, the vases cheap plastic. Everything was fake. So long as the myth of Mobutu's wealth was believed, he was universally powerful in Zaire. Only after he had died did anyone discover that the bank accounts were empty, the monuments hollow, the military badly trained and incapable of defending the country.

It was much the same with Togo's Gnassingbé Eyadéma. One of Africa's most durable dictators, he ruled Togo from 1967 until his death in 2005. He was in the French army in the 1950s, and later participated in two military coups in Togo, in 1963 and 1967. He managed to remain in power for so long with help from the French, who mostly ignored the abuses of his government and gave him military aid for decades.

Many talk about American adventures in Africa, but it is the French who have most aggressively propped up illegitimate governments and kept national institutions weak in their former colonies. The French especially support fatherly dictators who love French luxury goods and French military bases: Omar Bongo, who imported a French chateau to Gabon; Emperor Bokassa of the Central African Republic, who had an inauguration worthy of Louis XIV, and died in France; Léopold Sédar Senghor of Senegal, who was buried in France; and Félix Houphouët-Boigny of Côte d'Ivoire, who built the world's largest Catholic cathedral in his home village.

Gnassingbé Eyadéma outlasted them all. He was a Kabyé, the second largest ethnic group in Togo. In the first half of the twentieth century, many young Kabyé moved from their traditional arid and moutainous homeland around the northern city of Kara to work as sharecroppers on Ewe farms in the south. The wealthier Ewe looked down upon the Kabyé, but depended on them as laborers. Once in power, Eyadéma made sure to fill the military with Kabyé loyalists. It was called "The Army of Cousins," and armed by the French.

So Eyadéma had the loyalty of most Kabyé—and was happy, when threatened, to make much of the differences between the two ethnic groups. Ewe protesters were imprisoned or harassed in the 1990s. The Kabyé who were not directly related to the president benefited very little from his rule—but he held them hostage by fear. Like Kenya's former president Daniel arap Moi, he had so offended the rest of the country over the years that the Kabyé were terrified that if his family ceased to rule, there would be recriminations.

In 1974, he Africanized his name from Etienne and became General Gnassingbé Eyadéma. He survived a few assassination attempts, was well known for having "powerful medicine."

He threw political opponents to the crocodiles.

He had more than one hundred children.

He had the football stadium in Lomé named after him.

He was fond of alternative medicine.

He had four sons who matter:

Ernest, the eldest, is a military man, his late father's "enforcer." He was once the commander of the Green Berets, a commander of a military garrison. He was the favorite to take over from his father until he fell ill.

Faure, thirty-eight years old, is the son who most resembles his late father, and the one known to be "sober." He earned an MBA at George Washington University in Washington, D.C., before returning to Togo to manage his father's businesses and the family interests in phosphates, Togo's leading export.

Rock was the rebellious one—who disapproved of his father and avoided politics. He was put in charge of the Togolese Football Federation.

Kpatcha used to head the state body SAZOF, which oversees investments into and exports out of the country.

When Eyadéma died in 2005, the military installed Faure as president and Kpatcha became the minster of defense. There were riots in the streets, arrests, deaths; other states refused to recognize his government. But his late father's political machinery organized elections, which Faure Gnassingbé won. And he had good fortune on his side: amid all the unrest his younger brother Rock delivered the best gift his family has ever received: qualification for the World Cup. Faure Gnassingbé remained president, and Rock Gnassingbé was made a commander of the Order of Mono.

Driving past Lomé's main hospital I finally saw the first signs of sensible commerce. Lined along the hospital wall were secondhand imported goods: giant stereo speakers, a drum set, bananas, a small kiosk with a sign on its forehead that read TELEPHON INTERNATION, dog chains, lawn mowers, more dog chains, five or six big screen televisions, still more dog chains, crutches, a row of steam irons and a large faded oriental carpet.

An hour later, Hubert and I reached the market, and finally found ourselves in a functional and vibrant city. Currency dealers presented themselves at the window of the car—negotiations were quick, money changed hands. We set off to walk into the maze of stalls. It was hard to tell how big the market was, people were milling about everywhere, selling on the ground and setting up small rickety stalls in every available space.

There were stalls selling stoves and electronic goods, currency changers and traders from all over West Africa, tailors and cobblers and brokers and fixers and food and drink. Togo has always made its money as a free trade area, supplying traders from all over West Africa.

Markets like these have been in existence throughout West Africa for centuries. All of the ones in Lomé are run by the famous "Mama Benzes"—rich trading women who have chauffer-driven Mercedes Benzes. These days, after years of economic stagnation, the Mama Benz are called Mama Opel.

Most of all the stalls were bursting with fabrics. I have never seen so many—there were shapeless splotches of color, bold geometries, hot pinks on earth brown, ululating pinstripes. There were fabrics with thousands of embroidered coin-sized holes shaped like flowers. There were fabrics that promised wealth: one stall owner pointed out a strange design on a Togolese coin and showed me the same design on the fabric of an already busy shirt. There were fabrics for clinging, for flicking over a shoulder, for square shouldering, for floppy collaring, for marrying and some must surely have assured instant breakups.

We brushed past clothes that lapped against my ear, whispering, others licking my brow from hangers above my face.

Anywhere else in the world the fabric is secondary: it is the final architecture of the garment that makes a difference. But in Lomé, it is the fabric that matters. The fabric you buy can be sewed into a dress, a shirt, an evening outfit of headband, skirt and top in one afternoon, at no extra cost. It is all about the fabric. There was silk and cotton, fabrics from the Netherlands and China, mud cloth from Mali, kente from Northern Togo.

It was the stall selling bras that stopped my forward motion. It was a tiny open-air stall, with bras piled on a small table, bras hanging above, bras everywhere. Years ago, I had a part-time job as a translator for some Senegalese visitors to Kenya. Two of the older women, both quite large, asked me to take them shopping for bras. We walked into shop after shop in Nairobi's biggest mall. They probed and pulled and sighed and exclaimed—and I translated all this to the chichi young girls who looked offended that a woman of that age can ask questions about a bra that have nothing to do with its practical uses. We roamed for what seemed like hours, but these Francophone women failed to find a single bra in all the shops in Sarit Centre that combined uplifting engineering with the right aesthetic. They could not understand this Anglophone insistence on ugly bras for any woman over twenty-five.

Open air bra stalls in my country sell useful, practical white bras. All secondhand. Not in Togo. There were red strapless bras with snarling edges of black lace. I saw a daffodil yellow bra with curly green leaves running along its seam. Hanging down the middle of the line was the largest nursing bra I have ever seen—white and wired and ominous, with pulleys and pistons and a flying buttress or two. One red bra had bared black teeth around a nipple-sized pair of holes. Next to it was a corset in a delicate ivory color. I did not know people still wore corsets.

A group of women started laughing. I was gaping. Anglophone. Prude.

It took an hour for Hubert and I to move only a hundred meters or so. Wherever I looked, I was presented with goods to touch and feel. Hubert looked grim. I imitated him: heads down, we moved forward. But soon we saw what I was after: a stall specializing in Togo football team jerseys. There were long-sleeved yellow ones, short-sleeved ones, sleeveless ones. Shirts for kids. All of them had the same name on the back: Emmanuel Sheyi Adebayor.

I picked out a pair and while Hubert negotiated for them I ambled over to a nearby stall. An elegant, motherly woman dressed in pink lace smiled at me graciously. Her shirt stall looked cool and fresh. She invited me in to stand under the flapping clothes, and then dispatched a young man to get some cold mineral water. I admired one of the shirts—"Too small for you," she says. But I want it desperately! She was reluctant. Okay. Okay she said, "I will try to help you. When are you leaving?" Tomorrow I told her. Ahh. "I have a tailor—we will get the fabrics and sew the shirts up for you, a proper size."

It was then that I realized that I could settle in this place—I could cast my eyes about, express an interest and get a tailor-made solution to anything I wanted. I pointed at possible fabrics; she frowned and said, "Nooooo, this one without fancy collars. We will make it simple—let the fabric speak for itself." In French her opinion sounded very authoritative. Soon I found I had ordered six shirts. A group of leather-workers presented an array of handmade sandals: snakeskin, crocodile, every color imaginable. Madam thought the soft brown leather ones were good. She bent one shoe into a circle. Nodded. Good sole.

Her eyes narrowed at the salesman and asked, "How much?"

His reply elicited a shrug and a turn—she had already lost interest, no value for money. The price dropped and dropped again. Finally she nodded and I bought them. She summoned a Ghanaian cobbler, who reinforced the seams for me as I waited, glued the edges. She looked at me with compassion. "What about something for the woman you love?" I started to protest—no, I'm not into this love thing. . . . Her compassion deepened. The women's clothes! I saw a purple top with a purple fur collar. A hand-embroidered skirt and top of white cotton. It was clear to me that my two sisters would never be the same again if they had clothes like this. They each got two outfits. I couldn't believe how cheap the clothes were. What about Christmas presents for my nieces? And my brother Jim? And my nephews. And what about Jim's wife? The women in my life—they will be as gracious and powerful as the madam in pink lace, and cool in the heat. Queens, princesses. Sexy matriarchs. I spent four hours in her stall—and nearly $200.

The beach ran alongside a highway back to Ghana. Hundreds of scooter taxis chugged past us with 5 P.M. clients, mostly women, who seemed very comfortable. One woman rode sidesaddle. She was holding a baby and groceries, and her hair was tied up in one of Togo's ubiquitous knots of cloth. She seemed unbothered by the risks of two wheels. At the beach we sat on some rickety plastic chairs and discouraged a guitar-playing crooner, who wanted to give us a personal soundtrack for sunset. We ordered beers.

"Look," Hubert said, pointing at the fishermen. "They are about to pull in the net."

There must have been fifty people dragging in one long, long net.

"They do this every evening—then you will see people coming to buy fish for home and for the market."

It took at least half an hour for the net to come in. Hundreds of people gathered to buy fish. The crooner returned—and a group of Sierra Leoneans sitting next to us shouted at him to leave.

Hubert and I made our way to a beach bar.

On the way back to his family's house, I saw an old sign by the side of the road. Whatever it had previously advertised had rusted away, and somebody had painted on it in huge letters: TOGO 3–CONGO 2.

World Cup Record

FIFA Ranking: 56
World Cup Appearances: 0
World Cup Champions: 0
Federation Name: Federation Togolese de
  Football
Confederation: CAF
Founded: 1960
FIFA Affiliation: 1962
Nickname: Les Eperviers (Sparrow Hawks)
Manager: Otto Pfister
Website: www.ftf-enligne.tg
Stadium: Stade General Eyadema
Home Uniform: red/green/white
Away Uniform: yellow/green/white
Provider: Puma

1930:	Did not enter
1934:	Did not enter
1938:	Did not enter
1950:	Did not enter
1954:	Did not enter
1958:	Did not enter
1962:	Did not enter
1966:	Did not enter
1970:	Did not enter
1974:	Did not qualify
1978:	Did not qualify
1982:	Did not qualify
1986:	Withdrew
1990:	Withdrew
1994:	Did not qualify
1998:	Did not qualify
2002:	Did not qualify

Matches	Wins	Draws	Losses	GF	GA	GD	Points
0	0	0	0	0	0	0	0

Togo is appearing in the World Cup for the first time

Path to Qualification for World Cup 2006

11-Oct-03	Equatorial Guinea	1	Togo	0	**L**
16-Nov-03	Togo	2	Equatorial Guinea	0	**W**
5-Jun-04	Zambia	1	Togo	0	**L**
20-Jun-04	Togo	3	Senegal	1	**W**
4-Jul-04	Liberia	0	Togo	0	**D**
5-Sep-04	Togo	2	Congo	0	**W**
10-Oct-04	Togo	1	Mali	0	**W**
27-Mar-05	Mali	1	Togo	2	**W**
5-Jun-05	Togo	4	Zambia	1	**W**
18-Jun-05	Senegal	2	Togo	2	**D**
4-Sep-05	Togo	3	Liberia	0	**W**
8-Oct-05	Congo	2	Togo	3	**W**

Togo qualified by finishing first in Group 1 of the African Zone

Trinidad and Tobago

Capital: Port-of-Spain
Independence: August 31, 1962 (from the UK)
Area: 5,128 sq km
Population: 1,088,644
Median Age: 30.9 years
Life Expectancy at Birth: 66.7 years
Ethnic Groups: Indian (South Asian) 40%,
    African 37.5%, mixed 20.5%, other 1.2%,
    unspecified 0.8%
Religions: Roman Catholic 26%,
    Hindu 22.5%, Anglican 7.8%, Baptist 7.2%,
    Pentecostal 6.8%, Seventh Day
    Adventist 4%, other Christian 5.8%,
    Muslim 5.8%, other 10.8%,
    unspecified 1.4%, none 1.9%
Languages: English (official), Hindi, French,
    Spanish, Chinese
Suffrage: 18 years of age; universal
Military Obligation: 18 years of age for
    voluntary military service;
    no conscription
GDP Per Capita: $10,500
Budget: $3.193 billion
Military Expenditures: $66.7 million
    (0.6% of GDP)
Agriculture: cocoa, rice, citrus, coffee,
    vegetables, poultry
Industries: petroleum, chemicals, tourism,
    food processing, cement, beverage, cotton
    textiles
Currency: Trinidad and Tobago dollar

Source: *CIA World Factbook*

Trinidad and Tobago

Cressida Leyshon

"Anything other than three straight defeats will be a surprise." This was the judgment made by the Associated Press and published throughout the world, after Trinidad and Tobago became the last team to qualify for the 2006 World Cup. Bookmakers rated the Caribbean nation's chances of winning the trophy at 750–1, trailing well behind the other newcomers Angola, Ghana and Togo. The islands of Trinidad and Tobago make up the smallest country, with the smallest population, in the World Cup. It has taken eleven attempts for the country, better known for cricket than football, to make it to the finals. It took the return from international retirement of the thirty-four-year-old captain, Dwight Yorke, and the thirty-seven-year-old striker, Russell Latapy; a mid-campaign change of coaches, with the Dutch tactician Leo Beenhakker replacing the venerable Trinidadian Bertille St. Clair; a two-legged playoff against Bahrain; and the import of Christopher Birchall, a midfielder from England whose mother's birth in Port-of-Spain allowed him to become the first white player to start for the national team in twenty years. And after all this, after Trinidad and Tobago's epic journey to qualification, it was met by a one-line dismissal and relegation to the role of ultimate long shot. Yet with that sentence, with that relegation, came my support.

Something happens to me when sport becomes the clash of nations, rather than of teams. I can't help being moved by the idea that the whole world is watching, that within eleven men on a field you can see a nation's history. I was born in England, and if England is playing, I want England to win. But I'll pick other teams, other countries, too. I want to steal some of their joy in victory, their pain in defeat. Most of all, I want to see the long-shot triumph.

European travelers have been seduced by the islands at the mouth of the Orinoco River, where the clear water of the delta meets the salty water of the Caribbean, ever since Christopher Columbus sighted Trinidad on July 31, 1498. They've been sending back reports, making judgments, assessing the value of the land and its inhabitants. "There were houses and people and fine cultivated land, as green and lovely as the orchards of Valencia in March," Columbus wrote of Trinidad. The people he saw called their island Ieri, land of the hummingbird. To Columbus they were "handsome, with fine limbs and bodies." He tried to coax a canoe-full over to his ship:

> I greatly desired conversation with them, but it seemed that I had nothing left to show them which would induce them to come nearer still. So I had a tambourine brought up to the poop and played, and I made some of the young men dance, imagining that the Indians would draw closer to see the festivities. On observing the music and dancing, however, they dropped their oars, and picked up their bows, and strung them. Each one seized his shield, and they began to shoot arrows at us. I immediately stopped the music and dancing and ordered some crossbows to be fired.

Columbus thought he was on the verge of entering an earthly paradise, and wrote from the West Indies to his sponsors, King Ferdinand and Queen Isabella, of Spain: "I have come to the following conclusions concerning the world: that it is not round . . . but the shape of a pear, which is round everywhere except the stalk, where it juts out a long way; or that it is like a round ball, on part of which is something like the woman's nipple." Columbus imagined that this nipple formed the highest part of the earth's surface, closest to the sky and the sun. "For I believe that the earthly Paradise lies here, which no one can enter except by God's leave."

Eventually Columbus landed on Trinidad, was welcomed by men wearing gold and pearls, and given bread, fruit and wine. The Amerindians should have kept on shooting arrows.

V. S. Naipaul, Trinidad's great writer, described the Caribbean as "Europe's other sea, the Mediterranean of the New World . . . a Mediterranean which summoned up every dark human instinct without the complementary impulses towards nobility and beauty of older lands, a Mediterranean where civilization turned satanic, per-verting those it attracted . . . the aboriginal population of some millions wiped out; the insatiable plantations . . . the interminable wars . . . it would seem that simply to have survived in the West Indies is to have triumphed."

When the Spanish found none of the gold they desired, they harnessed paradise to cultivate another kind of gold. A gold that could be smoked or turned into chocolate or used to sweeten tea. A gold that required fields and labor. Slavery came to the islands, and over the next three centuries, as European powers vied with one another for control, the Caribbean became a tropical version of William Blake's dark, satanic mills.

To turn an island into a factory, laborers are needed. The indigenous population, disarmed by the Spanish, was forced into servitude. Sporadic revolts were put down, and the Amerindians—the Arawaks, the Chaimas, the Tamanaques, the Salives, the Chaguanas, the Quaquas and the Caribs—died of disease, hard labor and sadness. In the end, the conquistadors were never able to settle the islands effectively, and left them in a state of relatively benign neglect for well over a century. The French were invited to settle Trinidad, bringing with them sugar cane, African slaves and the minute classification of skin color. Tobago, the far smaller island, became a bargaining chip between the Europeans and changed hands as many as twenty-nine times, before it ended up in the hands of the English. Trinidad, too, was eventually taken over by Britain, whose efficiency in organizing the triangular trade in slaves from West Africa, sugar, tobacco and cotton from the West Indies and Americas, and goods from Europe, had made the cities of London, Liverpool and Bristol (where I grew up) flush with cash.

I moved to Bristol from Nottingham when I was ten. Nottingham was the home of Robin Hood and Maid Marion and an evil sheriff. Nottingham was the place where the rich were robbed to feed the poor. It was a city with a well-honed sense of its own mythology. What did Bristol have? Decaying docks and empty warehouses. The working port had moved far from the center, to Avonmouth, and it was easy to forget that Bristol was a port city. My father worked for Imperial Tobacco, a company with roots going back to 1786, though I never associated our move with the fact that ships had been delivering his livelihood to Bristol for hundreds of years.

If you turned right at the end of the street where my family lived, you would walk down Whiteladies Road; turn left, and you'd be walking up Blackboy Hill. I walked up and down Whiteladies Road and Blackboy Hill almost every day for eight years, and I barely thought about the possible significance of those names. By some estimates more than two thousand vessels unloaded their tobacco, cocoa and sugar on Bristol's docks, then sailed in search of slaves in West Africa. In the eighteenth century ships from Bristol, Liverpool and London carried two and a half million slaves to the new world—40 percent of the century's total.

Naipaul's literary predecessor in Trinidad, the incisive analyst of slavery, cricket and colonialism C. L. R. James, once described where all those ships went after leaving Bristol: "The slavers scoured the coasts of Guinea. . . . From the coast they organized expeditions far into the interior. They set the simple tribesmen fighting against each other with modern weapons over thousands of square miles. The propagandists of the time claimed that however cruel was the slave traffic, the African slave in America was happier than in his own African civilization."

When slavery was abolished, in 1834, the absentee sugar planters were forced to look elsewhere for a fresh source of labor, and the indentured laborers of China, and, in particular, India, changed the complexion of the West Indies once again. Trinidad became the paradoxical place that Naipaul, the descendant of agricultural laborers from India, describes at times with affection and at other times with disdain; where the songs and lamentations sung by West Africans in the camps and fields of the sugar plantations, called *kaiso,* laid the foundation for joyful, bawdy, political calypso; and where a buttoned-down English colony indulged in the wild celebration of a Roman Catholic pre-lenten carnival (a gift, in part, of French settlers). For James, the greatest paradox of colonialism was that it allowed him to embark upon the journey to becoming a writer: "I began to study

Latin and French, then Greek, and much else. But particularly we learnt, I learnt and obeyed and taught a code, the English public school code. Britain and her colonies and the colonial peoples. What do the British people know of what they have done there? Precious little. The colonial peoples, particularly the West Indians, scarcely know themselves as yet. It has taken me a long time to begin to understand."

Naipaul, like James, took his colonial education across the ocean, on a scholarship to Oxford, where he was determined to become a writer, if not through inspiration, then through will alone. As he wrote in the introduction to the reissue of his brilliant comic novel, *A House for Mr. Biswas*: "I had no gift. At least, I was aware of none. I had no precocious way with words, no talent for fantasy or storytelling. But I began to build my life around the writing ambition. The gift, I thought, was going to come later, when I grew up. Purely from wishing to be a writer, I thought of myself as a writer." From these beginnings, in the longest of all possible shots, he would go on to win the Nobel Prize for literature.

As Britain lost its share of the sugar market to America, and as the Caribbean islands lost their place in Europe's history, a Scottish immigrant named Thomas Boyd wrote to his family in Glasgow and asked them to send him a football, two bladders and an air pump. The writer Valentino Singh, in *The Story of Football in Trinidad and Tobago,* quotes an account of the first football game in Trinidad, in the early 1890s. "Thirty persons showed up and sides were formed. Jackets and caps were used as goalposts and the game started. After fifteen minutes, most of the players were *'hors de combat,'* and declared that the climatic conditions were against the winter sport. The remainder continued to play."

Cricket already established, football stuttered to life. Games were played on the Savannah, the grassy area in the middle of Port-of-Spain where cows grazed. Clubs were founded, and, as with everything else on the island, teams were organized on principles of religion, class and color. Boyd joined his Scottish compatriots in the

Clydesdale Cricket Club, playing football once the cricket season was over. An Irish priest founded the Shamrocks, for Catholics. A league was formed, affiliated with the football association back in England, and by 1911 deckchairs were available for spectators at a cost of six cents a game. Black and East Indian players, however, were excluded from the main clubs. Majestic, the only nonwhite team, was founded in 1909, but it didn't do well, conceding fifty-five goals and scoring only two in its first season.

It wasn't until the First World War, when British immigrants left Trinidad and Tobago to join the army, that the great local teams emerged. Singh's history is filled with detailed accounts of games played by now-defunct clubs, and rankings for leagues that no longer exist; but through all this old history, as deck chairs give way to stands, and white players to black (football never attracted Trinidadian Indians the same way that cricket does), you can feel institutions changing, the balance of power tilting, as London's hold over Port-of-Spain relaxes. And as the large-scale migrations of Trinidadians and Tobagonians to Britain began, in the years after the Second World War, the national football team also paid its first visit.

The Southampton *Evening News* of August 24, 1953, described the event: "Trinidad football team arrived in England today and the English weather provided a typical welcome. Dark mist caused by incessant fine rain hung over Southampton, as the SS *Golfito* nosed its way into the dock. But the weather could not dampen the lads' spirit. They sang their way into England with a specially written calypso entitled 'Fire Brigade water the road, Trinidad is coming down.'"

The calypso-singing team, having never played longer than sixty minutes, lost its first game, against Dorset County, 7–3. And in that one fact you can feel the isolation of Trinidad and Tobago, the way that football had developed along its own slightly ramshackle lines. At home, the rivalries were fierce; abroad the team became a charming puff of tropical air, a tonic for dreary, postwar England, not an opponent to be taken seriously. But the 1953 English tour, defeats and all, was part of an ambitious and successful program to improve the island game, initiated by Eric James, the first black secretary of the

Trinidad and Tobago Football Association, the man who set his country on its forty-two-year journey to the World Cup. He was also the brother of C. L. R. James.

When they were young, the two brothers watched cricket out of the window in their house by the recreation ground in the small town of Tunapuna. One would go on to become a great theorist of revolution and opponent of institutional organizations, spending much of his adult life outside Trinidad, in Britain and America; the other would spend his life at home, creating an institution for football free of color barriers.

If the James family represented the black middle classes, then Austin "Jack" Warner, the school teacher who became secretary of the football association in 1973, eleven years after the country gained its independence, is the man in whom the colonial legacy was finally shaken off. Warner, who speaks about cutting cane as a boy and walking six miles to school, identifies himself with the poor and dispossessed. "Football," he has said, "is still seen as a sport for the black, the destitute, the lower class. It does not endear itself to the people who have money." Warner reorganized the league system, expanded football throughout the islands, and, in 1983, became the youngest member of the FIFA executive. A few years later he resigned from his position at the football association to become a vice-president of FIFA and the president of CONCACAF (the group of North and Central American and Caribbean countries), though he retained a role as a "special adviser" to the national team. Along the way he also became very wealthy.

Warner has always presented himself as the fixer, the go-to guy, the man who can find girls to appear at an opening ceremony or help with the papers to make an English-born player eligible for the World Cup squad. There have been accusations of financial impropriety, and the Trinidad and Tobago *Express* has been investigating Warner's business practices, despite the euphoric haze of goodwill that surrounded the special adviser after Trinidad and Tobago won their final playoff game in November.

"Trinidad has always admired the 'sharp character'" Naipaul wrote in *The Middle Passage,* his account of returning to the West

Indies in 1960, "who, like the sixteenth-century picaroon of Spanish literature, survives and triumphs by his wits in a place where it is felt that all eminence is arrived at by crookedness." Naipaul's view of Trinidad is sometimes so harsh that it can be hard to read. He forgives nothing, damns everyone, is a scathing enumerator of the country's failings; a critic of all, whether East Indian, black or white. But in his fiction, especially his early novels, those same failings animate his writing. The moralist recedes and Naipaul revels in the sounds and textures, the arguments and entanglements, of a life left behind. Those early works are exhilarating, often joyous, sometimes tragic. I can't help wondering what Trinidad's Nobel laureate would make of a character like Jack Warner. Would he examine him with the eye of the moralist or the novelist?

Jack Warner and his Soca Warriors will be going to Germany this summer. The reception they can expect might not be that different from the one Eric James and the calypso-singing team received in 1953. The Soca Warriors are being billed as the party team. They come with Soca anthems, the faster, more aggressive combination of calypso melodies with East Indian rhythms, and a traveling drum section in the stands to accompany their games. They are the team to provide some excitement and flair off the field, but not necessarily much on it. Jamaica's Reggae Boyz livened up the 1998 World Cup; now it's the neighbors' turn. Or that's the expectation. The players have more serious ambitions: "I am not a party person. And a lot of the others aren't either," Kelvin Jack, one of the squad's goalkeepers, who plays for Dundee in Scotland's First Division, told the *Scotsman*. "And Dwight Yorke. He smiles on the pitch but he is my captain and I know how intense he is in the dressing room."

The World Cup is about one team of eleven men on the field facing another. It's not supposed to be about ticket sales and merchandise and FIFA vice-presidents using their positions to benefit financially. Of course, that view of the World Cup is a fantasy. It *is* about money and power and television rights and sponsorship deals and ticket allocations. It's about coaches being hired and coaches fired. It's about drug tests. It's about a few players being lionized and many more being vilified. It's about winners and losers. You can't help wishing for the fantasy, though. You can't help wishing there was an earthly paradise. Of falling into the trap that Columbus fell into.

The legacy of Trinidad and Tobago—and what England, Paraguay and Sweden should keep in mind before their first round games with the island nation—is its ability to beat the odds stacked against it. For four centuries, the country was at the receiving end of history, but it transformed everything it received. From *kaiso,* calypso; from colonization, cricket and carnival; and from labor riots, the powerful rhetoric of the trade-union movement, most recently put to use by Trinidadian Roger Toussaint, who led New York City's transit workers in an against-all-odds strike in December 2005. And if, at the end of their illustrious careers, Dwight Yorke and Russell Latapy can be a part of this legacy, can experience some of the World Cup glory they missed when they barely failed to qualify sixteen years ago; if a young, white Englishman from Staffordshire can discover his taste for Soca and carnival and score a couple of goals along the way; if a Dutchman can take a squad of Caribbeans who now play in teams scattered across the globe (and not necessarily in the best teams at that) and direct their joy and enthusiasm in playing for their country into a successful performance on the pitch; if Trinidad and Tobago could manage to win; if they could even beat England, when colony and colonizer meet in June, then, for an hour or two, the islands might be paradise. Because if you're the long-shot, victory is so much sweeter. Trinidad and Tobago once provided sweetness to Europe at the highest possible price. Perhaps it's time for them to take a little sweetness home.

World Cup Record

FIFA Ranking: 50
World Cup Appearances: 0
World Cup Champions: 0
Federation Name: Trinidad and Tobago Football
Federation
Confederation: CONCACAF
Founded: 1908
FIFA Affiliation: 1963
Nickname: Soca Warriors
Manager: Leo Beenhakker
Website: www.tnt.fifa.com
Stadium: Haseley Crawford Stadium
Home Uniform: black and red/red/red
Away Uniform: red and white/white/white
Provider: Adidas

1930:	Did not enter
1934:	Did not enter
1938:	Did not enter
1950:	Did not enter
1954:	Did not enter
1958:	Did not enter
1962:	Did not enter
1966:	Did not qualify
1970:	Did not qualify
1974:	Did not qualify
1978:	Did not qualify
1982:	Did not qualify
1986:	Did not qualify
1990:	Did not qualify
1994:	Did not qualify
1998:	Did not qualify
2002:	Did not qualify

Matches	Wins	Draws	Losses	GF	GA	GD	Points
0	0	0	0	0	0	0	0

Trinidad and Tobago is appearing in the World Cup for the first time

Path to Qualification for World Cup 2006

Date					
13-Jun-04	Dominican Republic	0	Trinidad & Tobago	2	W
20-Jun-04	Trinidad & Tobago	4	Dominican Republic	0	W
18-Aug-04	St. Vincent	0	Trinidad & Tobago	2	W
4-Sep-04	St. Kitts and Nevis	1	Trinidad & Tobago	2	W
8-Sep-04	Trinidad & Tobago	1	Mexico	3	L
10-Oct-04	Trinidad & Tobago	5	St. Kitts and Nevis	1	W
13-Oct-04	Mexico	3	Trinidad & Tobago	0	L
17-Nov-04	Trinidad & Tobago	2	St. Vincent	1	W
9-Feb-05	Trinidad & Tobago	1	United States	2	L
26-Mar-05	Guatemala	5	Trinidad & Tobago	1	L
30-Mar-05	Trinidad & Tobago	0	Costa Rica	0	D
4-Jun-05	Trinidad & Tobago	2	Panama	0	W
8-Jun-05	Mexico	2	Trinidad & Tobago	0	L
17-Aug-05	United States	1	Trinidad & Tobago	0	L
3-Sep-05	Trinidad & Tobago	3	Guatemala	2	W
7-Sep-05	Costa Rica	2	Trinidad & Tobago	0	L
8-Oct-05	Panama	0	Trinidad & Tobago	1	W
12-Oct-05	Trinidad & Tobago	2	Mexico	1	L
12-Nov-05	Trinidad & Tobago	1	Bahrain	1	D
16-Nov-05	Bahrain	0	Trinidad & Tobago	1	W

Trinidad and Tobago qualified by finishing fourth in the Concacaf Zone and beating Bahrain in a home-away playoff

Tunisia

Capital: Tunis
Independence: March 20, 1956
(from France)
Area: 163,610 sq km
Population: 10,074,951
Median Age: 27.3 years
Life Expectancy at Birth: 74.9 years
Ethnic Groups: Arab 98%, European 1%,
Jewish, other 1%
Religions: Muslim 98%, Christian 1%,
Jewish, other 1%
Languages: Arabic (official), French
Suffrage: 20 years of age; universal
Military Obligation: 20 years of age for
compulsory military service; conscript
service obligation: 12 months;
18 years of age for voluntary
military service
GDP Per Capita: $7,100
Budget: $7.573 billion
Military Expenditures: $356 million
(1.5% of GDP)
Agriculture: olives, olive oil, grain, dairy
products, tomatoes, citrus fruit, beef, sugar
beets, dates, almonds
Industries: petroleum, mining (particularly
phosphate and iron ore), tourism, textiles,
footwear, agribusiness, beverages
Currency: Tunisian dinar

Source: *CIA World Factbook*

Tunisia

Wendell Steavenson

Mourad Teyeb is smart and thin and lithe, with a face scored with lines after a decade of rumor and deadline. He is a sports journalist for the French paper *Le Temps* in Tunis. He wakes early and writes a story every morning. In the winter there is the Tunisian League and its four main protagonists: Sfax, from an industrial town; Etoile, from Sousse, the tourist boomtown of sun, sea and Mediterranean sand; and Espérance and Club Africain, old embittered rivals from the capital, Tunis. In the summer there are transfer rumors and the biannual "election" of club presidents, in which the head of the administration of every football club must be "elected" by a general assembly of club members—fans—although in practice, government officals, wise old men of the club (former presidents and board members) and vested business interests (sponsors, donors, pilferers and tax evaders) meet beforehand to decide on a candidate.

Mourad and I sat in a café on the Avenue Bourguiba, heart of the French Quarter of Tunis with its elegant white-painted turn-of-the-century buildings, sky blue shutters and wrought iron balconies, wafting smells of patisserie, trams and arbored boulevards. Everywhere patriotic bunting had been strung up to celebrate an international conference on the global future of technology and the Internet (never mind that human rights websites are routinely blocked by Tunisian servers). Tunisian flaglets, red and white, circle crescent and star, flapped next to portraits of President Ben Ali, who had two poses: one in a suit with his hand outstretched toward the future, the other in the full evening dress of a Ruritanian prince: white tie, purple sash and various clusters of medals and starburst orders. In both of them his hair was full and black. He was born in 1938. In reproduction, he looks about forty.

Mourad tried to explain the intersections of the elite families, politicians and business personalities that vied for the prestigious club presidencies and board membership. I wrote down names and he told me to use initials. "They can look through your book and they will know." I wrote down one name, the family of the wife of President Ben Ali. "Better you cross this one out," Mourad said, looking behind him.

Shots and goals, red cards, penalties and football boardroom politicking form a disproportionate part of the everyday soap opera of Tunisian life. In newspapers football comprises up to a third of the copy. Zouhair Hammami, a pilot for Tunisair, a former vice president of Club Africain, told me: "Football. Firstly, it's a good game, and it's cheap. You can watch on TV and then all week you can talk about the match. Secondly, with football you can dream: everyone is a coach, we have ten million coaches in Tunisia. In Tunisia it's the only thing you can discuss and give your opinion." Football, many in Tunis admit with a wry smile, is politics. Because there are no politics— President Ben Ali, won his last election with nearly 100 percent of the vote, and most newspapers routinely carry his previous day's engagements on the front page: *President Ben Ali received . . . President Ben Ali conferred . . . President Ben Ali chaired . . .* It sometimes seems as if football is the sum of all expression in the country. Another journalist friend of Mourad's who sat down with us for a coffee said, "The biggest freedom of expression in Tunisia is sports journalism." Mourad was not so encouraging: "But still we have self-censorship. There are red lines."

Most of the things Mourad knows about incompetent referees, double accounting on transfer deals, black market ticket links with club officials—he can't write about. One journalist apparently wrote about the corruption of referees for a foreign magazine. The issue was banned in Tunisia and its author was invited to an interview with the security services. They shouted at him, "Fuck your mother! Nothing like this happens in Tunisia! Where is your proof?"

No one owns Tunisian football clubs. They appear to float, suspended in a curious Tunisian ether-melange, simultaneously subsidized and exploited by the wise men, businessmen and the government. I tried to learn what I could. For a week I sat in cafés and at football stadiums, and talked to sports journalists, fans, players, coaches, presidents, ex presidents, federation officials, scouts, team doctors, radio commentators—several times I believed I had closed my fist around it all. "So: the men who want to be presidents of football clubs want this position to further their business interests, for self-fame, to engender power and influence."

"Ultimately club presidents are sanctioned by the government. So you can say that the government ultimately controls everything—"

"But it's possible to argue that the fans are the most important part of the equation because they represent the potential of the crowd. They represent the masses. The government is afraid of their potential so it uses the club presidents to control them."

In November 2004, Esperance, under the seventeen-year presidency of Slim Chiboub, son-in-law of President Ben Ali, lost a semifinal African Champions League match on penalties in Tunis. Angry chanting erupted against Chiboub. "Fuck you and fuck your father-in-law!" The crowd was unafraid, the match was being broadcast throughout the Arab world. Chiboub seemed to have lost face. A week later he resigned.

There were however, complications to any simple theory: As much as those in power at a top football club might be in a position to rake off cash they were also expected to attract donations from wealthy supporters and dip into their own pockets. As much as businessmen liked to use football clubs to raise their profile, they also exposed themselves to public scrutiny and ridicule if the results were not satisfactory. As much as the government seemed to maintain control over the appointments of the presidents of football clubs, it seemed more interested in simply having people who would run the game competently and smoothly. And after all, Tunisia is a stable North African country with a large and well-educated middle class, and Tunisian football has delivered a consistent winning national team and a competitive league into which European clubs regularly dip for talent, which is not something its neighbors—Algeria and Libya—can boast.

I tried to resist the idea that football in Tunisia was a substitute for politics; but it was too tantalizing. Zouhair the Tunisair pilot told me that before the war in Iraq he went to a Club Africain–Sfax match and unfurled a banner, as he had seen hundreds of thousands of anti-war demonstrators do in European and North American cities: NO WAR FOR MONEY. All the photographers snapped his picture. The police came and took his banner and spent thirty minutes calling to find out whether to jail him or not. They let him go but the picture never ran in any of the papers. While he was still unsure about his fate he explained to the policeman, "I am only expressing myself, I know everyone shares this sentiment about the war." The policeman said, "In Tunisia we need orders to express ideas." The pilot replied: "We should try to express the ideas first and then let the president react how he likes."

In March 2003, in the scant ultimatum period before the Americans bombed Iraq, there was a match the Tunisian authorities could not cancel, a friendly between Club Africain and Monaco in front of forty thousand people. It was the jubilee match for a retired Club Africain player, Lotfi Mhaissi, who was known as an elbowing, belligerent defender. The fans used to chant: "Lotfi Mhaissi—Saddam Hussein!" at matches; half admiringly, half ironically. On this occasion, the crowd chanted the name of Saddam Hussein for the whole match. The Monegasques played, intimidated, to a draw. Afterward Didier Deschamps, the Monaco coach, told Mourad, "It's proof that football can be an expression, or a reply, in time of war."

Cafés in Tunis were full of men, drinking coffee, smoking *shisha,* always a television on in the background: Fulham-Middlesbrough, a Spanish League game. The damp November air came in through the open door and the shisha men carefully ferried charcoal embers. Much of Tunis sits in a café through the winter to mooch and talk about football. "If there weren't cafés in Tunis, there would be civil war!" said Mourad, laughing.

On Thursday afternoon, it was raining and we went to a café owned by a man called Hassan Laabidi who wore impeccable tailored suits and stood, most of the time, behind the cash register in front of a blown up, framed photograph of himself with a former Club Africain president. On the walls were pictures of old Club Africain teams in red and white striped shirts. Hassan was bombastic and jolly, with a full range of Gallic gesticulation: shoulder shrugs and arm waving and eyebrow furrows.

There had been a demonstration of Club Africain fans the night before to protest the continuing lame presidency of Sherif Bellamine. But the police had found out and closed off all the roads around the club's headquarters. Still, the talk was everywhere that Bellamine would fall: He had failed to call a general assembly that summer, the players had not been paid and were threatening to strike and had turned up to play one match wearing black armbands.

Hassan pulled out a large stack of photographs from behind the bar and began to go through them for me—snaps from different years jumbled together, the sum of happy football times. Mourad bent over the pictures, interjecting, identifying: "This is the son of the former president of Club Africain . . . This man is a senior policeman—but don't write this . . . This is one of the officials who resigned two days ago . . . This one is the son of the man who owns Coca-Cola in Tunisia . . . This is the legendary Tunisian goalkeeper—you know him: Attouga! . . . Yes this man was a former vice president of Club Africain and now he is a government minister—but no one likes him." In one photograph taken in 1987, the year the current president Ben Ali replaced his predecessor in a bloodless coup, a player is wearing a Club Africain shirt with the slogan: "We are with Ben Ali for the Good of Tunisia." There were pictures of Hassan receiving an award for running a clean café from his district mayor, Hassan posing with the minister of tourism, a sports minister, various club presidents, football executives, the head of the Tunisian Football Federation, a famous Tunisian singer and even with Yasser Arafat, who was clasping a model of the Al Aqsa mosque in Jerusalem.

Hassan loved Club Africain. "It is thanks to Club Africain I know all those important people." Hassan rubbed his hands together. "Yes, you see!" he told me gleefully, foretelling Bellamine's demise, "we will have a big revolution!" There was a sense, Mourad explained to me, a point of exaggerated pride, among Club Africain fans, that their club was somehow democratic. "Oh yes, it's the largest opposition party in Tunisia!" one clubist, sitting around the table, joked.

"We have the club of the people; we can say what we want!" Another said: "Of course club presidents are more powerful than ministers. They have half the country behind them!"

The eight o'clock news came on, reporting the death of Bashir Manoubi, Tunisia's greatest football photographer and fan. Manoubi had traveled with Tunisia to the World Cup for decades and was famous for wearing a vast sombrero and a patchwork jacket adorned with multiserried badges and Tunisian flags. He had been decorated by President Ben Ali as a national cultural icon.

More powerful than government ministers? We went to see Mahmoud Mestiri, a wise man of Club Africain, in his eighties, venerable, but frail with soft, thin skin. He was wearing slippers and bathrobe and was watching basketball on television. On the table were pictures of him with President Ben Ali and Colin Powell. He had been a distinguished diplomat—to the UN, in Washington, ambassador to Belgium, Germany, Egypt, the Soviet Union. He came from one of the grand Tunis families who believed, he said with an admonishing twinkle, "they own Club Africain—but they do not!" One of his uncles had been chairman, another secretary general. He himself had been president of the club in the late 1980s. "It's true," laughed Mestiri, he was too old to care who heard, "club presidents are more powerful than ministers. The president changes his ministers every six months. I was foreign minister for eight months, so I know how it is!" All week people had been calling and asking who should replace Bellamine. He and Mourad began a detailed discussion of the combination of factors and personalities.

"Really the club belongs to the people, no one owns it. And one day they will make a revolution."

Mestiri waved his hands with excitement. "They often make intifada in the club! Its fan base is millions. It is some kind of popular movement."

"But it's just football—"

"Yes," Mestiri sighed. He said when he was in government, they had tried to rally football fans go out onto the street for National Day celebrations or presidential demonstrations. "But it never worked," he said laughing at the effort.

Mourad cried happily, "It's a democracy no?"
"Total democracy!"

On Friday George Best died and Bashir Manoubi was buried. On Saturday as we sat drinking orange juice, Mourad told me that overnight it had become apparent that a man called Kamel Idir was to succeed Bellamine as Club Africain president. Idir was already vice president, a reasonable bland technocrat with the right sort of political credentials.

Club Africain's headquarters at Parc A stood in contrast to the gleam and polish of next-door Parc B, where their rivals Esperance trained. The facilities were run down with cracked paint and dusty interiors; the training pitch was lumpy and a patio area comprised piles of dug up paving slabs and a dry fountain. Tacked up on the walls inside were photos of red and white striped jubilant mayhem: Club Africain fans holding up a giant number twelve shirt. No Club Africain player ever plays in a twelve shirt; twelve represents the fans; it is said that the fans are Club Africain's twelfth player.

All week, I had not heard the name of a single player. I mentioned this; Mourad laughed. "It's not a matter of players," he told me. "Football in Tunisia is played outside the ground." For all the quips about Club Africain democracy, the general assembly at which fans could shout and stamp would still not be held until the following summer.

After conferring with the wise men and government officials, Idir called a press conference to confirm Bellamine's resignation and his assumption of the presidency. He sat behind a dais decked in red and white Tunisian flag fabric. ". . . I legally, according to the law, become president, until the general assembly in June. I don't know of any president until now being forced to leave a club under pressure from fans. . . . we met people from the government this morning; we gained the support of the wise men . . . we need to restructure the club especially its finances . . . I will create a transfer committee independent of the board . . . I will reorganize the relationship with the media to avoid confusion and rumors."

Outside clumps of men, officials, journalists chatted. Most seemed happy with the coup. "It's the first step—" One shook his head. "Bellamine gambled too much on the first team, he forgot even to maintain minimum standards and conditions: look at the hostel for the young players! It's dirty, they have no woman working there even to bring them food!" "Anyone who comes home and sees the place is dirty, orders it to be cleaned up. But he didn't care!" The financial director of the club nodded quietly and admitted, "We're in a really bad financial situation. For now, all we have are promises for help with the money." One cynical sports journalist said: "Marx used to say religion was the opiate of the masses—for us it's football."

Afterward in a café with a loud clanging marble floor and metal chairs, there was a Portsmouth–Chelsea match on TV and a group of Esperance fans dealing cards to one another. The man who had run the sandwich stall outside Club Africain for thirty years sat in a corner with a cigarette. He was not convinced. "It's all the same as before; only the faces have changed," he said on hearing the news, "It's like peeling an onion."

On Sunday the big match was Espérance–Etoile. The stadium was constructed as an open-petaled flower of cantilevered concrete seating blocks. Esperance fans massed together at one end, Les Ultras at the Curva Sud. They chanted a wall of noise calling into question the sexual efficacy of the Etoile president, and jumped up and down so that whole blocks undulated. Bashir Manoubi's son donned his father's vast sombrero and glittering patchwork gypsy suit, and made a lap of the stadium to applauding fans. A banner hung over the side read: ESPERANTISTES SANS FRONTIERS. Black uniformed police laid their riot shields out on the grass.

This was all in expectation of what is known in Tunisian football as "the entrance." Just before the teams run out vast black banners embroidered with giant gold and silver trophies are unfurled over entire blocks of fans. Then the black banners retract and the crowd beneath hold up rectangles of colored cards to spell out the word GLORY. Then this formation dissolved in a fluttering hail of confetti. Mourad said he had seen entrances choreographed so elaborately that for the first fifteen minutes the game was entirely distracted:

referees, linesmen, coaches, players would look up at the stands at the unfolding spectacle. One French scout told me, "Many times I saw Rome–Lazio. I don't know any show that compares to the big Esperance–Club Africain game: maybe River Plate–Boca Juniors. That's all. You never saw anything like it."

The crowd during the match was vociferous: There were cries of "Burn the stadium!" Or to the goalkeeper: "Oooooooh! Son of a bitch!" "Bring him your sister!" An Esperance player was sent off for two yellow cards and the Esperantists were angry and yelled at the German referee: "Bring us those old rubbish Tunisian referees, they are better than these foreigners!"

"You see that man?" Mourad pointed to a black man taking pictures near the pitch. "He's Cameroonian. They say he makes black magic for the club. That is why, for the last few years, Esperance has always won." Except, apparently, when they lost five African Cup and Arab League matches during Ramadan. People said: "They cannot win in Ramadan because they cannot use their witchcraft in that holy month!" I rolled my eyes. "I know," said Mourad, "but many people believe these things."

Etoile came back from 1–0 down to win 2–1. "Etoile has a better wizard!" laughed Mourad. "Witchcraft! Black magic—"

I said, "It's only football!" Superstition, puffs of wind, luck, glances and chances: this is what football turns on the world over. But in Tunisia they have djinns and spirits and angels and a reasonable belief in the ability of supernatural disturbances to bend mortal experience.

Just two months before there had been, for example, a decisive World Cup qualifying match between Tunisia and Morocco. The Moroccans are well known in the Arab world as skilled occultists. Morocco took the lead twice, and twice Tunisia equalized (with supernatural help, as the newspapers subsequently said) for the 2–2 draw which ensured their qualification. In the second half, it was suggested—true, not true; only Allah knows—that some Tunisian wizard milled with the photographers behind the Morocco goal, enticing the ball into the net.

Mourad and I went to meet an agent for a Tunisian wizard at a café next to a highway access road. The wizard's agent was a large, fleshy jowly man, poor and ill educated, from the desert south. He wore a red and white scarf on his head and a dirty white shapeless burnoose. His eyeballs looked yellow and curdled, his brow was heavy. He was in Tunis to recommend auspices for a young man seeking a French visa.

Ah yes! Of course there were supernatural irregularities with the Morocco–Tunisia match. It was known to him that a wizard had wafted special verses from the Koran near the boots of the Moroccan players to protect their footwork. Tunisia, he declared, only started winning when one of the Moroccan players tumbled and lost his shoe in the second half, and the spell was broken.

He said his wizard had already helped a small club dropping in the Third Division to turn their losing streak. He was happy to recommend his services to Club Africain. He talked more about angels, "our guys" he called them, and incantations and ritual procedures.

Then he rang his wizard on his mobile phone. Greetings were exchanged, he put his master on speakerphone. "Ah, you have a woman with you there!" the wizard exclaimed through the handset. True. Me. His agent told him I had asked about the price for attracting a good boyfriend. "She doesn't need a boyfriend she already has one!" True. "She is very beautiful and intelligent," continued the wizard. True, obviously true. "She is kind, but sometimes she gets angry with people when they behave badly but she doesn't shout, she prefers to walk away." True. He told Mourad that he was a diligent journalist with a clean reputation, but that "They don't let you advance." Mourad nodded sagely. All true. Our mouths were hanging open.

The usual crowd in Hassan's café laughed at it all. "Perhaps in Esperance; but not in our team," said one fan. "Perhaps the Moroccans could have done it in that match against Tunisia: the Moroccans are known all over the world for that kind of thing," put in another fan, the headmaster of a primary school. Hassan weighed in. "The Moroccans use their ways, but the Tunisians always beat Morocco, and we win by football. We are the champions of Africa!"

There followed a discussion about Club Africain's apparent inability a few years previously to win in the new sixty thousand–seat national stadium, Rades. The headmaster teased Hassan: "And you were the one who brought the bull!" Hassan demurred, "Yes, but for luck; not for witchcraft." It transpired however, that after several years of losing matches at Rades stadium, Hassan had contributed 100 dinars (a little less than $100) to the 400 dinar price of a bull. Then he had taken it to the stadium, cut its throat on the touchline, and distributed its meat, as proscribed by the Koran, to the poor. "But we are not superstitious!" cried Hassan, shaking his head. "I pray, and religion forbids such things, even today I am fasting."

"Did it help?" I asked him.

"Yes," he raised his eyebrows knowingly, "we won afterwards."

Even Zouhair the pilot admitted to having asked a pilot friend to bring back a bottle of "special water" for a Club Africain player from Mali. The pilot, a good Muslim, refused to have anything to do with black magic and did not ferry the water. "And the player was injured in the very next match!"

On my last day in Tunis, a blowy afternoon, Club Africain beat a lower division side 6–1. The sparse crowd, huddled together on the long stretches of the stepped concrete tiers, cheered every goal. The radio commentors reported every foul and every missed chance into their microphones. The club officials, all volunteers, hoped the new president would manage things better, and everyone prayed, *inshallah*, that if nothing else they could beat Esperance that year.

World Cup Record

FIFA Ranking: 28
World Cup Appearances: 3
World Cup Champions: 0
Federation Name: Fédération Tunisienne de
  Football
Confederation: CAF
Founded: 1956
FIFA Affiliation: 1960
Nickname: The Eagles of Carthage
Manager: Roger Lemerre
Website: www.ftf.org.tn
Stadium: Stade 7 Novembre
Home Uniform: red/white/red
Away Uniform: all white
Provider: Puma

1930:	Did not enter
1934:	Did not enter
1938:	Did not enter
1950:	Did not enter
1954:	Did not enter
1958:	Did not enter
1962:	Did not qualify
1966:	Did not qualify
1970:	Did not qualify
1974:	Did not qualify
1978:	First round exit
1982:	Did not qualify
1986:	Did not qualify
1990:	Did not qualify
1994:	Did not qualify
1998:	First round exit
2002:	First round exit

Matches	Wins	Draws	Losses	GF	GA	GD	Points
9	1	3	5	5	11	-6	6

Tunisia is 45th on the all-time World Cup table

Path to Qualification for World Cup 2006

5-Jun-04	Tunisia	4	Botswana	1	**W**
20-Jun-04	Guinea	2	Tunisia	1	**L**
4-Sep-04	Morocco	1	Tunisia	1	**D**
9-Oct-04	Malawi	2	Tunisia	2	**D**
26-Mar-05	Tunisia	7	Malawi	0	**W**
4-Jun-05	Botswana	1	Tunisia	3	**W**
11-Jun-05	Tunisia	2	Guinea	0	**W**
17-Aug-05	Tunisia	1	Kenya	0	**W**
3-Sep-05	Kenya	0	Tunisia	2	**W**
8-Oct-05	Tunisia	2	Morocco	2	**D**

Tunisia qualified by finishing first in Group 5 of the African Zone

Ukraine

Capital: Kiev
Independence: August 24, 1991
 (from the Soviet Union)
Area: 603,700 sq km
Population: 47,425,336
Median Age: 38.2 years
Life Expectancy at Birth: 69.7 years
Ethnic Groups: Ukrainian 77.8%,
 Russian 17.3%, Belarusian 0.6%,
 Moldovan 0.5%, Crimean Tatar 0.5%,
 Bulgarian 0.4%, Hungarian 0.3%,
 Romanian 0.3%, Polish 0.3%,
 Jewish 0.2%, other 1.8%
Religions: Ukrainian Orthodox 52%,
 Protestant, Jewish, none 38%
Languages: Ukrainian (official) 67%, Russian
 24%; small Romanian-, Polish-,
 and Hungarian-speaking minorities
Suffrage: 18 years of age; universal
Military Obligation: 18–27 years of age for
 compulsory and voluntary military service;
 conscript service obligation: 18 months for
 army and air force, 24 months for navy
GDP Per Capita: $6,300
Budget: $12.26 billion
Military Expenditures: $617.9 million
 (1.4% of GDP)
Agriculture: grain, sugar beets, sunflower seeds,
 vegetables; beef, milk
Industries: coal, electric power, ferrous and
 nonferrous metals, machinery and transport
 equipment, chemicals, food processing
Currency: hryvnia

Source: *CIA World Factbook*

Ukraine

Benjamin Pauker

My interest in Ukraine began on a cold, rainy night in Milan. It was the second leg of the UEFA Cup semifinals, and AC Milan was playing Borussia Dortmund, a high-flying team from western Germany that had won the first fixture 4–0. The headline of the pink Italian daily *Corriere dello Sport* summed up the task: *"Missione Impossibile."* Several thousand traveling German supporters in black and yellow—Dortmund's colors—had traveled to Italy for the game, and, with nasty weather and the outcome already foretold, there was little local support at the cavernous San Siro stadium, save the *ultras* in my section (or rather me in theirs) smoking hash, lighting flares and throwing empty airplane bottles of grappa down on the pitch.

Though just returning to Milan from a month-long injury, Andriy Shevchenko—Sheva—lived up to his billing as perhaps the best striker in Europe. About ten minutes in he split the German defense open with a brilliant pass out to the left flank, releasing the Brazilian Serginho who crossed to Inzaghi for a headed goal. And though Sheva didn't score that evening, I remember his performance more than any other player's. He ran endlessly—creating intelligent pockets of space, unselfishly tracking back to midfield, making slashing off-the-ball runs behind defenders—crafting a poetry of graft and velocity that made everyone around him better.

Back home, in New York, I started to follow Shevchenko and Milan. On Sunday mornings, in an attempt at a continental lifestyle, I would throw on a scarf and head to an Italian bar to consume cappuccinos and wine, and watch Sheva lead Milan to the Italian *Scudetto* and the European Champions League title. Then I saw him voted European Footballer of the Year and awarded the *Ballon d'Or* in recognition of his prodigious talent.

Sheva was an easy target for my admiration—I like champions, dynasties, records that will never be broken, icons, the consistent display of greatness, overdogs. I've cheered for Brazil to demolish lesser nations, for France against Senegal, for England to score double-digits against the Faroe Islands. I followed Ferrari's F1 team when it was unstoppable, the Chicago Bulls with Michael Jordan, and the New York Yankees. Sheva fit right in. The truth is: I can't stomach the consistent losses that more noble fans must weather. I have never had to watch my heroes consigned to the second order of the minor leagues, to sub .500 seasons, to decades without trophies. But Shevchenko led me in an unexpected direction.

One day, walking in the East Village, I passed a picture of Sheva taped to the front door of an innocuous little townhouse on Second Avenue at St. Mark's Place, in the heart of New York's original Ukrainian diaspora. This was the Ukrainian Sports Club, which goes by its initials, YCK, pronounced "oosk." I opened the door and wandered in, past the dusty trophy case and empty card tables to the shabby bar in back. A couple of members swiveled to give me the once-over, then returned to their beers. One of the televisions behind the bar was showing AC Milan highlights; the other, recent footage from Independence Square in Kiev, where tens of thousands had successfully staged a peaceful democratic revolution. I had read a bit about it in the newspapers, but Shevchenko's involvement was what initially caught my attention.

In December 2004, Ukrainians massed in protest of rigged elections that had handed the country's leadership to Viktor Yanukovych, the twice-imprisoned, hand-picked successor of Leonid Kuchma, the country's crooked, long-serving president and puppet of the Kremlin. The popular choice, Victor Yushchenko, a westward-looking reformer who was most notable for surviving a dioxin poisoning that savaged his face and left him almost incapacitated, had been swindled out of the presidency. Though thirteen years had passed since Ukraine's independence, Moscow's shadow still loomed large: Ukrainians have not forgiven Stalin for the forced famine (caused by resistance to agricultural collectivization) in the early 1930s that killed roughly 7 million people. Nor have they forgiven the imposition of the Russian language, the millions of countrymen sent to Siberia, or decades of authoritarian rule under Moscow's edict. Sheva's fans recall bitterly how Ukraine was kept out of the World Cup in 1994, when Russia decided its team would be the sole representative of the

Commonwealth of Independent States. In December 2004, Ukrainians widely suspected that the Russian secret service was complicit in, if not outright responsible for, the electoral fraud. Tens of thousands gathered in the streets, donning orange, the color of Yushchenko's political party, and camped out for days in the cold, forcing a recount that eventually installed the new government.

Yushchenko's victory was a true upset in a country that has produced very few fairy tales. Sheva is another—an average kid from Kiev who became one of the stars of international football. He is "the world's most dangerous attacker," says Ronaldinho, the Brazil and Barcelona forward and current FIFA Player of the Year. But Sheva is no longer an underdog. And, perhaps because of his success, when revolution came to Ukraine, Sheva found himself on the wrong side of history.

In the run-up to the fixed elections, Sheva had campaigned on television for the establishment candidate, Yanukovych: eyes focused on a piece of paper, he read a prepared statement of support on state-sponsored Channel 1+1. His fans were aghast. Shortly thereafter, during a Champions League game against the Ukrainian club team Shakhtar Donetsk, supporters hung a banner that read, SHAME ON YOU, SHEVCHENKO, YOUR CHOICE MADE YOUR PEOPLE CRY. To avoid further politicizing the match, Shakhtar, a Ukrainian team named after a legendary coal miner, eschewed their traditional color—orange—in favor of a white strip. Three days later, Sheva apologized. "I've always tried to exist outside of politics because politics are for professionals elected by the people, and I stick to that position now," he said. "Yes, I live and play in Italy, but home remains close to me. I am not indifferent to the fate of Ukraine, to the future of my countrymen, my fans, whom I have never classified according to regional or political affiliation."

As one of Sheva's fans, I was also disappointed. I wanted him to be Ukraine's Johan Cruyff, a goal-scoring animal who stood for something, a moral compass for a nation in need. Instead, the revolution was a salt-of-the-earth movement, and though he was quickly forgiven by his admirers, Shevchenko wasn't a part of it.

• • •

I stopped going to the Italian café, and became a regular at YCK. The run-down bar suited me, despite my love of greatness. It was a warm and quiet place, entirely without pretense, where they passed around cold cuts on the weekends, and the drinks were cheap—a true rarity in New York. It was also populated with old men who were eager to tell me about their homeland. When I mentioned Dinamo Kiev and Shaktar Donetsk, the two heavyweight teams of Ukrainian football, they were pleased, but soon redirected me. "Those teams are run by oligarchs," said Jarowsalw "Jerry" Kurowyckyj, a godfather figure and fixture at the club. He pointed at the green and white scarf above the bar. Unknown to most west of the Carpathians Karpaty Lviv (who's scarf this was) is the storied team of western Ukraine's largest city, and the heart of its independence movement. "But now, they are second division."

My education at YCK went beyond sports. One winter afternoon, when I pulled out a book between halves of a game, a member turned to me and asked: "You know Shevchenko?"

"Sure," I said. "He's great. I saw him play once."

"No," he said, shaking his head. "Other Shevchenko."

He meant Taras Shevchenko, the Ukrainian poet, dead some 150 years, but as alive as Sheva to many Ukrainians. There's a Manhattan street named after him not a block from YCK. In a 2003 poll, Ukrainians voted Taras Shevchenko their most famous personality. That's akin to Americans picking Walt Whitman over Tom Cruise. (Sheva managed a respectable seventh.)

The poetry of Taras Shevchenko is Pushkin mixed with a little Thomas Paine: his mid-nineteenth-century nationalist stanzas of Cossacks on horseback and the bondage of serfdom inspired a national identity, revived the modern Ukrainian language and are still recited by schoolchildren. Here's a sample (translated by John Weir) that reaches typically abysmal lows and vainglorious heights (Shevchenko was in St. Petersburg at the time):

> *My thorny thoughts, my thorny thoughts,*
> *You bring me only woe!*

Why do you on the paper stand
So sadly row on row? . . .
Why did the winds not scatter you
Like dust across the steppes?
Why did ill-luck not cradle you
To sleep upon its breast? . . .

My thoughts, my melancholy thoughts,
My children, tender shoots!
I nursed you, brought you up—and now
What shall I do with you? . . .
Go to Ukraine, my homeless waifs!
Your way make to Ukraine
Along back roads like vagabonds,
But I'm doomed here to stay.

There you will find a heart that's true
And words of welcome kind,
There honesty, unvarnished truth
And, maybe, fame you'll find . . .
So welcome them, my Motherland,
Ukraine, into your home!
Accept my guileless, simple brood
And take them for your own!

Born into serfdom, he suffered in prison, and died in exile, without seeing his people freed: *"Such is our glory, sad and plain,/ The glory of our own Ukraine!"*

Ukraine is not what one would call a lucky country. Its forested plain has been a Eurasian crossroads, its history one of conquest and tragedy for a millennium. Pillaging Mongols were succeeded by proselytizing Lithuanians, in turn followed by Ruthenians, Poles and Tatars. Then came Russians, serfdom, Soviets, famine and, well, Chernobyl. (On Sheva's personal website, it notes that the disaster interrupted his training for a time as he was transferred to a school out of the danger zone.) Today, tour agencies offer sightseeing trips to the concrete sarcophagus that encloses the reactor, and the empty ghost towns nearby. Supposedly, the woods and lakes are lush again, but the locals tell you not to eat the fish. In the decade or so since the fall of communism, things haven't improved much: the country's two largest industries are human trafficking and rust.

The latter-day Shevchenko, Andriy, has fared considerably better: a house on Lake Como, a stunning American model for his wife and Silvio Berlusconi, the Italian prime minister, as his child's godfather. Sheva exists almost in opposition to his storied surname, which, for Ukrainians, now evokes not only suffering, serfdom and tears but also flash cars, euros and championships. Imagine England's David Beckham as, say, David Wordsworth.

After he got used to seeing me around the YCK bar, Willy, the club president, lent me tapes of Ukraine's early World Cup qualifying games. *Zbirna,* or the All-Stars, as the national team is affectionately known, were the first European side to book a place in Germany. Their coach, Oleg Blokhin, a former striker and icon of the Soviet teams of the 1970s and 1980s, has been either overconfident or abjectly defeatist ever since. When Ukraine beat Turkey (who finished third in the 2002 World Cup) to qualify at the head of their group, Blokhin boldly predicted that they would carry on to Germany and win the whole thing. Sheva, showing some media savvy, stepped in and told the press, "You have to understand that our coach was joking when he said that we're going to win the World Cup playing in our first finals." Blokhin reverted to pessimism: "This team needs backbone and Shevchenko can only put the finishing touches on it. We simply don't have enough players. . . . At this moment, we are simply not prepared to win the world championship."

But, as I watched the tapes, I found myself more impressed by Sheva's supporting cast than the superstar himself. Strikers Andrey Voronin of German powerhouse Bayer Leverkusen, and Andriy Vorobey of Shakhtar Donetsk, are among the best known, but midfielders Oleh Gusev, Anatoliy Tymoschuk and Ruslan Rotan are young and skilled, the latter contributing two match-winning goals in qualifying. They seem likely, given a good showing, to make the jump from their Ukrainian clubs to bigger European teams. And Ukraine is solid in defense: they conceded only four goals in the ten games it took them to qualify. Perhaps Blokhin, like Ukraine's most famous personality, embodies both the country's traditional world-weary pragmatism, and its grandiose sense of itself. No question he's canny—after all, he's a member of parliament despite his opposition to the Orange Revolution. *My thoughts, my melancholy thoughts . . .*

In December of last year, politics in Kiev again turned sour. Amid scandal and calls of corruption, Yushchenko disbanded his cabinet and fired his prime minister, Yulia Tymoshenko. A diplomatic tussle with Moscow over fuel imports threatened to install the crooked Yanukovich as head of a new government. Somewhere, Blokhin was smiling: word soon followed that the Ukrainian team would be based in Potsdam for the duration of the tournament—the only country to choose a site within the former Eastern bloc. It seemed a shocking reversal from the heights of a year before.

I stopped by the club to commiserate, but no one seemed unduly concerned. "Growing pains," said Willy, opening a round of beers. "At least we got a good draw. Spain, Tunisia and Saudi Arabia. For us, you must understand, this is enough."

World Cup Record

FIFA Ranking: 40
World Cup Appearances: 0
World Cup Champions: 0
Federation Name: Federatsija Futbola Ukraina
Confederation: UEFA
Founded: 1991
FIFA Affiliation: 1992
Nickname: Zbirna (The All-Stars)
Manager: Oleg Blokhin
Website: www.ffu.org.ua
Stadium: Olympic Stadium, Kiev
Home Uniform: yellow/blue/yellow
Away Uniform: blue/yellow/blue
Provider: Lotto

1930:	Did not enter
1934:	Did not enter
1938:	Did not enter
1950:	Did not enter
1954:	Did not enter
1958:	Did not enter
1962:	Did not enter
1966:	Did not enter
1970:	Did not enter
1974:	Did not enter
1978:	Did not enter
1982:	Did not enter
1986:	Did not enter
1990:	Did not enter
1994:	Did not enter
1998:	Did not qualify
2002:	Did not qualify

Matches	Wins	Draws	Losses	GF	GA	GD	Points
0	0	0	0	0	0	0	0

Ukraine is appearing in the World Cup for the first time

Path to Qualification for World Cup 2006

4-Sep-04	Denmark	1	Ukraine	1	D
8-Sep-04	Kazakhstan	1	Ukraine	2	W
9-Oct-04	Ukraine	1	Greece	1	D
13-Oct-04	Ukraine	2	Georgia	0	W
17-Nov-04	Turkey	0	Ukraine	3	W
9-Feb-05	Albania	0	Ukraine	2	W
30-Mar-05	Ukraine	1	Denmark	0	W
4-Jun-05	Ukraine	2	Kazakhstan	0	W
8-Jun-05	Greece	0	Ukraine	1	W
3-Sep-05	Georgia	1	Ukraine	1	D
7-Sep-05	Ukraine	0	Turkey	1	L
8-Oct-05	Ukraine	2	Albania	2	D

Ukraine qualified by finishing first in Group 2 of the European Zone

United States

Capital: Washington, DC
Independence: July 4, 1776
   (from Great Britain)
Area: 9,631,418 sq km
Population: 295,734,134
Median Age: 36.3 years
Life Expectancy at Birth: 77.7 years
Ethnic Groups: white 81.7%,
   black 12.9%, Asian 4.2%,
   Amerindian and Alaska
   native 1%, native Hawaiian and
   other Pacific islander 0.2%
Religions: Protestant 52%, Roman
   Catholic 24%, Mormon 2%, Jewish 1%,
   Muslim 1%, other 10%, none 10%
Languages: English 82.1%, Spanish 10.7%,
   other Indo-European 3.8%, Asian and
   Pacific island 2.7%, other 0.7%
Suffrage: 18 years of age; universal
Military Obligation: 18 years of age
GDP Per Capita: $40,100
Budget: $2.338 trillion
Military Expenditures: $370.7 billion (3.3% of GDP)
Agriculture: wheat, corn, other grains, fruits,
   vegetables, cotton; beef, pork, poultry, dairy
   products; forest products; fish
Industries: leading industrial power in the
   world, highly diversified and technologically
   advanced; petroleum, steel, motor vehicles,
   aerospace, telecommunications, chemicals,
   electronics, food processing, consumer
   goods, lumber, mining
Currency: US dollar

Source: *CIA World Factbook*

United States

Dave Eggers

When children in the United States are very young, they believe that soccer is the most popular sport in the world. They believe this because every single child in America plays soccer. It is a rule that they play, a rule set forth in the same hoary document, displayed in every state capital, which insists that six-year-olds also pledge allegiance to the flag—a practice which is terrifying to watch, by the way, good lord—and that once a year, they dress as tiny pilgrims with beards fashioned from cotton.

On Saturdays, every flat green space in the continental United States is covered with tiny people in shiny uniforms, chasing the patchwork ball up and down the field, to the delight and consternation of their parents, most of whom have no idea what is happening. The primary force behind all of this is the American Youth Soccer Organization, or AYSO. In the 1970s, AYSO was formed to popularize soccer among the youth of America, and they did this with startling efficiency. Within a few years, soccer was the sport of choice for parents everywhere, particularly those who harbored suspicions that their children had no athletic ability whatsoever.

The beauty of soccer for very young people is that, to create a simulacrum of the game, it requires very little skill. There is no other sport that can bear such incompetence. With soccer, twenty-two kids can be running around, most of them aimlessly, or picking weeds by the sidelines or crying for no apparent reason, and yet the game can have the general appearance of an actual soccer match. If there are three or four coordinated kids among the twenty-two flailing bodies, there will actually be dribbling, a few legal throw-ins and a couple times when the ball stretches the back of the net. It will be soccer, more or less.

Because they all play, most of America's children assume that soccer will always be a part of their lives. When I was eight, playing center midfielder for the undefeated Strikers (coached by the unparalleled Mr. Cooper), I harbored no life expectations other than that I would continue playing center midfielder until such time as I died. It never occurred to me that any of this would change.

But at about age ten, something happens to the children of the United States. Soccer is dropped, quickly and unceremoniously, by approximately 88 percent of all young people. The same kids who played at five, six, seven, move onto baseball, football, basketball, hockey, field hockey and, sadly, golf. Shortly thereafter, they stop playing these sports, too, and begin watching these sports on television, including, sadly, golf.

The abandonment of soccer is attributable, in part, to the fact that people of influence in America long believed that soccer was the chosen sport of Communists. When I was thirteen—this was 1983, long before glasnost, let alone the fall of the wall—I had a gym teacher, whom for now we'll call Moron McCheeby, who made a very compelling link between soccer and the architects of the Iron Curtain. I remember once asking him why there were no days of soccer in his gym units. His face darkened. He took me aside. He explained with quivering, barely mastered rage, that he preferred decent, honest American sports where *you used your hands.* Sports where one's hands were not used, he said, were commie sports played by Russians, Poles, Germans and other commies. To use one's hands in sports was American, to use one's feet was the purview of the followers of Marx and Lenin. I believe McCheeby went on to lecture widely on the subject.

It was, by most accounts, 1986 when the residents of the United States became aware of the thing called the World Cup. Isolated reports came from foreign correspondents, and we were frightened by these reports. We worried about domino effects and wondered aloud if the trend was something we could stop by placing a certain number of military advisers in Cologne or Marseilles. Then, in 1990, we realized that the World Cup might happen every four years, with or without us.

At the same time, high school soccer was booming in the suburbs of Chicago, due in large part to an influx of foreign exchange students.

My own high school team was ridiculously good by the standards of the day, stacked as it was with extraordinary players from other places. I can still remember the name of the forward who came from, I think, Rome: Alessandro Dazza. He was the best on the team, just ahead of Carlos Gutierrez (not his real name), who hailed from Spain and played midfield. Our best defender was a Vietnamese-American student named Tuan, and there was also Paul Beaupre, who was actually from our own WASP-filled town, but whose name sounded French. We were expected to win State, but we did not come very close. Homewood-Flossmoor, we heard, had a pair of twins from Brazil.

A short time later, after the growth of professional indoor soccer and some vague stabs at outdoor leagues, we proved to the world that the United States was serious, or relatively serious, about soccer, and the World Cup came to America in 1994. At least 4 to 5 percent of the country heard about this, and some commensurate percentage of them went to the games. This was enough to fill stadia, and the experiment was considered a success. In the wake of the Cup in America, other outdoor leagues have struggled to gain footing, and the current league seems more or less viable, though newspaper coverage of the games usually is found in the nether regions of the sports section, near the car ads and the biathalon roundups.

Our continued indifference to the sport worshiped around the world can be easily explained in two parts. First, as a nation of loony but determined inventors, we prefer things we thought of ourselves. The most popular sports in America are those we conceived and developed on our own: football, baseball, basketball. If we can claim at least part of the credit for something, as with tennis or the radio, we are willing to be passively interested. But we did not invent soccer, and so we are suspicious of it.

The second and greatest, by far, obstacle to the popularity of the World Cup, and of professional soccer in general, is the element of flopping. Americans may generally be arrogant, but there is one stance I stand behind, and that is the intense loathing of penalty-fakers. There are few examples of American sports where flopping is part of the game, much less accepted as such. Things are too complicated and dangerous in football to do much faking. Baseball? It's not possible, really—you can't fake getting hit by a baseball, and it's impossible to fake catching one. The only one of the big three sports that has a flop factor is basketball, where players can and do occasionally exaggerate a foul against them, but get this: the biggest flopper in the NBA is not an American at all. He's Argentinian! (Manu Ginobili, a phony to end all phonies, but otherwise a very good player.)

But flopping in soccer is a problem. Flopping is essentially a combination of acting, lying, begging and cheating, and these four behaviors make for an unappealing mix. The sheer theatricality of flopping is distasteful, as is the slow-motion way the chicanery unfolds. First there will be some incidental contact, and then there will be a long moment—enough to allow you to go and wash the car and return—after the contact and before the flopper decides to flop. When you've returned from washing the car and around the time you're making yourself a mini-bagel grilled cheese, the flopper will be leaping forward, his mouth Munch-wide and oval, bracing himself for contact with the earth beneath him. But this is just the beginning. Go and do the grocery shopping and perhaps open a new money-market account at the bank, and when you return, our flopper will still be on the ground, holding his shin, his head thrown back in mock agony. It's disgusting, all of it, particularly because, just as all of this fakery takes a good deal of time and melodrama to put over, the next step is so fast that special cameras are needed to capture it. Once the referees have decided either to issue a penalty or not to our Fakey McChumpland, he will jump up, suddenly and spectacular uninjured—excelsior!—and will kick the ball over to his teammate and move on.

American sports are, for better or worse, built upon transparency, or the appearance of transparency, and on the grind-it-out work ethic. This is why the most popular soccer player in American history is Sylvester Stallone. In fact, the two greatest moments in American soccer both involved Sylvester Stallone. The first came with *Victory,* the classic film about Allied soccer-playing POWs, and the all-star game they play against the Nazis. In that film, Stallone plays an American soldier who must, for some reason—no one can be expected to remember these things—replace the goalie on the POW team. Of course, Stallone knows nothing about soccer, so must learn to play goalie (somewhere, Moron McCheeby grins triumphantly). Stallone does this admirably, the Allies win (I think) and as the crowd surrounds them, they are hidden under coats and fans, and sneak away to freedom.

The second most significant moment was when the World Cup came to the United States, in 1994. It is reported that Stallone attended one of the games, and seemed to enjoy it.

It's inevitable, given the way the U.S. teams are improving every year, that eventually we will make it to the semifinals of the World Cup, and it's likely, one would think, that the United States will win it all in the near future. This is a country of limitless wealth and 300 million people, after all, and when we dedicate the proper resources to a project, we get the job done (see Vietnam, Lebanon, Iraq). But until we do win the Cup—and we have no chance this particular time around, being tossed into the Group of Death, which will consume us quickly and utterly—soccer will receive only the grudging acknowledgment of the general populace. Then again, do we really want—or can we even conceive of—an America where soccer enjoys wide popularity or even respect? If you were soccer, the sport of kings, would you *want* the adulation of a people who elected Bush and Cheney, not once but twice? You would not. You would rather return to your roots, communist or otherwise, and fight fascism with your feet.

World Cup Record

FIFA Ranking: 7
World Cup Appearances: 7
World Cup Champions: 0
Federation Name: United States Soccer
    Federation
Confederation: CONCACAF
Founded: 1913
FIFA Affiliation: 1913
Nickname: Sam's Army (for the fans)
Manager: Bruce Arena
Website: www.ussoccer.com
Stadium: Rose Bowl, Pasadena, CA
Home Uniform: all white
Away Uniform: all dark blue
Provider: Nike

1930: 3rd Place
1934: First round exit
1938: Did not participate
1950: First round exit
1954: Did not qualify
1958: Did not qualify
1962: Did not qualify
1966: Did not qualify
1970: Did not qualify
1974: Did not qualify
1978: Did not qualify
1982: Did not qualify
1986: Did not qualify
1990: First round exit
1994: Second round exit
1998: First round exit
2002: Quarterfinals

Matches	Wins	Draws	Losses	GF	GA	GD	Points
22	6	2	14	25	45	-20	20

United States is 25th on the all-time World Cup table

Path to Qualification for World Cup 2006

13-Jun-04	United States	3	Grenada	0	W
20-Jun-04	Grenada	2	United States	3	W
18-Aug-04	Jamaica	1	United States	1	D
4-Sep-04	United States	2	El Salvador	0	W
8-Sep-04	Panama	1	United States	1	D
9-Oct-04	El Salvador	0	United States	2	W
13-Oct-04	United States	6	Panama	0	W
17-Nov-04	United States	1	Jamaica	1	D
9-Feb-05	Trinidad	1	United States	2	W
27-Mar-05	Mexico	2	United States	1	L
30-Mar-05	United States	2	Guatemala	0	W
4-Jun-05	United States	3	Costa Rica	0	W
8-Jun-05	Panama	0	United States	3	W
17-Aug-05	United States	1	Trinidad	0	W
3-Sep-05	United States	2	Mexico	0	W
7-Sep-05	Guatemala	0	United States	0	D
8-Oct-05	Costa Rica	3	United States	0	L
12-Oct-05	United States	2	Panama	0	W

United States qualified by finishing in the top three in the CONCACAF Zone

The World Cup in Numbers

Past World Cup Results

	Host	Champion	2nd Place	3rd Place	4th Place
1930	Uruguay	**Uruguay**	Argentina	United States	Yugoslavia
1934	Italy	**Italy**	Czechoslovakia	Germany	Austria
1938	France	**Italy**	Hungary	Brazil	Sweden
1950	Brazil	**Uruguay**	Brazil	Sweden	Spain
1954	Switzerland	**W. Germany**	Hungary	Austria	Uruguay
1958	Sweden	**Brazil**	Sweden	France	W. Germany
1962	Chile	**Brazil**	Czechoslovakia	Chile	Yugoslavia
1966	England	**England**	W. Germany	Portugal	USSR
1970	Mexico	**Brazil**	Italy	W. Germany	Uruguay
1974	W. Germany	**W. Germany**	Holland	Poland	Brazil
1978	Argentina	**Argentina**	Holland	Brazil	Italy
1982	Spain	**Italy**	W. Germany	Poland	France
1986	Mexico	**Argentina**	W. Germany	France	Belgium
1990	Italy	**W. Germany**	Argentina	Italy	England
1994	United States	**Brazil**	Italy	Sweden	Bulgaria
1998	France	**France**	Brazil	Croatia	Netherlands
2002	Korea/Japan	**Brazil**	Germany	Turkey	South Korea

	Host	Nations	Matches	Goals	Goals Per Match	Attendance	Attendance Per Match
1930	Uruguay	13	18	70	3.9	434,500	24,139
1934	Italy	16	17	70	4.1	395,000	23,235
1938	France	15	18	84	4.7	483,000	26,833
1950	Brazil	13	22	88	4.0	1,337,000	60,773
1954	Switzerland	16	26	140	5.4	943,000	36,269
1958	Sweden	16	35	126	3.6	868,000	24,800
1962	Chile	16	32	89	2.8	776,000	24,250
1966	England	16	32	89	2.8	1,614,677	50,459
1970	Mexico	16	32	95	3.0	1,673,975	52,312
1974	West Germany	16	38	97	2.6	1,774,022	46,685
1978	Argentina	16	38	102	2.7	1,610,215	42,374
1982	Spain	24	52	146	2.8	1,856,277	35,698
1986	Mexico	24	52	132	2.5	2,407,431	46,297
1990	Italy	24	52	115	2.2	2,517,348	48,411
1994	United States	24	52	141	2.7	3,587,538	68,991
1998	France	32	64	171	2.7	2,785,100	43,517
2002	Korea/Japan	32	64	161	2.5	2,705,197	42,269

All-Time World Cup Table

	Nation	Matches	Wins	Draws	Losses	Goals For	Goals Against	Goal Difference	Points
1	Brazil	87	60	14	13	191	82	109	194
2	Germany	85	50	18	17	176	106	70	168
3	Italy	70	39	17	14	110	67	43	134
4	Argentina	60	30	11	19	102	71	31	101
5	England	50	22	15	13	68	45	23	81
6	France	44	21	7	16	86	61	25	70
7	Spain	45	19	12	14	71	53	18	69
8	Russia/USSR	37	17	6	14	64	44	20	57
9	Yugoslavia	37	16	8	13	60	46	14	56
	Sweden	42	15	11	16	71	65	6	56
11	Uruguay	40	15	10	15	65	57	8	55
12	Netherlands	32	14	9	9	56	36	20	51
13	Hungary	32	15	3	14	87	57	30	48
14	Poland	28	14	5	9	42	36	6	47
15	Mexico	41	10	11	20	43	79	-36	41
16	Austria	29	12	4	13	43	47	-4	40
17	Belgium	36	10	9	17	46	63	-17	39
18	Czechoslovakia	30	11	5	14	44	45	-1	38
19	Romania	21	8	5	8	30	32	-2	29
20	Chile	25	7	6	12	31	40	-9	27
21	Denmark	13	7	2	4	24	18	6	23
22	Paraguay	19	5	7	7	25	34	-9	22
23	Portugal	12	7	0	5	25	16	9	21
	Switzerland	22	6	3	13	33	51	-18	21
25	United States	22	6	2	14	25	45	-20	20
26	Cameroon	17	4	7	6	15	29	-14	19
	Scotland	23	4	7	12	25	41	-16	19
28	Croatia	10	6	0	4	13	8	5	18
29	Bulgaria	26	3	8	15	22	53	-31	17
30	Turkey	10	5	1	4	20	17	3	16
31	Peru	15	4	3	8	19	31	-12	15
	South Korea	21	3	6	12	19	49	-30	15
33	Ireland	13	2	8	3	10	10	0	14
	Northern Ireland	13	3	5	5	13	23	-10	14
35	Nigeria	11	4	1	6	14	16	-2	13
36	Colombia	13	3	2	8	14	23	-9	11
37	Costa Rica	7	3	1	3	9	12	-3	10
	Morocco	13	2	4	7	12	18	-6	10
39	Norway	8	2	3	3	7	8	-1	9
40	Senegal	5	2	2	1	7	6	1	8
	East Germany	6	2	2	2	5	5	0	8
42	Japan	7	2	1	4	6	7	-1	7

	Country	Matches	Wins	Draws	Losses	Goals For	Goals Against	Goal Difference	Points
	Algeria	6	2	1	3	6	10	-4	7
	Saudi Arabia	10	2	1	7	7	25	-18	7
45	Wales	5	1	3	1	4	4	0	6
	South Africa	6	1	3	2	8	11	-3	6
	Tunisia	9	1	3	5	5	11	-6	6
48	North Korea	4	1	1	2	5	9	-4	4
	Cuba	3	1	1	1	5	12	-7	4
	Iran	6	1	1	4	4	12	-8	4
51	Ecuador	3	1	0	2	2	4	-2	3
	Jamaica	3	1	0	2	3	9	-6	3
53	Honduras	3	0	2	1	2	3	-1	2
	Israel	3	0	2	1	1	3	-2	2
	Egypt	4	0	2	2	3	6	-3	2
56	Kuwait	3	0	1	2	2	6	-4	1
	Australia	3	0	1	2	0	5	-5	1
	Bolivia	6	0	1	5	1	20	-19	1
59	Iraq	3	0	0	3	1	4	-3	0
	Canada	3	0	0	3	0	5	-5	0
	Slovenia	3	0	0	3	2	7	-5	0
	Dutch East Indies	1	0	0	1	0	6	-6	0
	China	3	0	0	3	0	9	-9	0
	United Arab Emirates	3	0	0	3	2	11	-9	0
	Greece	3	0	0	3	0	10	-10	0
	New Zealand	3	0	0	3	2	12	-10	0
	Haiti	3	0	0	3	2	14	-12	0
	Zaïre	3	0	0	3	0	14	-14	0
	El Salvador	6	0	0	6	1	22	-21	0

Note: Three points for each win, one point for each draw

Most Goals in the World Cup

Player	Nation	Goals
Gerd Müller	Germany	14
Juste Fontaine	France	13
Pelé	Brazil	12
Ronaldo*	Brazil	12
Sandor Kocsis	Hungary	11
Jürgen Klinsmann	Germany	11
Helmut Rahn	Germany	10
Teofilio Cubillas	Peru	10
Gary Lineker	England	10
Grzegorz Lato	Poland	10
Gabriel Batistuta	Argentina	10
Roberto Baggio	Italy	9
Paolo Rossi	Italy	9
Uwe Seeler	Germany	9
Jairzinho	Brazil	9
Eusebio	Portugal	9
Karl-Heinz Rummenigge	Germany	9
Vava	Brazil	9
Ademir	Brazil	9
Christian Vieri*	Italy	9

Most Appearances in the World Cup

Player	Nation	Matches
Lothar Matthäus	Germany	25
Paolo Maldini*	Italy	23
Diego Maradona	Argentina	21
Wladislav Zmuda	Poland	21
Uwe Seeler	Germany	21
Grzegorz Lato	Poland	20
Berti Vogts	Germany	19
Karl-Heinz Rummenigge	Germany	19
Wolfgang Overath	Germany	19
Claudio Taffarel	Brazil	18
Franz Beckenbauer	Germany	18
Pierre Littbarski	Germany	18
Gaetano Scirea	Italy	18
Antonio Cabrini	Italy	18
Thomas Berthold	Germany	18
Mario Kempes	Argentina	18
Sepp Maier	Germany	18
Carlos Dunga	Brazil	18

*Still active

Penalty Shootouts

Nation	Wins	Losses	Shots	Goals	Goal Percentage
Germany	3	0	14	13	93%
Argentina	3	0	14	11	79%
Brazil	2	1	13	10	77%
France	2	1	16	12	75%
South Korea	1	0	5	5	100%
Belgium	1	0	5	5	100%
Sweden	1	0	6	5	83%
Bulgaria	1	0	4	3	75%
Ireland	1	1	10	7	70%
Spain	1	2	14	10	71%
Netherlands	0	1	4	2	50%
Yugoslavia	0	1	5	2	40%
Romania	0	2	11	8	73%
England	0	2	10	6	60%
Mexico	0	2	7	2	29%
Italy	0	3	15	8	53%
TOTAL			153	109	71%

Awards

FIFA World Player of the Year

Organized by FIFA and decided by votes cast by international team managers and, since 2004, by the captains of national soccer teams

2005

1. Ronaldo de Assis "Ronaldinho" (Brazil)
2. Frank Lampard (England)
3. Samuel Eto'o (Cameroon)
4. Thierry Henry (France)
5. Adriano Ribeiro Leite (Brazil)
6. Andriy Shevchenko (Ukraine)
7. Steven Gerrard (England)
8. Ricardo Izecson Santos "Kaka" (Brazil)
9. Paolo Maldini (Italy)
10. Didier Drogba (Côte d'Ivoire)

2004

1. Ronaldo de Assis "Ronaldinho" (Brazil)
2. Thierry Henry (France)
3. Andriy Shevchenko (Ukraine)
4. Pavel Nedved (Czech Republic)
5. Zinedine Zidane (France)
6. Adriano Ribeiro Leite (Brazil)
7. Anderson Luis de Sousa "Deco" (Portugal)
   Ronaldo Nazário de Lima (Brazil)
9. Ruud Van Nistelrooij (Netherlands)
10. Ricardo Izecson Santos "Kaka" (Brazil)
    Wayne Rooney (England)

2003

1. Zinedine Zidane (France)
2. Thierry Henry (France)
3. Ronaldo Nazário de Lima (Brazil)
4. Pavel Nedved (Czech Republic)
5. Roberto Carlos Da Silva (Brazil)
6. Ruud Van Nistelrooij (Netherlands)
7. David Beckham (England)
8. Raúl González Blanco (Spain)
9. Paolo Maldini (Italy)
10. Andrei Shevchenko (Ukraine)

2002

1. Ronaldo Nazário de Lima (Brazil)
2. Oliver Kahn (Germany)
3. Zinedine Zidane (France)
4. Roberto Carlos Da Silva (Brazil)
5. Rivaldo Vitor Borba Ferreira (Brazil)
6. Raúl González Blanco (Spain)
7. Michael Ballack (Germany)
8. David Beckham (England)
9. Thierry Henry (France)
10. Michael Owen (England)

2001

1. Luis Figo (Portugal)
2. David Beckham (England)
3. Raúl González Blanco (Spain)
4. Zinedine Zidane (France)
5. Rivaldo Vitor Borba Ferreira (Brazil)
6. Juan Sebastián Verón (Argentina)
7. Oliver Kahn (Germany)
8. Michael Owen (England)
9. Andrei Shevchenko (Ukraine)
10. Francesco Totti (Italy)

2000

1. Zinedine Zidane (France)
2. Luis Figo (Portugal)
3. Rivaldo Vitor Borba Ferreira (Brazil)
4. Gabriel Batistuta (Argentina)
5. Andrei Shevchenko (Ukraine)
6. David Beckham (England)
7. Thierry Henry (France)
8. Alessandro Nesta (Italy)
9. Patrick Kluivert (Netherlands)
10. Francesco Totti (Italy)
    Raúl González Blanco (Spain)

RSS Player of the Year

Awarded by the readers of RSSSF (the rec.sport.soccer newsgroup), organized by Kent Hedlundh, Umea, Sweden

2005   Ronaldinho (Brazil)
2004   Ronaldinho (Brazil)
2003   Pavel Nedved (Czech Republic)
2002   Ronaldo Nazário de Lima (Brazil)
2001   Michael Owen (England)
2000   Luis Figo (Portugal)

African Footballer of the Year

Awarded by the Confederation Africaine de Football

2004   Samuel Eto'o (Cameroon)
2003   Samuel Eto'o (Cameroon)
2002   El Hadji Diouf (Senegal)
2001   El Hadji Diouf (Senegal)
2000   Patrick Mboma (Cameroon)

Asian Player of the Year

Awarded by the Asian Football Confederation, officially called the "Sanyo Player of the Year Award"

2004   Ali Karimi (Iran)
2003   Mehdi Mahdavikia (Iran)
2002   Shinji Ono (Japan)
2001   Fan Zhiyi (China)
2000   Nawaf Al-Temyat (Saudi Arabia)

European Footballer of the Year

Organized by France Football; since 1995 non-European players who play in Europe are eligible

2005   Ronaldinho (Brazil)

2004   Andriy Shevchenko (Ukraine)

2003   Pavel Nedved (Czech Republic)

2002   Ronaldo (Brazil)

2001   Michael Owen (England)

2000   Luis Figo (Portugal)

Oceanian Player of the Year

Awarded by Oceania Football Confederation; open to all players originating from Oceania, no matter where they play

2004   Tim Cahill (Australia)

2003   Harry Kewell (Australia)

2002   Brett Emerton (Australia)

2001   Harry Kewell (Australia)

2000   Mark Viduka (Australia)

Rey del Futbol de America

Awarded by the Uruguayan newspaper El Pais since 1986; only South Americans who play for South American clubs are eligible

2005   Carlos Tevez (Argentina)

2004   Carlos Tevez (Argentina)

2003   Carlos Tevez (Argentina)

2002   Jose Cardozo (Paraguay)

2001   Juan Roman Riquelme (Argentina)

2000   Romario (Brazil)

World Cup "Lev Yashin" Award

Awarded by FIFA to the best goalkeeper of the tournament

World Cup 2002   Oliver Kahn (Germany)

World Cup 1998   Fabien Barthez (France)

World Cup 1994   Michel Preud'homme (Belgium)

World Cup Golden Ball

Awarded by journalists to the best player of the tournament (a "Silver Ball" is given to the runner-up and a "Bronze Ball" for third place)

World Cup 2002	Oliver Kahn (Germany)
World Cup 1998	Ronaldo Nazário de Lima (Brazil)
World Cup 1994	Romario da Souza (Brazil)
World Cup 1990	Salvatore Schillaci (Italy)
World Cup 1986	Diego Maradona (Argentina)
World Cup 1982	Paolo Rossi (Italy)
World Cup 1978	Mario Kempes (Argentina)

World Soccer's Player of the Year

Awarded by the English magazine World Soccer, *chosen by its readers*

2005	Ronaldinho (Brazil)
2004	Ronaldinho (Brazil)
2003	Pavel Nedved (Czech Republic)
2002	Ronaldo (Brazil)
2001	Michael Owen (England)
2000	Luis Figo (Portugal)

World's Best Goalkeeper of the Year

Awarded by the International Federation of Football History & Statistics (IFFHS)

2004	Gianluigi Buffon (Italy)
2003	Gianluigi Buffon (Italy)
2002	Oliver Kahn (Germany)
2001	Oliver Kahn (Germany)
2000	Fabien Barthez (France)

The 32 Nations in Numbers

Land Area (square km)

1	United States	9,631,418	17	Poland	312,685
2	Brazil	8,511,965	18	Italy	301,230
3	Australia	7,692,300	19	Ecuador	283,560
4	Argentina	2,766,890	20	Ghana	239,460
5	Mexico	1,972,550	21	Tunisia	163,610
6	Saudi Arabia	1,960,582	22	England	130,357
7	Iran	1,648,000	23	Serbia and Montenegro	102,350
8	Angola	1,246,700	24	South Korea	98,480
9	Ukraine	603,700	25	Portugal	92,391
10	France	547,030	26	Czech Republic	78,866
11	Spain	504,782	27	Togo	56,785
12	Sweden	449,964	28	Croatia	56,542
13	Paraguay	406,750	29	Costa Rica	51,100
14	Japan	377,835	30	Netherlands	41,526
15	Germany	357,021	31	Switzerland	41,290
16	Côte d'Ivoire	322,460	32	Trinidad and Tobago	5,128

Source: *CIA World Factbook 2005*

Population

1	United States	295,734,000	18	Côte d'Ivoire	17,298,000
2	Brazil	186,113,000	17	Australia	20,090,000
3	Japan	127,417,000	19	Netherlands	16,407,000
4	Mexico	106,203,000	20	Ecuador	13,364,000
5	Germany	82,431,000	21	Angola	11,827,000
6	Iran	68,018,000	22	Serbia and Montenegro	10,829,000
7	France	60,656,000	23	Portugal	10,566,000
8	Italy	58,103,000	24	Czech Republic	10,241,000
9	England	49,138,000	25	Tunisia	10,075,000
10	South Korea	48,641,000	26	Sweden	9,002,000
11	Ukraine	46,997,000	27	Switzerland	7,489,000
12	Spain	40,341,000	28	Paraguay	6,348,000
13	Argentina	39,538,000	29	Togo	5,400,000
14	Poland	38,558,000	30	Croatia	4,496,000
15	Saudi Arabia	26,418,000	31	Costa Rica	4,016,000
16	Ghana	21,946,000	32	Trinidad and Tobago	1,075,000

World Average: 24,160,000

Source: *CIA World Factbook 2005*, statistics.gov.uk

Population Annual Growth Rate

1	Paraguay	2.48%	17	Switzerland	0.49%
2	Saudi Arabia	2.31%	18	Portugal	0.39%
3	Togo	2.17%	19	South Korea	0.38%
4	Côte d'Ivoire	2.06%	20	France	0.37%
5	Angola	1.90%	21	England	0.28%
6	Costa Rica	1.48%	22	Sweden	0.17%
7	Ghana	1.25%	23	Spain	0.15%
8	Ecuador	1.24%	24	Italy	0.07%
9	Mexico	1.17%	25	Japan	0.05%
10	Brazil	1.06%	26	Poland	0.03%
11	Tunisia	0.99%	27	Serbia and Montenegro	0.03%
12	Argentina	0.98%	28	Germany	0.00%
13	United States	0.92%	29	Croatia	-0.02%
14	Australia	0.87%	30	Czech Republic	-0.05%
15	Iran	0.86%	31	Ukraine	-0.63%
16	Netherlands	0.53%	32	Trinidad and Tobago	-0.74%

World Average: 1.20%

Source: *CIA World Factbook 2005*. Figure for England is for the UK as a whole.

Definition: The average annual percent change in the population, resulting from a surplus (or deficit) of births over deaths and the balance of migrants entering and leaving a country

Population Density (per square km)

1	South Korea	491	17	Croatia	79
2	Netherlands	395	18	Costa Rica	78
3	England	378	19	Ukraine	78
4	Japan	337	20	Tunisia	61
5	Germany	230	21	Mexico	53
6	Trinidad and Tobago	212	22	Côte d'Ivoire	53
7	Italy	192	23	Ecuador	47
8	Switzerland	181	24	Iran	41
9	Czech Republic	129	25	United States	30
10	Poland	123	26	Brazil	21
11	Portugal	114	27	Sweden	20
12	France	110	28	Paraguay	15
13	Serbia and Montenegro	105	29	Argentina	14
14	Togo	100	30	Saudi Arabia	13
15	Ghana	87	31	Angola	8
16	Spain	85	32	Australia	2

World Average: 43

Source: *CIA World Factbook 2005*.

Birth Rate (births per 1,000 population)

1	Angola	45.6	17	France	12.2
2	Togo	37.2	18	Serbia and Montenegro	12.1
3	Côte d'Ivoire	35.5	19	Netherlands	11.1
4	Ghana	31.1	20	Portugal	10.8
5	Saudi Arabia	29.6	21	United Kingdom	10.8
6	Paraguay	29.4	22	Sweden	10.4
7	Ecuador	22.7	23	Spain	10.1
8	Mexico	21.0	24	South Korea	10.0
9	Costa Rica	18.6	25	Switzerland	9.8
10	Argentina	16.9	26	Poland	9.7
11	Brazil	16.8	27	Croatia	9.6
12	Iran	16.8	28	Japan	9.5
13	Tunisia	15.5	29	Czech Republic	9.1
14	United States	14.1	30	Italy	8.9
15	Trinidad and Tobago	12.7	31	Ukraine	8.7
16	Australia	12.3	32	Germany	8.3

World Average: 20.2

Source: *CIA World Factbook 2005*. Figure for England is for the UK as a whole.

Median Age

1	Japan	42.6	17	United States	36.3
2	Germany	42.2	18	South Korea	34.5
3	Italy	41.8	19	Trinidad and Tobago	30.9
4	Sweden	40.6	20	Argentina	29.4
5	Croatia	40.0	21	Brazil	27.8
6	Switzerland	39.8	22	Tunisia	27.3
7	Spain	39.5	23	Costa Rica	26.0
8	Netherlands	39.0	24	Mexico	24.9
9	England	39.0	25	Iran	24.2
10	Czech Republic	39.0	26	Ecuador	23.3
11	France	38.9	27	Saudi Arabia	21.3
12	Ukraine	38.2	28	Paraguay	21.2
13	Portugal	38.2	29	Ghana	20.5
14	Serbia and Montenegro	36.8	30	Côte d'Ivoire	19.1
15	Australia	36.6	31	Angola	18.1
16	Poland	36.4	32	Togo	17.8

World Average: 27.6

Source: *CIA World Factbook 2005*. Figure for England is for the UK as a whole.

Life Expectancy at Birth

1	Japan	80.9	17	Paraguay	74.4
2	Australia	80.1	18	Tunisia	74.4
3	Switzerland	80.0	19	Croatia	74.4
4	Sweden	80.0	20	Serbia and Montenegro	74.0
5	Italy	79.4	21	Poland	73.9
6	France	79.3	22	Mexico	72.3
7	Spain	79.2	23	Ecuador	71.9
8	Netherlands	78.7	24	Brazil	71.1
9	Germany	78.4	25	Trinidad and Tobago	69.6
10	England	78.2	26	Iran	69.4
11	United States	77.1	27	Saudi Arabia	68.7
12	Costa Rica	76.4	28	Ukraine	66.5
13	Portugal	76.4	29	Ghana	56.5
14	Argentina	75.5	30	Togo	53.4
15	South Korea	75.4	31	Côte d'Ivoire	42.7
16	Czech Republic	75.2	32	Angola	37.0

World Average: 67.4

Source: *CIA World Factbook 2005*. Figure for England is for the UK as a whole.

Infant Mortality Rate (deaths per 1,000 live births)

1	Sweden	2.8	17	Costa Rica	10.0
2	Japan	3.3	18	Ukraine	10.1
3	Czech Republic	3.9	19	Serbia and Montenegro	12.9
4	Germany	4.2	20	Saudi Arabia	13.2
5	France	4.3	21	Argentina	15.2
6	Switzerland	4.4	22	Mexico	20.9
7	Spain	4.4	23	Ecuador	23.7
8	Australia	4.7	24	Tunisia	24.8
9	Netherlands	5.0	25	Paraguay	25.6
10	Portugal	5.1	26	Trinidad and Tobago	25.8
11	England	5.2	27	Brazil	29.6
12	Italy	5.9	28	Iran	41.6
13	South Korea	6.3	29	Ghana	56.4
14	United States	6.5	30	Togo	62.2
15	Croatia	6.8	31	Côte d'Ivoire	90.8
16	Poland	7.4	32	Angola	187.5

World Average: 50.1

Source: *CIA World Factbook 2005*. Figure for England is for the UK as a whole.

Literacy Rate

1	Australia	100.0%	17	Argentina	97.1%
2	Poland	99.8%	18	United States	97.0%
3	Ukraine	99.7%	19	Costa Rica	96.0%
4	France	99.0%	20	Paraguay	94.0%
5	Germany	99.0%	21	Portugal	93.3%
6	England	99.0%	22	Serbia and Montenegro	93.0%
7	Sweden	99.0%	23	Ecuador	92.5%
8	Switzerland	99.0%	24	Mexico	92.2%
9	Japan	99.0%	25	Brazil	86.4%
10	Netherlands	99.0%	26	Iran	79.4%
11	Italy	98.6%	27	Saudi Arabia	78.8%
12	Trinidad and Tobago	98.6%	28	Ghana	74.8%
13	Croatia	98.5%	29	Tunisia	74.2%
14	Romania	98.4%	30	Togo	60.9%
15	South Korea	98.1%	31	Côte d'Ivoire	50.9%
16	Spain	97.9%	32	Angola	42.0%

World Average: 78.7%

Source: *CIA World Factbook 2005*. Figure for England is for the UK as a whole.

Executions (per year)

1	United States	68	17	Ghana	0
2	Iran	66	18	Italy	0
3	Saudi Arabia	29	19	Mexico	0
4	Japan	6	20	Netherlands	0
5	Angola	0	21	Paraguay	0
6	Argentina	0	22	Poland	0
7	Australia	0	23	Portugal	0
8	Brazil	0	24	Serbia and Montenegro	0
9	Costa Rica	0	25	South Korea	0
10	Côte d'Ivoire	0	26	Spain	0
11	Croatia	0	27	Sweden	0
12	Czech Republic	0	28	Switzerland	0
13	Ecuador	0	29	Togo	0
14	England	0	30	Trinidad and Tobago	0
15	France	0	31	Tunisia	0
16	Germany	0	32	Ukraine	0

Source: Amnesty International. Figure for England is for the UK as a whole.

Definition: Number of known executions in the country (data is for 1998). These figures include only documented cases; the true figures are likely to be much higher.

Armed Forces Personnel (per 1,000 population)

1	South Korea	14.0	17	Tunisia	3.5
2	Croatia	13.6	18	England	3.5
3	Angola	9.1	19	Netherlands	3.2
4	Saudi Arabia	7.6	20	Paraguay	3.2
5	Iran	7.5	21	Trinidad and Tobago	2.8
6	Ukraine	6.5	22	Germany	2.7
7	Sweden	5.9	23	Australia	2.5
8	Czech Republic	5.7	24	Japan	1.9
9	Poland	5.6	25	Argentina	1.8
10	France	4.8	26	Mexico	1.8
11	United States	4.6	27	Brazil	1.5
12	Ecuador	4.3	28	Togo	1.3
13	Italy	4.3	29	Côte d'Ivoire	0.5
14	Portugal	4.3	30	Ghana	0.3
15	Spain	4.1	31	Costa Rica	0.0
16	Switzerland	3.7	32	Serbia and Montenegro	NA

World Average: 3.1

Source: International Institute for Strategic Studies, *The Military Balance 2001–2002*. Figure for England is for the UK as a whole.

Prisoners (per 100,000 population)

1	United States	715	17	Italy	100
2	Ukraine	416	18	Germany	96
3	Trinidad and Tobago	351	19	France	95
4	Tunisia	253	20	Paraguay	75
5	Costa Rica	229	21	Sweden	75
6	Iran	226	22	Switzerland	72
7	Poland	210	23	Croatia	64
8	Czech Republic	178	24	Ecuador	59
9	Brazil	169	25	Japan	54
10	Mexico	169	26	Ghana	52
11	Spain	144	27	Togo	46
12	Portugal	130	28	Angola	44
13	Australia	116	29	Côte d'Ivoire	NA
14	Netherlands	112	30	England	NA
15	Saudi Arabia	110	31	Serbia and Montenegro	NA
16	Argentina	107	32	South Korea	NA

World Average: 148

Source: International Centre for Prison Studies

Definition: Number of prisoners held per 100,000 population (data is for 2003)

GDP Per Capita (in U.S. dollars)

1	United States	$39,732	17	Saudi Arabia	$11,742
2	Switzerland	$33,636	18	Croatia	$11,194
3	Australia	$30,700	19	Trinidad and Tobago	$10,679
4	England	$29,483	20	Mexico	$9,472
5	Japan	$29,392	21	Costa Rica	$9,455
6	Netherlands	$29,323	22	Brazil	$8,017
7	Germany	$28,654	23	Iran	$7,597
8	France	$28,637	24	Tunisia	$7,035
9	Sweden	$28,371	25	Ukraine	$6,364
10	Italy	$27,692	26	Paraguay	$4,715
11	Spain	$23,242	27	Ecuador	$3,705
12	South Korea	$19,019	28	Serbia and Montenegro	$2,426
13	Portugal	$17,859	29	Ghana	$2,199
14	Czech Republic	$16,815	30	Angola	$1,959
15	Argentina	$12,229	31	Togo	$1,608
16	Poland	$12,008	32	Côte d'Ivoire	$1,433

World Average: $8,625

Source: *CIA World Factbook 2005*. Figure for England is for the UK as a whole.

Annual GDP Real Growth Rate

1	Ukraine	12.0%	17	Croatia	3.7%
2	Angola	11.7%	18	Czech Republic	3.7%
3	Argentina	8.3%	19	Sweden	3.6%
4	Serbia and Montenegro	6.5%	20	Australia	3.5%
5	Iran	6.3%	21	England	3.2%
6	Ecuador	5.8%	22	Togo	3.0%
7	Trinidad and Tobago	5.7%	23	Japan	2.9%
8	Poland	5.6%	24	Paraguay	2.8%
9	Ghana	5.4%	25	Spain	2.6%
10	Brazil	5.1%	26	France	2.1%
11	Tunisia	5.1%	27	Switzerland	1.8%
12	Saudi Arabia	5.0%	28	Germany	1.7%
13	South Korea	4.6%	29	Italy	1.3%
14	United States	4.4%	30	Netherlands	1.2%
15	Mexico	4.1%	31	Portugal	1.1%
16	Costa Rica	3.9%	32	Côte d'Ivoire	-1.0%

World Average: 4.9%

Source: *CIA World Factbook 2005* (2004 estimates). Figure for England is for the UK as a whole.

Unemployment Rate

1	Mexico	3.2%	17	Czech Republic	10.6%
2	Switzerland	3.4%	18	Germany	10.6%
3	Ukraine	3.5%	19	Ecuador	11.1%
4	South Korea	3.6%	20	Iran	11.2%
5	Japan	4.7%	21	Brazil	11.5%
6	England	4.8%	22	Côte d'Ivoire	13.0%
7	Australia	5.1%	23	Croatia	13.8%
8	United States	5.5%	24	Tunisia	13.8%
9	Sweden	5.6%	25	Argentina	14.8%
10	Netherlands	6.0%	26	Paraguay	15.1%
11	Portugal	6.5%	27	Poland	19.5%
12	Costa Rica	6.6%	28	Ghana	20.0%
13	Italy	8.6%	29	Saudi Arabia	25.0%
14	France	10.1%	30	Serbia and Montenegro	30.0%
15	Spain	10.4%	31	Angola	NA
16	Trinidad and Tobago	10.4%	32	Togo	NA

World Average: 15.0%

Source: *CIA World Factbook 2005*. Figure for England is for the UK as a whole.

Exports (millions in U.S. dollars)

1	Germany	$893,300	18	Iran	$38,790
2	United States	$795,000	19	Portugal	$37,680
3	Japan	$538,800	20	Argentina	$33,780
4	France	$419,000	21	Ukraine	$32,910
5	England	$347,200	22	Angola	$12,760
6	Italy	$336,400	23	Tunisia	$9,926
7	Netherlands	$293,100	24	Croatia	$7,845
8	South Korea	$250,600	25	Ecuador	$7,560
9	Mexico	$182,400	26	Trinidad and Tobago	$6,671
10	Spain	$172,500			
11	Switzerland	$130,700	27	Costa Rica	$6,184
12	Sweden	$121,700	28	Côte d'Ivoire	$5,124
13	Saudi Arabia	$113,000	29	Serbia and Montenegro	$3,245
14	Brazil	$95,000			
15	Australia	$86,890	30	Ghana	$3,010
16	Poland	$75,980	31	Paraguay	$2,936
17	Czech Republic	$66,510	32	Togo	$663

World Average: $39,200

Source: *CIA World Factbook 2005*. Figure for England is for the UK as a whole.

Tourist Arrivals (per year)

1	France	67,310,000	17	Japan	4,218,000
2	United States	47,752,000	18	Croatia	3,834,000
3	Spain	43,252,000	19	Saudi Arabia	3,594,000
4	Italy	34,087,000	20	Brazil	2,850,000
5	England	25,515,000	21	Sweden	2,388,000
6	Poland	19,520,000	22	Portugal	1,072,000
7	Mexico	19,351,000	23	Costa Rica	811,000
8	Czech Republic	16,830,000	24	Iran	740,000
9	Germany	15,837,000	25	Ecuador	529,000
10	Netherlands	9,600,000	26	Paraguay	395,000
11	Ukraine	7,356,000	27	Ghana	325,000
12	Switzerland	6,530,000	28	Trinidad and Tobago	324,000
13	South Korea	5,800,000	29	Côte d'Ivoire	274,000
14	Australia	5,200,000	30	Togo	92,000
15	Argentina	4,540,000	31	Angola	45,000
16	Tunisia	4,263,000	32	Serbia and Montenegro	NA

World Average: 3,454,000

Source: *United Nations World Statistics Pocketbook and Statistical Yearbook,* Tourism Australia, World Tourism Organization. Figure for England is for the UK as a whole.

Tractors (per 1 million people)

1	Serbia and Montenegro	36,697	17	Ukraine	6,786
2	Poland	33,889	18	Brazil	4,331
3	Italy	30,119	19	Tunisia	3,484
4	Spain	21,938	20	Paraguay	2,599
5	France	20,839	21	Trinidad and Tobago	2,512
6	Sweden	18,329	22	Costa Rica	1,743
7	United States	16,231	23	Mexico	1,742
8	Portugal	15,995	24	Angola	871
9	Japan	15,916	25	Ecuador	666
10	Australia	15,679	26	Croatia	512
11	Switzerland	14,955	27	Saudi Arabia	360
12	Germany	12,505	28	Côte d'Ivoire	220
13	Czech Republic	9,444	29	Ghana	163
14	Netherlands	9,112	30	Togo	15
15	England	8,273	31	South Korea	NA
16	Argentina	7,082	32	Iran	NA

World Average: 6,498

Source: World Resources Institute. Figure for England is for the UK as a whole.

Military Expenditures (as a percentage of GDP)

1	Angola	10.6%	17	Sweden	1.7%
2	Saudi Arabia	10.0%	18	Netherlands	1.6%
3	Iran	3.3%	19	Germany	1.5%
4	United States	3.3%	20	Tunisia	1.5%
5	Australia	2.7%	21	Ukraine	1.4%
6	France	2.6%	22	Argentina	1.3%
7	South Korea	2.5%	23	Côte d'Ivoire	1.2%
8	England	2.4%	24	Spain	1.2%
9	Croatia	2.4%	25	Japan	1.0%
10	Portugal	2.3%	26	Switzerland	1.0%
11	Ecuador	2.2%	27	Mexico	0.9%
12	Togo	1.9%	28	Paraguay	0.9%
13	Czech Republic	1.8%	29	Ghana	0.6%
14	Brazil	1.8%	30	Trinidad and Tobago	0.6%
15	Italy	1.8%	31	Costa Rica	0.4%
16	Poland	1.7%	32	Serbia and Montenegro	NA

World Average: 2.0%

Source: *CIA World Factbook 2005*. Figure for England is for the UK as a whole.

Films Produced (per 1 million people)

1	France	13.4	17	Mexico	0.9
2	United States	13.1	18	Poland	0.7
3	Sweden	13.0	19	Brazil	0.5
4	England	12.7	20	Costa Rica	0.5
5	Netherlands	7.8	21	Iran	0.4
6	Australia	7.7	22	Tunisia	0.2
7	Germany	7.0	23	Ecuador	0.1
8	Switzerland	6.5	24	Ukraine	0.0
9	Czech Republic	5.9	25	Angola	NA
10	Spain	5.3	26	Côte d'Ivoire	NA
11	Argentina	5.2	27	Ghana	NA
12	Croatia	4.2	28	Paraguay	NA
13	Portugal	3.5	29	Saudi Arabia	NA
14	Italy	3.0	30	Serbia and Montenegro	NA
15	South Korea	1.5	31	Togo	NA
16	Japan	1.3	32	Trinidad and Tobago	NA

World Average: 1.7

Source: Internet Movie Database 2003. Figure for England is for the UK as a whole.

Televisions (per 1,000 people)

1	United States	740.5	17	Portugal	313.3
2	Japan	678.9	18	Croatia	271.4
3	Germany	623.6	19	Serbia and Montenegro	253.9
4	France	573.7	20	Mexico	241.0
5	Italy	521.5	21	Argentina	201.1
6	Sweden	511.0	22	Brazil	196.1
7	Australia	505.2	23	Saudi Arabia	193.1
8	England	504.6	24	Ecuador	187.1
9	Netherlands	493.7	25	Paraguay	156.0
10	Switzerland	442.0	26	Costa Rica	130.7
11	Spain	401.6	27	Tunisia	91.3
12	Trinidad and Tobago	395.3	28	Ghana	86.6
13	Ukraine	384.1	29	Iran	67.8
14	Poland	338.5	30	Côte d'Ivoire	63.0
15	Czech Republic	332.6	31	Angola	16.6
16	South Korea	326.9	32	Togo	13.5

World Average: 43.5

Source: *CIA World Factbook 2005*. Figure for England is for the UK as a whole.

Internet Users (per 1,000 people)

1	South Korea	600.7	17	Costa Rica	199.2
2	Sweden	569.3	18	Trinidad and Tobago	128.4
3	United States	537.6	19	Argentina	103.7
4	Netherlands	518.1	20	Mexico	94.5
5	England	508.8	21	Ukraine	80.9
6	Germany	473.1	22	Serbia and Montenegro	78.2
7	Australia	471.5	23	Brazil	76.8
8	Japan	448.9	24	Iran	63.2
9	France	361.1	25	Tunisia	62.5
10	Switzerland	341.3	26	Saudi Arabia	56.8
11	Portugal	340.7	27	Ecuador	42.6
12	Italy	318.4	28	Togo	38.9
13	Czech Republic	263.6	29	Paraguay	18.9
14	Spain	242.7	30	Ghana	7.7
15	Poland	232.6	31	Côte d'Ivoire	5.2
16	Croatia	225.5	32	Angola	3.5

World Average: 84.2

Source: *CIA World Factbook 2005*. Figure for England is for the UK as a whole.

Afterword: How to Win the World Cup

Franklin Foer

There have been revolutions to create socialism, democracy and authoritarian dictatorship. But humankind has yet to fight a revolution to guarantee one of the most vital elements, if not the most vital element, of the good life. That is, a winning soccer team.

If we were to take up arms for this reason, what kind of government would we want to install? Political theory, for all its talk about equality and virtue, has strangely evaded this question. But after seventeen World Cups, there's now a mass of empirical data, and using the most sophisticated methods available we can now determine the political and economic conditions that yield soccer glory.

To begin, we must first reach back into the dustbin of history. Communism, despite its gulags and show trials, produced great players and rock solid teams. The Hungarian squad of the early 1950s has gone down in history as one of the best to never win a championship. A few decades later, in 1982, the Poles advanced to the tournament's semifinals, drawing with Paolo Rossi's Italy and beating Michel Platini's France en route. These triumphs are reflected in the overall record. In World Cup matches against noncommunist countries, the red hordes bested their capitalist foes more often than not—46 wins, 32 draws, 40 losses.

But the fact remains that a Communist country has never won the World Cup. After watching the communists perform efficiently in preliminary rounds of the tournament, you could always count on them to collapse come the quarterfinals. There are many explanations for why communism never ascended higher. For starters, there's the Lobanovsky factor. Valeri Lobanovsky, the great Soviet and Ukrainian coach of the seventies and eighties, believed that science could provide underlying truths about the game. He would send technicians to games to evaluate players based on the number of "actions"—tackles, passes, shots—they performed. These evaluations perversely favored frenetic tackling over the creative construction of attack. Lobanovsky's method captures the pernicious way in which the rigidity of Marxism permeated the mentality of the Eastern bloc. Such rigidity might produce a great runner or gymnast, but it doesn't produce champions in a sport that requires regular flashes of individuality and risk taking. Then there's the misery of life under the hammer and sickle. Hungary, for instance, couldn't prevent its greatest players—László Kubala and Ferenc Puskas—from defecting to Spain in the fifties.

If the above data leads us to conclude that communism does not produce a superior soccer society, fascism has far more to recommend itself. Fascist governments can masterfully manufacture a sense of national purpose, and more than that, national superiority. This ethos, while not so appealing from the perspective of those who worry about individual rights, cultivates the perfect climate for a World Cup. Not only can it produce a healthy confidence, it can generate a powerful fear of losing. Who wants to disappoint a nation swept up in this kind of fervor? Or more to the point, who wants to disappoint a leader who might break your legs and imprison your grandmother? What's more, fascist governments subscribe to a cult of fitness and hygiene that leads them to siphon considerable national resources into sports programs. The fascist record speaks for itself. During the thirties, Il Duce's Italy claimed two trophies; Arrow-Cross Hungary finished second in 1938 and Germany took third in '34, as did Brazil in '38. (Under the reign of Getulio Vargas, Brazil was quasifascist or actually fascist, depending of who you ask.) Overall, fascism compiled a record of 17–4–5 in that decade.

But fascism has performed miserably since the fall of the Axis.

Proto-fascist regimes like Franco's Spain or Perón's Argentina presided over some of the great underachievers in the game's history. How could you squander the talent of Alfredo di Stefano? Salazar's Portugal who appeared in only one tournament during his thirty-six-year reign. (To be sure, it was a tremendous performance, with Eusebio leading the country to third place. But back in the days of Mussolini and Hitler, a good fascist dictator would have considered such a result an abomination—and would not have permitted Eusebio to play, in any case.) What accounts for the fall off? In the thirties, fascist nations were an independent force in the world. They were the most ferocious regimes on the planet. After the war, this swagger vanished. Suddenly, the power of these nations rested on their alliance with the United States. Once you become lapdogs of the Americans, it's hard to muster the same will to win.

There's an important corollary to this finding. No country has ever won a World Cup while committing genocide or gearing up to commit genocide. Germany and Yugoslavia both faltered on the eve of their mass murders. In 1938, Germany didn't win a single game. The greatest Yugoslavian team of all time lost in the quarterfinals of the 1990 tournament. Apparently, lusting after the blood of Jews and Muslims distracts vital energy from the more pressing task of scoring against Argentines and Italians.

Now, we've examined two of the most ubiquitous forms of command economy. That leaves a third: the good old-fashioned military junta. You can't find too many of these in the world today. But military juntas are historically superb at winning World Cups. The Brazilian and Argentine juntas presided over the most glorious victories in the tournament's history in the seventies and early eighties. It makes sense that juntas would excel at this. They are collective efforts, where even the strongmen are part of a broader apparatus. A good soccer team is, in a sense, a junta.

While military juntas have a tremendous record—three trophies in all—they still can't claim to be the most successful form of government. This is partly a problem of dilution. Military juntas must also claim credit for straggler countries like Paraguay and El Salvador. Their achievements, in the end, can't compete with the most effective soccer government known to man. Social democracy delivers more championships than the juntas—six in all. And even the worst social democratic teams—Belgium, Finland—win more consistently than their authoritarian peers.

To understand this success, one must understand the essence of the social democratic economy. Social democracies take root in heavily industrialized societies, and this is a great blessing. No country has won the World Cup without having a substantial industrial base. This base supplies a vast urban proletariat, which in turn supplies players for a team. Industrial economies also produce great wealth, which funds competitive domestic leagues that improve social democratic players by subjecting them to the highest quality day-to-day competition. And while the junta mindset nicely transposes itself to the pitch, the social democratic ethos is a far neater match. Social democracy celebrates individualism, while relentlessly patting itself on the back for its sense of solidarity—a coherent team with room for stars.

The new paradigm of political theory posited above cannot only help guide a revolution, it can help fill out a tournament prediction bracket. It is my contention that the outcome of each match in the World Cup can be forecast by analyzing the political and economics conditions of the countries represented on the pitch. This isn't quite an unbeatable system. But I have yet to see a method for filling out a tournament bracket that beats it. In addition to using the hierarchy above to guide your picks—fascism beats communism; military junta beats fascism; social democracy beats military junta—there are several other iron laws that can be applied:

1. EU means Experience Unlimited

Since its inception in 1992, the EU has racked up an impressive World Cup record of 44 wins, 24 draws and 36 losses. Western Europe has, of course, always dominated the tournament. But their recent performance is slightly better than the continent's past. In part, that's because FIFA has expanded the tournament from twenty-four teams to thirty-two. Old World powers have more minnows to devour. But the change can also be attributed to globalization. While most countries that qualify for the tournament have players in Spain, Italy and England, smaller European nations have benefited most from the opening of the big leagues to foreign talent. (To be sure, African and Latin American nations have also benefited greatly, but less so.) A country like Sweden has almost none of its starting eleven now playing for Swedish teams. Because of this migration of talent and exposure to superior competition, a European nation without much of a history of football success can suddenly transform itself into an impressive performer.

2. Liberated and in a winning mood

Countries that have just thrown off the yoke of communist or authoritarian oppression are extremely difficult to stop. The 1990 and 1994 tournaments were testament to this phenomenon, when postcommunist Bulgaria and Romania played deep into the knockout round. Poland had its most glorious run in '82, with the Solidarity movement playing in the background. And Germany won its last World Cup in the middle of its reunification.

3. Colonizers over colonized

These matches happen several times a tournament. Spain plays one of its old Latin American outposts. France faces the likes of Senegal or Cameroon. Portugal takes the field against Brazil. When these imperial overlords battle their old subjects, you'd expect that the colonized nation would play better. After all, imperialism is an inherently doomed venture. No colonial overlord can eternally resist their subject's demands for liberation. But that political reality doesn't translate into soccer. In fact, excepting Senegal's victory over France in the first game of the 2002 World Cup, the imperial powers historically win more often. Perhaps the imperial powers want to compensate for the psychological damage that accompanies the loss of empire and political decline. You might ask, shouldn't this trend benefit England, the greatest empire of the last two hundred years? It should except that England planted rugby and cricket more firmly than soccer in most of its colonies. Consequently, England can go whole tournaments without playing any commonwealth countries.

4. Never invest hope in an oil-producing nation

If a nation heavily exports oil—Nigeria, Russia, Mexico, Norway, the Gulf States, Iran—it's doomed to underachieve. When an economy can generate wealth so easily, even if that wealth only flows to a small oligarchy, a country can get lazy, thinking that riches will forever flow naturally to it. Political scientists call this the "paradox of plenty." And on the pitch, these countries lack a winning temperament and an innovative mindset. No oil-rich state has made it to the semifinals.

5. Neoliberal shock therapy is a buzz kill

Argentina hasn't made it to the quarterfinals since its government embarked on neoliberal reforms. Over the last decade, Brazil has only faltered once, in 1998, at the height of President Fernando Henrique Cardoso's push to open his country's markets. So, you should pick against any country that is in the midst of privatizing its banks and energy sector. But there's good news for Thomas Friedman and other proponents of classical liberalism. Countries normally bounce back from their liberal setbacks. Brazil is the locus classicus of the genre, but Poland and Ecuador also prove that neoliberalism only hurts soccer in the short-term.

6. The caveat

There's one iron law that overrides all the others. The political reality most likely to produce a Jules Rimet trophy at any given moment in history: whatever form of government has taken up residence in Brasilia that week.

	World Cup Champion	**Political System**
1930	Uruguay	Fragile Democracy
1934	Italy	Fascist Dictatorship
1938	Italy	Fascist Dictatorship
1950	Uruguay	Emerging Democracy
1954	West Germany	Christian Democracy
1958	Brazil	Populist Democracy
1962	Brazil	Populist Democracy
1966	England	Social Democracy
1970	Brazil	Military Junta
1974	West Germany	Social Democracy
1978	Argentina	Military Junta
1982	Italy	Social Democracy
1986	Argentina	Emerging Democracy
1990	West Germany	Social Democracy
1994	Brazil	Emerging Democracy
1998	France	Social Democracy
2002	Brazil	Neoliberal Democracy

About the Contributors

Tim Adams (Czech Republic) was deputy editor of *Granta* from 1988 to 1993 and is now a staff writer at the *Observer*. He is the author of *Being John McEnroe*. He lives in London.

Courtney Angela Brkic (Croatia) has worked as a forensic archeologist in Bosnia-Herzegovina and for the UN war crimes tribunal in the Hague. She is the author of *Stillness* and *The Stone Fields*, and teaches at Kenyon College in Ohio.

Jorge G. Castañeda (Mexico) is the author of *Utopia Unarmed: The Latin American Left After the Cold War* and *Compañero: The Life and Death of Che Guevara*. He is a Global Distinguished Professor of Politics and Latin American Studies at New York University, having served as Mexico's Foreign Minister from 2000 to 2003.

Robert Coover (Spain) is the author of *The Origin of the Brunists*, *Pricksongs and Descants*, *The Public Burning*, *Spanking the Maid*, *Gerald's Party* and other novels. His latest honor is the Dugannon Foundation's Rea Award for his lifetime contribution to the short story.

Geoff Dyer (Serbia and Montenegro) was born in 1958. His many books include *But Beautiful*, *Out of Sheer Rage*, *Yoga for People Who Can't Be Bothered to Do It* and *The Ongoing Moment*. He lives in London.

Dave Eggers (United States) is the editor of *McSweeney's* and of many books, including the yearly collection *The Best American Nonrequired Reading,* which he edits with high school students from 826 Valencia, a nonprofit educational center he founded. He is the author of four books, including *What Is the What?,* to be published in October 2006.

William Finnegan (Portugal) is a staff writer at *The New Yorker.* He is the author of *Crossing the Line, Dateline Soweto, A Complicated War* and *Cold New World.* He lives in New York.

Franklin Foer (Afterword) is the editor of *The New Republic* and the author of *How Soccer Explains the World.* He lives in Washington, D.C.

Jim Frederick (Japan) is Tokyo Bureau Chief of *Time Magazine.* He lives in Tokyo.

Aleksandar Hemon (France) was born in Sarajevo in 1964. He moved to Chicago in 1992 and began writing in English in 1995. His fiction has appeared in *The New Yorker, Granta* and *Best American Short Stories 1999* and *2000.* He lives in Chicago.

Isabel Hilton (Paraguay) is the author of *The Search for the Panchen Lama* and a columnist for the *Guardian.* She lives in London.

Peter Ho Davies (South Korea) was born to Welsh and Chinese parents in England in 1966. He is the author of two short-story collections, *The Ugliest House in the World* and *Equal Love,* and was named one of *Granta*'s Best of Young British Novelists. Davies directs the graduate program in creative writing at the University of Michigan, Ann Arbor.

Nick Hornby (England) is the author of the internationally bestselling novels *High Fidelity, About a Boy* and *How to Be Good,* and the memoir *Fever Pitch.* His fourth novel is *A Long Way Down.* He lives in London.

Thomas Jones (Argentina) is an editor on the *London Review of Books*. He lives in London.

Paul Laity (Côte d'Ivoire) is an editor on the *London Review of Books,* and edited the *Left Book Club Anthology.* He lives in London.

John Lanchester (Brazil) is the author of the novels *The Debt to Pleasure, Mr Phillips* and *Fragrant Harbour.* He used to write soccer match reports for British newspapers. He lives in London.

Cressida Leyshon (Trinidad and Tobago) is the deputy fiction editor of *The New Yorker.* She lives in New York.

Henning Mankell (Angola) was born in Sweden in 1948. He is the author of the Inspector Kurt Wallander mysteries. Mankell divides his time between Sweden and Mozambique.

Alexander Osang (Germany) was born in East Berlin in 1962. He is the author of several books, and he works for *Der Spiegel* in Brooklyn.

Tim Parks (Italy) was born in Manchester in 1954. In 1981 he moved to Italy where he has lived ever since. He has written eleven novels, three nonfiction accounts of life in northern Italy and a collection of essays.

Benjamin Pauker (Ukraine) is an editor and writer in New York. His writing has appeared in *Harper's,* the *Chicago Tribune* and *World Policy Journal.*

Caryl Phillips (Ghana) was born in St. Kitts and brought up in England. He is the author of three works of nonfiction and eight novels, including *Crossing the River,* which was short-listed for the Booker Prize. He has been named the Sunday Times Young Writer of the Year and one of *Granta*'s Best of Young British Novelists. He lives in New York.

Ben Rice (Australia) was born in Devon in 1972. He is the author of *Pobby and Dingan* and was named one of *Granta*'s Best of Young British Novelists in 2003. He lives in London.

Sukhdev Sandhu (Saudi Arabia) writes about film for the *Daily Telegraph* and teaches at New York University. He is a contributing editor at *Granta*, and the author of *London Calling: How Black and Asian Writers Imagined a City*. He lives in New York and London.

Saïd Sayrafiezadeh (Iran) was born in Brooklyn, New York, in 1968. His stories and essays have appeared in *The Paris Review, Granta, Open City* and *Columbia Journal of Literature and Art*, among others. His play about the Civil War draft riots was developed last year at the Sundance Theatre Lab. He is at work on a memoir about growing up in the Socialist Workers Party to be published by Dial Press. He lives in New York.

Eric Schlosser (Sweden) is the author of *Fast Food Nation* and *Reefer Madness*.

Jake Silverstein (Ecuador) is a contributing editor of *Harper's Magazine*. He lives in Austin, Texas.

Peter Stamm (Switzerland) was born in Switzerland in 1963. He is the author of two novels and several radio and stage plays. He lives in Winterthur, Switzerland.

Wendell Steavenson (Tunisia) is the author of *Stories I Stole*, about the Caucasus republic of Georgia. She has worked as a reporter for *Time* and has written for *Granta,* the *Telegraph* and *Prospect*. She lives in Beirut and London.

James Surowiecki (Poland) is a staff writer at *The New Yorker,* where he writes a regular business column. His work has appeared in the *New York Times,* the *Wall Street Journal, Artforum, Wired* and *Slate*. He lives in Brooklyn, New York.

Tom Vanderbilt (Netherlands) is the author of *Survival City: Adventures Among the Ruins of Atomic America* and *The Sneaker Book.* He lives in Brooklyn, New York.

Binyavanga Wainaina (Togo) was born in Kenya in 1971. He won the Caine Prize for African Writing in 2002, and is the founding editor of the literary magazine *Kwani?* He lives in Nairobi, Kenya.

Matt Weiland (co-editor) is the deputy editor of *Granta*. He has been an editor at the New Press in New York and managing editor of *The Baffler* magazine in Chicago, and he co-edited *Commodify Your Dissent: The Business of Culture in the New Gilded Age* with Thomas Frank. Originally from Minneapolis, he lives in London.

Sean Wilsey (co-editor) is the author of a memoir, *Oh the Glory of It All*. His writing has appeared in *The New Yorker, The London Review of Books,* and *McSweeney's* quarterly, where he is the editor at large. Before coming to *McSweeney's,* he worked as a fact checker at *Ladies' Home Journal* and as an apprentice gondolier in Venice, Italy. He lives in New York with his wife, Daphne Beal, and their son, Owen.

Matthew Yeomans (Costa Rica) is the author of *Oil: Anatomy of an Industry.* His writing has appeared in *Wired,* the *Village Voice* and *Doubletake.* He lives in Cardiff, Wales.

Acknowledgments

Thanks to Daphne Beal, Eugenia Bell, Deborah and Steven Weiland, Colin Hamilton, Buzz Lagos, Phil Nell and the rest at Minnesota Kicks soccer camp (1978–1983) for getting the ball rolling; to Linda Byrne, Horacio Herrera-Richmond, Eli Horowitz, Ian Jack, Deborah Treisman, Annie Falk, Leslie Falk, Dieter Janssen, Andrea Vazzano and the members of the George Best Society for Useful Wagers for pushing it down the pitch; and to Zoë Pagnamenta, Anne Jump, David McCormick, Simon Trewin, David Hirshey, John Williams and Tom Bromley for putting it in the net.